The Tennessee Locator

*********** CAR-RT SORT ** RR06
33272770 1041   MAA-DRM
FRED A WARRICK
OR CURRENT RESIDENT
1301 ASHBY DR
BRENTWOOD   TN 37027-6816

Published by BudRo
P.O. Box 2
Chattanooga, TN 37401-0002

Manufactured in the United States of America
ISBN 0-9634593-0-9

The Tennessee Locator

by HAROLD (BUD) ROHEN

Printed by
Quality Printing Services, Inc.
Athens, Tennessee 37303
(800) 688-8906

To: Mary Margaret
A loving and understanding wife, without whom I would never have found this beautiful State of Tennessee.

PREFACE

The idea for the Tennessee Locator first came to mind many years ago. Whenever I would read in the newspaper about happenings in certain areas of the State and I had no idea where those particular locations were, it was a little frustrating to me. Then in 1986, when Governor Lamar Alexander proclaimed that year as "Tennessee Homecoming Year," I thought how great it would be to have a reference book that would give the locations of the cities, towns, communities, mountains, rivers and lakes in the State of Tennessee.

I knew it would be next to impossible to locate all the communities, etc. in Tennessee, but I knew I had the time to try. My main concern was accuracy and it still is. I know there are typographical errors in this book, I tried to catch them all, but I know that I didn't. However, when I tell you that "Black Fox" is in the S central section of Bradley County, 3 mi E of McDonald, I expect that information to be correct and I feel comfortable that it is. However, I am as human as you and only ask that you leave me a little room for error.

Gathering this data was a one person effort and it became a monumental task. At first, I thought I could finish this book in a couple of years, but at that time I did not have a computer, so I had to do my own typing, collating, etc. After two years into the project, I became exhausted and at that point, I laid the project aside and I forgot about it until the Spring of 1990. I then had a Personal Computer and work on this project became a lot more comfortable.

For references, I used the Zip Code Directory, map indexes, transportation guides and any other publication that listed the names of cities, towns and communities. I made an index card for each community, etc., gathering approximately 7,000 cards. I went to Nashville and purchased a map of each county in Tennessee. With magnifying glass in hand, I then searched each county map finding the locations of each community, etc. When I located the community, I would measure the miles from the county seat or the nearest large community and in what direction it was located. For the communities I couldn't find on the county maps, I went to commercial maps and picked up their locations. There are several listings that cannot be found on any map, and in that event I have listed the general location within the county where it can be found.

In searching through the commercial maps, I also picked up the Hollows, Ridges, Gaps, Knobs, State Parks and several creeks. So now I have locations for Counties, Cities, Towns, Communities, Hollows, Mountains, Ridges, Knobs, State Parks, Rivers, Creeks and Lakes in Tennessee. Please keep in mind, I am not professing to have ALL locations within the State of Tennessee, but you won't find many that I have missed.

The intent of this book is to allow anyone to pick up a Tennessee Map and find with ease, the communities you are interested in, or at least place the general location in your mind.

Acknowledgments

I would like to thank the following for their time and patience in discussing their respective counties with me:

Mrs. Virginia Lindsey
Lawrence County

Mr. Larry Fox and
Mr. Herb Lawson
Sevier County

SECTION ONE:

Alphabetical Listing of all Locations
Pages 1 - 357

SECTION TWO:

Lakes, Rivers and Streams of Tennessee
Pages 358-382

SECTION ONE:
Alphabetical Listing of all Locations
Pages 1 - 357

The Tennessee Locator

COUNTY LOCATION MAP

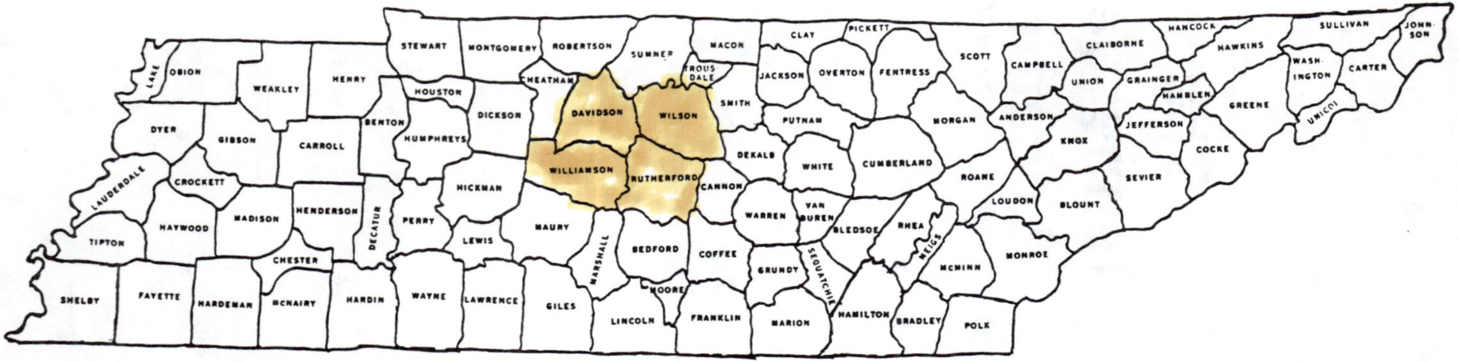

Abernathy Lake	Lake in near center of Giles County. N of Pulaski.
Abiff	Community in S area of Dickson County. 14 1/2 mi S SE of Charlotte.
Abrams Ridge	Ridge in S section of Blount County. 12 mi S of Maryville, SE of Happy Valley.
Acklin	Community within the city limits of Nashville in Davidson County.
Acorn	Community in central section of Monroe County. 8 1/2 mi E SE of Madisonville.
Acton	Community in SE corner of McNairy County. 13 1/2 mi SE of Selmer.
Adair	Community on NW border of Madison County. 10 mi NW of Jackson.
Adams	City in NW section of Robertson County. 11 mi W NW of Springfield. Incorporated in 1963.
Adams Crossroads	Community in W section of Dickson County. 10 mi W of Charlotte.
Adams Hollow	Located in W section of Bedford County.7
Adamson Hollow	Located in S section of Macon County. 1 mi N of Beech Bottom.
Adams Ridge	Ridge in W section of Hamilton County.
Adamsville	City in E NE section of McNairy County. 12 1/2 mi E NE of Selmer. Incorporated in 1870.
Adamsville Recreation Area	On middle E border of Hardin County. 7 mi W of Savannah on McNairy County line.
Addison	Community in middle SE section of McMinn County. 6 mi SE of Athens.
Adkins Mill	Community in W section of Morgan County. 2 mi N NW of Burlick.
Adkins Mountain	Mountain in W section of Campbell County, W of Turley.
Adolphus	Community in W section of Loudon County. 5 mi W of Loudon.
AEDC and Woods Reservoir Refuge	Located in N section of Franklin County near Coffee County Line.
Aethra	Community in E section of Lewis County, N of Bachelder.
Aetna	Community in S section of Hickman County. 8 1/2 mi S SW of Centerville.

Aetna	Community in SE section of Marion County. 8 mi E SE of Jasper near Raccoon Mountain.
Afton	Community in E central section of Greene County. 6 mi E NE of Greeneville.
Aiken Ridge	Ridge in middle E section of Maury County. 5 mi NE of Columbia.
Airshaft Hollow	Located in N section of Anderson County.
Akard Addition	Community in N NE section of Sullivan County, S of Maple Hill.
Akers Lake	Lake in NW section of Wilson County. 11 mi NW of Lebanon.
Akins Corner	Community in middle SW section of Tipton County. 8 1/2 mi SW of Covington.
Alamo	County of Seat of Crockett County. Located in S central section of county. Incorporated in 1911.
Alanthus Hill	Community in NW corner of Hancock County. 10 mi W NW of Sneedville.
Albany	Community in W NW central section of Greene County. 8 mi NW of Greeneville.
Alberton	Community in NE central section of Henderson County. 5 1/2 mi NE of Lexington.
Alcoa	City in N Central section of Blount County N of Maryville. Incorporated in 1919.
Alder	Community in SE area of Campbell County. 7 mi E SE of LaFollette.
Alders Branch	Community in middle NE section of Sevier County. Approx. 4 mi N of Sevierville.
Alder Springs	Community in SE area of Campbell County. 6 mi E of LaFollette.
Alder Springs	Community in central SW section of Union County. 4 mi S SE of Maynardville.
Alec Mountain	Mountain in E section of Hawkins County, E of Honeycutt.
Alexander Island	Island on Cumberland River, W NW section of Smith County. 4 mi W of Riddleton.
Alexander Knob	Located in E section of Loudon County, S of McMullens.
Alexander Springs	Community in NE section of Lawrence County. 10 mi N NE of Lawrenceburg.

Alexandria	City in NW section of DeKalb County. 15 mi NW of Smithville. Incorporated in 1831.
Algood	City in NE central section of Putnam County. 3 1/2 mi NE of Cookeville. Incorporated in 1901.
Algood Mountain	Mountain in NE section of Putman County. E of Algood.
Allardt	City in Central area of Fentress County. 4 mi SE of Jamestown. Incorporated in 1964.
Allen (Big Spring P.O.)	Community in S section of Meigs County. 7 mi S SW of Decatur.
Allen Grove	Community in SW area of Cocke County. 9 mi S of Newport and 2 mi W of Denton.
Allens	Community in middle NE section of Haywood County. 5 mi NE of Brownsville.
Allens Chapel	Community in central section of DeKalb County. 2 mi N NE of Smithville.
Allisona	Community in E SE section of Williamson County. 15 mi SE of Franklin.
Allnight Ridge	Ridge in SE section of Blount County. 4 mi E of Cades Cove.
Allons	Community in middle NW section of Overton County. 4 mi N NW of Livingston.
Alloway	Community in S area of Cumberland County. 12 mi S SE of Crossville.
Allred	Community in E SE section of Overton County. 8 1/2 mi E SE of Livingston.
Almaville	Community in W section of Rutherford County. 10 mi W of Murfreesboro.
Almy	Community in central N section of Scott County. 3 mi N of Huntsville.
Alnwick	Community in W Central section of Blount County. 2 mi W of Maryville.
Alpha	Community in W SW section of Hamblen County. 5 mi SW of Morristown.
Alpha Heights	Community in W SW section of Hamblen County. 6 mi W SW of Morristown.
Alpine	Community in middle E section of Overton County. 6 mi E of Livingston.
Alpine Mountain	Mountain in E section of Overton County. E SE of Livingston.

Altamont	County Seat of Grundy County. Located in N central section of County. Incorporated in 1853.
Alto	Community in NE area of Franklin County. 10 1/2 mi NE of Winchester.
Alton Park	Community within the city limits of Chattanooga. 3 1/2 mi S of downtown in Hamilton County.
Altonville	Community in W section of Hawkins County. 6 1/2 mi W of Rogersville.
Alumwell	Community in N central section of Hawkins County. 5 mi N of Rogersville.
Amburn Mountain	Mountain in SE corner of Polk County, E of Isabella.
Amerene	Community in N Central section of Blount County near Maryville.
American Knob	Mountain in W NW section of Anderson County.
Ames Plantation	Community on E SE border of Fayette County, E SE of Pattersonville.
Amherst	Community in middle W section of Knox County. 6 mi W of Knoxville.
Amis Chapel	Community in Central section of Hawkins County. 13 mi E NE of Rogersville.
Amqui	Community in NE section of Davidson County between Madison and Goodlettsville.
Anderson	Community in SW Central area of Carroll County. 6 mi SW of Huntingdon.
Anderson	Community in SE area of Franklin County. 18 mi SE of Winchester.
Anderson	Community on S SE border of Overton County. 15 1/2 mi S SE of Livingston.
Anderson County ANDERSON COUNTY	County Seat: Clinton. Zip Code: 37716. Located in NE Section of State. Bounded by Campbell, Union, Knox, Roane, Morgan and Scott Counties. Named in honor of Sen. Joseph Anderson.
Anderson Hallow	Located in SE corner of Wilson County. E of Prosperity.
Anderson Hollow	Located in W NW section of Humphreys County, E of Littleton Hollow. 3 mi S of Trinity.
Anderson Mountain	Mountain in SE section of Scott County. SE of Montgomery Junction.
Anderson Mountain	Mountain in N NE section of Scott County, N of

Anderson Mountain, (Cont.)	Ketchen.
Anderson Ridge	Ridge in S SE section of Marion County, N of Shellmound.
Anderson-Tully Wildlife Management Area	Located in W section of Lauderdale County. 18 mi W SW of Ripley, N of Fort Pillow State Park.
Andersonville	Community in NE area of Anderson County. Approximately 3 miles E of Norris.
Anderton Branch	Stream in W area of Franklin County, flows into Lost Creek.
Andrew Hollow Ridge	Located in middle W section of Stewart County, S of Fair View.
Andy Ridge	Ridge in N section of Anderson County.
Anes	Community in N central section of Marshall County. 8 mi N NE of Lewisburg.
Angeltown	Community in middle NE section of Sumner County. 12 1/2 mi N NE of Gallatin.
Annadel	Community in central NW section of Morgan County. 6 mi NW of Wartburg.
Ann Homer Ridge	Ridge in SE section of Perry County, E of Flatwoods.
Ansdale	Community in W Central area of Bradley County S of Cleveland.
Anthony Hill	Community in SW central section of Giles County. 6 mi SW of Pulaski.
Anthras	Community in NE area of Campbell County. 7 mi E SE of Jellico.
Antioch	Community in NE area of Crockett County.
Antioch	Community in SE Section of Davidson County.
Antioch	Community in SE section of DeKalb County. 9 mi SE of Smithville.
Antioch	Community in S SW section of Haywood County. 11 1/2 mi S SW of Brownsville. 3 1/2 mi E SE of Stanton.
Antioch	Community in NW central section of Henderson County. 3 1/2 mi NW of Lexington.
Antioch	Community in S section of Jackson County. 5 1/2 mi S of Gainesboro.
Antioch	Community in E section of Loudon County. 9 mi

Antioch, (Cont.)	E of Loudon.
Antioch	Community in middle SW section of Montgomery County. SW of Hilltop.
Antioch	Community in NE section of Tipton County. Approx. 6 mi E NE of Covington.
Apalachia	Community in E NE section of Polk County, N of Farner.
Apison	Community in SE area of Hamilton County near Collegedale. 16 mi S SE of Downtown Chattanooga.
Apple Lake	Lake is S section of Davidson County near Williamson County line.
Appleton	Community in SE corner of Lawrence County. 16 mi S SE of Lawrenceburg.
Applewood	Community on Signal Mountain in Hamilton County. 7 mi N NW of Chattanooga.
Arcadia	Community in N NW section of Sullivan County. 8 mi W NW of Blountville.
Archer	Community in S section of Marshall County. 8 1/2 mi S SE of Lewisburg.
Archer Center	Community in NE area of Campbell County.
Archville	Community in middle section of Polk County. 7 1/2 mi E SE of Benton.
Arcott	Community in Central section of Clay County. 3 1/2 mi SW of Celina.
Arden	Community on W border of Monroe County. W NW of Mount Vernon.
Ardmore	City in SE area of Giles County. 15 mi SE of Pulaski. Incorporated in 1949.
Arion Mountain	Mountain in N section of Fentress County, N of Pall Mall.
Arkland	Community in middle W section of Maury County. 10 mi W NW of Columbia.
Arline	Community in NW section of Blount County. 7 mi W NW of Maryville.
Arlington	City in E NE section of Shelby County. 25 mi E NE of Memphis. Incorporated in 1900.
Armathwaite	Community in E central section of Fentress County. 9 mi E SE of Jamestown.
Armindo	Community in middle NE section of Knox County.

Armindo, (Cont.)	6 mi NE of Knoxville.
Armona	Community in NW area of Blount County near Louisville.
Armour Village	Community in middle W section of Maury County. 6 mi W of Columbia.
Armstrong Bar	Located in SW tip of Shelby County on the Mississippi River.
Arno	Community in SE section of Williamson County. 11 mi SE of Franklin.
Arnold Air Force Base	Located in S section of Coffee County, part of Arnold Engineering Development Center.
Arnold Engineering Development Center	Located in S section of Coffee County, SE of Manchester.
Arnold Hollow	Located in N NE section of Humphreys County. 2 1/2 mi S of Woolworth.
Arnold Hollow	Located in W section of Wayne County. E of Houston.
Arp	Community in near center of Lauderdale County. 4 mi W NW of Ripley.
Arrington	Community in E section of Williamson County. 10 mi E SE of Franklin.
Arrow	Community in SW section of Maury County. 11 mi SW of Columbia.
Arrowhead	Community in S section of Knox County. 7 mi S of Knoxville. S of Crenshaw.
Arrowhead Estates	Community in NE section of Rhea County. 22 mi N NE of Dayton.
Arrow Lake	Lake in SW section of Maury County. 12 mi SW of Columbia.
Arthur	Community in N Central section of Claiborne County. 8 mi NW of Tazewell.
Asbury	Community in E central section of Coffee County. 6 mi E of Manchester.
Asbury	Community in middle SW section of Haywood County. 10 1/2 mi S SW of Brownsville. 4 1/2 mi E SE of Stanton.
Asbury	Community in SE section of Knox County, SW of Marbledale.
Asbury	Community in middle SE section of Lauderdale County. 2 1/2 mi W SW of Ripley.

Asbury	Community in N section of Pickett County. 3 1/2 mi E NE of Byrdstown.
Asbury	Community in S section of Stewart County. 7 mi S of Dover.
Asbury Estates	Community in middle section of Blount County. 3 mi E of Maryville.
Ashburn	Community in N section of Robertson County. 8 mi N NE of Springfield.
Ashburn Creek	Creek in E section of Clay County near Pickett County border.
Ash Hill	Located in S SE section of Williamson County near border. 2 mi S of Bethesda.
Ashland	Community in NE section of Wayne County. 9 1/2 mi N NE of Waynesboro.
Ashland City	County Seat of Cheatham County. Located in N Central area of county. Incorporated in 1859.
Ashland Hills	Community in middle section of Montgomery County. E of Clarksville.
Ashley Oaks	Community in Knox County. 10 mi W SW of Knoxville.
Ash Log Mountain	Mountain in SW area of Campbell County SW of Caryville.
Ashport	Community in W section of Lauderdale County. 14 1/2 mi W of Ripley.
Ashwood	Community in middle SW section of Maury County. 6 1/2 mi S SW of Columbia.
Asia	Community in N central section of Franklin County. 4 mi N of Winchester.
Askew Hollow	Located in W section of Houston County, N of Whiteoak Creek.
Aspen Hill	Community in S central section of Giles County. 7 mi S SE of Pulaski.
Athendale	Community in N central section of Maury County. 4 1/2 mi N NW of Columbia.
Athens	County Seat of McMinn County. Located in near center section of the County. Incorporated in 1829.
Atkins	Community in middle E NE section of Stewart County. 6 1/2 mi E NE of Dover.
Atkinson Ridge	Ridge in W SW section of Wayne County. W of Cromwell Crossroads.

Atnip Bluff Cabin Colony	Community in N central section of Dekalb County.
Atoka	City in S section of Tipton County. 12 mi S SW of Covington. Incorporated in 1911.
Atwood	City of W Border of Carroll County near Gibson County Line. 14 mi W of Huntingdon. Incorporated in 1941.
Auburntown	City in N area of Cannon County. 8 mi N of Woodbury. Incorporated in 1949.
Audubon Acres	Located in S section of the city of Chattanooga on Gunbarrel Road, in Concord Area of Hamilton County.
Ault Lake	Lake in W section of Jefferson County. 5 mi SW of Jefferson City.
Austin	Community in S section of Savannah in Hardin County.
Austin Farm	Community within the city limits of Chattanooga. 8 1/2 mi E NE of downtown. In Hamilton County.
Austin Farm	Community in S central section of Hawkins County. 2 mi S of Rogersville.
Austin Springs	Community in E NE section of Washington County. 10 mi NE of Jonesborough.
Austin Springs	Community in N NE section of Weakley County. 14 mi N NE of Dresden.
Avandale	Community within city limits of the City of Chattanooga. 2 1/2 mi E of downtown. In Hamilton County.
Avondale	Community in central section of Davidson County, approximately 3 mi N of Capital Bldg.
Avondale	Community in E central section of Grainger County. 3 1/2 mi E NE of Rutledge.
Avondale	Community in S SW section of Sumner County. Approx. 5 mi E NE of Hendersonville.
Avondale Springs	Community in E central section of Grainger County. 4 mi E NE of Rutledge.
Await	Community in NW section of Franklin County.
Ayers	Community in W area of Dyer County. 15 mi W of Dyersburg.
Aymett Town	Community in Central section of Giles County. 4 mi E SE of Pulaski.

Ayres Hollow — Located in E SE section of Benton County.

Babbs Mill — Community in N area of Greene County, near Baileyton.

Bacchus — Community in Central area of Claiborne County. 4 mi N of Tazewell.

Bachelder — Community in E section of Lewis County, S of Aethra.

Backbone Hollow — Located in N section of Anderson County.

Backbone Ridge — Ridge in N section of Anderson County.

Backbone Ridge — Ridge in E section of Dickson County, N of Claylick.

Backbone Ridge — Ridge in middle SE section of Jackson County, W of Freewill.

Backbone Ridge — Ridge in middle W section of Williamson County, W of Bingham.

Backwoods — Community in SW area of Carter County.

Bacon Ridge — Ridge in middle S section of Roane County. N of Stamp Creek Ridge.

Badger Spring Lake — Lake in S SW section of Maury County. 11 1/2 mi S SW of Columbia. S of Southport.

Baggettsville — Community in middle E SE section of Robertson County. 9 mi E SE of Springfield.

Bagwell City — Community in N central area of Chattanooga. 6 mi N NE of downtown in the area of Dupont Nylon Plant. In Hamilton County.

Bailey — Community in SE section of Shelby County. 19 E SE of Memphis.

Baileyton — City in N area of Greene County. 12 mi N of Greeneville. Incorporated in 1915.

Bailey Town — Community in W central section of Cocke County.

Bailey Town — Community in E SE section of Jefferson County near the border. 3 mi NE of Chestnut Hill.

Bain — Community in NW area of Benton County. 7 mi NW of Camden.

Bairds Mill — Community in S section of Wilson County. 7 1/2 mi S SW of Lebanon.

Baker Crossroads — Community in NW central section of Cumberland County. 6 mi W NW of Crossville.

Baker Mountain	Mountain in W section of Van Buren County, SW of Spencer.
Baker Mountain	Mountain in central SE section of White County, S of Rockhouse.
Baker Ridge	Ridge in SE section of Hamilton County.
Bakers	Community in N area of Davidson County. 4 mi N of Goodlettsville.
Bakers Crossroads	Community in NW section of White County. 7 1/2 mi NW of Sparta.
Bakers Gap	Community in S section of Johnson County. 8 mi S SW of Mountain City.
Bakersworks	Community in E SE area of Dickson County. 8 1/2 mi SE of Charlotte.
Bakerton	Community in SW corner of Clay County near Macon County line.
Bakertown	Community in E central section of Moore County. 3 mi SE of Lynchburg.
Bakerville	Community in SW section of Humphreys County. 10 1/2 mi S SW of Waverly.
Bakewell	Community in N area of Hamilton County. 23 mi N of Chattanooga and 7 mi N of Soddy Daisy.
Bakewell Mountain	Mountain in middle N section of Hamilton County. NW of Bakewell.
Bald Crossing	Community in W SW section of Washington County. 4 mi SW of Jonesborough.
Balding Knob	Located in central section of Humphreys County. 2 mi SE of New Hope.
Bald Knob	Mountain in E NE section of Johnson County, E of Wills.
Bald Mountain	Mountain in SE section of Cocke County, near border of North Carolina.
Bald Mountain	Mountain in SE area of Greene County near North Carolina border.
Bald Point	Community in NE section of Grainger County. 12 1/2 mi NE of Rutledge.
Bald River Gorge Wilderness	Located in central S SE section of Monroe County, S of Waucheesi. 7 mi SE of Tellico Plains.
Bales	Community near N NW border of Clay County. 2 1/2 mi NE of Oak Grove.

Ball Camp	Community in W section of Knox County. 11 mi W SW of Knoxville.
Ballplay	Community in central section of Monroe County. 9 1/2 mi E SE of Madisonville.
Ball Play	Community in SW section of Polk County. 10 1/2 mi S SW of Benton.
Balsam Point	Mountain in S section of Sevier County. 4 mi S SE of Gatlinburg, S of Bull Head.
Baltimore	Community in W central section of Cocke County. 7 mi E NE of Newport.
Bandmill Hollow	Located in W SW section of Sumner County. NE of Two Chestnut.
Bangham	Community in middle N section of Putnam County. 6 1/2 mi N NE of Cookeville.
Banner Hill	Community within the city limits of Erwin, S section of the city. In Unicoi County.
Banner Springs	Community in S area of Fentress County. 12 mi S of Jamestown.
Baptist Ridge	Community in S central section of Clay County. 5 mi S of Celina.
Baptist Ridge	Ridge in S central section of Clay County. 5 mi SW of Celina.
Barb Hollow	Located in N section of Anderson County.
Bards Creek	Creek in middle NW section of Stewart County. 7 mi NW of Dover. E of Tharpe.
Bards Lake	Lake in middle NW section of Stewart County. SE of Tharpe.
Barefoot	Community in NW corner of Macon County. 12 mi N NW of Lafayette.
Bare Knob	Located in S section of Rutherford County. S of Fosterville.
Barfield	Community in middle S section of Rutherford County. 4 1/2 mi S SW of Murfreesboro.
Barfield Knobs	Located in central SW section of Rutherford County. S of Barfield.
Bargerton	Community in NW central section of Henderson County. 7 1/2 mi NW of Lexington.
Barker Ridge	Ridge in W section of Hamilton County.
Barkertown	Community in E area of Grundy County. 10 mi E SE of Altamont.

Barkley Wildlife Management Area (State)	From near center of Stewart County to the Kentucky Border.
Barnardsville	Community in S SW section of Roane County. 9 mi S SW of Kingston.
Barnes	Community in W section of Pickett County. 6 1/2 mi W of Byrdstown.
Barnes	Community in E NE section of Washington County. 10 mi E NE of Jonesborough.
Barnes Hollow	Located in middle N NW section of Houston County, S of Stewart.
Barnes Hollow	Located in N NE section of Putnam County. 8 mi E of Cookeville. S of Willet Mountain.
Barnes Hollow	Located in S section of Stewart County, near Houston County line.
Barnes Store	Community in NW area of Coffee County.
Barnesville	Community on N border of Lawrence County. 13 1/2 mi N NW of Lawrenceburg.
Barnett Mountain	Mountain in E NE section of Warren County, S of Goodbars.
Barnetts	Community in SE section of Sullivan County. 9 mi SE of Blountville.
Barr	Community in NW section of Lauderdale County. 15 mi NW of Ripley.
Barren Plain	Community in middle N NW section of Robertson County. 6 1/2 mi N NW of Springfield.
Barren Spring	Community in NE Section of Carroll County.
Barretville	Community in N NE section of Shelby County. N NE of Rosemark.
Barrons Corner	Community in N central section of Gibson County. 6 mi N of Trenton.
Barthelia	Community in SW section of Trousdale County. 6 mi SW of Hartsville.
Bart Hollow	Located in W central section of Houston County, S of Tennessee Ridge community.
Bartlebaugh	Community in S central section of Hamilton County near Booker T. Washington State Park. 9 mi NE of downtown Chattanooga.
Bartlett	City in near center of Shelby County. 9 mi NE of Memphis. Incorporated in 1866.

Bartons Creek	Creek in N NW section of Wilson County, flows into Cumberland River.
Barton Springs	Community in mid E section of Hamblen County. 4 mi E of Morristown.
Bass Bay	Inlet off Kentucky Lake (Tennessee River) in E NE section of Benton County. Approx. 17 mi N NE of Camden.
Bass Bay	Community in E NE section of Benton County. Approx. 17 mi N NE of Camden.
Bat Creek Knobs	Located in N section of Monroe County, N of Fagin.
Bateman Hollow	Located in middle NE section of Humphreys County. 3 mi NW of McEwen.
Bates	Community in NE central section of Hickman County. Approx. 10 1/2 mi NE of Centerville.
Bates Hill	Community in W NW section of Warren County. 9 1/2 mi W NW of McMinnville.
Bates Mountain	Mountain in E section of Blount County, E of Watertown.
Bath Springs	Community in S area of Decatur County. 10 mi S SE of Decaturville.
Batley	Community in W Central area of Anderson County.
Batson Hollow	Located in W NW section of Humphreys County. 6 mi W of Waverly.
Battery Heights	Community within the city limits of Chattanooga. 4 1/2 mi E NE of downtown. In Hamilton County.
Baucom	Community located in W section of Coffee County, near Bedford County line, 9 mi W NW of Manchester.
Baugh	Community in SE section of Giles County. 13 1/2 mi SE of Pulaski.
Baugh Spring	Community on the W Central border of Bradley County. 6 mi W of Cleveland.
Bauxite Ridge	Ridge in SE section of Hamilton County.
Baxter	City in middle W section of Putnam County. 8 mi W of Cookeville. Incorporated in 1915.
Baxter Bottom	Located in SE section of Tipton County, E of Canaan Grove.
Baylor Lake	Lake in SW section of Hamilton County on

Baylor Lake, (Cont.)	Baylor School Campus in Chattanooga.
Bays Mountain	Mountain along N border of Greene County into Hawkins and the W NW section of Sullivan County.
Bays Mountain	Mountain across central section of Jefferson County.
Bays Mountain Park	Located in NE section of Hawkins County, E of McPheeters Bend.
Bazil Town	Community in N section of Roane County. N of Harriman.
Beacon	Community on W central border of Decatur County. 4 1/2 mi NW of Decaturville.
Bean Mountain	Mountain in NW section of Polk County.
Beans Creek	Community in SW area of Franklin County. 12 mi SW of Winchester.
Bean Station	Community in E NE section of Grainger County. 13 1/2 mi E NE of Rutledge.
Bear Creek	Creek in middle NW section of Stewart County. 4 mi NW of Dover.
Bear Creek Valley	Located in S SW section of Anderson County.
Bear Creek Waterfowl Management Area	Located in NW section of Stewart County, SE of Brandon Springs.
Beard Cane Mountain	Mountain in S SE section of Blount County. 5 mi S SW of Walland.
Bearden	Community within the city limits of Knoxville. 5 1/2 mi SW of downtown. In Knox County
Bear Den Mountain	Mountain in S section of Cumberland County, S of Brady Mountain.
Beardstown	Community in NE section of Perry County. 8 mi N NE of Linden.
Bear Hollow	Located in N section of Anderson County.
Bear Hollow	Located in NW section of Davidson County, S of Joelton.
Bear Knob	Located in SE section of Overton County, W of Twinton.
Bearpen Ridge	Ridge in S SW section of Cocke County, W of Raven Branch.
Bear Spring	Community in middle E SE section of Stewart County. 5 mi E of Dover.

Bear Stand	Community in E central section of Carter County.
Beartown	Community in W NW corner of Sullivan County. 15 mi W NW of Blountville.
Beartree Hollow	Located in S section of Anderson County.
Bearwallow	Community in NE area of Cheatham County.
Bearwallow Mountain	Mountain in NE central section of Sevier County, NE of Richardsons Cove.
Beasley	Community on NE border of Marshall County. 12 mi N NE of Oslin.
Beasley Crossroads	Community in SW corner of Williamson County. 3 mi S SE of Craigfield.
Beasleys Bend	Area in bend of Cumberland River, W section of Smith County. 7 mi W of Carthage.
Beasleys Bend	Area in bend of Cumberland River in S SW section of Trousdale County.
Beauty Hill	Community in middle N section of McNairy County. 7 mi N NE of Selmer.
Beaver	Community in W SW section of Tipton County. Approx. 10 mi W SW of Covington.
Beaver Creek Knobs	Mountain Range in N NE section of Sullivan County, W of Bristol.
Beaverdam Springs	Community in SW section of Hickman County. Approx. 10 mi SW of Centerville.
Beaver Hill	Community in S section of Overton County. 10 1/2 mi S SE of Livingston.
Beaver Ridge	Ridge in middle N section of Knox County, N of Knoxville.
Beckham Ridge	Ridge in W section of Wayne County. E of Gant Ridge.
Beckwith	Community in W section of Wilson County. 9 mi W of Lebanon.
Bedford	Community in W Central section of Bedford County. 6 mi W SW of Shelbyville.
Bedford County BEDFORD COUNTY	County Seat: Shelbyville. Zip Code 37160. Located in S Central section of the State. Bounded by Rutherford, Coffee, Moore, Lincoln and Marshall Counties. Named in honor of Thomas Bedford, Jr.
Bedford Lake	A small body of water located on the E border of Bedford County. 5 mi E SE of Wartrace.

Beech	Community in N central section of Obion County. 4 mi W SW of Union City.
Beech Bluff	Community on E border of Madison County. 10 1/2 mi E of Jackson.
Beech Bottom	Community in S section of Macon County. 4 mi S SE of Lafayette.
Beech Creek	Creek in SE area of Decatur County on Wayne County line.
Beech Fork	Community in SW section of Campbell County.
Beech Grove	Community in N area of Anderson County near Campbell County line. 2 mi NW of Lake City.
Beech Grove	Community in NW area of Cheatham County.
Beechgrove	Community in W NW area of Coffee County. 14 mi NW of Manchester, 3 mi S of Gossburg, near Bedford County line.
Beech Grove	Community in S SW section of Dyer County. 8 mi S SE of Dyersburg.
Beech Grove	Community in N area of Grainger County. 6 1/2 mi N NE of Rutledge.
Beech Grove	Community in S SW section of Hawkins County, S of Persia. 7 1/2 mi S of Rogersville.
Beech Grove	Community in N NW section of Knox County. 12 mi N of Knoxville.
Beech Grove	Community in E central section of Maury County. Approx. 3 mi E of Columbia.
Beech Grove	Community in N NE section of Trousdale County. 4 1/2 mi NE of Hartsville.
Beech Grove	Community in S SW section of Weakley County. Approx. 2 mi S of Greenfield.
Beech Hill	Community in W area of Franklin County. 10 1/2 mi W NW of Winchester.
Beech Hill	Community in E area of Giles County. 8 1/2 mi E NE of Pulaski.
Beech Hill	Community in S SW section of Macon County. 6 mi SW of Lafayette.
Beech Hollow	Located near E border of Cheatham County. 4 mi E of Ashland City.
Beech Island	Island on the Tennessee River in N NW section of Wayne County.
Beech Lake	Community in W Central section of Carroll

Beech Lake, (Cont.)	County W of Anderson.
Beech Lake	Lake in center of Henderson County, NW of Lexington.
Beechnut City	Community in N section of Sullivan County. Approx. 9 mi W of Bristol.
Beech River	River in central section of Decatur County. Flows across the county.
Beech Springs	Community in N NW section of Sevier County. 7 1/2 mi N NW of Sevierville.
Beechwood	Community in NE Section of Bedford County. 12 mi N NE of Shelbyville.
Beef Island Nos. 40 & 41	Island in Mississippi River, W NW border of Shelby County. W of Oaklawn.
Beeler Ridge	Ridge in middle E section of Bradley County, E of Cleveland.
Bee Ridge	Ridge in middle NE section of Cumberland County, S of Genesis.
Beersheba Springs	City in central area of Grundy County. 4 mi NE of Altamont. Incorporated in 1955.
Beetree Knob	Mountain in central section of Cocke County, S of Bridgeport.
Bee Tree Ridge	Ridge in S SE section of Overton County. 8 mi S SE of Livingston. SE of Highland.
Bel Air	Community in central W section of Maury County. 1 mi N of Columbia, N of Forest Hills.
Belcow Mountain	Mountain in S section of Greene County, W of Courtland Place.
Belfast	Community in E SE section of Marshall County. 5 1/2 mi E SE of Lewisburg.
Belinda City	Community in W SW section of Wilson County. 11 mi W SW of Lebanon.
Belk	Communiity in SE area of DeKalb County. 10 1/2 mi SE of Smithville.
Bell Bridge	Community in middle W NW section of Knox County. 7 mi W NW of Knoxville.
Bell Buckle	Town in NE area of Bedford County. 9 mi N NE of Wartrace. Incorporated in 1877.
Bell Campground	Located in middle W NW section of Knox County, W of Powell.
Belle Eagle	Community in middle N section of Haywood

Belle Eagle, (Cont.)	County. 6 1/2 mi N NE of Brownsville.
Bellefount	Community in NE Central section of Bradley County. 6 mi NE of Cleveland.
Belle Meade	Community in W central section of Blount County. 1 mi S of Maryville.
Belle Meade	City in SW section of Davidson County. 6 mi SE of Courthouse. Incorporated in 1938.
Belle Meade	Community in middle E section of Savannah in Hardin County.
Belleview	Community in S section of Lincoln County. 7 1/2 mi S of Fayetteville.
Belleville	Community in N section of Lincoln County. 8 1/2 mi N of Fayetteville.
Bellevue	Community in SW area of Davidson County. 11 mi SW of Courthouse, 4 mi SW of Belle Meade.
Bell Hollow	Located in SW section of Stewart County, N of Asbury.
Bell Mill	Located in SE section of Hamilton County.
Bell Ridge	Ridge in SE section of Hamilton County.
Bells	City in S SE area of Crockett County. 5 mi S of Almo. Incorporated in 1889.
Bells Bend	Located in S SW section of Cheatham County. 3 mi W of Shacklett.
Bells Bend	Located in W SW section of Davidson County. 2 mi N NW of West Meade.
Bellsburg	Community in NE area of Dickson County. 11 mi NE of Charlotte.
Bells Mill	Located in W SW section of Grundy County. 13 mi SW of Altamont. 1 1/2 mi S SW of Pelham.
Bell Spring	Community on N NE border of McMinn County. 9 1/2 mi NE of Athens.
Bell Town	Community in SW area of Cheatham County. 12 mi SW of Ashland City.
Belltown	Community in central section of Monroe County. 9 mi SE of Madisonville.
Belltown	Community in SE corner of Polk County. 20 1/2 mi S SE of Benton.
Belltown Hill	Community in S SE section of Polk County. 21 mi E SE of Benton, E of Isabella.

Bellview	Community in NW section of Bledsoe County. 9 mi N of Pikeville.
Bellview Estates	Community in S SE section of McMinn County, S of Carlock. 12 mi S SE of Athens.
Bellwood	Community in E NE section of Wilson County. 8 1/2 mi E NE of Lebanon.
Belmont	Community in NE area of Anderson County, 2 mi N of Gooseneck.
Belmont	Community in S central section of Coffee County. 4 mi S of Manchester.
Belmont	Community in N NW section of Fayette County. 12 1/2 mi N NW of Somerville.
Belmont	Community in E section of Jefferson County. 5 1/2 mi E of Dandridge.
Belmont	Community in Knox County. 11 mi W SW of Knoxville.
Belotes Bend	Located in SE section of Sumner County. Approx. 8 mi E SE of Gallatin.
Belvedere	Community in SW central section of Franklin County. 7 mi SW of Winchester.
Belvins	Community near center of Hawkins County. 5 1/2 mi NE of Rogersville.
Bemis	Community in S central section of Madison County. Approx. 3 mi S of Jackson.
Benbar	Community in SW section of Davidson County near Oak Hill.
Bench Mountain	Mountain in W section of Sevier County, S of DuPont Springs.
Bending Chestnut	Community in SW section of Williamson County. 13 mi W SW of Franklin.
Ben Henry Lake	Lake in NE corner of Hardeman County.
Benhill	Community in E section of Williamson County. 9 mi E SE of Franklin.
Benjamin Franklin Lake	Lake in W SW section of of Wilson County. 2 mi S SW of Silver Springs.
Benjestown	Community in W section of Shelby County. 7 1/2 mi N of Memphis.
Ben Lomond Mountain	Mountain in S section of Warren County. 5 mi S of McMinnville.
Bennett Hollow	Located in W section of Davidson County.

Bennett Lake	Lake in W central section of Lawrence County. N of Gandy.
Bent Arm	Mountain in SW section of Sevier County. 7 mi S SW of Gatlinburg, S SW of Burnt Mountain.
Benton	County Seat of Polk County. Located in W NW section of the County. Incorporated in 1915.
Benton County BENTON COUNTY	County Seat: Camden. Zip Code 38320. Located NW area of State. Bounded by Houston, Humphreys, Perry, Decatur, Carroll and Henry Counties. Named in honor of David Benton.
Benton Spring	Community in W section of Polk County. 2 1/2 mi S SE of Benton.
Benton Station	Community on W NW border of Polk County. 2 mi W NW of Benton.
Berea	Community in NE central section of Giles County. 5 1/2 mi NE of Pulaski.
Berea	Community in NE section of Warren County. 10 mi N NE of McMinnville.
Bergmantown	Community in SW section of Grundy County.
Berlin	Community in W section of Marshall County. 6 mi N NW of Lewisburg.
Berry	Community in central section of Dickson County. 2 mi W of Charlotte.
Berry Hill	City in S central section of Davidson County. 3 mi S of Courthouse. Incorporated in 1950.
Berrys Chapel	Community in N NW section of Williamson County. 4 mi N NW of Franklin.
Bessie	Community in NW corner of Lake County.
Beta	Community in middle S section of Meigs County. 8 mi S SW of Decatur.
Bethany	Community in SE area of Greene County, near Greystone. 7 1/2 mi SE of Greeneville.
Bethany	Community in middle W NW section of Warren County. 4 1/2 mi W NW of McMinnville.
Bethel	Community in NE section of Anderson County. 6 mi NE of Clinton.
Bethel	Community in Central area of Benton County. 2 mi NE of Camden.
Bethel	Community in E Central section of Blount County. 15 mi E SE of Maryville.

Bethel	Community in N Central section of Carroll County. 2 1/2 mi N of Huntingdon.
Bethel	Community in NW section of Cheatham County. 9 mi SW of Ashland City.
Bethel	Community in S area of DeKalb County. 7 1/2 mi S SE of Smithville.
Bethel	Community in S section of Giles County. 13 1/2 mi S of Pulaski.
Bethel	Community in SW section of Hardin County. 6 1/2 mi S of Savannah. 4 mi N of Pickwick Landing Dam.
Bethel	Community on N border of Haywood County. 10 mi N of Brownsville.
Bethel	Community in N NW section of Maury County. Approx. 13 mi N NW of Columbia.
Bethel	Community in central S section of Perry County. 2 1/2 mi S of Linden.
Bethel	Community in N section of Rutherford County. 8 mi N NE of Murfreesboro.
Bethel Springs	City in middle N NW section of McNairy County. 4 1/2 mi N NW of Selmer. Incorporated in 1927.
Bethel Valley	Located in S SW section of Anderson County.
Bethesda	Community in SE section of Williamson County. 12 mi S SE of Franklin.
Bethlehem	Community in SW area of Bedford County. 9 mi W SW of Shelbyville about 2 mi from Marshall County line.
Bethlehem	Community in E Central area of Campbell County. 8 mi E of LaFollette.
Bethlehem	Community in N Central area of Cheatham County.
Bethlehem	Community on W NW border of Hardin County. 7 mi W NW of Savannah.
Bethlehem	Community in N Section of Henry County. 12 mi N NE of Paris, E NE of Conyersville.
Bethlehem	Community in E SE section of Wayne County near the County Line. 15 mi SE of Waynesboro.
Bethlehem	Community in N section of Williamson County. 5 mi N NW of Franklin.
Bethpage	Community in E section of Sumner County. 10 mi NE of Gallatin.

Bethsalem	Community in middle SE section of McMinn County. 4 mi S SE of Athens.
Betsy Willis	Community in SE corner of Coffee County. 13 1/2 mi SE of Manchester.
Beulah	Community on W border of Greene County. 17 1/2 mi W of Greeneville, S of Creek Store.
Beulah	Community in SW section of Union County. 8 1/2 mi SW of Maynardville.
Beverly	Community within the city limits of Knoxville. 5 1/2 mi N NW of downtown. In Knox County.
Bible Hill	Community in W central section of Decatur County. 8 1/2 mi N of Decaturville.
Bidwell	Community in N NW section of Lincoln County. 9 mi N NW of Fayetteville.
Biffle Hollow	Located in E SE section of Houston County. Approx. 3 mi S of Yellow Creek.
Big Bald Mountain	Mountain in S section of Unicoi County. Ele. 5,516 ft.
Big Bend	Area in W section of Hamilton County.
Big Boy Junction	Community in W central section of Dyer County. 6 1/2 mi W of Dyersburg.
Big Brushy Mountain	Located in E section of Morgan County. S of Petros.
Big Bull Mountain	Mountain in S SE section of Cocke County, S of Tom Town.
Big Butte	Community in W Central area of Anderson County.
Bigbyville	Community in middle S section of Maury County. 7 mi S SW of Columbia.
Big Cherokee	Community in middle S section of Washington County. 4 mi S of Jonesborough.
Big Creek	Body of water in S section of Campbell County (Norris Lake).
Big Creek	Community on W central border of Hancock County. 8 mi W SW of Sneedville. 4 mi W SW of Evanston.
Big Creek	Community in central section of Hawkins County. 6 mi N NE of Rogersville.
Big Creek	Community in middle W section of Monroe County. 5 1/2 mi SE of Madisonville.

Big Creek Knobs	Located in W section of Monroe County, NE of Mount Vernon.
Big Creek Lake	Lake in central section of Grundy County, N of Coalmont. 4 mi S of Altamont.
Big Cypress Tree State Park	Located in SW section of Weakley County. SE of Sharon.
Big Eagle Creek	Creek on NE border of Overton County (Dale Hollow Lake).
Big Elk Creek	Creek in SE section of Stewart County. 3 mi E of Carlisle.
Big Flat Ridge	Ridge in S section of Cocke County, S of Raven Branch.
Big Fodderstack	Mountain in E section of Monroe County, E of Pine Ridge.
Big Fodderstack Mountain	Mountain in W section of Anderson County.
Big Fork Ridge	Ridge in N NW section of Anderson County.
Big Four Mountain	Mountain in N section of Campbell County. 3 mi S of Jellico.
Big Frog Mountain	Mountain in S section of Polk County, E of Ducktown.
Big Hill	Mountain in S SE section of Cocke County, S of Big Bull Mountain.
Big Hill Pond	Pond in SW corner of McNairy County. 11 mi SW of Selmer, in Big Hill Pond State Park.
Big Hill Pond State Park	Located in SW corner of McNairy County. 11 mi SW of Selmer.
Big Hill Pond Trail	Trail in SW section of McNairy County. In Big Hill Pond State Park.
Big Hurricane Creek	Creek in N central section of DeKalb County off Center Hill Lake.
Big Ivy	Community in SE section of Hardin County. 13 mi E SE of Savannah. 12 mi E NE of Pickwick Dam.
Big Lake	Lake in S SE section of Obion County. 12 mi S SW of Union City, S of Long Lake.
Big Laurel Branch Wilderness	Located in N central section of Carter County. 5 mi E of Elizabethton.
Big Lick	Community in S area of Cumberland County. 10 mi S of Crossville.

Big Mountain	Mountain in NW section of Greene County.
Big Mountain	Mountain in S section of Scott County, SE of Lone Mountain.
Big Oak Lake	Lake in middle NE section of Maury County. 8 mi NE of Columbia.
Big Pine Mountain	Mountain in E SE section of Carter County, NE of Laurel Fork.
Big Pine Mountain	Mountain in W section of Sevier County, S of DuPont.
Big Piney	Community in S section of Loudon County. 3 1/2 mi S of Loudon.
Big Possum Creek	Creek in W NW section of Hamilton County.
Big Richland Creek	Creek in NW section of Humphreys County. 8 mi NW of Waverly.
Big Ridge	Ridge in W SW section of Cocke County, SW of Cosby.
Big Ridge	Ridge in N section of Grainger County. 12 mi E NE of Rutledge.
Big Ridge	Community in N central section of Hamilton County in the Hixson area.
Big Ridge	Ridge in W NW section of Scott County in Scott State Forest.
Big Ridge	Ridge in S central section of Sevier County, N of Gatlinburg.
Big Ridge	Ridge in middle N section of Union County, S of Sharps Chapel.
Big Ridge Lake	Lake in W SW section of Union County in Big Ridge State Park.
Big Ridge State Park	Located in W section of Union County on Clinch River.
Big Rock	Community in NE section of Stewart County. 8 mi N NE of Dover.
Big Sandy	Community in NW area of Benton County. 11 mi N of Camden. Incorporated in 1903.
Big Sandy	Community in W section of Washington County. 6 mi W of Jonesborough.
Big Sandy River	River in NE section of Henry County. S of Paris Landing State Park.
Big Sinks	Community in N section of Union County. 9 mi N NW of Maynardville.

Big Soddy	Community in middle N section of Hamilton County, just N of Soddy Lake off Highway 27.
Big South Fork National River and Recreation Area	Located in E NE section of Fentress County and the NW section of Scott County.
Big Spring	Community in W NW central section of Carter County. 3 mi SE of Elizabethton.
Big Spring	Community in S section of Meigs County. 10 1/2 mi S SW of Decatur.
Big Spring Lake	Lake in S SE corner of Humphreys County near Perry County Line.
Big Springs	Community in W Central section of Blount County. 7 mi W of Maryville.
Big Springs	Community in NE corner of Hancock County. 17 mi NE of Sneedville. 7 mi E NE of Kyles Ford.
Big Springs	Community in middle NE section of Overton County. Approx. 4 mi NE of Livingston.
Big Springs	Community in SE corner of Rutherford County. Approx. 11 mi SE of Murfreesboro.
Big Spring Union	Community in NE area of Claiborne County. 9 1/2 mi NE of Tazewell.
Big Top	Located in SE section of Franklin County. E of Tally Top.
Bikerstaff Lake	Lake in SW area of Bledsoe County S of Fall Creek Falls State Park.
Bilbrey	Community in E NE section of Putnam County. Approx. 8 mi E of Cookeville.
Bill Wilks Swamp	Swamp in N NW section of Hardeman County, E of Vildo.
Biltmore	Community in NW area of Carter County. 2 mi N of Elizabethton.
Binfield	Community in W Central section of Blount County. 5 mi SW of Maryville.
Bingham	Community in central W section of Williamson County. 5 1/2 mi W of Franklin.
Birchwood	Community in NE area of Hamilton County near Meigs County line. 29 mi NE of downtown Chattanooga.
Bird Crossroads	Community in NE section of Sevier County. 11 1/2 mi E NE of Sevierville.
Bird Mill	Community in SE section of Lawrence County. E

Bird Mill, (Cont.)	SE of Center Point.
Bird Mountain	Mountain in middle E section of Morgan County.
Birds Bower	Community in SW corner of Haywood County, S SW of Stanton.
Birdsong Creek	Creek in SE section of Benton, W of Mt. Moriah. Flows into Tennessee River.
Birdsong Heights	Community in E SE section of Benton County, E of Chalklevel.
Bishop	Community in SE area of Dyer County. 4 mi E SE of Dyersburg.
Bitter End	Community in SE Section of Carter County. 12 mi SE of Elizabethton.
Bivens	Community in NE area of Giles County. 14 mi N NE of Pulaski.
Black Center	Community in Central area of Benton County. Approx. 1 mi NE of Camden.
Black Creek	Creek in SW section of Hamilton County, part of Lookout Creek.
Black Creek	Community in W SW section of Scott County. 7 mi W SW of Huntsville.
Black Fox	Community in S Central area of Bradley County. 3 mi E of McDonald.
Black Fox	Community in NW corner of Grainger County. 9 mi W NW of Rutledge.
Black Hallow	Located in S section of Houston County. Approx. 4 mi S of Erin.
Black Jack	Community in Central section of Coffee County. 2 1/2 mi S SW of Manchester.
Black John Hollow	Located in W section of Dickson County, N of Adams Crossroads.
Blackman	Community in middle W section of Rutherford County. 5 1/2 mi W NW of Murfreesboro.
Blackman Hollow	Located in E section of Bedford County.
Black Mountain	Mountain in SE section of Cumberland County, SE of Meridian.
Black Oak	Community within the city limits of Knoxville. 5 mi N NW of downtown. In Knox County.
Black Oak	Community in middle N NW section of Scott County. 8 1/2 mi NW of Huntsville.

Black Oak	Community in middle NW section of White County. Approx. 5 mi W NW of Sparta.
Blackoak Ridge	Ridge in S SW section of Anderson County.
Blackoak Ridge	Ridge in S section of Rhea County, E of Graysville.
Blackoak Ridge	Ridge in NE section of Roane County.
Black Sulphur Knobs	Mountain in S central section of Blount County, N of Sixmile.
Blaine	City in SW area of Grainger County. 14 mi SW of Rutledge. Incorporated in 1978.
Blair	Community in N NE section of Roane County. 10 mi N NE of Kingston.
Blair Gap	Community in SW corner of Sullivan County. 19 mi SW of Blountville.
Blair Lake	Lake in NE corner of Madison County. Approx. 11 mi NE of Jackson.
Blaker Towhead	Located in SW corner of Lake County and the NW corner of Dyer County.
B Lakes	Lake within the city limits of Coalmont in Grundy County. 6 mi S of Altamont.
Blakeville	Community in NW section of Lincoln County. 9 1/2 mi NW of Fayetteville.
Blanche	Community in SW section of Lincoln County. 12 mi SW of Fayetteville.
Blanket Mountain	Mountain in SW corner of Sevier County. 7 mi S SW of Gatlinburg.
Blanks Hollow	Located in E section of Benton County, S of Harmon Creek.
Blanton Chapel	Community in W area of Coffee County. 4 mi W of Manchester.
Blaylock Mountain	Mountain in N NE section of Putnam County. 2 mi E of Brotherton.
Bledsoe	Community in N section of Lincoln County. 12 1/2 mi N of Fayetteville.
Bledsoe	Community in E NE section of Sumner County. Approx. 3 mi S SW of Westmoreland.
Bledsoe County 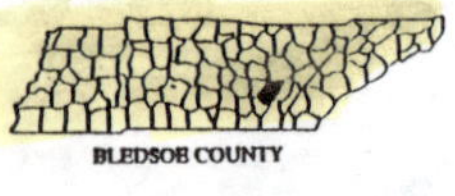 	County Seat: Pikeville. Zip Code: 37367. Located in SE area of the State. Bounded by Cumberland, Rhea, Hamilton, Sequatchie and Van Buren Counties. Named in honor of Anthony Bledsoe.

Bledsoe Creek	Creek in SE section of Sumner County. Flows into Cumberland River (Old Hickory Lake).
Bledsoe Creek State Park	Located in SE section of Sumner County. E of Gallatin.
Bledsoe Hollow	Located in S SW section of Bedford County.
Bledsoe State Forest	Located in NW area of Bledsoe County. 7 mi N NW of Pikeville.
Blevins	Community in S Central area of Carter County. 8 mi S of Elizabethton.
Block	Community in SW area of Campbell County.
Blockhouse	Community in near center of Blount County. 4 mi SE of Maryville.
Blockhouse Valley	Located in middle S section of Anderson County.
Blondy	Community in central section of Lewis County. N NE of Hohenwald.
Bloomingdale	Community in N NW section of Sullivan County. 9 1/2 mi W NW of Blountville.
Blooming Grove Creek	Creek in W section of Montgomery County, flows into Cumberland River. Runs E and N of Stringtown.
Bloomington	Community in NW section of Pickett County. 3 1/2 mi W NW of Byrdstown.
Bloomington Heights	Community in NW section of Sullivan County. 1 mi N of Kingsport.
Bloomington Springs	Community in middle NW section of Putnam County. 7 mi W NW of Cookeville.
Blossom	Community in E SE section of Hawkins County. 15 mi E NE of Rogersville. 1 mi SW of Goshen.
Blount Beach	Community in N Central section of Blount County near Maryville.
Blount County 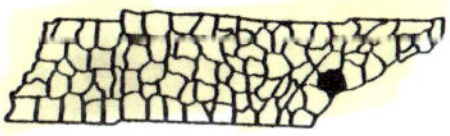 BLOUNT COUNTY	County Seat: Maryville. Zip Code: 37801. Located in SE section of the State. Bounded by Monroe, Loudon, Knox and Sevier Counties and North Carolina to the East. Named in honor of William Blount.
Blountville	County Seat of Sullivan County. Located near center of county.
Blowing Springs	Community in E central section of Anderson County. 3 mi N of Clinton.
Blowing Springs	Community in Wayne County located 7 1/2 mi E

Blowing Springs, (Cont.)	NE of Waynesboro,
Blue Bank	Community in middle E section of Lake County on Reelfoot Lake, N of Owl City.
Bluebird Ridge	Ridge in NE section of Anderson County and SW corner of Union County.
Blue Creek	Town in NE section of Giles County.
Blue Creek	Creek in S SW section of Humphreys County, flows into Tennessee River.
Blue Goose	Community on W NW border of Henderson County. 11 mi W NW of Lexington.
Blue Goose Hollow	Located on old W side of the City of Chattanooga on the E bank of the Tennessee River and W edge of Cameron Hill, N of Tannery Flats. In Hamilton County. Homeplace of the late great blues singer Bessie Smith.
Blue Grass	Community in S SW section of Knox County. 11 mi SW of Knoxville.
Bluegrass Ridge	Ridge in middle S section of Stewart County, N NE of Asbury.
Blue Hill	Community on NW border of Warren County. 11 1/2 mi NW of McMinnville.
Blue Knob	Located in W SW section of Smith County. 2 mi E of Flat Rock.
Blue Mill	Community in SE section of Cocke County.
Blue Pond	Pond in SW section of Lauderdale County, in the Anderson-Tully Wildlife Area.
Blue Ridge	Ridge in N section of Fentress County, SE of Pall Mall.
Blue Ridge Mountain	Mountain on S border of Polk County.
Blue Rock Mountain	Mountain in W section of Sevier County, N of Hornet.
Blue Sky	Community in N NW section of Perry County. Approx. 11 mi N NW of Linden.
Blue Spring	Community in N central section of Carter County. 5 mi E of Elizabethton.
Blue Springs	Community in S Central section of Bradley County. 4 mi S of Cleveland.
Blue Springs	Community in S area of DeKalb County. 6 1/2 mi S of Smithville.

Blue Springs	Community in E area of Hamilton County near Snow Hill.
Blue Springs Ridge	Ridge in S SW section of Bradley County, E of Lead Mine Ridge.
Bluestocking Hollow	Located in SW section of Bedford County.
Blue Water Lake	Located in E NE section of Williamson County. 14 mi E NE of Franklin.
Bluewing	Community in E Central section of Cannon County. 5 mi SE of Woodbury.
Bluff City	City in central SE section of Sullivan County. 7 1/2 mi SE of Blountville. Incorporated in 1870.
Bluff Creek	Community in middle S section of Smith County. 2 1/2 mi S of Carthage.
Bluff Springs	Community in N section of Warren County. 9 1/2 mi N of McMinnville.
Bluffton	Community in SW area of Cocke County. 10 mi S of Newport.
Bluhmtown	Community in SW area of DeKalb County. 5 1/2 mi SW of Smithville.
Blunts Landing	Community on W border of Perry County. 10 mi W of Linden.
Blythe Ferry	Ferry that crosses the Tennessee River from Meigs County to Rhea County at Dayton.
Blythe Ferry Goose Management Area	Located in S SW section of Meigs County, S of Hiwassee Island.
Board Camp Creek	Creek in W NW section of Hamilton County.
Board Camp Gulf	Area in W NW section of Hamilton County.
Board Valley	Community in N NE section of White County. 9 1/2 mi N NE of Sparta.
Bobtown	Community in E section of Franklin County.
Bodenham	Community in W area of Giles County. 7 1/2 mi W NW of Pulaski.
Boggess Crossroad	Community in middle NE section of Meigs County. 9 mi NE of Decatur.
Bogota	Community in N NW section of Dyer County. 9 1/2 mi N NW of Dyersburg.
Boiling Fork Creek	Creek in central section of Franklin County, flows NW to SE through Winchester.

Boiling Pond	Community in SW section of White County. 7 mi W SW of Sparta, E of Yateston.
Boiling Spring Hollow	Located in N NW section of Hamilton County.
Boiling Springs	Community in S SW section of Putnam County. 8 1/2 mi S SW of Cookeville.
Bold Spring	Community in SE section of Humphreys County. 10 mi SE of Waverly.
Bolens Chapel	Community in middle NW section of Henderson County. 3 1/2 mi NW of Lexington.
Bolivar	County seat of Hardeman County. Located in center of the County. Incorporated in 1827.
Bolton	Community in NE section of Shelby County. 20 1/2 mi NE of Memphis.
Boma	Community in SW section of Putnam County. 10 1/2 mi W SW of Cookeville.
Bomer Lake	Lake in central section of Haywood County, NW of Brownsville.
Bon Air	Community in N NE section of Sumner County. 15 mi N NE of Gallatin.
Bon Air	Community in middle E section of White County. 5 1/2 mi E NE of Sparta.
Bon Aqua	Community in N NE section of Hickman County. 14 1/2 mi N NW of Centerville.
Bon Aqua Junction	Community in NE section of Hickman County, E NE of Lyles.
Bond	Community in SE central section of Hickman County. 5 1/2 mi SE of Centerville.
Bon De Croft	Community in middle E section of White County. 7 1/2 mi E of Sparta.
Bone Cave	Community in NW corner of Van Buren County. 7 mi W NW of Spencer.
Bone Cave Mountain	Mountain in N NN W section of Van Buren County, NW of Spencer.
Bone Cave State Park	Located in NW section of Van Buren County.
Bone Hollow	Located in W SW section of Humphreys County. 2 mi W of Plant.
Bonham	Community in NW section of Rhea County. N NW of Spring City.
Bonicord	Community in SE area of Dyer County. 6 1/2 mi

Bonicord, (Cont.)	S SE of Dyersburg.
Bonnertown	Community on S SE border of Lawrence County. 16 mi S SE of Lawrenceburg. 4 mi W SW of Appleton.
Bonny Kate	Community in S section of Knox County. 6 1/2 mi S SE of Knoxville.
Bonny Oaks	Community in S central section of Hamilton County. 8 mi NE of downtown Chattanooga.
Bonsack	Community in SE section of Overton County. 15 mi S SE of Livingston.
Booker T. Washington State Park	Located in S central section of Hamilton County. 9 mi NE of downtown Chattanooga.
Boom	Community in SW section of Pickett County. Approx. 4 mi S SW of Byrdstown.
Boomer	Community in SE area of Cocke County. 5 mi SE of French Broad.
Boone	Community in middle NE section of Washington County. 6 mi N NE of Jonesborough.
Boone Lake	Lake in S SW section of Sullivan County, S of Holston.
Boones Creek	Community in NE section of Washington County. 7 1/2 mi N NE of Jonesborough.
Booneville	Community on NE border of Lincoln County. 10 1/2 mi NE of Fayetteville.
Boonshill	Community in W NW section of Lincoln County. 10 1/2 mi W NW of Fayetteville.
Boothspoint	Community in NW section of Dyer County on the Mississippi River.
Bordeaux	Community in central section of Davidson County. 4 mi NW of Courthouse.
Boring	Community in S SW section of Sullivan County. 7 1/2 mi S SW of Blountville.
Boston	Community in S SW section of Williamson County. 10 1/2 mi SW of Franklin.
Boston Branch Lake	Lake in W section of Hamilton County on Waldens Ridge. Approx. 5 mi N NE of Fairmount, Approx. 5 mi W of Daisy.
Boston Hollow	Located in middle section of Cheatham County. 2 mi E of Ashland City.
Bote Mountain	Mountain in SE section of Blount County. 5 mi E of Cades Cove.

Bottle Hollow	In SE section of Bedford County. 7 mi SE of Shelbyville.
Boulton Bend	Area in bend of Caney Fork River, S central section of Smith County. 2 mi SE of Carthage.
Bowers	Community in NW central section of Carter County.
Bowling	Community in Central section of Cumberland County. 4 mi E SE of Crossville.
Bowman	Community in N central section of Cumberland County. 8 mi N of Crossville.
Bowmantown	Community in W section of Washington County. 5 mi W of Jonesborough.
Box Elder	Community in middle W section of Hardin County. 4 mi W NW of Savannah.
Boxley Valley	Located in middle W section of Williamson County, E SE of Bingham.
Boxwell Reservation (B.S.A.)	Located in NW section of Wilson County. 12 mi NW of Lebanon.
Boxwood Hills	Community in W SW section of Knox County. 10 mi W SW of Knoxville. N of Lovell.
Boyce	Community within the city limits of Chattanooga. 3 mi NE of downtown in E Chattanooga, Hamilton County.
Boyd	Community in SW corner of Knox County. 16 mi SW of Knoxville, S of Virtue.
Boyd Bottoms	Located in NW section of Polk County, W of Patty.
Boyd Island	Island on Holston River in the E section of Knox County. E of Knoxville.
Boyds Creek	Community in NW section of Sevier County. 7 mi W NW of Sevierville.
Boyer Island	Island on French Broad River, N NE of Jimtown, in Cocke County.
Boynton Valley	Community in middle W NW section of Coffee County. 2 mi S SE of Farrar Hill.
Brace	Community in N section of Lawrence County. 9 mi N of Lawrenceburg.
Brackens Lake	Lake in SW area of Dyer County on Moss Island.
Brackentown	Community in N section of Sumner County 15 mi N NE of Gallatin.

Bradburn Hill	Community in central section of Greene County. 3 mi NE of Greeneville.
Bradbury	Community in middle E section of Roane County. 7 mi E of Kingston.
Braden	City in NW area of Fayette County. 16 mi NW of Somerville. Incorporated in 1969.
Braden	Community in N NW section of Union County. 12 mi N NW of Maynardville.
Braden Flats	Community in N Central section of Anderson County, between Frost Bottom and Briceville. 4 mi SW of Briceville.
Braden Mountain	Community in NW section of Campbell County near the Scott County Line.
Bradford	City in NE area of Gibson County. 10 mi NE of Trenton. Incorporated in 1913.
Bradley County	County Seat: Cleveland. Zip Code: 37311. Located in SE section of the State. Bounded by Hamilton, Meigs, McMinn and Polk counties and the State of Georgia to the South. Named in honor of Col. Edward Bradley of Shelby County.
Bradley Hill	Located in E NE section of Robertson County, E of Cross Plains.
Bradley Hollow	Located on S SW border of Stewart County, W of Redbank Hill.
Bradleytown	Community in SW area of Dyer County. 15 mi W SW of Dyersburg.
Bradshaw	Town in E section of Giles County.
Brady Mountain	Mountain in S section of Cumberland County, W of Grassy Cove.
Bradyville	Community in SW section of Cannon County. 8 mi SW of Woodbury.
Braemar	Community in middle W section of Carter County. 5 mi SE of Elizabethton.
Brainerd	Community within the city limits of Chattanooga. 5 mi E SE of downtown. Hamilton County.
Brainerd Hills	Community within the city limits of Chattanooga. 7 mi E SE of downtown. Hamilton County.
Brake Hollow	Located in W NW section of Humphreys County. S of Littleton Hollow. 6 mi W NW of Waverly.
Branchville	Community in SW section of Bedford County. 2 mi W SW of Richmond.

Branchville	Community in SW area of Franklin County. 13 1/2 mi SW of Winchester.
Brandon Spring	Located in NW section of Stewart County, W of Bear Creek Waterfowl Management Area.
Bransford	Community in E section of Sumner County. Approx. 4 mi S SW of Westoreland.
Branum	Community in N NE area of Fentress County.
Brashear Island	Island on Clinch River, 3 mi N NW of Union in Roane County.
Bratchers Crossroads	Community in W NW section of Warren County. 9 1/2 mi NW of McMinnville.
Brattontown	Community in near center of Macon County. 12 mi W NW of Lafayette.
Bray	Community in SW section of Hancock County. 10 mi SW of Sneedville. 5 1/2 mi W of Treadway.
Brayton	Community in SE area of Bledsoe County. 8 mi S of Pikeville.
Braytown	(Dovonia P.O.) in W NW section of Anderson County. 8 mi NW of Oliver Springs.
Brazil	Community in SW section of Gibson County. 8 mi SW of Trenton.
Breedenton	Community on W border of Meigs County. N NW of Decatur.
Brentwood	Community in S area of Davidson County.
Brentwood	Community within the city limits of Chattanooga. 7 mi E NE of downtown. In Hamilton County.
Brentwood	Community in Knox County. 9 mi W of Knoxville.
Brentwood	City in N NE section of Williamson County. 5 mi N NE of Franklin. Incorporated in 1969.
Brewer Gap	Located in middle N section of Hancock County. 4 mi W of Sneedville.
Brewstertown	Community in N section of Morgan County. 18 mi N NW of Wartburg.
Briarpatch Lake	Lake in W central section of Henry County. 7 mi W of Paris.
Briar Thicket	Community in NW section of Cocke County. 3 1/2 mi NE of Liberty Hill.
Briarwood	Community in central N section of Montgomery County. 2 1/2 mi S of Clarksville.

Briceville	Community in N Central area of Anderson County. 6 mi NW of Clinton.
Brick Church	Community in NE section of Giles County. 10 mi NE of Pulaski.
Brick Mill	Community in W Central section of Blount County near Binfield.
Brickyard Pond	Pond in SE section of Haywood County. 9 mi E SE of Brownsville. 6 1/2 NE of Eurekaton.
Bride	Community in N section of Tipton County. 4 1/2 mi W NW of Covington.
Bridgeport	Community in Central area of Cocke County. 3 mi E of Newport.
Bridwell Heights	Community in NW section of Sullivan County. Approx. 4 mi E of Kingsport.
Brier Hill	Community in N NE section of Lawrence County, approx. 7 mi N NW of Lawrenceburg.
Brier Knob	Located in SE corner of Blount County, in Great Smoky Mountains.
Brier Lick Knob	Located in S SE section of Blount County, near border. 11 mi S SW of Townsend.
Brigham Hill	Community in E SE section of Stewart County. 9 mi E SE of Dover.
Brigham Hollow	Located in N section of Humphreys County. 2 mi W SW of Woolworth.
Bright Hope	Community in SW section of Greene County, near Cedar Creek. 9 mi SW of Greeneville.
Brighton	Community in SE section of Lincoln County. 9 mi E SE of Fayetteville.
Brighton	City in near center of Tipton County. 7 mi S SW of Covington. Incorporated in 1860.
Brims Corner	Community in central section of Crockett County. 3 mi W NW of Alamo.
Brister Hollow	Located near N NW border of Humphreys County. 3 mi N of Halls Creek.
Bristol	City on N NE border of Sullivan County. 9 mi E NE of Blountville. Incorporated in 1855.
Britton Hill	Located in W NW section of Rutherford County. 1 mi W of Hilltop.
Brittontown	Community in middle N section of Greene County. 8 mi N of Greeneville.

Britts Hollow	Located in NE section of Benton County.
Britts Landing	Community in NW corner of Perry County. 14 mi N NW of Linden.
Brittsville	Community in S section of Meigs County. 13 mi S SW of Decatur.
Broad Acres	Community in Knox County. 8 1/2 mi NW of downtown Knoxville.
Broadmoor	Community in N NW section of Dyer County. 12 1/2 mi N NW of Dyersburg.
Broadview	Community in W area of Crockett County. 2 1/2 mi NW of Maury City, 9 mi W NW of Alamo.
Broadview	Community in W central section of Franklin County. 5 mi W of Winchester.
Broadview	Community in S section of Maury County. N of Southport.
Broadway	Community in NW central section of Henderson County. 4 1/2 mi W NW of Lexington.
Brockdell	Community in SW area of Bledsoe County. 9 mi SW of Pikeville.
Brock Hollow	Located in E SE section of Lawrence County. S of Prospect.
Brock Mountain	Mountain in central S section of Polk County.
Brookfield Acres	Community in middle NE section of Knox County. 2 mi W of Maloneyville.
Brooklin	Community in SE area of Davidson County.
Brooklyn Heights	Community in central section of Davidson County W of Nashville.
Brooks Bend	Area in bend of the Cumberland River, SW corner of Jackson County.
Brookside	Community in SW section of Campbell County.
Brotherton	Community in middle N NE section of Putnam County. 6 1/2 mi E NE of Cookeville.
Browder	Community in N central section of Loudon County. 3 mi N NE of Loudon.
Brown Crossroads	Community in S section of Lawrence County. 12 1/2 mi S SW of Lawrenceburg. 3 mi E SE of Lawrenceburg.
Brown Hollow	Located in E section of Humphreys County. 3 1/2 mi S SE of McEwen.

Brown Hollow	Located in NE section of Humphreys County. 3 1/2 mi N of Mc Ewen.
Browning Hollow	Located in NW section of Humphreys County, W of Mooney Hollow. 3 mi W NW of Halls Creek.
Brownington	Community in W NW section of Franklin County. 10 mi W NW of Winchester.
Brown Lake	Lake in E SE section of Lawrence County. NW of Gum Springs.
Brown Mill	Community in SW area of Franklin County. 11 1/2 mi SW of Winchester.
Brown Mountain	Mountain in S SE section of Knox County, S of Lake Forest.
Brown Mountain	Mountain in SE section of Warren County. 11 mi SE of McMinnville.
Brown Ridge	Ridge in N section of Smith County. 2 mi W of Cartwright.
Browns	Community located in S central section of Cocke County. 12 mi S SE of Newport.
Browns	Community in middle SE section of Macon County. 3 1/2 mi E SE of Lafayette.
Browns Chapel	Community in S section of Sequatchie County. 10 1/2 mi S of Dunlap.
Browns Creek Lake	Lake in NE section of Henderson County. 8 mi NE of Lexington.
Browns Ferry	Community in SW area of Hamilton County, W of Lookout Mountain.
Browns Hollow	Located in W section of Dickson County. 2 mi E of Thompsons Crossroads.
Browns Lake	Lake in N NW section of Davidson County on Robertson County line.
Browns Lake	Lake on S SE border of Robertson County. SW of Ridgetop.
Browns Shop	Community in SE section of Marshall County. Approx. 9 mi S SE of Lewisburg.
Brownsville	County Seat of Haywood County. Located in center of County. Incorporated in 1870.
Brownsville	Community on N border of Houston County. 3 1/2 mi N NW of Centerville.
Browntown	Community in W area of Cumberland County. 10 mi W of Crossville.

Browntown Ridge	Ridge in W section of Wayne County. E of Martins Mills.
Broyles	Community in NW Central section of Campbell County. 8 mi NW of LaFollette.
Broylesville	Community in W SW section of Washington County. 9 mi SW of Jonesborough.
Bruce Ridge	Ridge in NW section of Putnam County, E of Robinson Ridge. 2 mi S SE of Gentry.
Bruceton	City in NE area of Carroll County. 10 mi E of Huntingdon. Incorporated in 1925.
Brundige	Community in N NE section of Weakley County. Approx. 10 mi N NE of Dresden.
Bruner Grove	Community in N area of Cocke County. 9 mi N NE of Newport.
Brunswick	Community in middle NE section of Shelby County. 19 mi NE of Memphis.
Brush Creek	Community in middle N NE section of Sequatchie County. Approx. 3 mi N NE of Dunlap.
Brush Creek	Community in S SW section of Smith County. 10 mi S SW of Carthage.
Brush Creek	Community in NW section of Williamson County. 12 1/2 mi W NW of Franklin.
Brush Creek Mountain	Mountain in E section of Cocke County, N of Wolf Creek.
Brush Mountain	Mountain in E section of Monroe County, in Citico Creek Wilderness.
Brushy Mountain	Mountain in middle N section of Campbell County, N NE of Peabody.
Brushy Mountain	Mountain in W section of Campbell County, W of Silica.
Brushy Mountain	Mountain in SE area of Cocke County near border, E of Nough, in the Cherokee National Forest.
Brushy Mountain	Mountain in middle SE section of Overton County. 1 mi S SE of Livingston.
Brushy Mountain	Mountain in SE section of Sevier County. 6 mi E SE of Gatlinburg.
Brushy Mountain State Prison Farm	Located in midde E section of Morgan County. 3 mi E of Wartburg.
Brushy Ridge	Ridge in N central section of Hancock County, E of Sneedville.

Brushy Ridge	Ridge in SE section of Monroe County, E SE of Waucheesi.
Brushy Valley	Community in E Central area of Anderson County.
Bruton Branch	Community in S section of Hardin County on the Tennessee River (Pickwick Lake).
Bryan Mill	Located in S SW corner of Warren County. 12 mi SW of McMinnville, near county line.
Bryant	Community in middle SW section of Sequatchie County. 6 mi S SW of Dunlap.
Bryant Island	Island on French Broad River in NW section of Sevier County, N of Boyds Creek.
Bryant Station	Community in SE section of Maury County. 11 mi SE of Columbia.
Brydon Ridge	Ridge in SE section of Hamilton County.
Bryson	Community in E SE section of Giles County. 12 mi E SE of Pulaski.
Bryson Gap	Located in N section of Hancock County. 4 mi N NE of Sneedville.
Bryson Mountain	Community in N Central section of Claiborne County. 1 mi SW of Fork Ridge.
Brysonville	Community in NW section of Cannon County. 4 mi NW of Woodbury.
Buchanan	Community in NE section of Henry County. 12 mi NNE of Paris.
Buchanan Hollow	Located in S SW section of Houston County, S SE of Magnolia.
Buck Creek Lake	Lake in E NE section of White County near Putnam County Line. 11 mi E NE of Sparta.
Buckeye	Community in Central NW section of Campbell County. 9 mi W NW of LaFollette.
Buckeye Hollow	Located near W NW border of Dickson County. 3 mi N NW of Adams Crossroads.
Buckeye Lead	Mountain in SW corner of Cocke County.
Buckeye Ridge	Ridge in SE corner of Williamson County, SW of Riggs Crossroads.
Buckhorn Hollow	Located in E section of Humphreys County. 3 mi E SE of McEwen.
Buckingham Island	Island on French Broad River in N NW section of Sevier County, E of Boyds Creek.

Buck Knob	Mountain in SE section of Johnson County, N of Trade.
Bucklick	Community in W section of Morgan County. W SW of Deer Lodge.
Buck Lodge	Community in central NW section of Sumner County. 9 mi N NW of Gallatin.
Buck Mountain	Mountain in NW section of Fentress County, N of Fairview.
Buck Mountain	Mountain in middle E section of Putnam County. 4 mi E of Cookeville.
Buckner	Community in E central section of DeKalb County. 4 1/2 mi NE of Smithville.
Buckner Chapel	Community in E section of Putnam County. 14 1/2 E of Cookeville.
Bucksnort	Community in NW section of Hickman County. 14 1/2 mi W NW of Centerville near Interstate 40.
Bucksnort Ridge	Ridge in middle SE section of Wayne County. E of McGlamerys Stand.
Buck Tom Scout Camp	Community in SW section of Roane County. 11 mi SW of Kingston.
Bucktown	Community in N central section of Hardin County. 4 mi N NE of Savannah.
Bucktown	Community in NE section of Loudon County, S of Lenoir City.
Buena Vista	Community in E Central section of Carroll County. 8 mi E of Huntingdon.
Buffalo	Community in NW section of Anderson County.
Buffalo	Community in S section of Hickman County. Approx. 6 mi S of Centerville.
Buffalo	Community in S section of Humphreys County. 13 1/2 mi S of Waverly.
Buffalo	Community in middle E SE section of Scott County. 4 mi E SE of Huntsville.
Buffalo	Community in central section of Sullivan County. 3 mi S SE of Blountville.
Buffalo Mountain	Mountain in W section of Anderson County, E of Rosedale.
Buffalo Mountain	Mountain in E section of Scott County. S of New Salem.
Buffalo Mountain	Mountain in SE section of Washington County,

Buffalo Mountain, (Cont.)	near border. E of Dry Creek.
Buffalo River	Flows from Lawrence County through Lewis, Wayne, Perry and Humphreys Counties, where it flows into the Duck River.
Buffalo Springs	Community in S SW section of Grainger County. 5 mi S SW of Rutledge.
Buffalo Valley	Community in S SW section of Lewis County, W of Riverside.
Buffalo Valley	Community on W border of Putnam County. 17 mi W SW of Cookeville.
Buffat Heights	Community within the city limits of Knoxville. 5 mi N NE of downtown. In Knox County.
Bufords	Community in N central section of Giles County. 9 1/2 mi N of Pulaski.
Bug Hollow	Located in central W NW section of Sumner County. 1 1/2 mi N NE of Cottonwood.
Bug Hollow	Located in SE section of Wilson County. 2 mi E of Sherrilltown.
Bugscuffle	Community in E Central section of Bedford County. 8 mi E of Shelbyville, 1 1/2 mi S of Wartrace.
Bug Tussle	Community in middle E section of Macon County.
Buladeen	Community in NE area of Carter County. 12 mi NE of Elizabethton.
Bullet Mountain	Mountain in central section of Monroe County, S of Belltown.
Bullett Creek	Community on SW border of Monroe County. 19 mi S of Madisonville.
Bull Head	Mountain in S section of Sevier County. 3 1/2 mi S SE of Gatlinburg, S of Mount Le Conte.
Bull Hollow	Located in NW section of Humphreys County. 11 mi NW of Waverly.
Bullpen Landing	Located in W section of Shelby County, W of Ramsey.
Bull Run	Community in SE Area of Anderson County. 1 mi from Knox County Line. 5 mi SE of Clinton.
Bull Run	Community in NW area of Davidson County.
Bullrun Ridge	Ridge in S SE section of Anderson County and W section of Knox County.

Bull Run Steam Plant	(TVA) In SE section of Anderson County. 5 mi S of Clinton.
Bulls Gap	Community in W area of Greene County, near Mohawk.
Bulls Gap	City on S border of Hawkins County. 11 1/2 mi S SW of Rogersville. Incorporated in 1955.
Bullskin Ridge	Ridge in W SW section of Anderson County.
Bumpus Cove	Community in middle W section of Unicoi County. 4 mi W of Erwin.
Bumpus Mills	Community in N section of Stewart County. 8 1/2 mi N of Dover.
Buncombe	Community in N NE section of Sullivan County. Approx. 9 mi SW of Bristol.
Bungalow Town	Community in middle NW section of Blount County. 1 mi NW of Maryville.
Bunker Hill	Community in N NW section of Carter County, near border. 2 mi N NW of Keenburg.
Bunker Hill	Community in E SE section of Giles County. 9 1/2 mi E SE of Pulaski.
Bunker Hill	Located in E central section of Hawkins County, E of Striggersville.
Bunker Hill	Located in S SW section of Rutherford County. S of Puckett Store.
Buntontown	Community in SW corner of Johnson County. 16 mi SW of Mountain City.
Burbank	Community in S area of Carter County. 4 mi S SW of Roan Mountain.
Burchfield Heights	Community in W section of Knox County. 12 mi W of Knoxville, N of Solway.
Burem	Community near center of Hawkins County. 5 mi E of Rogersville.
Burge Mountain	Mountain in NW section of Anderson County.
Burgen	Community in SW section of Cannon County. 7 mi S SW of Woodbury.
Burger	Community in E SE section of McMinn County. 9 mi E SE of Athens. S SE of Englewood.
Burgess Falls Lake	Lake in NW corner of White County. 3 mi W of Macedonia.
Burgess Falls State Natural Area	Located in NW corner of White County. 3 mi W of Macedonia and extends into the S SW section

Burgess Falls State Natural Area, (Cont.)	of Putnam County.
Burgess Hollow	Located in E NE section of Humphreys County. 5 mi N NE of McEwen.
Burgess Knob	Located in SW section of Smith County. 2 mi N NE of Brush Creek.
Burke	Community in S area of Cumberland County. 12 mi S of Crossville.
Burke Hollow	Located in E section of Williamson County. 10 mi E of Franklin.
Burkett Siding	Community in W section of Madison County. Approx. 4 mi W SW of Jackson.
Burlington	Community within Knoxville City limits. 4 mi NE of downtown. In Knox County.
Burlington Heights	Community in E Central section of Bradley County near Cleveland.
Burlison	City in W NW section of Tipton County. 8 mi W of Covington. Incorporated in 1965.
Burnett	Community in S SE section of Putnam County. 8 mi SE of Cookeville.
Burnett Hollow	Located in middle W section of Williamson County, N of Bingham.
Burnett Mountain	Mountain in S SE section of Putnam County. 9 mi SE of Cookeville.
Burningham Hollow	Located in W NW section of Humphreys County, E of Anderson Hollow. 3 mi S of Trinity.
Burn Out Hollow	Located in N section of Anderson County.
Burns	City in SE central section of Dickson County. 9 mi S SE of Charlotte. Incorporated in 1953.
Burns Island	Island in S SW section of Marion County on the Tennessee River (Guntersville Lake).
Burnt Chruch	Community in E central section of Hardin County. 7 1/2 mi E SE of Savannah. 10 1/2 mi NE of Pickwick Dam.
Burnt Mountain	Mountain in SW section of Sevier County. 5 mi S SW of Gatlinburg.
Burristown	Community in E NE section of Jackson County. 7 mi E NE of Gainesboro.
Burrow Cove	Located in W SW section of Grundy County, W of Elkhead.

Burrville	Community in NW section of Morgan County. 16 mi NW of Wartburg.
Burt	Community in Central SW area of Cannon County. 5 mi SW of Woodbury.
Burton Hollow	Located in N NW section of Hamilton County.
Burwood	Community in S SW section of Williamson County. 10 mi S SW of Franklin.
Busby	Community in SW section of Lawrence County. Approx. 3 mi SE of Loretto.
Bush Town	Community within the city limits of Chattanooga. 2 mi E of downtown. In Hamilton County.
Bushwacker Hollow	Located in SW corner of Montgomery County.
Busselltown	Community in middle E section of Loudon County. 6 mi E NE of Loudon.
Busseltown	Community in E central section of Decatur County. 8 mi NE of Decaturville.
Busy Corner	Community in W central area of Coffee County. 6 mi NW of Manchester.
Butcher Ridge	Ridge in N section of Dickson County, NW of Cumberland Furnace.
Butler	Community in W SW section of Johnson County near the border. 15 mi SW of Mountain City.
Butler's Landing	Community in S central section of Clay County. 5 mi SW of Celina.
Butterstack Ridge	Ridge in N section of Marion County, W of Pine Hill.
Butts Hollow	Located in E central section of Humphreys County. 3 mi W NW of New Hope.
Buzzard Bluff Knob	Located in W section of Jackson County. 2 mi N NE of Rough Point.
Buzzard Point	Located in W section of Hamilton County on Walden Ridge.
Buzzard Point Ridge	Ridge in W SW section of Anderson County.
Buzzard Roost	Located in S section of Cocke County, NW of Hartford.
Buzzard Roost	Mountain in S section of Greene County, S of Rich Mountain.
Buzzard Roost	Located in NE section of Rutherford County. 2 mi S of Lofton.

Buzzard Roost Bottom	Located in middle W section of Gibson County. Approx. 3 mi W of Georgetown.
Bybee	Community in N NW area of Cocke County. 6 mi N of Newport.
Byerley Island	Island in NW corner of Jefferson County on the Holston River.
Byington	Community in W section of Knox County. 11 mi W of Knoxville, N of Ball Camp.
Byrd Bay	Lake in W NW section of Stewart County, inlet off the Tennessee River. S of Clay Bay.
Byrd Chapel	Community in W SW section of Knox County. 14 mi W SW of Knoxville.
Byrd Lake	Lake in SW central section of Cumberland County. S of Cumberland Mountain State Park.
Byrdstown	County Seat of Pickett County. Located in middle W section of the County. Incorporated in 1917.
Cabin Row	Community in S SE section of Montgomery County. 10 1/2 mi S SE of Clarksville.
Cabo	Community in E area of Chester County.
Cactus Cove	Community in N NW section of Blount County. 9 mi NW of Maryville.
Cades	Community in E area of Gibson County. 9 mi E of Trenton.
Cades Cove	In SE area of Blount County in the Smoky Mountains. 5 mi SW of Townsend.
Cades Cove Mountain	Mountain in S SE section of Blount County. 4 mi S SW of Kinzel Springs.
Caffey	Community in S SE section of McNairy County. 9 1/2 mi SE of Selmer.
Cages Bend	Area in bend of Cumberland River, middle W NW section of Smith County. 6 mi W NW of Carthage.
Cages Bend	Area in bend of the Cumberland River in S section of Sumner County.
Cagle	Community in middle NW section of Sequatchie County. 8 mi N NW of Dunlap.
Caigletown	Community in SW corner of Humphreys County. 2 1/2 mi S SE of Bakerville.
Cain Islands	Islands on French Broad River in NW section of Sevier County. 8 mi N NW of Sevierville.

Cain Mill	Community in NE section of Hamblen County. 6 mi NE of Morristown.
Cainsville	Communty in S SE section of Wilson County. 16 mi S SE of Lebanon.
Cairo	Community in central section of Crockett County. 3 1/2 mi NW of Alamo.
Cairo	Community in SE section of Sumner County. 5 mi E SE of Gallatin.
Calderwood	Community on the S Border of Blount County on Chilhowee Lake.
Calderwood Dam	Dam on E border of Monroe County on the Chilhowee River. 22 mi E of Madisonville.
Calditz Cove	Located in middle E section of Fentress County. 2 mi S of Allardt.
Caldwell	Community in N Central section of Bedford County. 3 mi E of Shelbyville.
Calfkiller	Community in SE section of Putnam County. 11 mi E SE of Cookeville.
Calfkiller River	Begins in Putnam County near the town of Calfkiller. Flows S into and through White County where it flows into the Caney Fork River.
Calhoun	City in SW corner of McMinn County. 12 mi SW of Athens. Incorporated in 1961.
Calico	Community in W central section of Meigs County. 2 1/2 mi W of Decatur.
California Hollow	Located in SE section of Macon County. 1 mi E SE of Gum Springs.
Calista	Community in E section of Robertson County. 12 mi E of Springfield.
Callie	Community in S section of Williamson County. 6 1/2 mi S SE of Franklin.
Calls	Community in S SE area of Coffee County. 10 mi SE of Manchester.
Calvary	Community in N NW section of Dyer County. 12 mi N NW of Dyersburg.
Camargo	Community in middle SW section of Lincoln County. 6 mi S SW of Fayetteville.
Cambria	Community on S SE border of McMinn County. Approx. 12 mi S SE of Athens.
Cambridge	Community in NE section of Warren County. 9 mi

Cambridge, (Cont.)	N NE of McMinnville.
Camden	County Seat of Benton County. Located in center of county. Incorporated in 1899.
Camden Wildlife Management Area	Located on E SE border of Benton County. Approx. 4 mi SE of Camden.
Camelot	Community in NW central section of Hawkins County. 4 mi NW of Rogersville.
Camelot	Community in Knox County. 11 mi W NW of downtown Knoxville.
Cameron Hill	Hill on old W side of the City of Chattanooga, E of Tennessee River. In Hamilton County.
Campaign	Community in NE section of Warren County. 10 mi NE of McMinnville.
Camp Austin	Community in S section of Morgan County. 5 mi S of Wartburg.
Campbell County CAMPBELL COUNTY	County Seat: Jacksboro. Zip Code 37757. Located in NE Section of State. Bounded by Claiborne, Union, Anderson, and Scott Counties and the State of Kentucky to the North. Named in honor of Col. Arthur Campbell.
Campbell County Park	Located in middle S section of Campbell County. 2 mi E of Jacksboro.
Campbell Cove Lake	Lake in middle SE section of Polk County, NE of Dogtown.
Campbell Hollow	Located in W SW section of Dickson County. 2 mi E NE of Tennessee City.
Campbell Junction	Community in W NW section of Cumberland County. 10 mi NW of Crossville.
Campbell Mountain	Mountain in N section of Fentress County. 4 mi NW of Jamestown.
Campbells Station	Community in S SE section of Maury County. 12 mi S SE of Columbia.
Campbellville	Community in W NW section of Giles County. 11 mi NW of Pulaski.
Camp Columbus	Recreation area on Dallas Bay in middle N section of Hamilton County. 13 1/2 mi N NE of Chattanooga.
Camp Creek	Community in SE area of Greene County. 8 mi SE of Greeneville.
Camp Ground	Community in SE area of Fentress County. 18 mi S SW of Jamestown.

Camp Ground	Community in middle NW section of Weakley County. 8 1/2 mi N NW of Dresden.
Camp Monterey	Located in E section of Putnam County, S of Monterey.
Camp Rock Island (BSA)	Located in NE corner of Warren County on Rocky River.
Camp Skymont	Boy Scout Camp in NW section of Grundy County. 8 mi W of Altamont.
Camps Lakes	Lakes in W NW section of Shelby County, S SE of Ramsey.
Camptown	Town in central section of Fentress County near Jamestown.
Camp Townsend	In E Central area of Blount County.
Canaan	Community in middle W SW section of Maury County. 8 1/2 mi W SW of Columbia.
Canaan	Community in SW section of Montgomery County. W of Oakridge.
Canaan Grove	Community in SE section of Tipton County. 9 mi S SE of Covington.
Canadaville	Community in W areaa of Fayette County. 15 mi W SW of Somerville.
Canby Hills	Community in Knox County. 9 1/2 mi W of Knoxville.
Cancel Mill	Community in N section of Claiborne County. 3 mi S SE of River View.
Candies Creek Ridge	Ridge in central section of Bradley County. Runs from Cleveland Northward.
Canebrake Mountain	Mountain in middle NE section of Monroe County in Cherokee National Forest.
Cane Creek	Flows from SW section of Bledsoe County, N through Van Buren County where it flows into the Caney Fork River.
Cane Creek	Creek on W border of Houston County, flows into Tennessee River.
Cane Hollow	Located in middle W section of Grundy County. 6 mi W SW of Altamont.
Cane Ridge	Community in SE section of Davidson County. 13 mi SE of Courthouse.
Caney Branch	Community in S SW section of Greene County. 12 mi SW of Greeneville.

Caney Creek	Community in N central section of Hawkins County. 2 1/2 mi N NE of Rogersville.
Caney Creek	Community in mid central section of Polk County. Approx. 7 1/2 mi SE of Benton.
Caney Fork River	Begins in SE corner of White County, flows W where it is joined by the Cane Creek and forms the boundary lines for White and Van Buren Counties. N into Dekalb County where it is backed up by the Center Hill Dam forming the Center Hill Lake. NW into Smith County where it flows into the Cumberland River.
Caney High Top	Mountain in SW central section of Sevier County. 4 mi S of Pigeon Forge.
Caney Spring	Community in N central section of Marshall County. 1 mi N of Lewisburg.
Caney Valley	Community in SE Corner of Claiborne County. 7 mi E SE of Tazewell.
Cannon County	County Seat: Woodbury. Zip Code 37190. Located in center of the State. Bounded by Wilson, DeKalb, Warren, Coffee and Rutherford countie-s. Named in honor of Newton Cannon.
CANNON COUNTY	
Cannon Creek	Community in S Central area of Bledsoe County.
Cantrell Ponds	Pond in W section of Stewart County, E of Mulbury Hill.
Cantrells Lake	Lake in central section of Davidson County. 2 1/2 mi NE of Bordeaux.
Capital Hill	Community in N area of Franklin County. 8 mi N NE of Winchester.
Capital Hill	Community in middle E section of Scott County. 3 mi E of Huntsville.
Capleville	Community in S SW section of Shelby County. S of Parkway Village.
Capling Ridge	Ridge in central N NW section of DeKalb County. 2 mi NE of Dowelltown.
Capps	Located in E SE section of Benton County.
Caraway Hills	Located in middle E section of Gibson County, W of Milan.
Cardiff	Community in middle NW section of Roane County. 6 1/2 mi W NW of Kingston.
Cardwell Mountain	Mountain in E section of Warren County. 5 mi E of McMinnville.
Cario Bend	Community in middle W NW section of Wilson

Cario Bend, (Cont.)	County. Approx. 5 mi W NW of Lebanon.
Carlisle	Community in SE section of Stewart County. 6 mi SE of Dover.
Carlock	Community in NE section of Jackson County. 8 mi NE of Gainesboro.
Carlock	Community in S SE section of McMinn County. 10 mi S SE of Athens.
Carlton	Community in NW area of Blount County near Louisville. 6 mi N NW of Maryville.
Carmichael Island	Island in Tennessee River. 3 mi E of Loudon.
Carole Cove	Community in E NE section of Fayette County. 4 mi E NE of Somerville.
Caroline Hollow	Located in N NW section of Humphreys County. 1 mi S of Concord.
Carol Lake	Lake in central section of Grundy County. S of Cumberland Heights. 2 1/2 mi SE of Altamont.
Carpenter	Community in Central area of Benton County. 5 mi N of Camden.
Carpenter Campground	In SW Central section of Blount County. 5 mi S of Maryville.
Carr Branch	Community in S section of Claiborne County. 9 mi SW of Tazewell.
Carrick Hollow	Located in middle S section of Cannon County. 5 mi S of Woodbury.
Carroll	Community in N central section of Madison County. 7 mi N of Jackson.
Carroll County 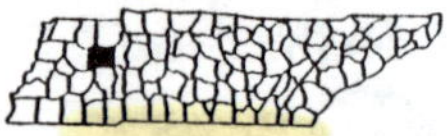 CARROLL COUNTY	County Seat: Huntingdon. Zip Code 38344. Located in NW section of the State. Bounded by Henry, Benton, Decatur, Henderson, Madison, Gibson and Weakley Counties. Named in honor of William Carroll.
Carroll Creek	Creek in SW section of Coffee County, flows into Duck River.
Carroll Hollow	Located near S SE border of Houston County. Approx. 3 mi S of Pollard.
Carroll Lake	Community in NW Section of Carroll County. 2 mi S of McKenzie.
Carr Ridge	Ridge in W section of Putnam County. 4 mi W of Baxter.
Carson Springs	Community in W area of Cocke County. 5 mi SE of Newport.

Carter — Community in NE aea of Carter County. 7 mi NE of Elizabethton.

Carter Chapel — Community in N central section of Greene County. 8 mi NW of Greeneville.

Carter County — County Seat: Elizabethton. Zip Code 37643. Located in NE section of the State. Bounded by Unicoi, Washington, Sullivan and Johnson Counties and the State of North Carolina to the East. Named in honor of Landon Carter.

CARTER COUNTY

Carters Creek — Community in N section of Maury County. 7 mi N NE of Columbia.

Cartersville — Community near W NW border of Maury County. 13 mi W NW of Columbia, 2 mi NW of Fikes Mill.

Cartertown — Community in S central section of Sevier County. Approx. 9 mi S SE of Sevierville.

Carter Valley — Located in middle N NE section of Hawkins County, NW of Surgoinsville.

Carthage — County Seat of Smith County. Located in near center of the County. Incorporated in 1817.

Carthage Junction (RR) — Located in S section of Gordonsville in Smith County.

Cartwright — Community in S SW section of Sequatchie County. 7 1/2 mi S SW of Dunlap.

Cartwright — Community in N NE section of Smith County. 11 mi N NE of Carthage.

Caryville — City in SW area of Campbell County, 3 mi SW of Jacksboro. Incorporated in 1968.

Casey Jones Home and Museum — Located on the NW outskirts of the City of Jackson. In Madison County.

Cash Point — Community in SW corner of Lincoln County. 17 mi SW of Fayetteville.

Casper Creek Park — Located in N section of Shelby County. N of Williams Chapel.

Casper Lake — Lake in N section of Shelby County, E SE of Kerrville.

Cassville — Community in W section of White County. 8 mi W NW of Sparta.

Castalion Springs — Community in SE section of Sumner County. 7 1/2 mi E of Gallatin.

Castle Heights — Community in W central section of Cocke County. 2 mi SE of Newport.

Cataska	Community on S SW border of Monroe County. 9 mi S of Tellico Plains.
Cataska Mountain	Mountain in the SW section of Monroe County.
Cat Corner	Community in SW corner of Obion County. 25 mi SW of Union City.
Cater Crossroads	Community in NW section of Bedford County. 13 mi N of Shelbyville, 3 mi NE of Taylor Crossroads.
Cates	Community in N section of Lake County. 4 1/2 mi N of Tiptonville.
Cates Pond	Pond in W section of Jefferson County. 1 mi S SE of Strawberry Plains.
Catfish Lake	Lake in SW section of Fayette County near Shelby County line, SW of Canadaville.
Cathey Ridge	Ridge in W section of Coffee County, SE of Baucom.
Cat Hollow	Located in E SE section of Benton County.
Catlettsburg (Cobtown)	Community in middle N NW section of Sevier County. 2 1/2 mi N NW of Sevierville.
Cato	Community in E section of Trousdale County. 7 1/2 mi E of Hartsville.
Caton Chapel	Community in central section of Sevier County. 7 1/2 mi E SE of Sevierville.
Catons Grove	Community in SW Section of Cocke County. 12 mi S of Newport, 1 1/2 mi W of Cosby.
Catoosa	Community in SW section of Morgan County. 5 mi SW of Wartburg.
Catoosa Wildlife Management Area	Located in N section of Cumberland County.
Catoosa Wildlife Management Area (State)	Located in SW section of Morgan County. 7 mi SW of Wartburg.
Cave	Community in S SW section of White County. 5 mi S of Sparta.
Cave Creek	Community in E SE section of Roane County. 8 mi E SE of Kingston.
Cave Ridge	Ridge in central section of Hamilton County, near Daisy.
Cave Ridge	Ridge in middle S section of Johnson County, SE of Pandora.

Cave Spring	Community in E Central section of Claiborne County. 2 1/2 mi NW of Tazewell.
Cave Spring	Community in W SW section of Montgomery County. W of Stringtown.
Cave Springs	Community in W central section of DeKalb County.
Cedar Bluff	Community in SW section of Knox County. 11 mi S SW of Knoxville.
Cedar Bluff	Community in SW section of Macon County. 6 mi W SW of Lafayette.
Cedar Bluff	Community in middle NE section of Sevier County. 7 mi E of Sevierville.
Cedar Bluff Mill	Community in central section of Franklin County, near Winchester.
Cedar Chapel	Community in NW corner of Hardeman County. 14 mi NW of Bolivar. 5 mi N of Whiteville.
Cedar Creek	Creek in SE section of Campbell County (Norris Lake).
Cedar Creek	Community in S area of Greene County. 10 mi S SW of Greeneville.
Cedar Creek Landing	Community on W SW border of Perry County. 9 mi W SW of Linden.
Cedar Crest North	Community in Knox County. 8 1/2 mi N NW of downtown Knoxville.
Cedar Fork	Community in SW section of Loudon County. 11 1/2 mi W SW of Loudon.
Cedar Fork	Community in S SW section of Roane County. Approx. 14 mi S of Kingston.
Cedar Gap	Town in S SW section of Franklin County.
Cedar Grove	Community in NW area of Bedford County. 2 1/2 mi W of Taylor Crossroads
Cedar Grove	Community in N Central section of Benton County.
Cedar Grove	Community in SW Corner of Carroll County. 15 mi SW of Huntingdon.
Cedar Grove	Community in SE corner of Henderson County. 13 1/2 mi SE of Lexington. 3 mi N NE of Sardis.
Cedar Grove	Community in S central section of Humphreys County. 9 1/2 mi S of Waverly.
Cedar Grove	Community in NW section of Knox County. 11 mi

Cedar Grove, (Cont.)	N NW of Knoxville.
Cedar Grove	Community in middle section of Pickett County. 4 mi E SE of Byrdstown.
Cedar Grove	Community in middle E section of Roane County. 4 mi SE of Kingston.
Cedar Grove	Community in SW section of Rutherford County. 13 mi W SW of Murfreesboro.
Cedar Grove	Community in middle SE section of Sullivan County. 8 1/2 mi E SE of Blountville.
Cedar Grove	Community in S section of Sumner County. 3 mi S of Gallatin.
Cedar Grove	Community within the limits of Johnson City, W section of town. In Washington County.
Cedar Hill	Community in central section of Greene County. 4 mi SW of Greeneville.
Cedar Hill	Community within the city limits of Chattanooga. 4 1/2 mi S SE of downtown. In Hamilton County.
Cedar Hill	Community in middle W section of Putnam County. 9 1/2 mi W of Cookeville.
Cedar Hill	City in middle W NW section of Robertson County. 7 mi W NW of Springfield. Incorporated in 1963.
Cedar Knob	Located in W section of Smith County near border. 3 1/2 mi W NW of Rock City.
Cedar Lake	Lake in NE central section of Henderson County. 4 1/2 mi E NE of Lexington.
Cedar Lane	Community in NE area of Greene County. 17 mi N NE of Greeneville.
Cedar Mountain	Mountain in middle W section of Carter County, S of Braemar.
Cedar Ridge	Ridge in SW corner of Franklin County. S of Huntland.
Cedars of Lebanon State Park and Forest	Located in S SW section of Wilson County. W of Bairds Mill.
Cedar Spring	Community in SE area of Bradley County near Felker.
Cedar Springs	Community in central SW section of McMinn County. 2 mi SW of Athens.
Cedercroft Hill	Located in W section of Sumner County. 2 1/2

Cedercroft Hill, (Cont.)	mi S of Mulloy.
Celina	County Seat of Clay County. Located in the E center of the county. Incorporated in 1909.
Center	Community in E central section of Crockett County. 4 1/2 mi E NE of Alamo.
Center	Community in NW corner of Henry County. 12 1/2 mi NW of Paris.
Center	Community in NW section of Lawrence County. 10 1/2 mi NW of Lawrenceburg.
Center	Community in W section of Monroe County. 3 mi S of Madisonville.
Center Grove	Community in NW area of Franklin County. 10 mi NW of Winchester.
Center Grove	Community in SE section of Jackson County. 7 mi SE of Gainesboro.
Center Hill	Community in E area of Cannon County near Warren County line. 6 1/2 mi E SE of Woodbury.
Center Hill	Community in S section of Henderson County. 7 1/2 mi S of Lexington, E of Pine Lake.
Center Hill	Community in SE section of Warren County. 11 mi SE of McMinnville.
Center Hill Dam	Located in N area of DeKalb County on the Caney Fork River.
Center Hill Lake	Lake in N Central section of DeKalb County on the Caney Fork River.
Center Point	Community on E border of Chester County near the Henderson County line. 15 mi E of Henderson.
Center Point	Community in NW section of Fayette County. 13 1/2 mi W NW of Somerville.
Center Point	Community in E area of Giles County. 10 1/2 mi E NE of Pulaski.
Center Point	Community in SE section of Hardeman County. 14 mi SW of Bolivar. 3 mi S SW of Hickory Valley.
Center Point	Community in SE central section of Lawrence County. 9 1/2 mi S of Lawrenceburg.
Center Point	Community in NE section of Meigs County. S of Ten Mile.
Center Point	Community in W SW section of White County. 9 mi W SW of Sparta.

Center Star	Community in middle NE section of Hardin County. 4 mi E NE of Burnt Church.
Center Star	Community in SE section of Hickman County, SW of Shady Grove.
Centersville	Community in E section of Loudon County. 7 1/2 mi E SE of Loudon.
Centertown	City in W section of Warren County. 8 1/2 mi W NW of McMinnville. Incorporated in 1951.
Centerview	Community in N central section of Hardin County, SE of Cerro Gordo.
Center View	Community in SE corner of Johnson County. 8 mi S SE of Mountain City.
Centerville	Community in SE area of Gibson County. 14 1/2 mi SE of Trenton.
Centerville	Community in E NE section of Greene County. 12 mi NE of Greeneville.
Centerville	County Seat of Hickman County. Located in center of County. Incorporated in 1911.
Centerville	Community in NE section of Wilson County. 7 1/2 mi NE of Lebanon.
Central	Community in W area of Carter County. 3 mi W SW of Elizabethton.
Central	Community in W area of Gibson County. 10 mi W of Trenton.
Central	Community in middle E section of Lauderdale County. 4 mi N of Ripley.
Central	Community on E border of Obion County. 7 1/2 mi S SE of Union City.
Central Point	Community in S central section of Grainger County. 2 mi SE of Rutledge.
Central Point (Mill Point)	Community in N section of Sullivan County. 10 mi E NE of Kingsport.
Cerro Gordo	Community in N central section of Hardin County. 7 1/2 mi N NE of Savannah.
Chalet Village	Chalet community in middle SW section of Sevier County. 2 mi W of Gatlinburg.
Chalklevel	Community in S Central section of Benton County. 5 mi SE of Camden.
Chalk Level	Community in S section of Hawkins County. SW of McCloud.

Chalybeate	Community in S section of Van Buren County. Approx. 13 mi S SW of Spencer.
Chambers	Community on E SE border of McNairy County. 13 mi E SE of Selmer.
Chambers	Community in NE section of Obion County. 6 mi E NE of Union City.
Chambers Hill	Located in middle S section of Williamson County, W of Callie.
Champ	Community on E border of Lincoln County. 10 1/2 mi E of Fayetteville.
Champion Lake	Lake in SW section of Lauderdale County. Approx. 1 1/2 mi SE of Fulton.
Chanceytown	Community in SE section of Polk County in the Copper Basin, N of Ducktown.
Chandler	Community in N Central section of Blount County near Maryville.
Chantay Acres	Community in central section of Maury County. 2 mi N of Columbia, N of River Heights.
Chanute	Community in N section of Pickett County. 4 1/2 mi NW of Byrdstown.
Chapel Hill	Community in SW section of Henderson County. 7 mi SW of Lexington, SW of Life.
Chapel Hill	City in N NE central section of Marshall County. 13 1/2 mi N NE of Lewisburg. Incorporated in 1849.
Chapel Hill	Community in W section of Maury County. 12 mi W of Columbia.
Chapel Hollow	Located in S central section of Houston County. Approx. 4 1/2 mi SW of Erin.
Chapmanboro P.O. (Cheap Hill)	Located in NW area of Cheatham County. 6 mi NW of Ashland City.
Chapman Grove	Community in W section of Roane County. 6 mi E SE of Rockwood.
Chapmans	Community in central area of Giles County. 2 mi SE of Pulaski.
Chapman Swamp	Swamp in N NW section of Hardeman County near Madison County line.
Charleston	City on N border of Bradley County. 10 mi N of Cleveland. Incorporated in 1956.
Charleston	Community in E section of Tipton County. 9 mi E SE of Covington.

Charleys Branch	Community in NW area of Anderson County. 10 mi N of Oliver Springs.
Charlotte	County seat of Dickson County. Located in N central section of County. Incorporated in 1837.
Chaseville	Community in SE area of Benton County. Approx. 5 mi S of Gismonda.
Chaska	Community in N Central section of Campbell County. 5 mi SE of Jellico.
Chattanooga	County Seat of Hamilton County. Located in S area of County on the Georgia Border. Incorporated in 1839.
Cheap Hill	Community in NW area of Cheatham County. 6 mi NW of Ashland City.
Cheatham County CHEATHAM COUNTY	County Seat: Ashland City. Zip Code 37015. Located in North Central area of the State. Bounded by Robertson, Davidson, Williamson, Dickson and Montgomery Counties. Named in honor of Edward S. Cheatham.
Cheatham Lake	Lake in NW area of Cheatham County on Cumberland River.
Cheatham Wildlife Management Area	Located in S Central section of Cheatham County.
Cheek Lake	Lake in middle NE section of Davidson County, SE of Montague.
Cherokee	Community in S SE area of Grainger County.
Cherokee	Community in S section of Grainger County. 5 mi S SE of Rutledge.
Cherokee	Community in E SE section of Washington County. 5 mi E SE of Jonesborough.
Cherokee Dam	Dam in S area of Grainger County, on Holston River near Oakland.
Cherokee Dam	Dam on Holston River in the N NW section of Jefferson County, N of Mill Spring.
Cherokee Hills	Community in middle N section of Sevier County. Approx. 2 1/2 mi E of Sevierville.
Cherokee Lake	Lake (Holston River) in NW section of Jefferson County, SE section of Grainger County, NW section of Hamblin County and SW section of Hawkins County.
Cherokee Mountain	Mountain in S SE section of Washington County, SE of Greenwood.

Cherokee National Forest — Begins in Polk County near Ocoee and runs in a NE direction through Monroe, Cocke, Greene, Unicoi, Carter and Johnson Counties.

Cherokee Park — In N Central section of Blount County near Maryville.

Cherokee Reservation (U.S.-T.V.A.) — Located in S area of Grainger County, E of Oakland.

Cherokee Ridge — Community in Knox County. 6 1/2 mi W NW of downtown Knoxville.

Cherokee Wildlife Management Area — Runs through center of Johnson County.

Cherry — Community in middle SW section of Lauderdale County. 11 mi W SW of Ripley.

Cherry Brook — Community in Knox County. 6 mi W NW of downtown Knoxville.

Cherry Chapel — Community in SE section of Hardin County. 13 mi SE of Savannah. 4 1/2 mi N of Walnut Grove.

Cherry Corner — Community in S SW section of Marshall County. Approx. 8 mi S SW of Lewisburg.

Cherry Crossroads — Town in NW area of Clay County.

Cherry Grove — Community in E Central section of Benton County. 7 mi NE of Camden.

Cherry Hill — Comunity in NE area of DeKalb County. 9 mi N NE of Smithville.

Cherry Valley — Community in middle SE section of Wilson County. 10 mi SE of Lebanon.

Cherrywood — Community in NW section of Carroll County.

Chesney — Community in E SE section of Union County. 5 mi E SE of Maynardsville.

Chester County — County Seat: Henderson. Zip Code 38340. Located in SW section of State. Bounded by Henderson, Hardin, McNairy, Hardeman and Madison Counties. Named in honor of Col. Robert I. Chester.

CHESTER COUNTY

Chesterfield — Community in middle E section of Henderson County. 7 1/2 mi E of Lexington. 3 mi W of Darden.

Chester Frost Park — Also known as Hamilton County Park is located in central section of Hamilton County on the Tennessee River. 12 mi NE of downtown Chattanooga. In Hamilton County.

Chester Hollow — Located in E section of Benton County.

Chestnut Bluff	Community in W area of Crockett County. 13 mi W NW of Alamo.
Chestnut Glade	Community in N NW section of Weakley County. 11 1/2 mi N NW of Dresden.
Chestnut Grove	Community in E area of Grainger County. 11 1/2 mi E NE of Rutledge.
Chestnut Grove	Community in NW section of Grundy County. 7 mi N NW of Altamont.
Chestnut Grove	Community in SE section of Hancock County on Hawkins County border. 6 mi E of Sneedville.
Chestnut Grove	Community in middle N section of Jefferson County. 3 mi N of Dandridge.
Chestnut Grove	Community in central SE section of Perry County. 1 1/2 mi E NE of Linden.
Chestnut Grove	Community in S section of Robertson County. 6 1/2 mi S SW of Springfield.
Chestnut Grove	Community in middle N NW section of Stewart County. 5 mi N NW of Dover.
Chestnut Grove	Community in W NW section of Sumner County. 11 mi NW of Gallatin.
Chestnut Grove	Community in E section of Union County. 3 1/2 mi NW of Maynardville.
Chestnut Grove	Community on S SW border of Warren County. 12 mi S of McMinnville.
Chestnut Hill	Community in E section of Benton County. Approx. 6 mi E NE of Camden.
Chestnut Hill	Community in E central section of Cumberland County. 6 mi E NE of Crossville.
Chestnut Hill	Community in SE corner of Jefferson County. 7 1/2 mi SE of Dandridge.
Chestnut Hill	Community in middle N section of Sumner County. 11 mi N of Gallatin.
Chestnut Mound	Community in E SE section of Smith County. 8 mi E SE of Carthage.
Chestnut Mountain	Mountain in S SW section of Cocke County, E of Catons Grove.
Chestnut Mountain	Mountain in N section of Polk County.
Chestnut Mountain	Mountain in SE section of White County, SW of Stringtown.
Chestnut Orchard	Community in middle S section of Robertson

Chestnut Orchard, (Cont.)	County. 4 mi S of Springfield.
Chestnut Ridge	Ridge in S SE section of Anderson County.
Chestnut Ridge	Ridge in NE section of Anderson County and SW section of Union County.
Chestnut Ridge	Ridge in middle NE section of Blount County. W of Melrose.
Chestnut Ridge	Ridge in central section of Cocke County, S of West Myers.
Chestnut Ridge	Community in E area of Greene County. 7 1/2 mi E SE of Greeneville.
Chestnut Ridge	Ridge in W section of Hamilton County.
Chestnut Ridge	Ridge in SW corner of Hancock County.
Chestnut Ridge	Ridge in E section of Hancock County. 5 mi E of Sneedville.
Chestnut Ridge	Located in the N section of Lincoln County, S of Bledsoe.
Chestnut Ridge	Ridge in middle E section of Roane County.
Chestnut Ridge	Ridge in E NE section of Sevier County, S of Jones Cove.
Chestnut Ridge	Ridge in W SW section of Sumner County. 3 mi S of Two Chestnut.
Chestnut Top	Mountain in SE section of Blount County. 2 mi S SE of Townsend.
Chestnut Valley	Community in central section of Monroe County. NE of Tellico Plains.
Chestoa	Community in middle S section of Unicoi County. 3 1/2 mi SW of Erwin.
Chestuee	Community in E Central section of Bradley County. 4 mi E of Cleveland.
Chestuee	Community in W section of Monroe County. S of Gudger.
Chestuee	Community in NW corner of Polk County. Approx. 5 mi N NW of Benton.
Chewalla	Community on S SW border of McNairy County. 11 mi S SW of Selmer.
Chic	Community in SW area of Dyer County. 16 mi W SW of Dyersburg.
Chickamauga	Community within the city limits of

Chickamauga, (Cont.)	Chattanooga, in Airport Road and Lee Highway area. In Hamilton County.
Chickamauga and Chattanooga National Military Park	Located on top of Lookout Mountain and South into the State of Georgia in the Fort Oglethorpe-Chickamauga area.
Chickamauga Dam	Dam on the Tennessee River in S section of Hamilton County in Chattanooga. Forms Chickamauga Lake.
Chickamauga Gulch	Located in W section of Hamilton County on Waldens Ridge, W of Daisy.
Chickamauga Lake	Formed by the Chickamauga Dam in the Tennessee River backs up to the Watts Bar Dam in Rhea County. Chickamauga Dam is located in the City of Chattanooga, County of Hamilton.
Chickasaw Bluff Trail	Located in NW corner of Shelby County.
Chickasaw Heights	Community in central section of Henry County, N of Paris.
Chickasaw National Wildlife Refuge	Located on W NW section of Lauderdale County.
Chickasaw State Park and Forest	Located in W area of Chester County. 7 mi SW of Henderson.
Chickasaw State Park and Forest Wildlife Management Area	Located in NE section of Hardeman County. 10 mi N NE of Bolivar. 3 mi NE of Silerton.
Chigger Point	Located in E section of Hamilton on the bank of Lake Chickamauga, near Loret Villa.
Childers Hill	Community in SW corner of Hardin County. 11 mi S SW of Savannah. 4 1/2 mi W of Pickwick Landing Dam.
Childress	Community in S SE section of Sullivan County. 8 mi S SE of Blountville.
Chilhowee	Community in S SW area of Blount County. 14 mi S of Maryville.
Chilhowee Dam	Located in SE corner of Blount County on Chilhowee Lake near Tallassee.
Chilhowee Lake	Lake in the SW corner of Blount County on the Monroe County line.
Chilhowee Lake (Little Tennessee River)	Located on E NE border of Monroe County.
Chilhowee Mountain	Mountain in middle W section of Polk County.

Chilhowee Mountain aka Bluff Mountain	Mountain located in S Central section of Blount County and extends into W section of Sevier County.
Chilhowee Mountain Wildlife Management Area	Located in E NE section of Blount County, SE of Prospect.
Chilhowee Park	Park in E central section of Knoxville. 3 mi NE of downtown. In Knox County.
Chilhowee View	Community in Central section of Blount County. 4 1/2 mi SE of Maryville.
Chilly Spring Knob	Mountain in S section of Blount County.
Chimney Mountain	Mountain in E NE section of Scott County. N of Buffalo Mountain.
Chimney Mountain	Mountain in N NE section of Scott County. 9 mi E of Oneida.
Chimneytop Mountain	Mountain in E SE section of Hawkins County near Greene and Washington County lines. E of Light Mill.
Chimney Top Mountain	Located in E section of Morgan County. NW of Petros.
China Grove	Community in N area of Gibson County. 11 mi N of Trenton.
Chinquapin	Community in Sevier County at the head of Waldens Creek, approx. 4 mi. W of Pigeon Forge.
Chinquapin Grove	Community in SE section of Sullivan County. 9 mi SE of Blountville.
Chinquapin Hill	Located in E section of Williamson County. 1 mi N of Franklin, E of Burke Hollow.
Chinquapin Knob	Mountain in SW section of Sevier County. 5 mi W SW of Gatlinburg.
Chinquapin Ridge	Ridge in S SE section of Monroe County, S of Henderson Top.
Chinubee	Community in SW section of Lawrence County. 13 mi SW of Lawrenceburg. 6 mi NW of Loretto.
Chipman	Community in E section of Sumner County. Approx. 10 mi E NE of Gallatin.
Chisholm Lake	Lake in NW section of Lauderdale County. Approx. 8 mi N NW of Ripley.
Chittum	Community in S central section of Claiborne County. 2 mi S of Tazewell.

Chitwood Mountain	Mountain in NE section of Scott County, SE of Pleasant Grove.
Choptack	Community in W section of Hawkins County. 4 mi W of Rogersville.
Chota	Community in S SW section of Blount County. 10 mi S SW of Maryville.
Christiana	Community in S section of Rutherford County. 10 mi S of Murfreesboro.
Christian Bend	Community in E section of Hawkins County. 13 mi E NE of Rogersville.
Christianburg	Community in W NW section of Monroe County. 4 1/2 mi W NW of Madisonville.
Christian Chapel	Community in SW section of Gibson County. 8 mi S SW of Trenton.
Christie Hill	Community in SW Central section of Blount County. 8 mi S of Maryville.
Christmasville	Community in NW area of Carroll County near Weakley County line. 13 mi NW of Huntingdon.
Christmasville	Community in middle NW section of Haywood County. 7 1/2 mi NW of Brownsville.
Chuckey	Community in E area of Greene County. 9 mi E NE of Greeneville.
Chuck Swan State Forest and Wildlife Management Area	Located in W section of Union County on Norris Lake. N of Big Ridge State Park.
Chucky Mountain	Mountain in S section of Greene County, N of Paint Mountain.
Church Hill	City in NE section of Hawkins County. 18 mi E NE of Rogersville. Incorporated in 1958.
Churchton	Community in E NE section of Dyer County. 13 mi E NE of Dyersburg.
Circle H Ranch Lake	Lake in S section of Lincoln Couonty. 9 mi S of Fayetteville.
Citico Beach	Community in NE section of Monroe County. 14 1/2 mi E of Madisonville.
Citico Creek Wilderness	Located in E section of Monroe County, E of Flats Mountain.
City Lake	Lake in central SW section of Overton County. S of Livingston.
City Lake	Lake in middle E section of Putnam County. 5 mi SE of Cookeville.

City Lake	Lake in NW section of Sumner County. NE of Portland.
Clack Branch	Community in SW section of Lawrence County. Approx. 2 mi NW of Loretto.
Clacks Gap	Community in N NE section of Roane County. 6 1/2 mi N NE of Kingston.
Clacks Gap Ridge	Ridge in N NE section of Roane County.
Claiborne County CLAIBORNE COUNTY	County Seat: Tazewell. Zip Code 37879. Located in NE section of the State. Bounded by Hancock, Grainger, Union and Campbell Counties and the States of Kentucky and Virginia to the North. Named in honor of William C. Claiborne.
Clairfield	Community in NW corner of Claiborne County. 7 mi NW of Speedwell.
Clampit Hollow	Located in W SW section of Macon County. 1 mi E of Fairview.
Claridge	Community on Signal Mountain in Hamilton County. 7 1/2 mi N of Chattanooga.
Clarkrange	Community in S area of Fentress County. 17 1/2 mi S SW of Jamestown.
Clarksburg	City in S Central section of Carroll County. 9 mi S of Huntingdon. Incorporated in 1969.
Clarksville	County Seat of Montgomery County. Located in N central section of the County. Incorporated in 1785.
Clarksville Lake	Lake in middle W section of Montgomery County. 9 mi W SW of Clarksville.
Clarktown	Community in SW area of Carter County.
Clarktown	Community in E section of White County. 8 1/2 mi E of Sparta.
Claxton	Community in S Central section of Anderson County. 4 mi S SE of Clinton.
Claxton	Community in S SW central section of McMinn County. Approx. 10 mi S SW of Athens.
Clay Bay	Lake in W NW section of Stewart County, inlet off the Tennessee River. S of Ginger Bay.
Claybrook	Community in NE section of Madison County. Approx. 1 mi E NE of Jackson.
Clay County CLAY COUNTY	County Seat: Celina. Zip Code 38551. Located in the N Central Border of the State. Bounded by Pickett, Overton, Jackson and Macon Counties and the State of Kentucky to the

Clay County, (Cont.)	North. Named in honor of Henry Clay.
Clay Hill	Community in E NE section of Marshall County. 10 mi N NE of Lewisburg.
Claylick	Community in E area of Dickson County. 7 1/2 mi E SE of Charlotte.
Claysville	Community in W section of Cumberland County. 7 mi W NW of Crossville.
Clayton	Community in NW section of Obion County. 10 1/2 mi W NW of Union City.
Clear Branch	Community in middle S section of Unicoi County. 8 1/2 mi SW of Erwin.
Clear Creek Lake	Lake in N NE central section of Giles County. SE of Bufords.
Clear Creek Mill	Community in NE section of Greene County, near Jearoldstown.
Clear Lake	Community in N area of Carroll County. Between McKenzie and Macedonia.
Clearmont	Community in W section of Warren County. 12 mi W NW of McMinnville.
Clear Springs	Community in N section of Knox County. 12 mi N NE of Knoxville.
Clear Springs	Community in W SW section of McMinn County. Approx. 12 mi W of Athens.
Clearview	Community in W NW section of Sumner County. 14 mi NW of Gallatin.
Clearwater	Community in NW section of McMinn County. 5 1/2 mi NW of Athens.
Clement Lake	Lake in W NW section of Williamson County. 1 mi N NW of Fairview.
Clementsville	Community in NW area of Clay County. 11 1/2 mi NW of Oak Grove.
Clemon Point	Located in NW section of Hamilton County.
Cleveland	County Seat of Bradley County located in the center of the county. Incorporated in 1893.
Clevenger	Community on W border of Cocke County. 4 mi W of Newport.
Click Mill	Community in S central section of Cocke County. 7 1/2 mi SE of Newport, 5 mi W of Harmony Grove.
Cliff Springs	Community in SE corner of Overton County. 16

Cliff Springs, (Cont.)	1/2 mi SE of Livingston.
Clifton	City in W NW section of Wayne County. 14 mi W NW of Waynesboro. Incorporated in 1946.
Clifton Bend	Community in SE area of Decatur County.
Clifton Hills	Community within the city limits of Chattanooga. 3 mi S SE of downtown in East Lake area of Hamilton County.
Clifton Junction	Community in W NW section of Wayne County. 10 1/2 mi W of Waynesboro.
Clifty	Community in W central section of Cumberland County.
Clifty	Community in E section of White County. Approx. 14 mi E of Sparta.
Climer	Community in NE area of Bradley County. 6 mi E of Cleveland.
Clinchmore	Community in SW area of Campbell County.
Clinch Mountain	Range running from SW through NE section of Grainger County into NW section of Hawkins County.
Clinch River	Flows from the State of Virginia into Hawkins and Hancock Counties, forms boundary for Claiborne and Grainger Counties, flows through Union County forms boundary for Campbell and Anderson Counties, flows into Roane County where in flows into the Tennessee River.
Clingmans Dome	Mountain on S border of Sevier County. In the Great Smoky Mountains. Ele. 6,643.
Clinton	County Seat of Anderson County. Located in E Central area of county. 4 mi from Knox County line. Incorporated in 1835.
Clopton	Community in S section of Tipton County. 7 1/2 mi S of Covington.
Cloud Creek	Community in W central section of Hawkins County. 7 1/2 mi W of Rogersville.
Clouds	Community in middle S area of Claiborne County 4 mi W of Tazewell.
Clovercroft	Community in central NE section of Williamson County. 6 mi E of Franklin.
Clovercroft Lake	Lake in middle E NE section of Williamson County. 6 1/2 mi E of Franklin.
Cloverdale	Community within the city limits of Chattanoo-

Cloverdale, (Cont.)	ga in the Hixson area near Northgate Shopping Center.
Cloverdale	Community in S SW section of Obion County. 10 mi SW of Union City.
Clover Hill	Community in W Central section of Blount County. 4 mi SW of Maryville.
Cloverhill	Community in central section of Davidson County, E of Nashville.
Clover Lakes	Community in N NW section of Hardeman County. 9 mi N NW of Bolivar. 7 mi NE of Whiteville.
Cloverport	Community in N central section of Hardeman County. 9 1/2 mi N of Bolivar. 9 mi NW of Whiteville.
Club Springs	Community in SE section of Smith County. 8 mi SE of Carthage.
Coalfield	Community in SE section of Morgan County. 11 mi E SE of Wartburg.
Coal Hill	Community on SE border of Morgan County. 10 1/2 mi SE of Wartburg.
Coal Hill Mountain	Mountain in W SW section of Scott County, SE of Glenmary.
Coaling	Community in N NE section of Dickson County. 9 1/2 mi N NE of Charlotte.
Coaling Grounds Ridge	Ridge in W section of Roane County.
Coalmont	City in S central section of Grundy County. 6 mi S of Altamont. Incorporated in 1957.
Coalpit Hollow	Located in middle N NW section of Humphreys County. 5 mi N NE of Waverly.
Cobb Hollow	Located in S SE section of Williamson County, E of Riggs Crossroads. 16 mi SE of Franklin.
Coble	Community in W section of Hickman County. 9 1/2 mi W of Centerville.
Cochran	Community in S central section of Marshall County. Approx. 2 mi S of Lewisburg.
Cocke County COCKE COUNTY	County Seat: Newport. Zip Code 37821. Located in NE section of the State. Bounded by Sevier, Jefferson, Hamblem and Greene Counties and North Carolina to the East. Named in honor of Sen. William Cocke.
Cockrill Bend	Located in middle W section of Davidson County. 3 mi W of Bordeaux.

Coffee County 	County Seat: Manchester. Zip Code 37355. Located in South Central area of the State. Bounded by Cannon, Warren, Grundy, Franklin, Moore, Bedford and Rutherford Counties. Named in honor of Major General John Coffee.
Coffee Lake	Lake in S section of Haywood County, E of Ko Ko.
Coffee Landing	Community in middle NW section of Hardin County on the Tennessee River. 4 mi NW of Savannah.
Coffee Ridge	Located in S section of Unicoi County. 10 mi S SW of Erwin.
Coffman Camp	Community in N area of Grainger County. 5 mi N of Rutledge.
Cog Hill	Community on S SE border of McMinn County. Approx. 12 mi S SE of Athens.
Cohutta Wilderness	Located on S border of Polk County.
Coile	Community in middle W section of McMinn County. Approx. 4 mi W of Athens.
Coker Creek	Community in S SW section of Monroe County. 7 mi S SW of Tellico Plains.
Coldbranch Hollow	Located in E SE section of Benton County.
Cold Ridge	Ridge in W NW section of Coffee County. 2 1/2 mi N of Noah.
Cold Spring	Community in N Central section of Bledsoe County. 4 mi NE of Pikeville.
Cold Spring	Community in N NE section of Johnson County, SW of Wills.
Cold Spring	Community in NE section of Sullivan County. N of Holston Valley.
Cold Spring Knob	Mountain in S SW section of Sevier County near border, S of Miry Ridge. 10 mi S SW of Gatlinburg.
Cold Springs	Community in NE Section of Blount County. 9 mi E of Maryville.
Cold Springs	Community in middle NE section of Hawkins County. 12 mi NE of Rogersville.
Cold Springs Knob	Mountain in S SW section of Sevier County. In the Great Smoky Mountains. Ele. 5,240.
Coldwater	Community in W SW section of Lincoln County. Approx. 10 mi W SW of Fayetteville.

Cold Water Knob	Located in SE section of Blount County. 5 mi E SE of Cades Cove.
Coldwell	Community in central section of Bedford County.
Cole Hollow	Located in middle W SW section of Stewart County, N NW of Asbury.
Colesburg	Community in S central section of Dickson County. 8 1/2 mi S of Charlotte.
Coletown	Community in SE section of Polk County in Copper Basin, S of Ducktown.
Collegedale	City in SE area of Hamilton County. 15 mi E of downtown Chattanooga. Formerly Thatcher's Switch. Incorporated 1969.
College Grove	Community in E SE section of Williamson County. 14 mi E of Franklin.
College Park Estates	Community in E central section of Blount County. 3 mi S SE of Maryville.
College Port	Community in W area of Carter County.
College Station	Community in S Central area of Bledsoe County. 8 mi SW of Pikeville.
Collier Hill	Located in central NW section of Humphreys County. 3 1/2 mi N NW of Waverly.
Collier Hollow	Located in NW section of Humphreys County. 2 mi SE of Trinity.
Collier Lake	Lake in center E section of Madison County, between Jackson and Lake Graham.
Colliers Corners	Community in middle NE section of Jefferson County. 6 mi N NE of Dandridge.
Colliersville	City in SE section of Shelby County. 22 mi E SE of downtown Memphis. Incorporated in 1903.
Collins	Community in E section of Grundy County. 9 mi E SE of Altamont.
Collins Cove	Located near center of Overton County. 3 mi S of Livingston.
Collins Lake	Community in SW area of Davidson County. 11 mi W of Downtown Nashville.
Collins Mill	Community in N NW section of McMinn County. 10 1/2 mi N NE of Athens.
Collins River	Begins in the NE section of Warren County and flows NE into the Caney Fork River. SW of Walling.

Collinwood	City in central section of Wayne County. 10 mi S SE of Waynesboro. Incorporated in 1947.
Colonial Heights	Community in SW section of Sullivan County. 11 mi W SW of Blountville.
Colonial Village	Community within the city limits of Chattanooga. Approx. 4 mi N NE of downtown.
Colonial Village	Community within the city limits of Knoxville. 3 1/2 mi SE of downtown. In Knox County.
Columbia	County seat of Maury County. Located in center of county. Incorporated in 1817.
Columbia Gardens	Community in central W section of Maury County. 2 mi W of Columbia, N of West Haven.
Columbia Hill	Community in S SE section of Overton County. Approx. 14 mi S SE of Livingston.
Columbus Hill	Community in middle E section of Jackson County. E NE of Gainsboro.
Colverts Lake	Lake in center of DeKalb County, E of Smithville.
Comb Ridge	Ridge in SE section of Union County, NW of Copper Ridge.
Combs	Community in S area of Claiborne County SW of Tazewell.
Comby Ridge	Ridge in SE area of Claiborne County, NE of Love Mountain and SW section of Hancock County.
Commerce	Community in E SE section of Wilson County. 11 1/2 mi E SE of Lebanon.
Commissary Ridge	Ridge in middle E section of Stewart County, NE of Bear Spring.
Community Center	Community in N central section of Gibson County.
Como	Community on W border of Henry County. 10 1/2 mi W of Paris.
Compton	Community in central NE section of Rutherford County. 5 1/2 mi NE of Murfreesboro.
Conasauga	Community in SW corner of Polk County. 13 mi S SW of Benton.
Concord	Community in S Central section of Carroll County. 6 mi S SE of Huntingdon.
Concord	Community in E central section of Gibson County. 6 mi E of Trenton.

Concord	Community within the city limits of Chattanooga. 8 mi E SE of downtown. In Hamilton County.
Concord	Community on N border of Humphreys County. 10 mi N NE of Waverly.
Concord	Community in SW section of Knox County. 13 mi SW of Knoxville.
Concord	Community in central section of Rhea County. 9 mi N NE of Dayton.
Concord	Community in SW section of Rutherford County. 11 1/2 mi SW of Murfreesboro.
Condon	Community in S SE section of Union County. 4 1/2 mi S of Maynardville.
Condra	Community on NE border of Marion County. 17 mi NE of Jasper.
Conkintown	Community in SW corner of Sullivan County, on Hawkins County Line.
Conklin	Community in S SW section of Washington County. 8 mi S SW of Jonesborough.
Conrad Ridge	Ridge in N section of Decatur County, N of Jeannette.
Consauga	Community in SE corner of McMinn County. Approx. 10 mi SE of Athens. E of Etowah.
Conservation League Lake	Lake in middle NW section of Scott County. 8 1/2 mi N NW of Huntsville.
Convict Lake	Lake in SW section of Lauderdale County, E of Anderson-Tully Wildlife Area at the Ft. Pillow State Prison Farm.
Conway	Community in SE area of Giles County.
Conyearsville	Community in N section of Henry County. 10 mi N of Paris.
Cookeville	County Seat of Putnam County. Located in near center of the County. Incorporated in 1855.
Cook Hollow	Located in S central section of Stewart County, S of Parker Hollow.
Cooktown	Community on E border of Overton County. 11 mi E SE of Livingston.
Cooley Hill	Hill in middle W section of Houston County, N NE of New Hope.
Cooley Hollow	Located in E section of Benton County. Approx. 3 mi SE of Faxon.

Cool Springs	Community in NW area of Gibson County. 16 1/2 mi NW of Trenton.
Coon Hollow	Located in E SE section of Houston County, N of Yellow Creek.
Cooper	Community in W area of Fentress County. 8 1/2 mi W of Jamestown.
Cooper Chapel	Town in W NW section of Fentress County.
Cooper Hollow	Located in S section of Cannon County. 1 mi S of Burgen, 7 mi S SW of Woodbury.
Cooper Lake	Lake in middle NW section of Scott County. 7 mi NW of Huntsville.
Cooper Mill	Community in N central section of Bledsoe County. 3 mi NE of Pikeville.
Coopers Spur	Community in E section of Carroll County. Approx. 7 mi E of Huntingdon.
Coopertown	Community in middle S SW section of Robertson County. 7 mi SW of Springfield.
Copeland Cove	Located in central section of Overton County. 4 mi S of Livingston. Between Collins Cove and Hartsaw Cove.
Copeland Devide	Located in E SE section of Sevier County, S of Pittman Center.
Copeland Ridge	Ridge in middle W section of Wayne County. W NW of Collinwood.
Copperhill	City in SE corner of Polk County. 21 mi SE of Benton. Incorporated in 1913.
Copper Ridge	Ridge in NE section of Grainger County and SW section of Hancock County.
Copper Ridge	Ridge in N section of Hawkins County, NW of Eidson.
Copper Ridge	Community in N NW section of Knox County. S of Beech Grove.
Copper Ridge	Ridge in NW section of Knox County. N of Knoxville.
Copper Ridge	Ridge in SE section of Union County, SE of Alder Springs.
Coptown	Town in S SW section of Franklin County.
Cora Lake	Lake in SW corner of Shelby County. N of Robco Lake.
Coran	Community in S section of Hawkins County. N of

Coran, (Cont.)	Persia, 12 mi S of Rogersville.
Corbin Lake	Lake in W area of Grainger County. 4 1/2 mi W SW of Rutledge.
Corbondale	Community in SW section of Montgomery County. SE of Stringtown.
Cordell	Community in middle S SE section of Scott County. 6 mi S SE of Huntsville.
Cordell Hull Birthplace	Community in NW section of Pickett County. 3 mi W NW of Byrdstown.
Cordell Hull Dam	Dam on the Cumberland River. 2 1/2 mi N of Carthage in Smith County.
Cordell Hull Lake	Lake in central E section of Smith County (Cumberland River).
Cordell Hull Wildlife Refuge	Located in middle NW section of Jackson County. 4 mi NW of Gainesboro.
Cordell Mountain	Mountain in E section of Scott County, NE of Cordell.
Corders Crossroads	Community in middle SE section of Lincoln County. 7 mi SE of Fayetteville.
Cordova	Community in middle SE section of Shelby County. 16 mi E of Memphis.
Corinth	Community in middle N section of Knox County. 6 1/2 mi N NE of Knoxville.
Corinth	Community in middle N section of Sumner County. 13 mi N of Gallatin.
Cornersville	City in SW corner of Marshall County. 7 mi S SW of Lewisburg. Incorporated in 1849.
Corning	Community in E SE section of Wayne County. 18 mi S SE of Waynesboro.
Cornpone - aka Cove Creek Cascades	Community in middle W SW section of Sevier County. 8 mi S SW of Sevierville.
Corryton	Community in NE section of Knox County. 14 mi N NE of Knoxville.
Cortner	Community in SE section of Bedford County. 2 mi W of Normandy Lake, 10 mi E of Shelbyville.
Cosby	Community in SW area of Cocke County. 12 1/2 mi S of Newport.
Cosby Knob	Mountain in SW area of Cocke County on North Carolina Line in Great Smoky Mountains. Elev. 5145 ft.

Cottage Grove	City in W NW section of Henry County. 10 mi W NW of Paris. Incorporated in 1909.
Cottage Home	Community in SE corner of Wilson County. 20 mi SE of Lebanon.
Cotton Lake	Community in E NE section of Tipton County. 8 mi E of Covington.
Cotton Patch Crossroads	Community in NW corner of Houston County. Approx. 14 mi W NW of Erin.
Cotton Port Ridge	Ridge in W SW section of Meigs County, W of Goodfield.
Cottontown	Community in middle W section of Sumner County. 7 mi W NW of Gallatin.
Cottonwood Grove	Community in S section of Lake County. 10 1/2 mi S SW of Tiptonville.
Cotula	Community in NE Central area of Campbell County. 9 mi NE of LaFollette.
Couchville	Located in E SE section of Davidson County.
Coultersville	Community in N area of Hamilton County. 28 mi N NE of downtown Chattanooga.
Counce	Community in SW section of Hardin County. 13 mi S of Savannah. 2 mi SW of Pickwick Dam.
County Corner	Community in SE corner of Carroll County.
County Line	Community in E area of Grainger County. 13 1/2 mi E NE of Rutledge.
Countyline	Community in NW section of Moore County. 2 1/2 mi N of Lynchburg.
County Line Island	Island on Obey River on W border of Pickett County and E border of Clay County.
Courthouse Hollow	Located in NE section of Wayne County. S of Ashland.
Courtland	Community in central SE section of Robertson County. Approx. 2 1/2 mi SE of Springfield.
Courtland Place	Community in S section of Greene County, near North Carolina border.
Cove Creek	Community in S Central area of Campbell County. 4 mi SE of Caryville.
Cove Creek	Creek in S area Campbell County (Norris Lake).
Cove Creek	Community in S area of Carter County near North Carolina border. 16 mi S SE of Elizabethton.

Cove Creek Cascades - aka Cornpone	Community in middle W SW section of Sevier County. 8 mi S SW of Sevierville.
Cove Lake State Park	Located in SW area of Campbell County near Caryville.
Cove Mountain	Mountain in SW section of Sevier County.
Covington	County seat of Tipton County. Located in middle NE section of county. Incorporated in 1826.
Covington Hollow	Located in W section of Montgomery County.
Cowan	City in E central section of Franklin County. 6 mi S SE of Winchester. Incorporated in 1921.
Cowcamp Ridge	Ridge in E section of Monroe County, S of Salt Spring Mountain.
Cowden	Community in N central section of Marshall County. S SW of Oslin.
Cowen Point	Located in W section of Grundy County. 6 1/2 mi W SW of Altamont.
Coxbury	Community in S section of Benton County. Apporx. 3 mi S SW of Rockport.
Coxville	Community in N NE section of Crockett County. 6 mi N NE of Alamo.
Cozette	Community in N central area of Decatur County. 12 mi N of Decaturville.
Crab Hollow	Located in central W NW section of Sumner County. 1 mi E of Cottonwood.
Crab Orchard	City in E central section of Cumberland County. 8 mi E SE of Crossville. Incorporated in 1973.
Crab Orchard Mountain	Mountain in SW section of Morgan County.
Crab Orchard Mountains	Mountains in SE area of Cumberland County.
Crabtree	Community in S central area of Carter County. 2 mi W of Roan Mountain. 12 mi SE of Elizabethton.
Crackerbox Ridge	Ridge in SE section of Hamilton County.
Crackers Neck	Community in S SE section of Johnson County. 5 mi S of Mountain City.
Craft Hollow	Located in middle E SE section of Humphreys County. 2 mi NW of New Hope.

Craft Spring	Community in N area of Greene County near Baileyton.
Craggie Hope	Community in SW area of Cheatham County. 13 mi S of Ashland City.
Craigfield	Community in W SW section of Williamson County. 18 mi W of Franklin.
Craig Hollow	Located in SE section of Benton County.
Craig Hollow	Located in NW section of Humphreys County. 2 mi N of Trinity.
Craig Lake	Lake in S section of Cheatham County, near the border.
Crandull	Community in NW section of Johnson County. 7 mi NW of Mountain City.
Cranford Hollow	Located in middle E section of Maury County. 3 mi N of Union Grove.
Cranmore Cove	Community in SW section of Rhea County. 2 1/2 mi W of Dayton.
Cravenstown	Community on E SE border of Overton County. Approx. 12 mi E SE of Livingston.
Crawfish Valley	Community in N central section of Lawrence County. 4 mi N NW of Lawrenceburg.
Crawford	Community in SE section of Overton County. 12 1/2 mi E SE of Livingston.
Creasy Hollow	Located in middle W SW section of Macon County. 1 mi S of Cross Lanes.
Creek Side	Community within the city of Columbia, SE section of town, in Maury County.
Creek Store	Community on W border of Greene County. 18 mi W of Greeneville.
Crenshaw	Community in S section of Knox County, S of Mt. Olive. 6 mi S of Knoxville.
Cresent	Community in middle section of Rutherford County. Approx. 7 mi S SW of Murfreesboro.
Cresent View	Community in central section of Giles County.
Creston	Community in NW section of Cumberland County. 5 mi N NW of Crossville.
Crestwood Hills	Community in Knox County. 8 1/2 mi W SW of Knoxville.
Crews Store	Community in NE area of Carroll County.

Crewstown Community in middle SW section of Lawrence County. 7 1/2 SW of Lawrenceburg.

Crippen Gap Community in middle N section of Knox County. 5 1/2 mi N of Knoxville.

Crisp Spring Community in middle W section of Warren County. Approx. 6 mi W of McMinnville.

Crocker Hollow Located in E section of Cheatham County. 4 mi E NE of Ashland City.

Crocker Springs Lake Lake in NW area of Davidson County, E of Joelton.

Crockett Community in middle SE section of Obion County. 9 mi S of Union City.

Crockett Bay Lake in N NW section of Stewart County near the Kentucky border. NW of Tobaccopart.

Crockett County County Seat: Alamo. Zip Code 38001. Located in Western section of the State. Bounded by Dyer, Gibson, Madison, Haywood and Lauderdale counties. Named in honor of David Crockett.

CROCKETT COUNTY

Crockett Mills Community in N central section of Crockett County. 6 mi N NW of Alamo.

Crockett Ridge Ridge in W section of Hamblen County. 2 mi W of Morristown.

Crockettsville Community in middle NE section of Sevier County. 10 mi E of Sevierville.

Cromwell Crossroads Community in middle W SW section of Wayne County. 13 mi S SW of Waynesboro.

Cronanville Community in N section of Lake County. 4 mi N of Tiptonville.

Crooked Creek Located in N NW corner of Perry County. 13 1/2 mi N NW of Linden.

Crosby Community in E area of Grainer County. 13 mi E of Rutledge.

Cross Community in N NE section of Sullivan County. Approx. 6 mi W SW of Bristol.

Cross Anchor Community in middle N central section of Greene County. 7 mi N of Greeneville.

Cross Bridges Community in middle W section of Maury County. 10 mi W of Columbia.

Cross Creek Community within the city limits of Chattanooga, located in N section of city. Approx. 8 mi N NE of downtown. In Hamilton County.

Cross Creek National Wildlife Refuge	Located in E SE section of Stewart County on the Cumberland River.
Crossfield	Community in Knox County. 6 mi E SE of downtown Knoxville.
Cross Keys	Community in SE section of Williamson County. 13 mi S SE of Franklin.
Crossland	Community on N border of Henry County. 14 mi N NW of Paris.
Cross Lanes	Communtiy in middle W section of Macon County. 7 mi W of Lafayette.
Crosslin Hollow	Located in NW section of Coffee County. 2 mi N of Noah.
Cross Mountain	Mountain in SW section of Campbell County near Anderson County Line.
Cross Mountain	Mountain in E section of Cocke County, SW of Lanceville.
Crossno Ridge	Ridge in N NW section of Wayne County. N of Mooney.
Cross Plains	City in E NE section of Robertson County. 10 1/2 mi E NE of Springfield. Incorporated in 1973.
Cross Road	Community in N section of Scott County. 12 mi N NW of Huntsville.
Cross Road	Community on S border of Stewart County. 9 1/2 mi S of Dover.
Crossroads	Community in S Central section of Benton County. 4 mi SW of Camden.
Crossroads	Community in E area of Cannon County. 7 1/2 mi E of Woodbury.
Crossroads	Community in S central section of Crockett County. 3 mi S SW of Alamo.
Cross Roads	Community in central section of DeKalb County. 3 mi W of Smithville.
Cross Roads	Community in S SE section of Dyer County. 10 1/2 mi S SE of Dyersburg.
Crossroads	Community in N central section of Hardin County. 9 mi NE of Savannah. 3 mi E of Cerro Gordo.
Crossroads	Community in S central Section of Hickman County. Approx. 4 1/2 mi S SW of Centerville.
Cross Roads	Community in N central section of Lawrence

Cross Roads, (Cont.)	County. 5 1/2 mi N of Lawrenceburg.
Crossroads	Community in E SE section of Lawrence County. N of Oak Hill, S SE of Lawrenceburg.
Cross Roads	Community in NW corner of Macon County. 9 1/2 mi NW of Lafayette.
Crossroads	Community in E SE section of Shelby County. 2 mi E of Memphis.
Crossroads	Community in S section of Wayne County. 18 mi S SE of Waynesboro.
Crosstown	Community in S SW section of Tipton County. Approx. 5 mi SW of Brighton.
Crossville	County Seat of Cumberland County. Located near center of county. Incorporated in 1901.
Crouch Crossroad	Community in middle N NE section of Washington County. 7 mi N NE of Jonesborough.
Crowley Store	Community in S section of Weakley County. 10 1/2 mi S of Dresden.
Crow Pond	Pond in NW section of Hamilton County.
Crucifer	Community on W border of Henderson County. 9 mi W of Lexington. 4 mi N NW of Huron.
Crump	Community on W central border of Hardin County. 4 1/2 mi W of Savannah.
Crunk	Community in S section of Robertson County. Approx. 5 mi S of Springfield.
Crutcher Lake	Lake in SW section of Lauderdale County, W of Anderson-Tully Wildlife Area.
Crutcher Lake	Lake in SW section of Sumner County. 7 mi W of Gallatin.
Crystal	Community in N section of Obion County. 7 mi W NW of Union City.
Crystal Ridge	Ridge on E NE border of Lincoln County, S of Gattistown.
Crystal Springs	Community in SE section of Lincoln County. 8 1/2 mi SE of Fayetteville.
Crystal Springs Lake	Lake in SE section of Lincoln County. E of Crystal Springs.
Cuba	Community in W SW section of Hawkins County. 7 mi W SW of Rogersville.
Cuba	Community in NW section of Shelby County. 15 mi N of Memphis.

Cub Creek	Creek in NE central section of Decatur County.
Cub Creek	Community in middle NW section of Jackson County. 4 1/2 mi NW of Gainesboro.
Cub Creek	Creek in middle E section of Stewart County. SW of Atkins.
Cub Creek Lake	Lake in NE corner of Henderson County. 13 mi NE of Lexington.
Cub Knob	Located in W SW section of Smith County. 6 mi W SW of Carthage.
Culleoka	Community in S SE section of Maury County. 9 1/2 mi S SE of Columbia.
Cullom Hollow	Located in W section of Davidson County.
Culpepper	Community in W Central section of Cannon County. 4 mi W of Woodbury.
Cumberland City	City in SE corner of Stewart County. 14 mi E SE of Dover. Incorporated in 1903.
Cumberland City Steamplant (U.S. - TVA)	Located in S SE section of Stewart County. 12 mi SE of Dover.
Cumberland County CUMBERLAND COUNTY	County Seat: Crossville. Zip Code 38555. Located in Middle Ease section of the State. Bounded by Fentress, Morgan, Roane, Rhea, Bledsoe, White and Putnam Counties. Named in honor of the Cumberland Mountains.
Cumberland Cove	Located in SE section of Putnam County. 7 mi S of Monterey.
Cumberland Estates	Community within the city limits of Knoxville. 5 mi W NW of downtown. In Knox County.
Cumberland Furnace	Community in N section of Dickson County. 6 mi N of Charlotte.
Cumberland Gap	City in upper N central section of Claiborne County on the Kentucky Line. Incorporated in 1907.
Cumberland Gap National Historical Park	Located in upper N central section of Claiborne County on Kentucky Line.
Cumberland Grove	Community in central area of Fentress County. 3 mi S of Jamestown.
Cumberland Heights	Community in central section of Davidson County, W of Nashville.
Cumberland Heights	Community in central section of Grundy County. 2 mi SE of Altamont.

Cumberland Heights	Community in central NW section of Montgomery County. 2 1/2 mi SW of Clarksville.
Cumberland Mountain State Park	Located in S central section of Cumberland County. 2 mi S of Crossville.
Cumberland Plateau	Mountain Range in SE section of Cumberland County.
Cumberland River	Flows from Kentucky into Clay County, South into Jackson County, Southwest into Smith County where it is backed up by the Cordell Hull Dam. Flows Westward into Trousdale, Wilson and Sumner Counties where it forms county lines, into Davidson County, thru Cheatham, Montgomery and Stewart Counties and into Kentucky where it flows into the Ohio River.
Cumberland Springs	Community in NE section of Moore County. 6 mi NE of Lynchburg.
Cumberland Springs	Community in SW section of Rhea County. 3 1/2 mi NW of Dayton.
Cumberland Springs Wildlife Management Area	Located in N section of of Moore County. S of Ledford Mills.
Cumberland View	Community in S Central section of Campbell County. 4 mi S of LaFollette.
Cummings	Community in middle S section of White County. 2 1/2 mi S of Sparta.
Cummings Creek	Creek in middle W section of Montgomery County, flows into Cumberland River, E of Dotsonville.
Cummings Crossroads	Community in W section of Sumner County. 9 mi W NW of Gallatin.
Cummings Hollow	Located in N NE section of Humphreys County. 3 mi E SE of Woolworth.
Cummingsville	Community in N section of Van Buren County. 4 mi N of Spencer.
Cunningham	Community in S section of Montgomery County. 9 1/2 mi S of Clarksville.
Cunningham Broadbent Lake	Lake in middle W NW section of Montgomery County. 2 mi S of Woodlawn.
Cupp Mill	Community in lower central section of Claiborne County. 8 mi SW of Tazewell.
Curlee	Community in SW area of Cannon County. 5 1/2 mi SW of Woodbury.

Currie	Community in W area of Gibson County. 7 mi NW of Trenton.
Curry He Mountain	Mountain in W SW section of Sevier County, N of Curry She Mountain. 3 mi S of Wears Valley.
Curry Pond	Pond in E NE section of Hamilton County. W of Highway 58 and Dolly Pond Road. Approx. 1 1/2 mi SE of Skull Island.
Curry She Mountain	Mountain in SW section of Sevier County, S of Curry He Mountain. 7 mi SW of Gatlinburg.
Curtis Mountain	Mountain in SW section of Johnson County, E of Butler.
Curtistown	Located in SE corner of Warren County. 2 mi E NE of Spring Creek.
Curve	Community in E NE section of Lauderdale County. 6 mi NE of Ripley.
Cusick	Community in W section of Sevier County. 8 mi W SW of Sevierville.
Cusik	Community in NE section of Loudon County. 11 mi NE of Loudon.
Cuthbert Switch	Community in middle SW section of Haywood County. 5 mi S SW of Brownsville.
Cypress	Community in E central section of Crockett County.
Cypress	Community in SW corner of McNairy County. 12 mi S SW of Selmer.
Cypress Bottom	Located in NW section of Fayette County.
Cypress Creek	Community in NE corner of Henry County. 18 mi NE of Paris.
Cypress Grove Nature Park	Located on the NW outskirts of the City of Jackson.
Cypress Inn	Community in S section of Wayne County. 21 1/2 mi S SW of Waynesboro, near the county line.
Daddy Ridge	Ridge in E SE section of Overton County, W of Crawford.
Daddys Creek	Flows from S section of Cumberland County in NE direction into Morgan County where it flows into the Obed River.
Daisy	See Soddy Daisy
Dale Hallow Lake	Located in the E central section of Clay County (Obey River).

Dale Hollow — Community in E central section of Clay County. 3 mi E of Celina.

Dale Hollow Dam — Located in E central section of Clay County on the Obey River. 3 mi E of Celina.

Dalewood — Community in central section of Davidson County, E of Nashville.

Dalewood — Community within the city limits of Chattanooga, in East Chattanooga area near Wilcox Blvd.

Dallas Bay — Community in middle NE section of Hamilton County on Dallas Bay (Lake Chickamauga). 13 mi N NE of Chattanooga.

Dallas Bay — Inlet off Lake Chickamauga in Hamilton County. 13 mi N NE of Chattanooga.

Dallas Heights — Community within the city limits of Chattanooga. 3 mi N NE of downtown. In Hamilton County.

Dallas Hills — Community in central area of Hamilton County. 14 mi N NE of downtown Chattanooga.

Dallas Hollow — Community in Hamilton County. 14 mi N NE of Chattanooga.

Dallas Island — Island on Lake Chickamauga near Dallas Bay. Part of Chester Frost Park in Hamilton County. 15 mi N NE of downtown Chattanooga.

Dalton Hollow — Located in N section of Trousdale County. 1 mi N of Hartsville.

Damascus — Community in W section of Johnson County. 6 mi W SW of Mountain City.

Damon — Community in SW corner of Hardin County, S of Southside.

Dancyville — Community on S border of Haywood County. 13 mi S of Brownsville. 7 1/2 mi E SE of Stanton.

Dandridge N.E. of Koxville — County Seat of Jefferson County. Located in S central section of the County. Incorporated in 1843.

Daniel Hollow — Located in SE section of Bedford County.

Danner Town — Community in NE area of Dickson County. 8 mi NE of Charlotte.

Dante — Community in NW central section of Knox County. 5 mi NW of Knoxville.

Dan Top — Mountain in S section of Cocke County, S of Midway.

Darden	Community on E border of Henderson County. 10 mi E of Lexington. 8 1/2 mi N NE of Scotts Hill.
Darkey Spring	Community in W SW section of White County. 7 mi W SW of Sparta.
Darks Mill	Community in middle N section of Maury County. 5 mi N NE of Columbia.
Darnall Towhead	Located in NW section of Lake County.
Darrow Mill	Community in W area of Greene County near Mohawk.
Darwin	Community in SW corner of Shelby County. 8 1/2 mi S SW of Memphis.
Daus	Community in middle S SW section of Sequatchie County. 5 mi S SW of Dunlap.
Davenport	Community in W NW section of Warren County. 11 1/2 mi W NW of McMinnville.
Davenport Hollow	Located in central section of Cannon County. 2 mi S of Woodbury.
David Crockett State Park	Located near center of Lawrence County. W of Lawrenceburg.
Davids Knob	Mountain in N central section of Sevier County, SE of Middle Creek.
Davidson	Community in SW section of Fentress County. 14 mi SW of Jamestown.
Davidson	Community in N central section of Grainger County.
Davidson	Community in middle section of Pickett County. 6 mi E of Byrdstown.
Davidson Chapel	Community in Central section of Gibson County. 5 1/2 mi E NE of Trenton.
Davidson County 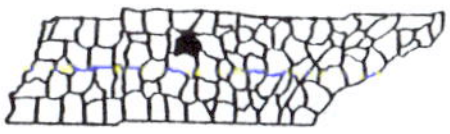 DAVIDSON COUNTY	County Seat: Nashville. Zip Code 37201. Located in North Central area of the State. Bounded by Robertson, Sumner, Wilson, Rutherford, Williamson and Cheatham Counties. Named in honor of Brig. General William Lee Davidson.
Davidson Cove	Located in E SE section of Putnam County. 5 mi S SW of Monterey.
Davis Chapel	Community in Central area of Campbell County. 3 1/2 mi E of LaFollette.
Davis Creek	Community in E Central area of Campbell County S of Well Spring on Norris Lake.

Davis Lake	Lake in S Central section of Bedford County. 6 mi S of Shelbyville.
Davis Ridge	Ridge in SW corner of Sevier County. 11 mi S SW of Gatlinburg.
Davis Springs	Community in NE section of Unicoi County. Approx. 7 mi E NE of Erwin.
Davy Crockett Birthplace State Park	Located in E section of Greene County, SE of Chucky. 9 mi E NE of Greeneville.
Davy Crockett Lake	Lake in S central section of Greene County on Nolichucky River.
Day Hollow	Located in W section of Houston County, S of McKinnon.
Day Lake	Lake in E area of Franklin County. 13 mi E of Winchester, S of Jackson Lake.
Day Lake	Lake on N NW border of Marion County. 16 mi W NW of Jasper partly in Franklin County.
Daylight	Community in middle NW section of Warren County. 6 mi NW of McMinnville.
Days Crossroads	Community in near center of Macon County. 2 mi E SE of Lafayette.
Daysville	Community in SE section of Cumberland County. 15 mi E SE of Crossville.
Dayton	County Seat of Rhea County. Located in middle SW section of the County. Incorporated in 1895.
Daytona Heights	Community in S central section of Hamilton County. 10 mi N NE of downtown Chattanooga.
Dayton Spur	Community in E central section of Cumberland County. 2 1/2 mi E NE of Crossville.
Deadrick Ridge	Ridge in S section of Blount County.
Dean	Community in E SE section of Scott County. Approx. 13 mi SE of Oneida.
Deanburg	Community in W section of Chester County near Hardeman County line, NW of Chickasaw State Park.
Deane Hill	Community within the city limits of Knoxville. 6 mi W SW of downtown. In Knox County.
Deans	Community in E center section of Hickman County. 3 mi S of Centerville.
Dearfield Acres	Community in N NE section of Sullivan County.

Dearfield Acres, (Cont.) S of Bristol.

De Armond Community in N section of Roane County. 7 mi N NE of Kingston.

Deason Community in N Central section of Bedford County. 8 mi N of Shelbyville, 4 1/2 mi W of Bell Buckle.

DeBusk Community in Central section of Greene County. 4 1/2 mi SE of Greeneville.

Decatur County seat of Meigs County. Located near center of County. Incorporated in 1838.

Decatur County County Seat: Decaturville. Zip Code 38329. Located in Middle Western area of the State. Bounded by Benton, Perry, Wayne, Hardin, Henderson and Carroll Counties. Named in honor of Commodore Stephen Decatur.

DECATUR COUNTY

Decaturville County Seat of Decatur County. Located near center of County. Incorporated in 1903.

Decherd City in central section of Franklin County. NE of Winchester. Incorporated in 1867.

Deep Springs Community in E Central section of Anderson County. 3 mi from Knox County line. 2 mi NE of Clinton.

Deep Springs Community in S section of Jefferson County. 6 mi W SW of Dandridge.

Deep Springs Hollow Located in middle S section of Cheatham County. 3 mi S of Germantown.

Deerfield Community in middle NW section of Lawrence County. 9 mi W NW of Lawrenceburg.

Deering Hollow Located in SW section of Macon County. 1 mi W of New Harmony.

Deer Lodge Community in middle NW section of Morgan County. 11 mi NW of Wartburg.

Deermont Community in S section of Morgan County. 5 1/2 mi S of Wartburg.

Defeated Community in middle N NE section of Smith County. 6 mi N NE of Carthage.

Defeated Ridge Ridge in SE section of Blount County. 6 mi S SE of Townsend.

Defense Depot - U.S. Located in Downtown Memphis, in Shelby County.

DeKalb County County Seat: Smithville. Zip Code 37166. Located in Middle Central section of the

DeKalb County, State. Bounded by Smith, Putnam, White, Warren, Cannon and Wilson Counties. Named in honor of Baron Johann DeKalb.

Delano Community in N NW section of Polk County. 8 mi N NE of Benton.

De Lap Community in SW Central area of Campbell County.

Delina Community on S border of Marshall County. 13 mi S SE of Lewisburg.

Dellrose Community in W SW section of Lincoln County. 13 mi W SW of Fayetteville.

Dellwood Community in middle E NE section of Blount County. 4 mi E of Maryville.

Del Rio Community in Central E area of Cocke County on French Broad River. 9 1/2 mi E SE of Newport.

Demory Community in SE section of Campbell County. 4 mi E SE of LaFollette.

Demoss Hollow Located in SW section of Davidson County. 4 mi N of Bellevue.

Denmark Community in N central section of Houston County. Approx. 2 mi W NW of Erin.

Denmark City in SW section of Madison County. 11 1/2 mi W SW of Jackson. Incorporated in 1839.

Dennis Cove Community in middle W SW section of Carter County, SE of Braemar.

Denson Island Island on the Tennessee River on E NE border of Decatur County, E of Cozette.

Densons Landing Community on W NW border of Perry County. 12 1/2 mi NW of Linden.

Denton Community in SW area of Cocke County. 8 mi S of Newport.

Denton Crossroads Town in NW area of Clay County.

Denton Knob Mountain in W SW section of Cocke County, W NW of Allen Grove.

Dentville Community on S border of McMinn County. 11 mi S of Athens.

Denver Community on W border of Humphreys County. 8 mi W SW of Waverly.

DePriest Bend Located in central NE section of Perry County. Approx. 9 mi N NE of Linden.

DeRossett	Community in E NE section of White County. 9 mi E NE of Sparta.
Desha	Community in middle E section of Sumner County. Approx. 5 mi NE of Gallatin.
Detroit	Community in NW section of Tipton County. 9 mi W NW of Covington.
Devils Elbow	Area in N section of Davidson County.
Devils Nose	Community in N central section of Hawkins County. 3 1/2 mi N of Rogersville.
Devils Tater Patch	Located in S SE section of Blount County, near border. 4 mi S SE of Cades Cove.
Devonia	See Braytown
Diamond Island	On the Tennessee River in W SW section of Hardin County, N of Pittsburg Landing.
Diana	Community in E NE section of Giles County. 12 mi E NE of Pulaski.
Dibrell	Community in N section of Warren County. 9 mi N of McMinnville.
Dibrell	Community in central SW section of White County. 3 mi SW of Sparta.
Dick Cabin Ridge	Ridge in E section of Wayne County. E of Waynesboro.
Dick Hollow	Located in middle N NW section of Macon County. 1 mi E NE of Gap of the Ridge.
Dickinson Island	Island on the Tennessee River, in the E section of Knoxville. 3 mi E of downtown Knoxville.
Dickson	City in SW central section of Dickson County. 8 mi S SW of Charlotte. Incorporated in 1899.
Dickson County DICKSON COUNTY	County Seat: Charlotte. Zip Code 37036. Located in the Middle of the State. Bounded by Montgomery, Cheatham, Williamson, Hickman, Humphreys and Houston Counties. Named in honor of Dr. William Dickson.
Dickson Town	Town in SE area of Giles County.
Difficult	Community in N NE section of Smith County. 9 mi N NE of Carthage.
Diggs Hollow	Located in S section of Benton County.
Dill	Community in SW area of Bledsoe County. 10 mi W SW of Pikeville.

Dillon Pond	Pond in N section of the city of Livingston. In Overton County.
Dillton	Community in central SE section of Rutherford County. 5 1/2 mi SE of Murfreesboro.
Disco	Community in NW area of Blount County near Mt Vernon. 11 mi W NW of Maryville.
Dismal	Community in NW area of DeKalb County. 9 1/2 mi W NW of Smithvivlle.
Dismal Hollow	Located in SE corner of Rutherford County.
Dismal Swamp	Swamp in SW corner of McNairy County. 12 mi SW of Selmer, in Big Hill Pond State Park.
Disney	Community in S Central section of Campbell County near Anderson County Line. 5 mi SE of Caryville.
Ditney Mountain	Mountain in E NE section of Polk County.
Ditney Mountain	Mountain in middle NE section of Scott County. 5 mmi E of Huntsville.
Ditty	Community in S SW section of Putnam County. 6 1/2 mi S SW of Cookeville.
Dividing Ridge	Ridge in E section of Hamilton County, S of Grasshopper.
Dixie	Community in middle NW section of Obion County. 8 mi W of Union City.
Dixie Lee Junction	Community in N NE section of Loudon County. 10 mi N NE of Loudon.
Dixie Mills	Community in W central section of Decatur County.
Dixon Cove	Located in middle N NW section of Marion County. Approx. 6 mi N of Jasper.
Dixon Island	Island on Cumberland River near W NW border of Smith County. 4 mi W NW of Riddleton.
Dixon Mountain	Mountain in E NE section of Sevier County. 12 mi E SE of Sevierville.
Dixon Springs	Community in NW section of Smith County. 9 mi NW of Carthage.
Dixonville	Community in SW corner of Tipton County. 19 1/2 mi SW of Covington.
Doaks Crossroads	Community in S section of Wilson County. 7 1/2 mi S SE of Lebanon.
Doc Jones Hollow	Located in S SW section of Williamson County.

Doc Jones Hollow, (Cont.)	1 mi N of Burwood.
Doctor Hollow	Located in central N NW section of Macon County. N NW of Pleasant Hill.
Doddsville	Community in NW area of Cheatham County. 4 mi W of Cheap Hill.
Dodson	Community in S SE section of White County. 8 mi S SE of Sparta.
Dodson Branch	Community in E SE section of Jackson County. 7 1/2 mi E SE of Gainesboro.
Doe Creek	Creek in SW section of Decatur County on Harden County line.
Doe Creek Lake	Lake in E NE section of White County. 9 1/2 mi E NE of Sparta, N of DeRossett.
Doe Mountain	Mountain in SW central section of Johnson County, NE of Doeville.
Doe Mountain Wildlife Management Area	Located in middle SW section of Johnson County, S of Pandora.
Doeville	Community in W SW section of Johnson County. 10 1/2 mi SW of Mountain City.
Dog Hill	Community in W area of Crockett County. 11 mi W NW of Alamo.
Dog Hollow	Located in SW section of Montgomery County, N of Tarsus.
Dogtown	Community near center of Carter County, 4 mi SE of Elizabethton.
Dogtown	Community in SE section of Grundy County, near Tracy City.
Dogtown	Community in SE section of Polk County. 17 mi SE of Benton.
Dogwood	Community in SE area of Cumberland County. 15 mi SE of Crossville.
Dogwood	Community in SE section of Roane County. 7 1/2 mi SE of Kingston.
Dogwood Flat	Community in middle NE section of Hickman County, W of Little Rock Mills.
Dogwood Lake	Lake in E NE section of Henderson County. 9 mi E NE of Lexington.
Dogwood Lakes	Lake in SW section of Cumberland County. Between Midway and New Era. 12 mi S SW of

Dogwood Lakes, (Cont.)	Crossville.
Dogwood Mudhole	Community in E section of Wayne County. 10 mi E SE of Waynesboro.
Dollar	Community in SE Area of Carroll County. 8 mi E NE of Clarksburg.
Dolly Pond	Community in middle NE section of Hamilton County, S of Grasshopper.
Dolomite	Community in N NE section of Houston County. Approx. 3 mi N NE of Erin.
Donegan Crossing	Community in middle W SW section of Dickson County. 3 mi E of Tennessee City.
Donelson	Community in E section of Davidson County. 7 mi E of Courthouse.
Donnell Chapel	Community on E SE border of Rutherford County. 12 1/2 mi SE of Murfreesboro.
Donoho	Community in middle NE section of Smith County. 6 1/2 mi NE of Carthage.
Dorton	Community in central section of Cumberland County. 4 mi E of Crossville.
Dorton Lake	Lake in SW area of Cumberland County. N of Tansi Lake.
Dossett	Community in S Central section of Anderson County. 6 mi SW of Clinton.
Doss Hollow	Located in W NW corner of Macon County. 12 mi W NW of Lafayette.
Dotson	Community in N central section of Grainger County. 4 mi N of Rutledge.
Dotsontown	Town in E area of Greene County. 11 1/2 mi E NE of Greeneville.
Dotsonville	Community in middle W section of Montgomery County. 7 1/2 mi W SW of Clarksville.
Doty Chapel	Community in NE central section of Greene County. 9 mi NE of Greeneville.
Double Bridges	Community in NE section of Lauderdale County. 11 1/2 mi N NE of Ripley.
Double Bridges	Community in middle W section of Tipton County. 11 mi W SW of Covington.
Double Springs	Community in S SW section of McMinn County. 9 mi S SW of Athens.

Double Springs	Community in central W section of Putnam County. 5 1/2 mi W of Cookeville.
Double Springs	Community in central E SE section of Rutherford County. 4 mi E SE of Murfreesboro.
Double Springs	Community in SW section of Sullivan County. Approx. 5 mi SW of Colonial Heights.
Double Top	Community in NW area of Fentress County. 8 mi W NW of Jamestown.
Douglas	Community in middle E section of Franklin County. E of Fayetteville.
Douglas	Community in S central section of Williamson County. 3 1/2 mi S SE of Franklin.
Douglas Dam	Dam in N section of Sevier County. 6 1/2 mi N of Sevierville.
Douglas Estates	Community in SE section of Jefferson County. 4 mi E SE of Dandridge, E of Henderson Island.
Douglas Lake	Lake in NW area of Cocke County and the S SE section of Jefferson County. (French Broad River)
Douglass Hollow	Located in E section of Humphreys County. 1 mi E of New Hope.
Dover	Community in E central section of Hamblen County. 4 mi E of Morristown.
Dover	County Seat of Stewart County. Located in near center of County. Incorporated in 1820.
Dover Island	Island on Cumberland River in middle N section of Stewart County.
Dowelltown	City in W central section of DeKalb County. 8 mi W NW of Smithville. Incorporated in 1949.
Doyle	City in S SW section of White County. 6 mi S SW of Sparta. Incorporated in 1963.
Dozier Hollow	Located in W SW section of Davidson County, NE of Collins Lake.
Drake Hollow	Located in W section of Coffee County. 2 mi SE of Busy Corner.
Drakes Creek	Creek in S SW corner of Sumner County. Flows into Cumberland River.
Drane Lake	Lake in W NW section of Shelby County. N of Frayser.
Drapers Crossroads	Community in middle E section of Macon County. 6 1/2 mi E of Lafayette.

Dresden	County Seat of Weakley County. Located in near center of county. Incorporated in 1827.
Dripping Spring	Community in W section of Sevier County, near DuPont.
Dripping Springs	Community in NW section of Cumberland County.
Druard Hollow	Located in N section of Davidson County.
Drummonds	Community in W SW section of Tipton County. 16 mi W SW of Covington.
Dry Branch	Community on N central border of Hancock County. 5 mi NE of Sneedville. 2 mi from Virginia Line.
Dry Creek	Creek in central area of Franklin County, W of Winchester.
Dry Creek	Community in S SE section of Washington County. 6 mi S SE of Jonesborough.
Dry Fork Bay	Lake in W section of Stewart County, inlet off the Tennessee River. N of Fort Henry.
Dry Gap	Community in middle NW section of Knox County. 6 mi N NW of Knoxville.
Dry Hill	Community in SW corner of Johnson County. 13 mi SW of Mountain City.
Dry Hill	Community in middle NE section of Lauderdale County. 7 mi N NE of Ripley.
Dry Hill	Community in N NW section of Roane County. 3 mi N NE of Rockwood.
Dry Hollow	Located in W section of Dickson County. 1 mi W of Ruskin.
Dry Hollow	Located in NW section of Houston County, SE of McKinnon.
Dry Hollow	Located in middle N NE section of Humphreys County. 3 1/2 mi N of Gorman.
Dry Hollow	Located in S section of Overton County. 10 mi S SE of Livingston, NE of Beaver Hill.
Dry Leaf Ridge	Ridge on S border of Johnson County.
Dry Run Mountain	Mountain in S section of Johnson County, N of Stone Mountain.
Dry Valley	Located in S SE section of Putnam County. S of Goffton.
Duck Creek	Community in center of Hancock County. 2 1/2 mi S of Sneedville.

Duckett Ridge	Mountain in NE section of Polk County.
Duck Island	Island on Piney River in E NE section of Rhea County.
Duck River	Flows from Coffee County where it is backed up by the Normandy Dam forming Normandy Lake, into Bedford, Marshall, Maury, Hickman and Humphreys Counties where it flows into the Tennessee River.
Duck River Ridge	Ridge across S section of Williamson County, near Maury County line.
Ducktown	Community in E NE section of Greene County. 15 mi NE of Greeneville, near county line.
Ducktown	City in SE section of Polk County. 17 mi SE of Benton. Incorporated in 1951.
Ducktown	Community in W NW section of Washington County. 9 mi W NW of Jonesborough.
Dudley Hollow	Located on N NW border of Houston County, E of Sykes Hollow.
Dudney Hill	Community in middle SE section of Jackson County. 2 1/2 mi SE of Gainesboro.
Duff	Community in E Central area of Campbell County. 6 mi NE of LaFollette.
Dug Ridge	Ridge in middle E section of Roane County.
Dukedom	Community on N border of Weakley County. 14 1/2 mi N of Dresden.
Dulaney	Community in central area of Greene County. 5 mi SW of Greeneville.
Dull	Community in E NE central section of Dickson County. 5 mi E NE of Charlotte.
Dumplin	Community in SW section of Jefferson County. 8 mi W SE of Dandridge.
Dumplin	Community in N section of Sevier County. N of Sevierville near Jefferson County Line.
Dunaway Ridge	Ridge in S central section of Stewart County, S of Dover.
Dunbar	Community in S area of Decatur County. 9 mi S of Decaturville.
Dunbar Cave	Community in central NE section of Montgomery County. 3 mi E NE of Clarksville.
Dunbar Cave State Natural Area	Located in NE section of Montgomery County. 3 mi N NE of Clarksville.

Dunbar Lake	Lake in middle NE section of Montgomery County. 3 1/2 mi E NE of Clarksville.
Duncan	Community in N Central area of Blount County near Maryville.
Duncan Hills	Community in the S section of the City of Red Bank. Hamilton County, Tennessee.
Duncan Hollow	Located in SW section of Johnson County, W of Dry Hill.
Duncan Lake	Lake in central area of Franklin County. 6 mi N of Winchester.
Duncantown	Community in N area of Franklin County. 10 1/2 mi N NE of Winchester.
Duncanville	Community in middle W section of Marshall County. 2 mi W of Lewisburg.
Dunham Lake	Lake in SW section of Dyer County, SE of Bradleytown.
Dunlap	County seat of Sequatchie County. Located near center of County. Incorporated in 1909.
Dunn	Community in middle S SE section of Lawrence County. Approx. 3 mi S of Lawrenceburg.
Dunns Chapel	Community in NE area of Dickson County.
Duo	Community in S area of Claiborne County. 3 mi NW of Tazewell.
Duplex	Community in S SE section of Williamson County. 12 1/2 mi S SE of Franklin.
Dupont	Community in W section of Sevier County. 8 mi W SW of Sevierville.
Dupont Springs	Community in W section of Sevier County. 8 mi SW of Sevierville.
Durham Hollow	Located in W section of Sumner County. 2 mi SW of Cummings Crossroads.
Durhamville	Community in SE section of Lauderdale County. 5 1/2 mi S SE of Ripley.
Dutch	Community in N NW section of Giles County. 5 mi N NW of Rutledge.
Dutch Valley	Community in near center of Anderson County. 4 mi W of Clinton.
Dyer	City in NW central section of Gibson County. 6 1/2 mi N NW of Trenton. Incorporated in 1899.
Dyer County	County Seat: Dyersburg. Zip Code 38024.

Dyer County, (Cont.)	Located in NW area of the State. Bounded by Lake, Obion, Gibson, Crockett and Lauderdale Counties and the Mississippi River to the West. Named in honor of Col. Robert Henry Dyer.
Dyersburg	County Seat of Dyer County. Located near center of county. Incorporated in 1836.
Dykes	Community in N section of Union County. Approx. 2 mi E of Big Sinks.
Dykes Crossroads	Community in W central area of Cumberland County. 4 1/2 mi NW of Crossville.
Dykes Mountain	Mountain in N section of Grundy County, near Warren County border.
Dyllis	Community in NE section of Roane County. 8 1/2 mi N of Kingston.
Eads	Community on E border of Shelby County. 23 mi E NE of Memphis.
Eagan	Community in NW corner of Claiborne County near Campbell County line. 8 mi NW of Speedwell.
Eagle Bluff Lake	Lake in S Central area of Campbell County N of Jacksboro.
Eagle Creek	Community in SE section of Benton County. 12 mi SE of Camden.
Eagle Creek	Creek in SE section of Benton County, flows into Tennessee River. E of Eagle Creek community.
Eagle Creek	Creek in W section of DeKalb County, flows into Caney Fork River. E of Philippi.
Eagle Creek	Inlet off Kentucky Lake (Tennessee River) in NE section of Henry County, SW of Paris Landing State Park.
Eagle Creek Wildlife Management Area	Located in middle NW section of Wayne County. NW of Waynesboro.
Eagle Furnace	Community on W SW border of Roane County. 14 mi W SW of Kingston.
Eagle Lake	Lake in W NW section of Shelby County. SW of Poplar Tree Lake.
Eagle Nest Island	Island on Tennessee River on S border of Decatur County.
Eagletown	
Eagleville	City in SW corner of Rutherford County. 16 mi

Eagleville, (Cont.) W SW of Murfreesboro. Incorporated in 1949.

Earleyville Community in middle NW section of Warren County. 7 m i NW of McMinnville.

East Brainerd Community in SE area of Hamilton County. 11 mi E of downtown Chattanooga.

EastBrook Community in NW central section of Franklin County. 4 1/2 mi NW of Winchester.

East Camp Creek Creek S of Gallatin, flows into Old Hickory Lake. In Sumner County.

East Chapel Community in E SE section of Grainger County. 8 mi E of Rutledge.

East Chattanooga Communitiy within the city limits of Chattanooga. 4 mi E NE of downtown. In Hamilton County.

East Cyruston Community in W section of Lincoln County. 8 mi W of Fayetteville.

Eastdale Community with city limits of Chattanooga. 3 1/2 mi E of downtown near Ridgeside. In Hamilton County.

East Etowah Community in SE section of McMinn County. 9 mi S SE of Athens. SE of Etowah.

East Fork Community in middle E NE of Sevier County. 8 mi E SE of Sevierville.

East Jamestown Community in N central section of Fentress County. 4 mi NE of Jamestown.

East Junction Community in SW section of Memphis. In Shelby County.

East Kingsport Community in N NW section of Sullivan County. 11 mi W NW of Kingsport.

East Lake Community within the city limits of Chattanooga. 3 1/2 mi SE of downtown. In Hamilton County.

Eastland Community in E section of White County. 13 mi E of Sparta.

East Miller Cove In NE section of Blount County. 11 mi E of Maryville.

Eastport Community in W central section of Cocke County.

Eastport Community in SW section of Pickett County. 8 1/2 mi S of Byrdstown.

East Ridge City in S area of Hamilton County. East of

East Ridge, (Cont.)	Chattanooga on the Georgia Border. Incorporated in 1921.
East Side	Community in NW central section of Carter County.
East Side	Community in SE area of Dickson County. 11 mi S SE of Charlotte.
East Springbrook	Community in N Central section of Blount County near Maryville.
East Sweetwater	Community in NW section of Monroe County. E of Sweetwater.
East Union	Community in E central section of Madison County. 3 mi E SE of Jackson.
Eastview	Community in central section of Greene County near Greeneville.
Eastview	City in middle S section of McNairy County. 7 mi S SE of Selmer. Incorporated in 1969.
East View	Community in S section of Meigs County. 15 mi S SW of Decatur.
Eastwood	Community in Knox County. 9 mi E NE of downtown Knoxville.
Eaton	Community in W area of Gibson County. 10 1/2 mi W of Trenton.
Eaton Crossroad	Community in N section of Loudon County. 7 1/2 mi N of Loudon.
Eaton Forest	Community in N section of Loudon County. 7 mi N of Loudon, W of Eaton Crossroads.
Eaton Hollow	Located in SE corner of Rutherford County.
Ebenezer	Community in S SW section of Knox County. 10 mi SW of Knoxville.
Ebenezer	Community in S central section of Marion County. 3 mi E of Jasper.
Ebenezer	Community in W SW section of Monroe County. 9 1/2 mi S of Madisonville.
Ebenezer	Community in S SE section of Tipton County. 10 1/2 mi S of Covington.
Echo Lake	Lake in central area of Giles County. NW of Pulaski.
Echo Meadows	Community in NE section of Davidson County.
Eden Corner	Community in middle E section of Robertson County. 7 1/2 mi E of Springfield.

Edenwold	Community in NE area of Davidson County. 10 mi NE of Courthouse.
Edgar Evins State Park	Located in N area of DeKalb County on Center Hill Lake. W of Silver Point.
Edgemont	Community in W central section of Cocke County. 3 1/2 mi W of Newport.
Edgemoor	Community in S Central area of Anderson County.
Edgewood	Community in W area of Dickson County. 11 mi N NW of Dickson.
Edgewood	Community in E area of Dyer County. 9 1/2 mi E NE of Dyersburg.
Edgewood Acres	Community in N central section of Blount County. 3 mi NE of Maryville.
Edgoten	Community on N NW border of Montgomery County. 8 mi N NW of Clarksville.
Edison	Community in S SW section of Gibson County. 6 1/2 mi S of Trenton.
Edith	Community in N central section of Lauderdale County. 7 mi N of Ripley.
Edward Grove	Community on middle NW border of Haywood County. 12 mi NW of Brownsville.
Edwards Lake	Lake in NW section of Shelby County. E NE of Locke.
Edwards Point	Community in W section of Hamilton County on Signal Mountain near Sequatchie County and Marion County Lines.
Edwina	Community in W central section of Cocke County. 4 mi S of Newport.
Egam	Community in central NW section of Lincoln County. 5 mi W NW of Fayetteville.
Egan	Community in central NW section of Wilson County. Approx. 3 mi W NW of Lebanon.
Egypt	Community in central NW section of Shelby County. 10 1/2 mi from Downtown Memphis.
Egypt	Community in middle SW section of Tipton County. Approx. 3 mi E of Double Bridges.
Egypt Hill	Located in middle W SW section of Wilson County. 2 mi S SE of Holloway.
Egypt Hollow	Located in middle W NW section of Williamson County, W of Montpier Farms.

Egypt Knob	Located in E section of Overton County. S of Treet Mountain.
Eidson	Community in N section of Hawkins County. 7 1/2 mi N NE of Rogersville.
Elaine lake	Lake located in SE area of Bedford County near Hilltop. 8 mi SE of Shelbyville.
Elba	Community in W SW section of Fayette County. 16 mi SW of Somerville.
Elbethel	Community in W Central section of Bedford County. 3 mi NW of Shelbyville.
Elbridge	Community in SW section of Obion County. 18 mi SW of Union City.
Elder Island	Island in Woods Reservoir in N section of Franklin County. N of Capital Hill.
Elder Mountain	Mountain in SW area of Hamilton County. 4 mi W of downtown Chattanooga. Part of Raccoon Mountain.
Eldridge Cove	Located in S section of Overton County. 2 mi NW of Beaver Hill.
Eledge Ridge	Ridge in SW section of McMinn County, W of Calhoun.
Elgin	Community in W SW section of Scott County. Approx. 13 mi S SW of Oneida.
Elizabeth	Community in N section of Crockett County. 13 mi N NW of Alamo.
Elizabeth	Community in E central section of Morgan County. 3 1/2 mi N NE of Wartburg.
Elizabethton	County seat of Carter County. Located in NW section of county. Incorporated in 1799.
Elkhead	Community in W section of Grundy County. 8 mi SW of Altamont.
Elkhorn	Community in E section of Henry County. 9 1/2 mi E of Paris.
Elkins	Community in Middle N section of Hickman County. 3 mi N NW of Centerville.
Elk Mills	Community on E Border of Carter County near North Carolina line. 3 mi SE of Little Milligan.
Elkmont	Community in SW section of Sevier County. Approx. 14 mi S of Sevierville.
Elkmont Springs	Town in SE area of Giles County.

Elk River	Community near E border of Carter County E of Little Milligan.
Elk River	Flows from Grundy County near Elkhead into Coffee County where it is backed up of the Elk River Dam forming Woods Reservoir and by the Tims Ford Dam forming the Tims Ford Lake, into Moore, Lincoln and Giles Counties where it flows into the State of Mississippi.
Elk River Dam	Dam in N section of Franklin County, forms Woods Reservoir. N NE of Estill Springs.
Elkton	City in SE area of Giles County. 12 mi E of Pulaski. Incorporated in 1831.
Elk Valley	Community in N Central area of Campbell County, E of Zeb Mountain.
Ellejoy	Community in NE Area of Blount County. 12 mi NE of Maryville.
Ellendale	Community in middle N section of Shelby County. NE of Bartlett.
Ellington Park	Located in S central section of Williamson County. 4 mi S SE of Franklin.
Ellis Mill	Community in W section of Monroe County, S of Mount Vernon.
Ellis Mills	Community in E NE section of Houston County. Approx. 6 1/2 mi E of Erin.
Ellis Ridge	Ridge in N section of Hamilton County.
Ellistown	Community in middle NE section of Knox County. 8 1/2 mi NE of Knoxville.
Elm Grove	Community in NW section of Tipton County. 9 mi W of Covington.
Elmore	Community in W area of Crockett County. 12 mi W of Alamo.
Elmore	Community in N central section of Cumberland County.
Elmore Park	Community within the city limits of Memphis, SE of Bartlett. In Shelby County.
Elm Springs	Community in NW area of Grainger County. 6 mi NW of Rutledge.
Elmwood	Community in Central SE section of Smith County. 4 mi E SE of Carthage.
Elora	Community in SE corner of Lincoln County. 15 mi SE of Fayetteville.

Elverton	Community on N NE border of Roane County. 8 1/2 mi N NE of Kingston.
Elza	Community in S Central area of Anderson County. 2 mi E SE of Dossett.
Embreeville	Community in S section of Washington County. 8 mi S of Jonesborough.
Embreeville Mountain	Mountain in S SW section of Washington County, SW of Embreeville.
Emerts Cove	Located in central E NE section of Sevier County, S of Richardsons Cove.
Emery Mill	Community in Central section of Bledsoe County. 2 mi N of Pikeville.
Emmett	Community in E section of Sullivan County. 12 mi E of Blountville.
Emory Gap	Community in N NW section of Roane County. 4 1/2 mi NW of Kingston.
Emory Heights	Community in N section of Roane County. 4 mi N of Kingston.
Emory River	River in N section of Roane County, N of Kingston, off Tennessee River.
England Hollow	Located near E border of Dickson County. 2 mi S of Harpeth Valley.
Engleton Heights	Community within the city limits of Chattanooga. Approx. 10 mi E SE of downtown, near East Brainerd.
Englewood	City in E section of McMinn County. 6 1/2 mi E of Athens. Incorporated in 1919.
Englewood	Community in near center of Obion County. 7 mi SW of Union City.
Englewood Lake	Lake in NW center of Obion County. 7 mi W SW of Union City.
English Creek	Community in W central section of Cocke County.
English Mountain	Mountain in E NE section of Sevier County and into Cocke County.
Enigma	Community in E section of Smith County. 9 mi E of Carthage.
Enka Dam	Dam on Nolichucky River in N NW section of Cocke County. N of Point Pleasant.
Eno	Community in SW section of Dickson County. 10 1/2 mi S SW of Charlotte.

Enon	Community in N NE section of Macon County. 8 1/2 mi NE of Lafayette.
Ensor	Community in W NW section of Putnam County. N of Baxter.
Enterprise	Community in S SW section of Maury County. 13 mi S SW of Columbia.
Enterprize	Community on S border of Hawkins County. 6 mi SE of Rogersville. 1 mi NE of Needmore.
Enville	City in lower E section of Chester County. 8 mi E of Oak Grove. Incorporated in 1943.
Ephesus	Community in NE corner of Carroll County. 11 mi NE of Huntingdon.
Epperson	Community in SW section of Monroe County. 6 1/2 mi S SW of Tellico Plains.
Epworth	Community in Williamson County. 1/2 mi S of Millview, 5 mi E SE of Franklin.
Erasmus	Community in W central section of Cumberland County. 9 1/2 mi W SW of Crossville.
Erie	Community in SW corner of Loudon County. 15 mi W SW of Loudon.
Erin	County Seat of Houston County. Located in N central section of County. Incorporated in 1909.
Ernestville	Community in middle S section of Unicoi County. 7 mi SW of Erwin.
Erwin	County seat of Unicoi County. Located near center of county. Incorporated in 1903.
Essary Springs	Community in SE corner of Hardeman County. 20 mi SE of Bolivar. 3 mi S of Pocahontas.
Estes Pond	Located on N border of Lake County, N of Proctor City.
Estill Springs	City in NW central section of Franklin County. 6 mi N NW of Winchester. Incorporated in 1948.
Ethridge	Community in N NE section of Lawrence County. 6 mi N NE of Lawrenceburg. Incorporated in 1973.
Etowah	City in SE corner of McMinn County. 8 1/2 mi S SE of Athens. Incorporated in 1909.
Etter	Community in middle W section of Pickett County. 1 1/2 mi SE of Byrdstown.
Euchee	Community in N section of Meigs County. N of

Euchee, (Cont.)	Pleasant Hill.
Eulia	Community in W SW section of Macon County. 8 mi W of Lafayette.
Eureka	Community in N Central section of Bradley County. 8 mi N of Cleveland.
Eureka	Community in middle W section of Roane County. 9 mi W SW of Kingston.
Eurekaton	Community in S section of Haywood County. 10 1/2 mi S SE of Brownsville. 11 mi W of Stanton.
Eva	Community on E Border of Benton County on Kentucky Lake. 5 mi E of Camden.
Eva Lake	Lake in E section of Franklin County. 12 mi E of Winchester, SW of Jackson Lake.
Evans Island	Island on Nolichucky River, SE of Pate Hill. In Greene County.
Evans Mountain	Mountain in SW section of Smith County. 1 1/2 mi S of New Middleton.
Evanston	Community in W central section of Hancock County. 4 1/2 mi SW of Sneedville.
Evansville	Community in central section of Dyer County near Dyersburg.
Eve Mill	Community in N NW section of Monroe County. 9 mi N NE of Madisonville.
Evensville	Community in S central section of Rhea County. 6 mi N NE of Dayton.
Everett Lake	Lake in W section of Dyer County, W SW of Ayers.
Evergreen	Community in SE area of Carter County. SE of Shell Creek.
Ewingville	Community in central section of Williamson County. E of Franklin.
Excell	Community in middle SE section of Montgomery County. N of Hickory Point.
Eyola	Community in NE area of Bradley County near Georgetown.
Factory	Community in E section of Wayne County. 8 1/2 mi E SE of Waynesboro.
Fagin	Community in middle NW section of Monroe County. 3 1/2 mi NE of Madisonville.

Fairfax Heights	Community within the city limits of Chattanooga. Approx. 5 mi N NE of downtown. 2 mi E of Red Bank.
Fairfield	Community in NE area of Bedford County. 11 mi NE of Shelbyville, 4 mi NE of Wartrace.
Fairfield	Community in N central section of Hickman County. Approx. 4 mi N NW of Centerville.
Fairfield	Community in N NE section of Sumner County. 17 mi N NE of Gallatin.
Fairfield Glade	Community in E central section of Cumberland County. 9 mi NE of Crossville.
Fairmont	Community in W area of Hamilton County on Walden's Ridge. 9 mi N of downtown Chattanooga.
Fair Oaks	Community within the city limits of Knoxville. 6 1/2 mi W NW of downtown. In Knox County.
Fairview	Community in W Central section of Blount County. 3 mi SW of Maryville.
Fairview	Community in N Central section of Bradley County near Cleveland.
Fairview	Community in N area of Carroll County. 5 mi N of Huntingdon.
Fairview	Community in SW corner of Carter County near Unicoi County line. 10 mi S of Elizabethton.
Fairview	Community in E area of Clay County. 11 mi E of Celina.
Fairview	Community in SW area of Coffee County. 8 mi W SW of Manchester.
Fairview	Community in NW section of Fentress County. 6 1/2 mi NW of Jamestown.
Fairview	Community in E area of Gibson County.
Fairview	Community in NE section of Grainger County. 11 1/2 mi NE of Rutledge.
Fairview	Community in E central section of Greene County. 6 mi NE of Greeneville.
Fairview	Community in S SW section of Lawrence County. 16 mi S SW of Lawrenceburg. 2 1/2 mi S SW of Loretto.
Fair View	Community in middle W section of Lincoln County. 6 mi W NW of Fayetteville.
Fairview	Community in W SW section of Macon County. 8

Fairview, (Cont.)	1/2 mi W SW of Lafayette.
Fairview	Community in N NW section of Madison County. 10 mi N of Jackson.
Fairview	Community in middle E section of McMinn County. Approx. 2 mi E of Athens.
Fairview	Community in N central section of Meigs County. 4 mi N NE of Decatur.
Fairview	Community in SW section of Pickett County. 3 1/2 mi W SW of Byrdstown.
Fairview	Community in middle SW section of Roane County. 5 1/2 mi S SW of Kingston.
Fairview	Community in middle E SE section of Scott County. 6 mi E SE of Huntsville.
Fairview	Community in central W section of Stewart County. 3 mi W of Dover.
Fairview	Community in central section of Sullivan County. 3 mi S SW of Blountville.
Fairview	Community in middle SE section of Warren County. 4 mi SE of McMinnville.
Fairview	Community in middle W NW section of Washington County. 3 1/2 mi W NW of Jonesborough.
Fairview	Community in SE section of Wayne County. 19 mi S SE of Waynesboro.
Fairview	City in W section of Williamson County. 15 mi W NW of Franklin. Incorporated in 1959.
Fairview Heights	Community in S section of Jefferson County. Approx. 7 1/2 mi W SW of Dandridge, SW of Deep Springs.
Fairview Heights	Community within the City of Columbia, N section. In Maury County.
Faix	Community in SW section of Pickett County. SW of Mount Union. 4 mi S of Byrdstown.
Falcon	Community in near center of McNairy County. 2 mi S of Selmer.
Fall Branch	Community in NW corner of Washington County. 12 mi NW of Jonesborough.
Fall Creek	Community in W Central section of Bedford County.
Fall Creek	Creek in E central section of DeKalb County, flows into Caney Fork River.

Fall Creek Falls State Park	Located on E SE border of Van Buren County. Approx. 8 mi SE of Spencer. 10 mi W of Pikeville.
Fall Creek Lake	Lake in Fall Creek Falls State Park.
Falling Water	Community in W central section of Hamilton County. 13 mi N of downtown Chattanooga.
Falling Water Falls	Located on Walden Ridge in Hamilton County. Approx. 2 mi N of Town of Walden.
Falling Water River	River in E area of DeKalb County, flows into Caney Fork River.
Falling Water River	River on S SW border of Putnam County.
Fall River	Community in E SE section of Lawrence County. 9 1/2 mi SE of Lawrenceburg.
Falls Mill	Community in SW area of Franklin County. 10 mi SW of Winchester.
Fanchers Mills	Community in W NW section of White County. Approx. 9 mi W NW of Sparta.
Fancy	Community in middle NW section of Weakley County. 6 mi NW of Dresden.
Farmers Exchange	Community in SW corner of Hickman County. 14 mi SW of Centerville.
Farmington	Community in central section of Marshall County. 6 mi NE of Lewisburg.
Farner	Community on E border of Polk County. 19 mi E of Benton.
Farragut	City in SW section of Knox County. 15 mi SW of Knoxville. Incorporated in 1980.
Farrar Hill	Community in W NW section of Coffee County. 2 mi NW of Boynton Valley.
Farris Chappel	Community in SW central section of Franklin County. 4 mi S of Winchester.
Farrport	Community in N section of Blount County. 4 mi N of Maryville.
Faulkner Springs	Community in central NE section of Warren County. 3 mi N NE of McMinnville.
Faxon	Community in N area of Benton County. 14 mi NE of Camden.
Fayette Corners	Community in NE section of Fayette County. 11 1/2 mi NE of Somerville.
Fayette County	County Seat: Somerville. Zip Code 38068.

Fayette County, Located in SW corner of the State. Bounded by Shelby, Tipton, Haywood and Hardeman Counties and by the State of Mississippi to the South. Named in honor of Marquis De La Fayette.

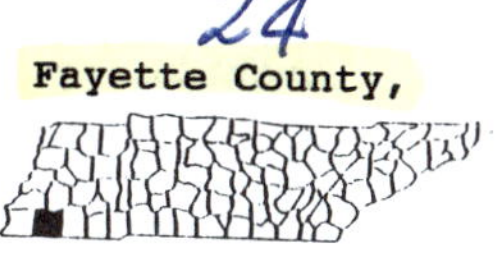

Fayetteville County Seat of Lincoln County. Located near center of county. Incorporated in 1889.

Feathers Chapel Community in central section of Fayette County. 4 mi W NW of Somerville.

Felker Community in SE area of Bradley County. 8 mi SE of Cleveland.

Felldown Hollow Located in middle S SE section of Stewart County, S of Carlisle.

Fentress County County Seat: Jamestown. Zip Code 38556. Located in North Central area of the State. Bounded by Pickett, Scott, Morgan, Cumberland and Overton Counties. Named in honor of James Fentress.

FENTRESS COUNTY

Ferguson Creek Creek in E area of DeKalb County, flows into Caney Fork Creek.

Fern Lake Lake in N central border of Claiborne County on Kentucky Line. 3 mi W of Harrogate.

Fernvale Community in midddle W section of Williamson County. 11 1/2 mi W of Franklin.

Fernwood Community in S section of Hamblen County. 4 mi S of Morristown.

Fessey Hollow Located in W section of Montgomery County.

Few Chapel Community in E NE section of Humphreys County. 12 mi E of Waverly.

Few Hollow Located in SW section of Dickson County. 4 mi S of Tennessee City.

Field Crest Community in central W SW section of Maury County. 2 mi W of Columbia, S of West Haven.

Fikes Mill Community in W NW section of Marshall County. Approx. 11 mi W NW of Columbia.

Fiketon Community in middle NW section of McMinn County. 6 1/2 mi W NW of Athens.

Fincastle Community in E Central section of Campbell County. 5 mi NE of LaFollette.

Findlay Community in central section of White County. 2 mi N of Sparta.

Finger City in N NW section of McNairy County. 13 mi N of Selmer. Incorporated in 1970.

Finley	Community in W central section of Dyer County. 5 1/2 mi W of Dyersburg.
First Island	Island on Dale Hollow Lake. 7 mi E NE of Celina in Clay County.
Fisher Knob	Located in S SE section of Wilson County. E of Turney Knob.
Fisherville	Community in E section of Shelby County. 22 mi E of Memphis.
Fishgap Hill	Community in NW corner of Obion County. 13 mi W NW of Union City.
Fish Springs	Community in E area of Carter County. 8 mi E SE of Elizabethton.
Five Forks	Community in W section of Decatur County. Approx. 8 mi N NW of Decaturville.
Five Forks	Community in NW section of Hardin County, W of Saltillo.
Five Point	Community in SE section of Lawrence County. 13 1/2 mi S SE of Lawrenceburg.
Five Points	Community in E central section of Giles County. 5 1/2 mi E of Pulaski.
Five Points	Community on SE border of Madison County. 10 1/2 mi SE of Jackson.
Five Points	Community in S section of Rhea County. 3 1/2 mi S of Dayton.
Flag Branch	Community in S central section of Greene County. 7 mi S of Greeneville.
Flag Pond	Community in S section of Unicoi County. 12 mi SW of Erwin.
Flat Branch	Community in S central section of Grundy County. 8 mi S of Altamont.
Flat Creek	Community in S Central section of Bedford County. 7 mi SE of Shelbyville.
Flat Creek	Community in middle W section of Overton County. 3 mi W of Livingston.
Flat Creek	Creek in N section of Sevier County (Douglas Lake).
Flat Gap	Community in S central section of Hancock County. 1 mi N of Treadway, 6 mi S of Sneedville.
Flat Gap	Community in near center of Jefferson County. 5 mi NW of Dandridge.

Flat Hollow	Community in E Central section of Campbell County. 10 mi E of LaFollette.
Flat Mountain	Mountain in NE section of Coffee County. 1 mi W NW of Summitville.
Flatrock	Community in SW area of Cumberland County. 11 mi W SW of Crossville.
Flat Rock	Community on W border of Morgan County. 15 mi W NW of Wartburg.
Flat Rock	Community in W section of Smith County. 8 1/2 mi W SW of Carthage.
Flats Mountain	Mountain in E section of Monroe County in Cherokee National Forest, SE of Indian Boundary Lake.
Flat Top	Located in S section of Franklin County. N of Grassy Glade Ridge.
Flattop	Community in NW section of Hamilton County on Walden's Ridge. 22 mi N of downtown Chattanooga.
Flatwood	Community in W NW section of Warren County. 9 1/2 mi NW of McMinnville.
Flat Woods	Community in Central section of Campbell County near Jacksboro.
Flatwoods	Community in N central section of Lawrence County. 4 mi N NW of Lawrenceburg.
Flatwoods	Community on S border of Perry County. 9 1/2 mi S of Linden.
Fletcher Lake	Lake in SW section of Lauderdale County, W of Anderson-Tully Wildlife Area.
Flewellyn	Community in middle SW section of Robertson County. 5 1/2 mi W SW of Springfield.
Flint Mountain	Mountain in S section of Unicoi County, W of Rocky Fork.
Flint Rock	Ridge in E SE section of Carter County, N of Laurel Fork.
Flint Springs	Community in S Central section of Bradley County. 7 mi S of Cleveland.
Flintville	Community in SE section of Lincoln County. 10 1/2 mi E SE of Fayetteville.
Flipper Bend	Located in central section of Hamilton County.
Flippin	Community in E NE section of Lauderdale County. 4 mi NE of Ripley.

Floraton	Community in middle E SE section of Rutherford County. 9 mi E SE of Murfreesboro.
Florence	Community in central NW section of Rutherford County. 6 mi NW of Murfreesboro.
Flourville	Community in NE section of Washington County. 8 mi N NE of Jonesborough.
Flowertown	Community in SW area of Coffee County.
Fly	Community in NW corner of Maury County. Approx. 13 mi N NW of Columbia.
Flynns Lick	Community in middle SW section of Jackson County. 3 1/2 mi SW of Gainesboro.
Fodderstack Mountain	Mountain in E SE section of Blount County, N of Tremont.
Fodderstack Mountain	Mountain on NE border of Greene County N of Pine Grove and extends into E SE section of Hawkins County, S of Light Mill.
Fodderstack Mountain	Mountain in N NE section of Johnson County, N of Laurel Bloomery.
Fogg Hollow	Located in W SW section of Giles County. N of Anthony Hill.
Fooshee Pass	Community in NW corner of Meigs County. Below Watts Bar.
Forbus	Community in NW corner of Fentress County. 10 mi N NW of Jamestown.
Ford	Community in NE section of Loudon County. 9 mi NE of Loudon.
Ford Chapel	Community in S Central section of Claiborne County. 7 mi W SW of Tazewell.
Ford Crossing	Community in W SW section of Washington County. 2 1/2 mi SW of Jonesborough.
Ford Hill	Located in W NW section of Sevier County near Seymour, S of Shooks Gap.
Fordtown	Community in SE area of Campbell County.
Fordtown	Community in SW section of Sullivan County. 11 mi SW of Blountville.
Forest Grove	Community in NW area of Davidson County. 15 mi NW of Courthouse. 9 mi W of Goodlettsville.
Forest Grove	Community in middle NW section of Meigs County. 4 1/2 mi N of Decatur.
Forest Highland	Community within the city limits of

Forest Highland, (Cont.)	Chattanooga. Approx. 6 mi N NE of downtown, near Hixson.
Forest Hill	Community in Center of Blount County. 3 mi S of Maryville.
Forest Hill	Community in NW central section of Humphreys County. 1 1/2 mi N of Waverly.
Forest Hill	Community in SE section of Shelby County. 18 mi E SE of Memphis.
Forest Hills	City in S area of Davidson County. 7 mi S of Courthouse. SE of Belle Meade. Incorporated in 1957.
Forest Hills	Community within the city limits of Knoxville. 3 1/2 mi W SW of downtown. In Knox County.
Forest Home	Community in N NW section of Williamson County. 4 1/2 mi NW of Franklin.
Forest Mill	Community near center of Coffee County. 4 mi NE of Manchester.
Forest Park	Community in W section of Hamilton County.
Forge Knob	Located in S SE section of Blount County, near border. 11 mi S SW of Townsend.
Forge Mountain	Mountain in E section of Johnson County, E of Mountain City.
Forge Ridge	Community in NE central section of Claiborne County. 8 mi N of Tazewell.
Forked Deer	Community in NW corner of Haywood County. 14 1/2 mi N NW of Brownsville.
Forked Deer Island	Island on W border of Lauderdale County, N of Ashport.
Forked Deer River	River on SW border of Dyer County. Flows into Obion River.
Fork Mountain	In W section of Anderson County, near Morgan County line. 7 mi NW of Oliver Springs.
Fork Mountain	Mountain in SW section of Carter County, S of Hampton.
Fork Ridge	Community in upper NW area of Claiborne County near Kentucky State Line. 16 mi NW of Tazewell.
Forks of River	Community in SE section of Knox County, S of Knoxville, W of Marbledale.
Forrest Hills	Community within the city of Columbia, N section of town. In Maury County.

Fort Campbell Military Reservation	Army Base in NE Stewart County and NW section of Montgomery County.
Fort Cheatham	Community within the city limits of Chattanooga. 3 1/2 mi S SE of downtown near East Lake. In Hamilton County.
Fort Donelson National Battlefield	Located in near center of Stewart County. 1 1/2 mi SW of Dover.
Fortescue Hill	Located on S SW border of Haywood County, S SE of Meux Corner.
Fort Henry	Community in W section of Stewart County. 10 mi W of Dover.
Fort Loudoun	Located in N NE section of Monroe County, E of Vonore.
Fort Loudoun Dam	Located in NE section of Loudon County on Tennessee River.
Fort Loudoun Lake	Lake in E NE section of Loudon County, E of Lenoir City (Tennessee River).
Fort Loudoun State Park	Located in N NE section of Monroe County, E of Fort Loudoun.
Fort Patrick Henry Lake	Lake in W NW section of Sullivan County, SE of Kingsport.
Fort Pillow	Community in SW corner of Lauderdale County.
Fort Pillow State Park	Located in SW section of Lauderdale County, W of Oak Grove. 16 mi W of Henning.
Fort Pillow State Prison Farm	Located in S SW section of Lauderdale County. 13 mi W SW of Ripley.
Fort Robinson	Community within the city of Kingsport, NW section of town. In Sullivan County.
Forty Five	Community in SE section of Fayette County. 13 mi S of Somerville.
Forty Forks	Community in middle N NW section of McNairy County. 8 1/2 mi N of Selmer.
Foster Corners	Community in SE area of Davidson County.
Foster Crossroads	Community in N section of Scott County. Approx. 6 mi N NW of Oneida.
Foster Falls	Located in N NW section of Marion County. Approx. 7 mi N of Jasper.
Fosterville	Community in S section of Rutherford County. 13 1/2 mi S of Murfreesboro.
Foundry Hill	Community in N NW section of Henry County. 8

Foundry Hill, (Cont.)	mi N NW of Paris and SW of Puryear.
Fountain City	Community within the city limits of Knoxville. 5 1/2 mi N NW of downtown. In Knox County.
Fountaincrest	Community in Knox County. 8 mi N of downtown Knoxville.
Fountain Grove	Community in NE area of Coffee County. 9 mi. NE of Manchester.
Fountain Head	Community in middle NW section of Sumner County. 11 mi N NW of Gallatin.
Fountain Heights	Community in middle SE section of Maury County. 6 1/2 mi SE of Columbia.
Four Corners	Community in SE area of Campbell County. 5 mi SE of Jacksboro.
Four Corners	Community in SE area of Davidson County.
Fourmile Board Hill	Community in NE section of Wayne County. 3 1/2 mi E NE of Waynesboro.
Fourmile Hill	Located in middle S SW section of Wilson County. 1 mi N of Holloway.
Four Points	Community in S area of Dyer County. 4 mi S SE of Dyersburg.
Four Points	Community in N NE area of Gibson County. 10 mi N NE of Trenton.
Four Points	Community in SW section of Jefferson County near border. 11 mi W of Dandridge.
Fowler Grove	Community in N Central area of Cocke County. 7 mi N NE of Newport.
Fowler Hollow	Located in W NW section of Dickson County. 1 mi NW of Adams Crossroads.
Fowlkes	Community in S area of Dyer County. 4 1/2 mi S of Dyersburg.
Fox Bluff	Community in NW area of Cheatham County.
Fox Branch	Community in NE central section of Hancock County on Virginia Border. 7 1/2 mi NE of Sneedville. 4 mi NW of Kyles Ford.
Fox Creek Lake	Lake in middle N section of Cumberland County. 4 mi N NE of Crossville.
Fox Hills	Community in N section of Blount County. 8 mi N NW of Maryville.
Fox Hollow	Located in SE section of Rutherford County. S

Fox Hollow, (Cont.) of Big Springs.

Foxwood Heights Community within the city limits of Chattanooga. 3 1/2 mi E of downtown. In Hamilton County.

Frances Lake Lake in N central section of Cumberland County. 7 mi N NE of Crossville.

Frankewing Community in E area of Giles County. 10 mi E of Pulaski.

Frankfort Community in W section of Morgan County. 11 1/2 mi W of Wartburg.

Franklin County seat of Williamson County. Located near center of county. Incorporated in 1815.

Franklin County County Seat: Winchester. Zip Code 37398. Located in S central section of the State. Bounded by Lincoln, Moore, Coffee, Grundy and Marion Counties and the State of Alabama to the South. Named in honor of Benjamin Franklin.

FRANKLIN COUNTY

Franklin - Marion State Forest Located in SE area of Franklin County. 12 mi NE of Cowan.

Fraterville Community in N Central section of Anderson County. 2 mi S of Lake City.

Frayser Community in W section of Shelby County. 6 mi N of Downtown Memphis.

Frederick Ridge Ridge in SE section of Sequatchie County.

Fredonia Community in central area of Coffee County. 4 1/2 mi N NW of Manchester.

Fredonia Community in SW corner of Haywood County. 16 mi SW of Brownsvile. 4 mi SW of Stanton.

Fredonia Community in middle E SE section of Montgomery County. 10 mi SE of Clarksville.

Fredonia Community in NW central section of Sequatchie County. 3 mi NW of Dunlap.

Free Communion Community in N section of Overton County. 7 mi N NE of Livingston.

Free Hill Community in N central section of Clay County, 2 mi NE of Celina.

Freeland Community on N border of Henry County. 16 mi N NE of Paris.

Freeman Hollow Located in W section of Dickson County, E of Adams Crossroads.

Freeman Ridge	Ridge in W section of Hamilton County.
Freemont	Community in SE section of Grundy County, near Tracy City.
Freewill	Community in W Central section of Bradley County. 3 mi NW of Cleveland.
Freewill	Community in SE section of Jackson County. 5 1/2 mi SE of Gainesboro.
Fremont	Community in middle N NW section of Obion County. 7 1/2 mi W of Union City.
French Broad	Community in Central E area of Cocke County on the French Broad River. 12 mi E SE of Newport.
French Broad	Community in E section of Jefferson County. 6 mi E of Dandridge.
French Broad River	Flows from the State of North Carolina into Cocke County, where the Nolichucky River flows into it. Flows into Jefferson County where it is backed up by the Douglas Dam, forming Douglas Lake, and into Sevier County, westward into Knox County where it joins the Holston River forming the Tennessee River.
French Hollow	Located in NE section of Benton County.
Frese Pond	Pond in S central section of Hardeman County. W of Roger Springs. 14 mi S of Bolivar.
Friendship	Community in E Central section of Bledsoe County. 6 mi E of Pikeville.
Friendship	Community in Blount County.
Friendship	City in NW section of Crockett County. 11 mi NW of Alamo. Incorporated in 1899.
Friendship	Community in E area of Giles County.
Friendship	Community in NW section of Hawkins County. 9 1/2 mi W NW of Rogersville.
Friendship	Community in NE corner of Sullivan County. E of South Holston Lake.
Friends Station	Community in middle W NW section of Jefferson County. 10 mi W NW of Dandridge.
Friendsville	City in W area of Blount County. 8 mi W of Maryville. Incorporated in 1953.
Frierson Town	Community in W SW section of Maury County. Approx. 10 mi SW of Columbia.
Frog Alley	Community in SE corner of Benton County.

Frogge Mountain	Mountain in W NW section of Fentress County, S SW of Pall Mall.
Frog Jump	Community in W area of Crockett County. 12 1/2 Mi W of Alamo.
Frog Jump	Community in SW section of Gibson County. 6 mi NW of Trenton.
Frog Level	Community on N border of Hawkins County. 9 1/2 mi N of Rogersville.
Frog Pond	Community in E area of Dickson County. 8 mi E NE of Dickson.
Frog Pond	Community in NE central section of Macon County. 3 1/2 mi N NE of Lafayette.
Frost	Community in W SW central section of Anderson County. 8 mi W of Clinton.
Frost Bottom	Community in W SW central section of Anderson County. 4 1/2 mi NE of Oliver Springs.
Frozen Head State Park	Located in E section of Morgan County. N of Petros. 5 mi E of Wartburg.
Fruedenburg Ridge	Ridge in S section of Sequatchie County.
Fruitland	Community in S central section of Gibson County. 6 mi S of Trenton.
Fruitvale	Community in SE section of Crockett County. 5 1/2 mi E SE of Alamo.
Fry Hollow	Located in E SE section of Benton County.
Fuller Ridge	Ridge in SE section of Hamilton County.
Fulton	Community in SW section of Lauderdale County, SW of Fort Pillow State Park.
Fuqua Hollow	Located in SE section of Humphreys County. 2 1/2 mi S SE of New Hope.
Furnace	Community in NW section of Hickman County. Approx. 12 mi NW of Centerville.
Furnace Hollow	Located in SE section of Stewart County, E of Brigham Hill.
Gabtown	Community in N NW corner of Washington County. Approx. 11 mi NW of Jonesborough.
Gadsden	City in E central section of Crockett County. 7 mi E of Alamo. Incorporated in 1867.
Gailor	Community in SE section of Tipton County. 12 1/2 mi SE of Covington.

Gainesboro	County Seat of Jackson County. Located near center of County. Incorporated in 1817.
Gaines Cove	Located in W section of Marion County, S of Martin Springs.
Gainesville	Community in S SE section of Tipton County. 10 1/2 mi S SE of Covington.
Gaitherville	Community on W border of Lawrenceburg in Lawrence County.
Galbraith Springs	Community in W SW section of Hawkins County. 10 mi W SW of Rogersville.
Galen	Community in N NE central section of Macon County. 5 1/2 mi N NE of Lafayette.
Gallatin	County seat of Sumner County. Located in S section of County. Incorporated in 1815.
Gallaway Mill	Community in central section of Sullivan County. 2 1/2 mi S SE of Blountville.
Galloway	City in NW area of Fayette County. 16 mi W NW of Somerville. Incorporated in 1966.
Gandy	Community in middle W section of Lawrence County. Approximately 10 mi N NE of Loretto. 3 mi SW of Lawrenceburg.
Gann	Community in E area of Gibson County. 12 mi E NE of Trenton.
Gant	Community in middle W NW section of Maury County. Approx. 7 mi W NW of Columbia.
Gant Ridge	Ridge in W section of Wayne County. W of Beckham Ridge.
Gap Creek	Community in W Central area of Carter County. 4 mi SW of Elizabethton.
Gap of the Knob	Located in E NE section of Greene County. 9 mi NE of Greeneville.
Gap of the Ridge	Community in W central section of Macon County. 5 mi W of Lafayette.
Gap Springs	Community in SE area of Bradley County near Felker.
Garber	Community in S SW section of Washington County. 5 1/2 mi S of Jonesborough.
Garding Hollow	Located in S central section of Cheatham County. 3 mi N of Shacklett.
Gardner	Community in W NW section of Weakley County. 11 1/2 mi W NW of Dresden.

Garland	Community in SW section of Knox County, S of Lakewood. 13 mi SW of Knoxville.
Garland	City in N NW section of Tipton County. 6 1/2 mi W NW of Covington. Incorporated in 1913.
Garner Hollow	Located in E NE section of Benton County. Approx. 1 1/2 mi N of Bass Bay.
Garrett	Community in W central section of Decatur County.
Garrett Knob	Located in middle SW section of Rutherford County. E of Rockvale.
Garrett Lake	Lake in E NE section of Weakley County, E of Jewell.
Garrettsburg	Community in E central section of Carroll County.
Gassaway	Community in NE section of Cannon County. 5 1/2 mi E of Auburntown.
Gates	City in E NE section of Lauderdale County. 9 1/2 mi NE of Ripley. Incorporated in 1901.
Gath	Community in middle N section of Warren County. 6 1/2 mi N of McMinnville.
Gatlinburg	City in middle S section of Sevier County. 11 mi S SE of Sevierville. Incorporated in 1945.
Gatlin Point	Located in NW section of Stewart County, NE of Brandon Springs.
Gattistown	Community on E NE border of Lincoln County. 10 1/2 mi E NE of Fayetteville.
Gause	Community in SW section of Robertson County. 10 1/2 mi SW of Springfield.
Gaylon Heights	Community within the city limits of Chattanooga. 5 mi E NE of downtown. In Hamilton County.
Gee Creek Wilderness	Located in N section of polk County. Approx. 8 mi N NE of Benton.
Genesis	Community in N central section of Cumberland County.
Geneva	Community in E SE section of Wayne County. Approx. 15 mi S SE of Waynesboro.
Gentry	Community in W section of Putnam County. 13 1/2 mi W of Cookeville.
Gentry Mountains	Mountains in S section of Johnson County. 2 mi S of Mountain City.

Gentry Park	Community in SE section of Dickson County.
Georgetown	Community in NW section of Bradley County. 7 mi NE of Cleveland.
Georgetown	Community in central section of Gibson County. 2 mi N NW of Trenton.
Georgetown	Community in NE area of Hamilton County near Bradley County line. 27 mi NE of downtown Chattanooga.
Georgetown	Community in middle SW section of McMinn County. Approx. 6 mi W SW of Athens. SW of Suburban Hills.
Georgia Crossing	Community in central section of Franklin County. 4 mi E of Winchester.
German Creek	Creek in E area of Grainger County. S of Tate Springs.
Germantown	Community in W Central section of Cheatham County. 5 mi SW of Ashland City.
Germantown	Community in NW area of Davidson County. 10 mi N NW of Courthouse.
Germantown	City in middle S SE section of Shelby County. 14 mi E SE of Memphis. Incorporated in 1903.
Gernt	Community in N central section of Fentress County.
Gerren Heights	Community in E Central section of Bledsoe County. 3 1/2 mi E SE of Pikeville.
Gettys Ridge	Ridge in SW section of McMinn County, SE of Sanford.
Gibbs	Community in E section of Obion County. Approx. 3 mi E SE of Union City.
Gibbs Crossroads	Community in SE corner of Macon County. 9 1/2 mi E SE of Lafayette.
Gibbs Knob	Located in W section of Rutherford County. 2 mi S of Little Hope.
Gibson	City in S SE section of Gibson County. 9 mi SE of Trenton. Incorporated in 1909.
Gibson County GIBSON COUNTY	County Seat: Trenton. Zip Code 38382. Located in NW area of the State. Bounded by Obion, Weakley, Carroll, Madison, Crockett and Dyer Counties. Named in honor of Col. John Gibson.
Gibson Gap	Located in W section of Hancock County. 5 mi W of Sneedville.

Gibson Hall	Community in NE area of Claiborne County. 7 mi NE of Tazewell.
Gibson Inn	Community in SE area of Cumberland County.
Gibson Mountain	Mountain in SW section of Johnson County, SW of Doeville.
Gibson Pond	Pond in Hardeman County E NE of Bolivar.
Gibsontown	Community within the city of Kingsport, middle N section of town. In Sullivan County.
Gibson Wells	Community in SW area of Gibson County. 9 mi NW of Trenton.
Gift	Community in NE section of Tipton County. 5 mi E of Covington.
Gilbreath	Community in NW area of Greene County. 10 mi NW of Greeneville. 1 1/2 mi SE of Marvin.
Gilchrist	Community on E border of McNairy County. 9 1/2 mi E NE of Selmer.
Gildfield	Community in N NE section of Shelby County. 18 1/2 mi NE of Memphis.
Giles County GILES COUNTY	County Seat: Pulaski. Zip Code 38478. Located in South Central section of the State. Bounded by Lawrence, Maury, Marshall and Lincoln Counties and the State of Alabama to the South. Named in honor of William B. Giles.
Giles Hill	Located in E SE corner of Williamson County. 2 mi N of Riggs Crossroads.
Giles Town	Community in NW section of Shelby County. 13 1/2 mi N of Memphis.
Gillespie Bend	Area in bend of Tennessee River, 6 mi E SE of Dayton in Rhea County.
Gilliam Hollow	Located in W SW section of Dickson County. 1 mi E NE of Tennessee City.
Gilliland Ridge	Ridge in SW section of Cocke County, S of Catons Grove.
Gillises Mill	Community in E SE section of Hardin County. Approx. 12 mi E SE of Savannah.
Gilmore	Community in N central section of Madison County. 5 mi N of Jackson.
Gilt Edge	City in W section of Tipton County. 10 mi S SW of Covington. Incorporated in 1966.
Ginger Bay	Lake in NW section of Stewart County, inlet off the Tennessee River. S of Rushing Bay.

Gin House Lake	Lake in SW section of Tipton County. Approx. 2 mi N of Munford.
Gismonda	Community in SW section of Benton County. Approx. 3 1/2 mi W SW of Chalklevel.
Gizzard Cove	Located in N NW section of Marion County, E of Martin Springs.
Gladdice	Community on W SW border of Jackson County. 8 mi W SW of Gainesboro.
Glade Creek	Community in SE corner of Putnam County. 17 mi SE of Cookeville.
Glades	Community in NW section of Morgan County. 14 mi NW of Wartburg.
Glades	Community in central section of Sevier County. Approx. 9 1/2 mi S SE of Sevierville.
Gladeville	Community in SW section of Wilson County. 10 mi S SW of Lebanon.
Glass	Community in middle S SW section of Obion County. 16 mi S SW of Union City.
Glass Hollow	Located in S section of Dickson County. 2 mi S SW of Pomona.
Glass Knob	Located in SE section of Knox County. E SE of Shooks.
Gleason	City in middle SE section of Weakley County. 7 1/2 mi SE of Dresden. Incorporated in 1903.
Glen	Community SE area of Coffee County. 12 1/2 mi SE of Manchester.
Glen Alice	Community in W section of Roane County. 13 1/2 mi W SW of Kingston.
Glencliff	Community in SE section of Davidson County.
Glendale	Community in N central section of Chester County. 5 mi N NE of Henderson.
Glendale	Community in S area of Davidson County.
Glendale	Community within the city limits of Chattanooga. 5 mi N of downtown Chattanooga at the foot of Signal Mountain. Hamilton County.
Glendale	Community in central SW section of Lawrence County. Approx. 4 mi NE of Loretto.
Glendale	Community in E section of Loudon County. 7 1/2 mi E of Loudon.
Glendale	Community in central S SE section of Maury

Glendale, (Cont.) — County. 5 1/2 mi S SE of Columbia.

Glendale — Community in W NW section of Washington County. 8 mi W NW of Jonesborough.

Glendale Estates — Community in near center of Giles County. E of Pulaski.

Glengary Lake — Lake in central section of Fayette County. 4 mi W of Somerville.

Glenmary — Community on SW border of Scott County. 10 mi SW of Huntsville.

Glenmore Estates — Community in N section of Blount County. 5 mi N of Maryville.

Glenobey — Community in W NW section of Fentress County.

Glenview — Community in central area of Coffee County.

Glenview — Community in Central section of Davidson County, E of Nashville.

Glenview Lake — Lake in SW section of Tipton County. Approx. 2 mi NW of Munford.

Glenwood — Community within the city limits of Chattanooga. 3 mi E of downtown. In Hamilton County.

Glenwood — Community in SW central section of Humphreys County. 4 mi S SW of Waverly.

Glenwood — Community in Knox County. 7 mi N NW of downtown Knoxville.

Glenwylde — Community in N section of Dickson County. 8 mi N of Charlotte.

Glimp — Community in S section of Lauderdale County. 7 1/2 mi SW of Ripley.

Globe — Community in W section of Marshall County. Approx. 4 mi W SW of Lewisburg.

Glover Crossroads — Community in middle S SW section of Robertson County. 5 1/2 mi S SW of Springfield.

Glynnwood Lake — Community in E SE section of Shelby County. 20 mi E of Memphis.

Gnat Grove — Community in S section of Marshall County. Approx. 10 mi S of Lewisburg.

Gnat Hill — Community in N area of Coffee County. 10 1/2 mi N NW of Manchester.

Goad — Community in E area of Fentress County. 11 1/2 mi E of Jamestown.

Goat City	Community in SE section of Gibson County. 14 mi NE of Trenton.
Goat Hill	Community in Marion County located 6 1/2 mi N of Whitwell.
Gobey	Community in central section of Morgan County. 3 mi N of Wartburg.
Godsey Ridge	Ridge in SW section of Hamilton County within the City of Red Bank.
Godwin	Community in near center of Maury County. 2 1/2 mi N of Columbia.
Goffton	Community in S SE section of Putnam County. 5 mi SE of Cookeville.
Goin	Community in S central section of Claiborne County. 9 mi W SW of Tazewell.
Golddust	Community in W section of Lauderdale County. 18 1/2 mi W of Ripley.
Golden Mountain	Mountain in N section of White County. 5 mi N of Sparta.
Golden Mountain	Mountain in N section of White County. 3 mi E of Bakers Crossroads.
Gold Mine Ridge	Ridge in E section of Cocke County, W of Brush Creek Mountain.
Gold Point Ridge	Ridge in central section of Hamilton County.
Gooch Waterfowl Management Area (State)	Located in S SE section of Obion County.
Goodbars	Community on E NE border of Warren County. 11 mi E NE of McMinnville.
Goodfield	Community in S central section of Meigs County. 4 mi S SW of Decatur.
Good Hope	Community in N area of Campbell County. 1 1/2 mi E SE of Jellico.
Good Hope	Community in E central section of Dyer County.
Good Hope	Community in middle NE section of McNairy County. Approx. 8 mi NE of Selmer.
Goodlettsville	City in NE section of Davidson County. 13 mi N NE of Courthouse. Incorporated in 1958. Boundaries extend into Sumner County.
Good Luck	Community in N section of Gibson County. 10 mi N of Trenton.

Goodman Ridge	Ridge in middle E section of Pickett County. 1 1/2 mi NE of Travisville.
Good Pasture Mountain	Mountain in W NW section of Overton County. 8 mi W NW of Livingston.
Goodrich	Community in N central section of Hickman County. 4 1/2 mi N of Centerville.
Goodrich Hollow	Located in S central section of Humphreys County. 5 mi S SE of Waverly.
Good Ridge	Ridge in SE section of Macon County, N NW of Russell Hill.
Goodspring	Community in SW central area of Giles County. 5 1/2 mi SW of Pulaski.
Good Springs	Community in S section of McMinn County. 8 mi S SE of Athens.
Goose Gap	Community in W section of Sevier County, N of Waldens Creek.
Goose Horn	Community in SE corner of Macon County. 11 1/2 mi E SE of Lafayette.
Goose Horn Ridge	Ridge on W border of Jackson County. 2 mi N of Milltown.
Goose Lake	Lake in NE section of Dyer County near Obion County line.
Gooseneck	Community in NE area of Anderson County. 10 mi NE of Clinton.
Gooseneck	Community in NW Section of Blount County near Louisville. 8 mi W of Maryville.
Goose Pond	Pond in SE section of Coffee County, on Arnold Engineering Development Center.
Goose Pond	Lake in SW section of Grundy County, S of Mt. View.
Goose Pond	Pond in W section of Lauderdale County, S of Right Hand Arm Lake. Approx. 8 mi W NW of Ripley.
Gordon Hill	Located in SE corner of Fayette County.
Gordonsburg	Community in middle NE section of Lewis County. 8 mi E NE of Hohenwald.
Gordonsville	City in middle S section of Smith County. 4 mi S of Carthage. Incorporated in 1909.
Gorman	Community in NE section of Humphreys County. 5 mi E NE of Waverly.

Gosey Hill Located in SE section of Williamson County. 8 mi SE of Franklin. 1/2 mi N of Peytonsville.

Goshen Community in E SE section of Hawkins County. 16 mi E NE of Rogersville. 1 mi NE of Blossom.

Goshen Ridge Ridge in S section of Marshall County. 3 mi N NW of Delina.

Goshen Ridge Ridge in S SW section of Sevier County near border. 8 mi S of Gatlinburg.

Gossburg Community in NW corner of Coffee County. 15 mi NW of Manchester.

Gould Hollow Located in W section of Humphreys County. 1 mi N of Denver.

Gowen Knob Located in E SE section of Rutherford County. W of Donnell Chapel.

Gower Community in SW area of Davidson County. 8 1/2 mi W SW of Courthouse.

Gower Island Island on Cumberland River, in W section of Davidson County. 3 mi W of Scottsboro.

Grabal Community in SE section of Gibson County. 13 mi E SE of Trenton.

Graball Community in S section of Marshall County. 10 mi S of Lewisburg.

Graball Community in near center of Sumner County. 6 1/2 mi N of Gallatin.

Graceland Located in SW section of Memphis, N of Whitehaven.

Graham Community in N central section of Hickman County. 6 1/2 mi N of Centerville.

Grainger County County Seat: Rutledge. Zip Code 37861. Located in NE area of the State. Bounded by Claiborne, Hancock, Hawkins, Hamblen, Jefferson, Knox and Union Counties. Named in honor of Mary Grainger.

GRAINGER COUNTY

Grainger County Park Located in S section of Grainger County. 4 1/2 mi S SE of Rutledge, W of Wa-No Village.

Grandfather Knob Located in S section of Wilson County. W of Cainsville.

Grand Junction City in SW corner of Hardeman County. 18 mi SW of Bolivar. 12 mi W of Roger Springs. Incorporated in 1901. Boundaries extend into Fayette County.

Grand Valley Lake Lake in Hardeman County. 8 mi S of Bolivar. 4

Grand Valley Lake, (Cont.)	mi E NE of Van Buren.
Grandview	Community in E NE area of Greene County. 9 1/2 mi NE of Greeneville.
Grandview	Community on N NE border of Hardin County on the Tennessee River, N of Swift.
Grandview	Community in Knox County. 5 mi SE of downtown Knoxville.
Grandview	Community in N section of Rhea County. 20 mi N NE of Dayton on the mountain.
Granite	Community in near center of Anderson County. 3 mi NW of Clinton.
Grant	Community in W NW section of Hamilton County. 20 mi N of downtown Chattanooga.
Grant	Community in W SW section of Smith County. 8 mi SW of Carthage.
Grantsboro	Community in SE area of Campbell County. 4 mi SE of LaFollette.
Grants Chapel	Community near center of Jefferson County. 2 mi NW of Dandridge.
Granville	Community in SW corner of Jackson County. 9 1/2 mi SW of Gainesboro.
Grapeyard Ridge	Ridge in middle SE section of Sevier County. 4 mi E of Gatlinburg.
Grasshopper	Community in NE area of Hamilton County. 26 mi NE of Chattanooga.
Grasshopper Creek	Creek in NE section of Hamilton County, N of Grasshopper, flows into Chickamauga Lake.
Grassy Cove	Community in S SE section of Cumberland County. 9 mi S SE of Crossville.
Grassy Creek	Community in S SE section of Polk County. 17 mi SE of Benton.
Grassy Fork	Community in S central section of Cocke County. 11 mi S SE of Newport. 4 mi SW of Sandy Gap.
Grassy Glade Ridge	Ridge in S SW section of Franklin County. E of Bean Creek.
Grassy Hollow	Located in SE section of Benton County.
Grassy Mountain	Mountain in middle E section of Hawkins County, SE of Slide.

Grassy Mountain	Mountain in N NE section of Morgan County, E of Sunbright.
Grassy Ridge	Ridge in S section of Greene County, N of Courtland Place.
Grassy Valley	Community in Central section of Greene County 4 mi N of Greeneville.
Gratio	Community on W SW border of Obion County. 23 1/2 mi SW of Union City.
Gravel Field Hollow	Located in E NE section of Benton County.
Gravel Hill	Community in middle S SE section of McNairy County. 7 mi S SE of Selmer.
Gravelly Hill	Community in N central section of Jefferson County, S of Jefferson City.
Gravelly Hills	Community in NW area of Blount County. 10 mi NW of Maryville.
Gravelly Mountain	Mountain in N section of Blount County, E of Rockford.
Gravelstand Top	Mountain in S section of Monroe County, E NE of Smithfield.
Graveltown	Community in middle N section of Smith County. 7 mi N of Carthage.
Graveston	Community in N NE section of Knox County. 13 1/2 mi N NE of Knoxville.
Gravley Hill	Located in N section of Trousdale County and SW corner of Macon County.
Gray	Community in S Central section of Bedford County.
Gray	Community in N section of Washington County. 8 1/2 mi N of Jonesborough.
Gray Hollow	Located in SW section of Dickson County. 1 mi E of Oak Grove.
Gray Hollow	Located in S section of Trousdale County. 2 mi S of Providence.
Graymere Manor	Community in central W section of Maury County. 2 mi SW of Columbia, S of Field Crest.
Gray Mountain	Mountain in E SE section of Scott County. S of Straight Fork.
Gray Mountain	Mountain in E section of Scott County, NE of Norma.
Graysburg	Community in NE area of Greene County near

Graysburg, (Cont.)	Jearoldstown. 13 mi N NE of Greeneville.
Graysburg Knobs	Mountain in E NE section of Greene County, E of Graysburg.
Grays Camp	Community on NE border of Lake County. 8 1/2 mi NE of Tiptonville.
Grays Crossing	Community on N central border of Houston County. Approx. 2 1/2 mi W NW of Erin.
Graysville	City on SW border of Rhea County. 5 1/2 mi SW of Dayton. Incorporated in 1917.
Graytown	Community in center of Hickman County. 4 mi E NE of Centerville.
Great Falls Dam	Dam in NE corner of Warren County on Caney Fork River.
Great Falls Dam	Dam in S SW section of White County, on the Caney Fork River. SW of Walling.
Great Smoky Mountains National Park	Located in E SE section of the State, in Blount, Sevier and Cocke Counties and the State of North Carolina. Gatlinburg is considered the focal point of the Smokies.
Green Acres	Community within the city of Kingsport, S section of town. In Sullivan County.
Greenback	City in SE corner of Loudon County. 11 mi E SE of Loudon. Incorporated in 1957.
Green Briar	Community in N NW section of Pickett County. 3 mi N of Byrdstown.
Greenbriar Lake	Lake in middle N section of Wilson County. 4 mi N NW of Lebanon.
Greenbrier	Community in W Central section of Cheatham County. 3 mi W of Ashland City.
Greenbrier	City in SE section of Robertson County. 7 mi SE of Springfield. Incorporated in 1937.
Greenbrier	Community in S SW section of Williamson County. 16 mi SW of Franklin.
Greenbrier Cover	Located in SE section of Sevier County. 3 mi S SE of Pinnacle.
Greenbrier Lake	Lake in SE section of Robertson County, E of Greenbrier.
Greenbrier Pinnacle	Located in E SE section of Sevier County. 5 mi SE of Pittman Center.
Greene County	County Seat: Greeneville Zip Code 37743 Located in Northeast section of the State.

Greene County, — Bounded by Cocke, Hamblen, Hawkins, Washington and Unicoi Counties and the State of North Carolina to the East. Names in honor of Nathaniel Greene.

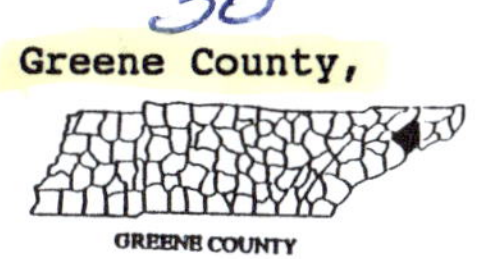

Greene Mountain — Mountain in SE area of Greene County S of Camp Creek.

Greeneville — County seat of Greene County. Located in center of county. Incorporated in 1817.

Green Field — Community in central S SW section of Giles County. Approx. 4 mi S SW of Pulaski.

Greenfield — City in S SW section of Weakley County. 11 1/2 mi S SW of Dresden. Incorporated in 1891.

Greenfield Bend — Community on W NW border of Maury County. Approx. 13 mi W NW of Columbia.

Greenfields — Community within the city of Kingsport, middle S section of town. In Sullivan County.

Green Grove — Community in SW corner of Macon County. 9 mi SW of Lafayette.

Greenhaw — Community in central section of Franklin County. 6 1/2 mi E NE of Winchester.

Greenhill — Community in S section of Jefferson County. 4 mi W NW of Dandridge.

Green Hill — Community in N section of Warren County. 10 mi N of McMinnville.

Green Hill — Community in W section of Wilson County. 14 mi W of Lebanon.

Green Hills — Community in S area of Davidson County.

Green Island — Island in NE section of Lake County on Reelfoot Lake.

Green Lake — Lake in S central section of Claiborne County W of Chittum and S of Tazewell.

Greenland — Community in NE section of Hawkins County. W SW of Church Hill.

Greenlawn — Community in W NW section of Wilson County. 2 mi N NW of Green Hill.

Green Mountain — Mountain in SW area of Cocke County, N of Cosby in Cherokee National Forest.

Green Mountain — Mountain in N section of Putnam County. 5 mi N NE of Cookeville.

Green Pine — Community in W area of Carter County. 5 mi S SW of Elizabethton.

Green Pond	Community in SE section of Overton County. 14 1/2 mi SE of Livingston.
Greens Crossroads	Community in NE section of Warren County. 8 mi N NE of McMinnville.
Greens Mill	Community in central section of Hamilton County near Soddy Daisy.
Greentop	Mountain in W section of Sevier County, N of DuPont Springs.
Greentown	Community on N border of Marion County, N of Oak Grove.
Greenvale	Community in S SE section of Wilson County. 15 mi S SE of Lebanon.
Green Valley	Community in N section of Macon County. 6 mi N NW of Lafayette.
Greenville	Community in NW section of Davidson County. 1 mi NW of Courthouse.
Greenwood	Town in E section of Macon County. 9 1/2 mi E of Lafayette.
Greenwood	Community in SW corner of Rutherford County.
Greenwood	Community in middle SE section of Washington County. 3 mi SE of Jonesborough.
Greenwood	Community in central SE section of Wilson County. 5 mi SE of Lebanon.
Greenwood Forest	Community in Knox County. 7 mi N of downtown Knoxville.
Greenwood Heights	Community within the city limits of Knoxville. 5 1/2 mi W NW of downtown. In Knox County.
Greer Mountain	Mountain in E SE section of Johnson County, near border. SE of Midway.
Gregory Bald	Mountain located on S border of Blount County on the North Carolina line. Elevation 4,948 ft.
Gregory Hollow	Located in E section of Sumner County, N NE of Bledsoe.
Greystone	Community in SE area of Greene County. 8 mi E SE of Greeneville.
Grices Creek	Creek in SE corner of Stewart County. N of Cumberland City.
Griffin	Community in NW central section of Fayette County. 9 mi W NW of Somerville.

Griffin Corner	Community in NW section of Shelby County. 13 1/2 mi N NE of Memphis.
Griffin Hollow	Located in SE section of Wilson County. 1 mi E of Sherrilltown.
Griffintown	Community in W Central area of Cheatham County. 8 mi SW of Ashland City.
Griffith	Community in W Central section of Bledsoe County. 4 mi W of Pikeville.
Griffith Creek	Community in N NE section of Marion County. 15 mi N NE of Jasper.
Griffith Mountain	Mountain in S SW section of Scott County, W of Lone Mountain.
Grigsby	Community in S section of Hawkins County. S of Chalk Level.
Grimsley	Community in S central section of Fentress County. 11 1/2 mi S of Jamestown.
Grinders Switch	Community in center of Hickman County. 1 1/2 mi NW of Centerville.
Grindstone Knob	Located in W NW section of Rutherford County. W of Little Hope.
Grindstone Mountain	Mountain in W section of Cocke County, N of Carson Springs.
Grindstone Mountain	Mountain in SE section of Hamilton County near Collegedale.
Grindstone Mountain	Mountain in SE section of Hamilton County.
Grindstone Ridge	Ridge in W central section of Sevier County, S of Pigeon Forge.
Grizzard	Community in Central section of Gibson County. 4 mi NW of Trenton.
Gross Lake	Lake in SW section of Cumberland County. SE of Midway. 12 mi SW of Crossville.
Groundhog Mountain	Mountain in W SW section of Monroe County, W SW of Tellico Plains.
Grove	Community in SE section of Morgan County. 5 mi SE of Wartburg.
Gruetli - Laager	City in central section of Grundy County. 5 mi SE of Altamont. Incorporated in 1980.
Grundy County GRUNDY COUNTY	County Seat: Altamont. Zip Code 37301. Located in South Central section of the State. Bounded by Warren, Sequatchie, Marion, Franklin and Coffee Counties. Named in honor of Felix

Grundy County, (Cont.)	Grundy.
Grundy Lakes Game Preserve	In S section of Grundy County N of Tracy City.
Grundy State Forest	In S section of Grundy County, W SW of Tracy City. 12 mi S SW of Altamont.
Gudger	Community in W section of Monroe County. 4 1/2 mi SW of Madisonville.
Guild	Community in S SE section of Marion County. 6 mi E SE of Jasper.
Gulf Island	Island on Norris Lake in W section of Union County.
Gulf Park	Community in Knox County. 11 mi W SW of Knoxville.
Gullet Mountain	Mountain near center of Overton County. 3 mi SE of Livingston.
Gum	Community in central S SE section of Rutherford County. 8 mi S SE of Murfreesboro.
Gum Creek	Community in NE area of Franklin County. 9 1/2 mi NE of Winchester.
Gumdale	Community in E central section of Decatur County near county line.
Gum Flat	Community in SE section of Crockett County. 9 mi SE of Alamo.
Gum Fork	Community in NE section of Scott County. 14 mi N NE of Huntsville.
Gum Pond	Pond in NW section of Lauderdale County, SE of Lake Chisholm.
Gum Spring	Community in W central area of Cocke County. 2 1/2 mi NW of Newport.
Gum Spring	Community in SW section of White County. 7 mi SW of Sparta.
Gum Spring Mountain	Mountain in middle W section of White County, W of Sparta.
Gum Springs	Community in E SE central section of Lawrence County. 4 mi SE of Lawrenceburg.
Gum Springs	Community in central SE section of Lincoln County. N of Flintville.
Gum Springs	Community in S SE section of Macon County. 7 mi SE of Lafayette.

Gum Stand	Community in Sevier County, S of Pigeon Forge, midway between Pigeon Forge and Gatlinburg.
Gunn Hollow	Located in W NW section of Wayne County. W of Waynesboro.
Gunnings	Community in N NW section of Sullivan County. Approx. 8 mi E of Kingsport.
Gunsight Mountain	Mountain on E border of Scott County.
Gunter Mountain	Mountain in S SE section of Overton County, S of Columbia Hill.
Guntersville Lake	Lake in S SW section of Marion County, E of South Pittsburg (Tennessee River).
Guntown	Community in central section of Hawkins County. 1 mi SE of Rogersville.
Guys	City in S section of McNairy County. 10 mi S SE of Selmer. Incorporated in
Habersham	Community in N Central section of Campbell County. 6 mi S SE of Jellico.
Hackberry	Community in SW section of Montgomery County. SW of Hilltop.
Hagersville Hollow	Located in middle NE section of Houston County, W of Spring Hill.
Hagys Corner	Community on S border of Tipton County. 13 mi S SW of Covington. S of Atoka.
Haigler Ridge	Community in E section of Henry County, S of Old Springville.
Hale	Community in central N section of Washington County. 2 mi N of Jonesborough.
Hale Mill	Community in SW area of Cumberland County. 9 1/2 mi SW of Crossville.
Hales Camp	Located in NW section of Rutherford County. 11 mi N NW of Murfreesboro.
Hales Crossroads	Community in S SE section of Hamblen County. 6 mi S SW of Morristown.
Hales Point	Community in N NW section of Lauderdale County. 13 mi N NW of Ripley.
Haletown (Guild P.O.)	Community in S SE section of Marion County. 6 mi E SE of Jasper.
Haley	Community in E Central section of Bedford County. 3 mi S of Wartrace, 8 mi E of Shelbyville.

Haley Mountain	Mountain in S SE section of Cumberland County, S of Crab Orchard.
Half Acre	Community in E NE section of Cannon County. 9 mi E NE of Woodbury.
Halladay	Community in SW corner of Benton County. 12 mi S of Camden.
Hallmark Hollow	Located in E section of Benton County.
Halls	Community in Mid-Western area of Benton County. 5 mi NW of Camden.
Halls	Community in N section of Knox County. 7 1/2 mi N NW of Knoxville.
Halls	City in NE corner of Lauderdale County. 12 mi N NE of Ripley. Incorporated in 1901.
Halls Creek	Community in NW section of Humphreys County. 7 1/2 mi N NW of Waverly.
Halls Crossroads	Community in Knox County. 8 1/2 mi N of downtown Knoxville.
Halls Hill	Community in E section of Rutherford County. 9 1/2 mi E NE of Murfreesboro.
Halls Mill	Community in W Central area of Bedford County. 4 mi from Marshall County line, 8 mi NW of Shelybville.
Halls Mill	Community in SW section of Sullivan County. 9 1/2 mi SW of Blountville.
Hall Town	Community in W section of Sumner County. 10 mi NW of Gallatin.
Halltown	Community in N section of Trousdale County. 3 mi N NE of Hartsville.
Hamble	Community in N section of Dickson County. 9 mi N NE of Charlotte.
32 Hamblen County HAMBLEN COUNTY	County Seat: Morristown. Zip Code 37814. Located in North East section of the State. Bounded by Hawkins, Greene, Cocke, Jefferson & Grainger Counties. Names in honor of Hezekiah Hamblen.
Hambright	Community in middle W section of Polk County, N of Reliance.
Hamburg	Community in SW corner of Hardin County. 10 mi S SW of Savannah. 3 1/2 mi W NW of Pickwick Landing Dam.
Hamillville	Community within city limits of Chattanooga. 8 mi N of downtown near Hixson. In Hamilton

Hamillville, (Cont.) County.

Hamilton County County Seat: Chattanooga. Zip Code 37402. Located in SE section of the State. Bounded by Marion, Sequatchie, Bledsoe, Rhea, Meigs and Bradley Counties and by the State of Georgia to the South. Named in honor of Alexander Hamilton.

HAMILTON COUNTY

Hamilton Mill Community in SW section of Lincoln County. 12 mi W SW of Fayetteville.

Hamlin Town Community in NW corner of Claiborne County. 8 mi NW of Speedwell.

Hammon Chapel Community in E section of Johnson County. 4 1/2 mi E of Mountain City.

Hampshire Community on W border of Maury County. 14 1/2 mi W of Columbia.

Hampton Community in W central section of Carter County. 4 mi S SE of Elizabethton.

Hampton Hill Community in SE area of Greene County near Greystone.

Hampton Mountain Mountain in S section of Overton County, near border. NW of Anderson.

Hamptons Crossroads Community in N NW section of White County. 9 1/2 mi N NW of Sparta.

Hampton Station Community in N NE section of Montgomery County. 9 1/2 mi NE of Clarksville.

Hancock County County Seat: Sneedville. Zip Code 37869. Located in North East section of the State. Bounded by Hawkins, Grainger, Claiborne Counties and the State of Virginia to the North. Named in honor of John Hancock.

HANCOCK COUNTY

Handleyton Community in NE section of Robertson County. 15 mi E NE of Springfield.

Haney Community in W central section of Decatur County.

Hanging Limb Community in SE section of Overton County. 13 1/2 mi SE of Livingston.

Hanging Rock Hollow Located near N NW border of Macon County. 1 mi N NE of Cross Roads.

Hannah Mountain Mountain in S section of Blount County.

Happy Hill Community in NE area of Giles County.

Happy Holler Located in W SW section of Sevier County, between Wares Valley and Chinquapin.

Happy Hollow	Located in E central section of Overton County. 6 mi E SE of Livingston.
Happy Valley	Community in NE section of Bedford County. 2 mi NE of Bell Buckle.
Happy Valley	In S Central section of Blount County. 10 mi S of Maryville.
Happy Valley Ridge	Ridge in S section of Blount County. 10 mi S of Maryville.
Harbin	Community in W NW section of Roane County. 2 mi E of Harbin.
Harbison Crossroads	Community in N section of Knox County. 10 1/2 mi N NE of Knoxville.
Harbor Channel	Channel off Lake McKellar, in SW section of Shelby County.
Harbuck	Community in E SE section of Polk County. 17 mi S SE of Benton.
Hardeman County HARDEMAN COUNTY	County Seat: Bolivar. Zip Code 38008. Located in South West section of the State. Bounded by Fayette, Haywood, Madison, Chester and McNairy Counties and by the State of Mississipi to the South. Named in honor of Thomas Jones Hardeman.
Hardin Bottom	Located in SW corner of Perry County.
Hardin County HARDIN COUNTY	County Seat: Savannah. Zip Code 38372. Located in South West section of the State. Bounded by McNairy, Chester, Henderson, Decatur and Wayne Counties and the the State of Mississippi and Alabama to the South. Named in honor of Col. Joseph Hardin.
Hardin Ford	Community in SW section of Lawrence County. S of Chinubee.
Hardison Mill	Community on E border of Maury County. Approx. 11 mi E of Columbia.
Hardscrabble	Community in NW area of Cannon County. 5 mi N NW of Woodbury.
Hard Scratch Hill	Located in S SW section of Macon County. 1 mi S of New Harmony.
Hardy	Community in Middle W SW section of Overton County. 8 mi SW of Livingston.
Hardy Acres	Community in central section of Maury County. 3 mi N of Columbia, NE of Chantay Acres.
Harlan Knob	Mountain in central section of Hawkins County, NE of Striggersville.

Harlan Mountain	Mountain in central section of Monroe County. 9 mi E SE of Madisonville.
Harmon	Community in W NW section of Johnson County. 6 1/2 mi W NW of Mountain City.
Harmon Creek	Creek in E NE section of Benton County. Approx. 11 mi E NE of Camden. Flows into Tennessee River.
Harmony	Community in W area of Franklin County. 8 mi W of Winchester.
Harmony	Community in W NW section of Van Buren County. 7 mi W of Spencer.
Harmony	Community in NW section of Washington County. 8 1/2 mi NW of Jonesborough.
Harmony Grove	Community in SE central section of Cocke County. 1 1/2 mi S of French Broad, 12 mi SE of Newport.
Harms	Community in W central section of Lincoln County. 4 1/2 mi W of Fayetteville.
Harpeth	Community in S section of Williamson County. 8 1/2 mi S SE of Franklin.
Harpeth River	River on W border of Cheatham County. Flows into Cumberland River.
Harpeth Valley	Community in SW corner of Davidson County. 13 mi SW of Courthouse.
Harpeth Valley	Community in E area of Dickson County. 10 mi E of Charlotte.
Harpeth Valley Ridge	Ridge in NE section of Dickson County, W of Bellsburg.
Harr	Community on N NE border of Sullivan County, on the Virginia Border, N of Twin Oaks.
Harrill Hills	Community within the city limits of Knoxville. 6 mi N of downtown. In Knox County.
Harriman	City in N section of Roane County. 5 mi N of Kingston. Incorporated in 1891.
Harriman Junction	Community in N NW section of Roane County. 7 mi NE of Rockwood.
Harris	Community in NE section of Obion County. 6 1/2 mi E NE of Union City.
Harrisburg	Community in middle N section of Sevier County. 4 1/2 mi E of Sevierville.
Harris Hills	Community within the city limits of East Ridge

Harris Hills, (Cont.)	on the Georgia State Line. 9 mi Se of downtown Chattanooga. In Hamilton County.
Harris Hollow	Located in W section of Humphreys County. 1 mi W NW of Pursley.
Harris Mountain	Community in middle SE section of Overton County. SE of Highland.
Harrison	Community in E central section of Hamilton County. 15 mi NE of downtown Chattanooga.
Harrison Bay State Park	Located in central section of Hamilton County on the Tennessee River. 16 mi NE of downtown Chattanooga in the Harrison Community.
Harrison Bluff	Community in Lake Chickamauga. 11 1/2 mi NE of downtown Chattanooga. North of Bartlebaugh. In Hamilton County.
Harrison Ferry Mountain	Mountain in E SE section of Warren County. 7 mi E SE of McMinnville.
Harrison Hills	Community in middle N section of Loudon County. 6 mi N NE of Loudon.
Harrison Hollow	Located in central section of Houston County. Approx. 3 mi W SW of Erin.
Harrison Knob	Mountain in W SW section of Cocke County, W of Allen Grove.
Harrogate	Community in N central section of Claiborne County. 10 mi NW of Tazewell.
Harrtown	Community in N NW section of Sullivan County. Approx. 8 mi E NE of Kingsport.
Hartford	Community in SW central section of Cocke County. 10 mi S SE of Newport, 3 mi W SW of Grassy Fork.
Hart Gulf	Valley in E section of Hamilton County.
Hartmantown	Community in NW section of Washington County. 7 mi NW of Jonesborough.
Hartsaw Cove	Located in S section of Overton County. 5 mi S of Livingston.
Hartsville	County seat of Trousdale County. Located near center of County. Incorporated in 1833.
Hartsville Island	Island on Cumberland River in S section of Trousdale County. 2 1/2 mi S SW of Hartsville.
Hartsville Junction	Community in E section of Sumner County. Approx. 8 mi E NE of Gallatin.
Harwell	Community in S area of Giles County.

Haskins Chapel	Community in W Central section of Bedford County on Haskins Chapel Road at Rattlesnake Lodge Road. 10 mi W of Shelbyville.
Haskins Hollow	Located in W NW section of Macon County. 2 mi W SW of Rocky Mound.
Hatcher Hollow	Located in E NE section of Humphreys County. 3 mi N NE of McEwen.
Hatcher Mountain	Mountain in S SE section of Blount County.
Hatcher Mountain	Mountain in W section of Sevier County, S SW of Cove Creek Cascades.
Hatchertown	Community in W SW section of Sevier County. Approx. 9 mi S SW of Sevierville.
Hatchett Hollow	Located in NE section of Bedford County.
Hatchie	Community in SW corner of Madison County. 19 mi SW of Jackson.
Hatchie Bottom	Swamp in N NW section of Hardeman County. From N into S section of Haywood County.
Hatchie National Wildlife Refuse	Located in SE section of Haywood County.
Hatfield Mountain	Mountain in SW section of Morgan County.
Hatfield Ridge	Ridge in NW section of Scott County.
Hathaway	Community in S SW section of Lake County. 12 1/2 mi S SW of Tiptonville.
Hava Lakotu Lakes	Lakes in E section of Dickson County. 1 mi NW of Claylick.
Havana	Community in NE section of Hardin County, NE of Swift.
Haw	Community in SW section of Giles County.
Hawkins County HAWKINS COUNTY	County Seat: Rogersville. Zip Code 37857. Located in NE section of the State. Bounded by Sullivan, Washington, Greene, Hamblen, Grainger and Hancock Counties and the State of Virginia to the North. Named in honor of Benjamin Hawkins.
Hawkins Island	Island on Holston River, SE of Church Hill.
Hawkinsville	Community in SE area of Dyer County. 10 1/2 mi SE of Dyersburg.
Hawkinsville	Located in S section of Hamilton County.
Haw Ridge	Ridge in S corner of Anderson County, S SE of Oak Ridge.

Haws Crossroads Community in NW section of Washington County. 10 mi NW of Jonesborough.

Hawthorne Community in S Central section of Bedford County. 8 mi S of Shelbyville.

Haydenburg Community in middle W NW section of Jackson County. 6 1/2 mi NW of Gainesboro.

Haydenburg Ridge Ridge in middle NW section of Jackson County, N of Haydenburg.

Hayesville Community in S area of Greene County near Davy Crockett Lake.

Hayne Pinnacle Located in W section of Smith County. 2 1/2 mi W of Tanglewood.

Haynes Community in S central section of Lake County, S of Wynnburg, N of Ridgely.

Hays Community in S SW section of Fayette County. 15 mi S SW of Somerville.

Haysboro Located in middle E section of Davidson County.

Hays Crossing Community in S SW section of Fayette County, W of Moscow.

Haysville Community on N NW border of Macon County. 7 1/2 mi N NW of Lafayette.

Haywood County County Seat: Brownsville. Zip Code 38012. Located in South West section of the State. Bounded by Crockett, Madison, Hardeman, Fayette, Tipton and Lauderdale Counties. Named in honor of Judge John Haywood.

HAYWOOD COUNTY

Hazel Community on N border of Henry County near Mason Lake.

Hazel Hollow Located in E NE section of Benton County. Approx. 1 mi E of Faxon.

Heard Ridge Ridge in SE corner of Clay County and N border of Overton County.

Heath Community in E section of Johnson County. 3 mi E SE of Mountain City.

Heath Hollow Located in E NE section of Humphreys County. 3 mi E of McEwen.

Hebbertsburg Community in E area of Cumberland County. 13 mi E NE of Crossville.

Hebron Community in N area of Fayette County. 10 1/2 mi N NW of Somerville.

Hebron	Community in SE central section of Hardeman County. 8 mi SE of Bolivar, SW of Hornsby.
Heddy Hollow	Located in middle S section of Stewart County, W SW of Bear Spring.
Hedge Hollow	Located in central E SE section of Humphreys County. W of New Hope.
Heiskell	Community in NW section of Knox County. 10 mi NW of Knoxville.
Helena	Community in N NW section of Fentress County. 5 mi W of Jamestown.
Helenwood	Community in central W NW section of Scott County. 3 mi W NW of Huntsville.
Hell Bend	Area in bend of Caney Fork River in S central section of Smith County. 2 1/2 mi S of Carthage.
Hellhole	Community in NE area of Bledsoe County.
Hellican (The)	Located in W section of Hamilton County.
Hells Point Ridge	Ridge in NW section of Campbell County, S of Newcomb.
Heloise	Community in W area of Dyer County. 16 1/2 mi W of Dyersburg.
Helton	Community in NW area of DeKalb County. 10 mi NW of Smithville.
Heltonville	Community in E SE section of Grainger County. 6 1/2 mi E of Rutledge.
Hematite	Community in SW section of Montgomery County. W of Hilltop.
Hembree	Community in SE corner of Scott County. 13 mi S SE of Huntsville.
Hemlock Knob	Located in E section of Monroe County, in Cherokee National Forest E of Waucheesi.
Henardtown	Community in S central section of Hawkins County. 2 mi S of Rogersville.
Henderson	County Seat of Chester County. Located near center of county. Incorporated in 1901.
Henderson County HENDERSON COUNTY	County Seat: Lexington. Zip Code 38351. Located in middle West section of the State. Bounded by Carroll, Decatur, Hardin, Chester and Madison Counties. Named in honor of Col. James Henderson.
Henderson Island	Island in SE section of Jefferson County. 2 mi

Henderson Island, (Cont.)	S of Dandridge.
Henderson Springs	Community in central section of Sevier County. Approx. 6 mi SW of Sevierville.
Henderson Top	Mountain in SE section of Monroe County, SE of Bald River Gorge.
Hendersonville	City in S SW section of Sumner County. 11 mi SW of Gallatin. Incorporated in 1968.
Hendon	Community in SE Section of Bledsoe County. 13 mi S of Pikeville.
Hendron	Community in S SE section of Knox County. 8 1/2 mi SE of Knoxville.
Henning	City in S SE section of Lauderdale County. 4 1/2 mi S SW of Ripley. Incorporated in 1901.
Henrietta	Community in NW section of Cheatham County. 4 mi W of Thomasville.
Henry	City in SW section of Henry County. 8 1/2 mi SW of Paris. Incorporated in 1907.
Henry County HENRY COUNTY	County Seat: Paris. Zip Code 38242. Located in North West section of the State. Bounded by Stewart, Benton, Carroll and Weakley Counties and by the State of Kentucky to the North. Names in honor of Patrick Henry.
Henry Crossing	Community in N NW area of Grainger County.
Henry Crossroads	Community in N NW section of Sevier County. 6 1/2 mi N of Sevierville.
Henry Horton State Park	Located in E NE section of Marshall County. 10 mi N NE of Lewisburg, at Chapel Hill.
Henry Town	Community in E section of Sevier County, S of Jones Cove.
Henryville	Community in N section of Lawrence County. 11 mi N NW of Lawrenceburg.
Hensley Chapel	Community in central SW section of White County. 4 mi W SW of Sparta.
Henson Hollow	Located in E section of Sumner County, S of Phillips Hollow. 2 1/2 mi E of Bransford.
Herb Parsons Lake	Lake in W SW section of Fayette County near Shelby County line SW of Canadaville.
Heritage Hills	Community in central section of Blount County. 4 mi S of Maryville.
Heritage Hills	Community in Hamilton County. 11 mi E NE of

Heritage Hills, (Cont.) Chattanooga.

Heritage Landing Community within the city limits of Chattanooga on the banks of the Tennessee River. 1 mi N NE of downtown. In Hamilton County.

Hermitage Community in E area of Davidson County. 9 mi E NE of Courthouse.

Hermitage Springs Community in W area of Clay County near Macon County line. 15 mi W of Celina.

Herndon Hollow Located in E SE section of Benton County.

Hew Hope Community in S central section of Gibson County. 3 mi SE of Trenton.

Hiawassee Community in SW section of Warren County. 8 1/2 mi SW of McMinnville.

Hice Station Community in NW section of Carroll County. Approx. 5 mi NW of Huntingdon.

Hickerson Station Community in SW Central section of Coffee County. 5 1/2 mi S SW of Manchester.

Hickey Community in SW area of Campbell County.

Hickey Community in SW section of Putnam County. 12 1/2 mi W SW of Cookeville.

Hickman Community in S section of Smith County. 7 1/2 mi S SE of Carthage.

Hickman Bar Located in W section of Shelby County on the Mississippi River, W of Benjestown.

Hickman County County Seat: Centerville. Zip Code 37033. Located in middle West section of the State. Bounded by Dickson, Williamson, Maury, Lewis, Perry and Humphrey Counties. Named in honor of Edwin Hickman.

HICKMAN COUNTY

Hickman Creek Hill Located on central W section of Stewart County, S SW of Fair View.

Hickory Community in W section of Jefferson County, S SE of Strawberry Plains.

Hickory Corners Community in SW area of Chester County. 8 mi SW of Henderson.

Hickory Flat Community in SW section of Carroll County. 15 mi SW of Huntingdon near Henderson County line.

Hickory Flats Community in SE section of Henderson County. 13 mi S SE of Lexington. 4 mi W NW of Sardis.

Hickory Flats	Community in middle E NE section of McNairy County. 10 mi E NE of Selmer.
Hickory Forks	Community in W section of Decatur County. Approx. 7 mi N NW of Decaturville.
Hickory Grove	Community in S section of Bledsoe County, E of Smithtown.
HIckory Grove	Community in SW area of Franklin County. 11 mi S SW of Winchester.
Hickory Grove	Community in W central section of Gibson County. 4 mi W of Trenton.
Hickory Grove	Community in N NW section of Rutherford County. 10 mi N NW of Murfreesboro.
Hickory Grove	Community in E SE section of Sumner County. Approx. 8 mi E of Gallatin.
Hickory Hieghts	Community in central section of Lawrence County. SE of Lawrenceburg.
Hickory Hill	Community in near center of Moore County. 2 1/2 mi SE of Lynchburg.
Hickory Hill	Located in S section of Rutherford County. E of Fosterville.
Hickory Hills	Community within the city limits of Knoxville. 6 mi SW of downtown. In Knox County.
Hickory Nut Mountain	Mountain in SW corner of White County, N of Joppa.
Hickory Point	Community in S section of Haywood County. 10 1/2 mi S SW of Brownsville. 1 1/2 mi W of Spring Hill.
Hickory Point	Community in SE section of Montgomery County. 9 mi SE of Clarksville.
Hickory Star Landing	Community in central SW section of Union County. 4 1/2 mi W NW of Maynardville.
Hickory Top	Mountain in S section of Blount County.
Hickory Tree	Community in SE section of Sullivan County. 10 mi E SE of Blountville.
Hickory Valley	Community within the city limits of Chattanooga. 9 mi E of downtown in Hamilton County.
Hickory Valley	City in SW section of Hardeman County. 11 mi SW of Bolivar. 3 1/2 mi E of Fayette Couty line. Incorporated in 1951.
Hickory Valley	Community in central SW section of Union

Hickory Valley, (Cont.)	County. 4 1/2 mi W of Maynardville.
Hickory Withe	Community in W area of Fayette County. 13 1/2 mi W of Somerville.
Hicks Chapel	Community in NE section of Marion County. 13 mi NE of Jasper.
Hicks Crossing	Community in W NW section of Sevier County. 10 mi W NW of Sevierville.
Hicks Hollow	Located in W section of Macon County. 2 mi W of Fairview.
Hicksville	Community within the city limits of Jackson, middle NW section of town. In Madison County.
Hico	Community in N area of Carroll County. 7 mi N NW of Huntingdon.
Hidden Cove Lake	Lake in W section of Wilson County. 12 mi W SW of Lebanon.
Hidden Harbor	Community on Lake Chickamauga in Hamilton County. 11 1/2 mi NE of downtown Chattanooga. Near Gold Point Estates.
High Bluff	Community in S section of Knox County. 7 1/2 mi S SE of Knoxville.
Highcliff	Community in N area of Campbell County. 3 mi E of Jellico.
Highland	Community in W SW area of Fentress County.
Highland	Community on W section of Jackson County. 6 1/2 mi W of Gainesboro.
Highland	Community in E section of Obion County. Approx. 2 mi E SE of Union City.
Highland	Community in S section of Overton County. 7 mi S SE of Livingston.
Highland	Community in N NE section of Sumner County. N of Brackentown.
Highland	Community in central section of Wayne County. 6 mi S SE of Waynesboro.
Highland Academy	Community in middle NW section of Sumner County. 9 mi N NW of Gallatin.
Highland Acres	Community in middle W section of Blount County. 3 mi SW of Maryville.
Highland Heights	Community in central W section of Giles County. Approx. 2 mi SW of Pulaski.

Highland Heights	Community within the city of Columbia, S section of town. In Maury County.
Highland Park	Community in Central section of Campbell County near Jacksboro.
Highland Park	Community within the city limits of Chattanooga. 2 mi SE of downtown. In Hamilton County.
Highland Park	Community within the city limits of Knoxville. 6 1/2 mi N of downtown. In Knox County.
Highland Park	Community in NE section of Loudon County, N of Lenoir City.
Highland Park	Community within the City of Columbia, near center of town. In Maury County.
Highland Springs	Community in W section of Grainger County. 7 mi W SW of Rutledge.
High Point	Community in Central section of Campbell County near Jacksboro.
High Point	Community in NW section of Cocke County. 10 mi N of Newport, 3 mi E of Point Pleasant.
High Point	Community in W section of Morgan County. 13 mi W NW of Wartburg.
High Point	Community in central NW section of Scott County. 5 mi N NW of Huntsville.
High Point	Located in S section of Scott County, S SW of Hembree.
Highstand Ridge	Ridge in E section of Benton County, S of Harmon Creek.
Hil-A-Wa Lake	Lake in central SW section of Marshall County. 2 mi W SW of Lewisburg.
Hilham	Community in W NW section of Overton County. 7 mi W NW of Livingston.
Hill	Community in SE section of Maury County. 7 mi E SE of Columbia.
Hillard	Community in central area of Carroll County. 4 mi SE of Huntingdon.
Hill City	Community within the city limits of Chattanooga. Just N of River. 1 mi from downtown. In Hamilton County.
Hillcrest	Community in S central section of Coffee County. 2 mi S of Manchester.
Hillcrest	Community near Morristown in central section

Hillcrest, (Cont.)	of Hamblen County.
Hillcrest	Community in S section of Sullivan County. 6 mi S SE of Blountville.
Hillcrest	Community in NW section of Sullivan County, E of Kingsport.
Hillsboro	Community in SE central section of Coffee County. 7 1/2 mi SE of Manchester.
Hills Chapel	Community in SE area of Davidson County.
Hillsdale	Community near S border of Macon County. 5 1/2 mi S of Lafayette.
Hillsview	Community in W SW section of McMinn County. 12 mi W SW of Athens.
Hilltop	Community in SE section of Bedford County. 9 mi SE of Shelbyville.
Hilltop	Community in middle SW section of Montgomery County. 4 1/2 mi S SW of Clarksville.
Hilltop	Community in W NW section of Rutherford County. W of Smyrna.
Hill Town	Community in NW section of Maury County. 12 mi N NW of Columbia.
Hillvale	Community in NE Central section of Anderson County. 5 mi N of Clinton.
Hillville	Community in SE section of Haywood County. 11 mi S SE of Brownsville. 13 mi E of Stanton.
Himesville	Community in S Central section of Bedford County. 4 mi S SE of Shelbyville.
Hinch Mountain	Mountain in S section of Cumberland County, E of Burke.
Hinds Chapel	Town in W NW section of Fentress County.
Hinds Ridge	Ridge in S section of Union County, S of Lone Mountain.
Hinkle	Community on N NW border of Hardin County. 13 1/2 mi N NW of Savannah. 7 1/2 mi N of Right.
Hinkledale	Community in NW section of Carroll County.
Hinson Springs	Community in center of Henderson County, SW of Lexington.
Hinton Crossing	Community in NW area of Cheatham County.
Hitchcox	Community in W Central area of Bledsoe County.

Hitch Pond	Pond in NW section of Blount County. 9 mi W NW of Maryville. N of Mt. Vernon.
Hiwassee College	College located in Monroe County, N of Madisonville.
Hiwassee Island	Island in area where Hiwassee River flows into the Tennessee River, in Meigs County.
Hiwassee River	Flows from Hiwassee Lake in North Carolina into Polk County, forms county lines for Bradley and McMinn Counties, into Meigs County where it flows into the Tennessee River.
Hiwassee Wildlife Refuge	Located in SW and W section of Meigs County.
Hixon	Community in NW section of Grundy County. 5 mi W of Altamont.
Hixson	Community within the city limits of Chattanooga. 8 1/2 mi N of downtown. In Hamilton County.
Hobbs Hill	Community in SE section of Grundy County N of Tracy City.
Hodges	Community in W section of Jefferson County. 12 mi W NW of Dandridge.
Hodges Lake	Lake in W section of Jefferson County, SW of Hodges.
Hodgetown	Community in central area of Hamilton County near Soddy Daisy.
Hodson	Community in N section of Crockett County. 10 mi N NW of Alamo.
Hogback Mountain	Mountain in S central section of Polk County, E of Sylco Ridge.
Hogback Ridge	Ridge in SW corner of Monroe County.
Hoggtown	Community in middle N NE section of Smith County. 5 1/2 mi N NE of Carthage.
Hog Wallow Ridge	Ridge in central E SE section of Overton County. 6 mi SE of Livingston.
Hohenwald	County Seat of Lewis County. Located in W central section of the County. Incorporated in 1911.
Holland Mill	Community in NE area of Greene County. 10 mi N NE of Greeneville.
Holland Pond	Pond in N central section of Franklin County. 5 1/2 mi N NE of Winchester.

Holleman Bend	Area in bend of the Cumberland River, S of Gladdice.
Holloway	Community in middle S section of Wilson County. 5 mi S SW of Lebanon.
Hollow Rock	City in NE area of Carroll County. 8 mi E NE of Huntingdon. Incorporated in 1911.
Hollow Springs	Community in SW section of Cannon County near Coffee County line. 10 mi S of Woodbury.
Holly Creek	Community in E SE section of Wayne County. Approx. 18 mi S SE of Waynesboro.
Holly Grove	Community in NE corner of Haywood County. 8 1/2 mi NE of Brownsville. 1 1/2 mi S SE of Jones.
Holly Grove	Community in middle E section of Marshall County. Approx. 3 mi E NE of Lewisburg.
Holly Grove	Community in W center section of Tipton County. 5 1/2 mi W SW of Covington.
Holly Leaf	Community in E NE area of Gibson County. 15 mi E NE of Trenton.
Holly Springs	Community in SW section of Monroe County. 8 mi S SW of Tellico Plains.
Holly Springs	Community in middle NW section of Overton County. 4 1/2 mi W NW of Livingston.
Hollywood	Community in S section of Maury County. 9 mi S of Columbia.
Holman Ridge	Ridge in N section of Hawkins County, W of Frog Level.
Holmes Creek	Creek in N central section of DeKalb County, flows into Center Hill Lake.
Holmes Gap	Located near E SE border of Wilson County. 14 mi E SE of Lebanon.
Holmes Hollow	Located in W section of Houston County, N NW of Magnolia.
Holston	Community in middle S SW section of Sullivan County. 5 mi SW of Blountville.
Holston Hills	Community within city limits of Knoxville in E section of the City, 5 mi E NE of downtown. In Knox County.
Holston Mountain	Mountain in NE area of Carter County near Sullivan County line.
Holston Mountain	Mountain on NW border of Johnson County.

Holston Mountain	Mountain on NE border of Sullivan County, near Johnson County line.
Holston River	Flows from the State of Virginia, southward into Sullivan County forming South Holston Lake, west into Hawkins County, southwest into Grainger, Hamblen and Jefferson Counties forming Cherokee Lake, flows southwest into Knox County where it joins the French Broad River forming the Tennessee River.
Holston Valley	Community in N NE section of Sullivan County. 14 1/2 mi E NE of Blountville.
Holt	Community in S SW section of Wayne County. 19 mi S SW of Waynesboro.
Holt Knob	Located in N NE section of Williamson County. 3 mi SE of Brentwood.
Holtland (Holts Corner)	Community on N NE border of Marshall County. 12 1/2 mi N NE of Oslin. 19 mi N NE of Lewisburg.
Holton	Community in NE Section of Campbell County near Jellico.
Holts Corner (Holtland P.O.)	Community on N NE border of Marshall County. 19 mi N NE of Lewisburg. 12 1/2 mi N NE of Oslin.
Holtsville	Community in N central section of Hardin County, SW of Hookers Bend N of Savannah.
Holttown	Community in NW area of Cocke County. 8 mi N of Newport.
Holy Hill	Community in central section of Johnson County, NW of Mountain City.
Homer Hollow	Located in NE section of Benton County.
Homestead	Community in S central section of Cumberland County. E of Cumberland Mountain State Park. 4 mi SE of Crossville.
Honeycutt	Community in central section of Hawkins County. 7 mi E of Rogersville.
Hood Lakes	Lakes in S central section of Lawrence County. S of Lawrenceburg.
Hoodoo	Community in NW area of Coffee County. 12 mi NW of Manchester.
Hookers Bend	Community in N central section of Hardin County. 7 mi N of Savannah.
Hooper Mountain	Mountain in W central section of Polk County.

Hoopers Lake	Located in SW area of Carroll County, between Howley and Hickory Flat.
Hoovers Gap	Community in S SE section of Rutherford County. 14 mi S SE of Murfreesboro.
Hopewell	Community in N Central section of Bradley County. 4 mi N of Cleveland.
Hopewell	Community in SW section of Carroll County. 13 mi SW of Huntingdon.
Hopewell	Community in NE area of Claiborne County. 10 mi NE of Tazewell.
Hopewell	Community in E area of Davidson County. 10 mi E NE of Courthouse.
Hopewell	Community in NW area of Gibson County. 10 1/2 mi NW of Trenton.
Hopewell	Community in middle W section of Tipton County. 12 mi W SW of Covington.
Hopewell Springs	Community in central N NW section of Monroe County. 5 1/2 mi E of Madisonville.
Hopson	Community in SW area of Carter County. 9 mi SE of Elizabethton.
Hornbeak	City in middle W SW section of Obion County. 14 1/2 mi W SW of Union City. Incorporated in 1923.
Horner	Community in SW section of Perry County. 7 mi S SW of Linden.
Hornertown	Community on S SW border of Hickman County. 11 mi S SW of Centerville.
Hornet	Community on W SW border of Sevier County. Approx. 11 mi SW of Sevierville.
Hornet Tree Top	Mountain in E SE section of Blount County, S of Tremont.
Horn Hollow	Located in W NW section of Cumberland County, S of Mayland.
Horn Lake	Lake in SW corner of Shelby County. S of Robco Lake.
Hornsby	City in E central section of Hardeman County. 8 1/2 mi E SE of Bolivar. Incorporated in 1920.
Hornsby Hollow	Located in W NW section of Meigs County, S SW of Maple Grove.
Horn Springs	Community in middle N NW section of Wilson

Horn Springs, (Cont.)	County. 4 1/2 mi W NW of Lebanon.
Horse Creek	Community in E area of Greene County. 9 mi E of Greensville.
Horse Creek	Community in S SW corner of of Sullivan County. 18 mi W SW of Blountville.
Horsehead Knob	Located in N section of Jackson County. 2 mi N NE of Whitleyville.
Horse Island	Island in NE section of Lake County in Reelfoot Wildlife Area.
Horse Mountain	Mountain in middle N section of Bedford County. 2 mi E of Shelbyville.
Horseshoe	Community in E central area of Carter County. 5 mi E of Elizabethton.
Horseshoe Bend	Located in S SW section of Cheatham County. 3 mi N NW of Shacklett.
Horseshoe Bend	Area in bend of Cumberland River, N central section of Smith County. 2 mi N NE of Carthage.
Horseshoe Lake	Lake in NE section of Dyer County, S of Poplar Ridge.
Horseshoe Mountain	Mountain in S SE section of Sevier County, near border. 9 mi E SE of Gatlinburg.
Horseshoe Ridge	Ridge in SE section of Blount County. 3 mi SE of Cades Cove.
Horsleys	Community in SW section of Macon County. 6 mi SW of Lafayette.
Hortense	Community in W central section of Dickson County. 5 1/2 mi W SW of Charlotte.
House Mountain	Mountain in N section of Knox County. 11 mi N NE of Knoxville.
Housley	Community in NE area of Carter County. 3 mi SW of Buladeen.
Houston	Community in W section Wayne County. 10 mi W SW of Waynesboro.
Houston County 	County Seat: Erin. Zip Code 37061. Located in North West section of the State. Bounded by Stewart, Montgomery, Dickson, Humphreys and Benton Counties. Named in honor of Sam Houston.
Houston Valley	Located in E section of Cocke County and S section of Greene County, N of Wolf Creek.

Houston Valley	Community in S area of Greene County. 15 mi S SE of Greeneville near Cocke County line.
Howard	Community in N NE section of Monroe County on Tellico Lake. 12 mi E NE of Madisonville.
Howard	Community in W section of Perry County. Approx. 10 mi W of Linden.
Howard Chapel	Community in middle N section of Overton County. 3 1/2 mi N NE of Livingston.
Howard H. Baker, Sr. Lake	Lake in middle N section of Scott County. 7 mi N NW of Huntsville.
Howard Quarter	Community in E central section of Claiborne County. 9 mi E of Tazewell.
Howards Landing	Island on Mississippi River, W NW section of Shelby County.
Howard Springs	Community in W central section of Cumberland County. 3 mi W of Crossville.
Howardville	Community in SE section of Hamilton County near Bradley County line. Due E of Apison on Southern Railway.
Howell	Community in NW central section of Lincoln County. 5 1/2 mi N NW of Fayetteville.
Howell Hill	Community in S SE section of Lincoln County. 7 mi S SE of Fayetteville.
Howley	Community in SW area of Carroll County. 11 mi SW of Huntingdon.
Hubbard	Community in NE Section of Blount County. 5 mi E of Maryville.
Hubbard Cove	Located in NW corner of Grundy County. 8 mi W NW of Altamont.
Hubertville	Community in central NE section of Robertson County. 5 1/2 mi NE of Springfield.
Huckleberry	Community in W central section of Hamilton County. 2 mi W of Soddy Daisy. 16 mi N NE of downtown Chattanooga.
Huckleberry Creek Dam	Located in N area of Arnold Engineering Development Center in Coffee County.
Huckleberry Lake	Lake in SW section of Dickson County. 2 mi S SE of Tennessee City.
Huckleberry Ridge	Ridge in central section of Monroe County, W of Rafter.
Hudson	Community in N central section of Lawrence

Hudson, (Cont.)	County. 7 1/2 mi NW of Lawrenceburg.
Huffine Island	Island on Tennessee River, 7 mi S SE of Kingston in Roane County.
Huffman	Community in N section of Morgan County. 12 1/2 mi N NW of Lynchburg.
Huffman Hollow	Located in W NW section of Coffee County, SE of Noah.
Hughell Crossing	Community in N central section of Cumberland County.
Hughes Bay	Lake in W NW section of Stewart County, inlet off the Tennessee River. S of Byrd Bay.
Hughes Loop	Community in E central section of Gibson County.
Hughes Ridge	Ridge in NW section of Hamilton County. N of Flat Top.
Hughey	Community in W NW section of Lincoln County. 7 1/2 mi W NW of Fayetteville.
Hull Mill	Community in NW central section of Greene County near Mosheim.
Humbolt	City in S area of Gibson County. 11 mi S SE of Trenton. Incorporated in 1865.
Humbolt Lake	Lake in NE area of Crockett County. 8 mi E NE of Alamo on Gibson County line.
Humphreys County HUMPHREYS COUNTY	County Seat: Waverly. Zip Code 37185. Located in middle West section of the State. Bounded by Houston, Dickson, Hickman, Perry and Benton Counties. Named in honor of Parry W. Humphreys.
Hunt Creek Dam	Located in N area of Arnold Engineering Development Center in Coffee County.
Hunter	Community in Central area of Campbell County near Jacksboro.
Hunter	Community in N central section of Carter County E NE of Elizabethton.
Hunter Cove	Located in S SE section of Putnam County. 7 mi SE of Cookeville. N of Burnett Mountain.
Hunter Hills	Community in E area of Hamilton County near Snow Hill.
Hunter Lake	Lake in NE section of Maury County. 7 mi N NE of Columbia.
Hunters Point	Community in N section of Wilson County. 6 mi

Hunters Point, (Cont.)	N of Lebanon.
Hunters Point Bend	Area in bend of the Cumberland River, in the SW corner of Trousdale County.
Huntersville	Community in W section of Madison County. 9 1/2 mi W of Jackson.
Huntingdon	County Seat of Carroll County. Located near center of county. Incorporated in 1911.
Hunting Hills West	Community in Knox County. 7 1/2 mi W of Knoxville.
Huntington Forest	Community in central section of Hamilton County. Apporx. 10 mi N NE of downtown Chattanooga. Approx. 3 1/2 mi N NE of Hixson.
Huntland	City in SW area of Franklin County. 13 mi SW of Winchester. Incorporated in 1907.
Huntsville	County Seat of Scott County. Located in near center of County. Incorporated in 1965.
Hurdlow	Community in S section of Moore County. N of Liberty Hill.
Hurley	Community on W SW border of Hardin County. 9 mi SW of Savannah near Shiloh National Military Park.
Huron	Community in SW section of Henderson County. 9 mi W SW of Lexington.
Hurricane	Community in W NW area of Coffee County.
Hurricane	Community in middle N section of Jackson County. 4 mi N or Gainesboro.
Hurricane	Community in S SW section of Wilson County. 2 1/2 mi S SE of Major.
Hurricane Creek	Creek in NW section of Franklin County, flows into Elk River.
Hurricane Creek	Community within the city limits of Chattanooga, in the E Brainerd area. In Hamilton County.
Hurricane Creek	Creek in NW corner of Houston County, flows into the Tennessee River.
Hurricane Creek	Creek in SW section of Putnam County off Center Hill Lake, SW of Silver Point.
Hurricane Hollow	Located in NW section of Humphreys County, S of Rushing Hollow. 10 mi W NW of Waverly.
Hurricane Hollow	Located in S central section of Stewart

Hurricane Hollow, (Cont.)	County, S SW of Dover. S of Lindsey Hollow.
Hurricane Mills	Community in S central section of Humphreys County. 8 mi S SE of Waverly.
Hurricane Ridge	Ridge in central section of Giles County. N of Pulaski.
Hurricane Ridge	Ridge in E section of Hancock County, SW of Livesay Mill.
Hurricane Ridge	Ridge in S section of Roane County.
Huskeys Grove	Community in Sevier County, halfway between Pigeon Forge and Gatlinburg.
Hustburg	Community in W section of Humphreys County. 11 1/2 mi SW of Waverly.
Hutchins College	Community in W NW section of White County. 9 mi W NW of Sparta.
Hydro	Community in NW area of Decatur County. 14 mi N NW of Decaturville.
Hygeia Springs	Community in SE section of Robertson County. 7 1/2 mi SW of Springfield.
Hyndsver	Community in middle N section of Weakley County. 6 mi N NW of Dresden.
Iconium	Community in Central section of Cannon County. 4 mi SE of Woodbury.
Icy Cove	Located in SE section of Putnam County. 6 mi S SW of Monterey.
Idaho	Community in SE section of Lawrence County. Approx. 10 mi S SE of Lawrenceburg.
Idaville	Community in S section of Tipton County. 10 mi S SW of Covington. E of Atoka.
Ideal Valley	Community in middle W NW section of Rhea County. W of Spring City.
Idlewild	Community in NE area of Gibson County. 8 mi E NE of Trenton.
Idlewild	Community in central W section of Maury County. 2 mi NW of Columbia, W of Fairview Heights.
Idlewild	Community in W NW section of McMinn County. 7 mi W NW of Athens.
Idlewood Acres	Community in Knox County. 6 1/2 mi NW of downtown Knoxville.

Idol	Community in N NE central section of Grainger County. 9 mi NE of Rutledge.
Igou Gap	Located in SE section of Hamilton County.
Ilford	Community in Central section of Campbell County near LaFollette.
Inadu Knob	Mountain in SW corner of Cocke County on North Carolina line in the Great Smoky Mountains. Elev. 5941 ft.
Independance	Community in NE corner of Hancock County. 16 mi E of Sneedville. 6 mi E SE of Kyles Ford.
Independence	Community in N section of Overton County. 8 mi N of Livingston.
India	Community in central section of Henry County. 4 mi NE of Paris.
Indian Boundary Lake	Lake in middle E section of Monroe County in Cherokee National Forest.
Indian Cave	Community in SW area of Grainger County. 9 1/2 mi S SW of Rutledge.
Indian Cove	Located in N NW section of Marion County, NE of Foster Falls. Approx. 8 mi N of Jasper.
Indian Creek	Community in S Central section of Campbell County. 5 mi S of LaFollette.
Indian Creek	Creek in N central area of DeKalb County, flows into the Caney Fork River.
Indian Creek	Creek on W SW border of Humphreys County. 12 mi W SW of Waverly.
Indian Mound	Community in E area of DeKalb County. 8 mi E SE of Smithville.
Indian Mound	Community in E section of Stewart County. 8 mi E of Dover.
Indian Mountain	Mountain in W SW section of Rutherford County. 2 1/2 mi S of Almaville. S of Scales Mountain.
Indian Mountain State Park	Located in N Central section of Campbell County on Kentucky Line W of Jellico.
Indian Ridge	Community in SW area of Grainger County. 9 1/2 mi SW of Rutledge.
Indian Ridge	Ridge in N NE section of Hancock County near Fox Branch.
Indian Ridge	Ridge in middle NE section of Washington County. 3 mi W NW of Johnson City.

Indian Rock Lake	Lake in SW area of Cumberland County. E of Newton. 12 mi S SW of Crossville.
Indian Springs	Community in middle W section of Sullivan County. 6 mi W of Blountville.
Inglewood	Community in central area of Davidson County. 5 mi N NE of Courthouse.
Ingram Lake	Lake in middle N section of Maury County. 6 mi N NE of Columbia, W of Neapolis.
Inman Ridge	Ridge in NW section of Decatur County, W of Yellow Springs.
Inskip	Community within the city limits of Knoxville. 4 mi N NW of downtown. In Knox County.
Interstate West	Community in SW section of Cheatham County.
Irish Cut	Community in N NW section of Cocke County. 1 mi E of Newport.
Iron City	City in SW corner of Lawrence County. 21 1/2 mi SW of Lawrenceburg. 4 1/2 mi W SW of St. Joseph. Incorporated in 1962.
Iron Hill	Community in S SE area of Dickson County. 13 mi S of Charlotte.
Iron Hill Island	Island on Watts Bar Lake in NE section of Rhea County.
Iron Mountain	Community in NE area of Carter County near Johnson County line.
Iron Mountain	Mountain on W SW border of Carter County on North Carolina line and into NE section of Unicoi County.
Iron Mountain	Mountain in N section of Johnson County, N of Cold Spring.
Iron Mountain	Mountain in W SW section of Polk County, E of Willis Springs.
Iron Mountains	Mountain on W and NW border of Johnson County, N of Mountain City.
Ironsburg	Community on S SW border of Monroe County. 9 mi S SW of Tellico Plains.
Irons Creek	Creek in E section of Clay County, off Dale Hollow Lake.
Irving College	Community in S SE section of Warren County. 7 1/2 mi S SE of McMinnville.
Irwin	Community in middle N NE section of Union County, 6 mi N NW of Maynardville.

Isabella	Community in SE section of Polk County. 19 mi E SE of Benton.
Isaiah Hollow	Located in W section of Montgomery County.
Isbell	Community in middle SW section of Maury County. 8 1/2 mi SW of Columbia.
Isham	Community on N border of Scott County. Approx. 8 mi N NE of Oneida.
Ish Creek	Creek in W NW section of Blount County, flows into the Tennessee River. S of Mt. Vernon.
Island Home	Community within the city limits of Knoxville. 2 mi E of downtown. In Knox County.
Isoline	Community in NW central section of Cumberland County. 10 mi N NW of Crossville.
Isom	Community on W border of Maury County. 15 mi W of Columbia.
Ivory	Community in NE area of Anderson County. 2 mi E of Andersonville.
Ivy	Community on SW border of Monroe County. W of Epperson.
Ivy Bluff	Community in S area of Cannon County. 11 mi S of Woodbury.
Ivy Branch Hollow	Located in W section of Davidson County.
Ivydell	Community near center of Campbell County, 1 mi NW of LaFollette.
Ivy Hill	Located in middle NW section of Humphreys County. 4 mi E of Trinity.
Ivy Point	Community in NE section of Davidson County. 4 mi NW of Goodlettsville.
Ivyton	Community on E section of Overton County. 9 mi E of Livingston.
Jabez Knob	Mountain in N central section of Hancock County. 2 mi N of Sneedville.
Jackass Hollow	Located in W section of Montgomery County.
Jack Hollow	Located in NE section of Humphreys County. 5 mi N of McEwen.
Jacksboro	County Seat of Campbell County. Located in SW section of County. Incorporated in 1968.
Jacksboro	Community in W SW section of Warren County. 9 1/2 mi W of McMinnville.

Jacks Creek	Community in middle NE section of Chester County. Approx. 7 mi E NE of Henderson.
Jackson	County Seat of Madison County. Located in near center of County. Incorporated in 1845.
Jackson Bend	Community in NW Section of Blount County on Loudon Lake.
Jackson Chapel	Community in NE section of Dickson County. 8 mi NE of Charlotte.
Jackson County JACKSON COUNTY	County Seat: Gainesboro. Zip Code 38562. Located in North central section of the State. Bounded by Clay, Overton, Putnam, Smith and Macon Counties. Named in honor of Andrew Jackson.
Jackson Heights	Community in central section of Maury County. 3 mi N NE of Columbia, E of Hardy Acres.
Jackson Lake	Lake in E area of Franklin County. 13 mi E of Winchester, E of Sewanee.
Jackson Lake	Located in middle N section of Williamson County. 3 mi N NE of Franklin.
Jackson Ridge	Community in SW section of Rutherford County. 11 1/2 mi SW of Murfreesboro.
Jackson Square	Community located within Oak Ridge, Anderson County.
Jacksonville	Community in middle SW section of Obion County. Approx. 7 mi W NW of Obion.
Jake Hollow	Located in E section of Putnam County. 10 mi E SE of Cookeville. S of Sand Springs.
Jakes Mountain	Mountain in N section of Sequatchie County.
Jalapa	Community in SW section of Monroe County. 12 1/2 mi S of Madisonville. 5 mi W of Tellico Plains.
Jameson	Community in N section of Maury County. 10 mi N of Columbia.
James Point	Located in SW section of Hamilton County.
Jamestown	County Seat of Fentress County. Located in N central section of county. Incorporated in 1835.
Jamestown	Community on E NE border of Lawrence County. Approx. 12 mi N NE of Lawrenceburg.
Jamestown	Community in W NW section of Tipton County. 12 mi W of Covington.

Jamison Hollow	Located in NE section of Humphreys County. 5 1/2 mi N of Mc Ewen.
Jane Hollow	Located in E NE section of Benton County.
Jarman Hollow	Located in SW section of Montgomery County. 1 1/2 mi SE of Tarsus.
Jarrell	Community in NW section of Carroll County. 9 mi NW of Huntingdon.
Jarrett Knob	Located in middle S SW section of Rutherford County. 2 mi N of Rockvale.
Jasper	County seat of Marion County. Located in middle S section of the County. Incorporated in 1959.
Jaybird	Community W central section of Cocke County.
Jaybird	Community in N central section of Hamblen County. 4 mi NE of Morristown.
Jay Ell	Community in middle N section of Sevier County between Middle Creek and Murphys Chapel.
Jeannette	Community in N central section of Decatur County. 1 mi N of Decaturville.
Jearoldstown	Community in N NE section of Greene County. 16 mi N NE of Greeneville.
Jefferson	Community in SE section of DeKalb County. 7 1/2 mi SE of Smithville.
Jefferson City	City in N NW section of Jefferson County. 8 mi N NW of Dandridge. Incorporated in 1901.
Jefferson County JEFFERSON COUNTY	County Seat: Dandridge. Zip Code 37725. Located in Northeast section of the State. Bounded by Grainger, Hamblen, Cocke, Sevier and Knox Counties. Names on honor of Thomas Jefferson.
Jefferson Springs	Community in N NW section of Rutherford County. NW of Hickory Grove.
Jellico	City in N Central section of Campbell County on Kentucky Line. Incorporated in 1903.
Jellico Mountain	Mountain in NW section of Campbell County.
Jena	Community in SE section of Loudon County. 12 mi E SE of Loudon.
Jenkins Hill	Located in E section of Williamson County. 11 1/2 mi E of Franklin, S of Morton Knob.
Jenkins Mill	Community in SW section of Cocke County.

Jenkins Mountain	Mountain in SW central section of Carter County. 5 mi S of Elizabethton.
Jenkins Village	Community in SW corner of Clay County, N of Bakertown.
Jenkinsville	Community in central section of Dyer County. 2 mi W NW of Dyersburg.
Jennings Knob	Located in central SE section of Wilson County. 5 mi SE of Lebanon.
Jennings Pond	Pond in NW section of Lauderdale County, E of Lake Chisholm.
Jeremiah	Community on N border of Putnam County. Approx. 7 mi NE of Cookeville.
Jernigan Town	Community in E section of Robertson County. Approx. 11 mi E of Springfield.
Jersey	Community within the city limits of Chattanooga. 7 mi E of downtown near Lake Hills in Hamilton County.
Jessie	Community in middle NE section of Warren County. 5 1/2 mi N NE of McMinnville.
Jewell	Community in E NE section of Weakley County. 6 1/2 mi E NE of Dresden.
Jewell Cave	Community in W area of Dickson County. 10 mi W of Charlotte.
Jewett	Community in S area of Cumberland County. 13 mi S SE of Crossville.
Jimtown	Community in W NW section of Cocke County. 2 mi E of Newport.
Jockey	Community in E NE section of Greene County. 12 1/2 mi NE of Greeneville.
Joel Hollow	Located in central W NW section of Sumner County. 1 1/2 mi me E NE of Cottonwood.
Joelton	Community in NW area of Davidson County. 11 mi N NW of Courthouse. 3 mi S of Forest Grove.
John Allen Hollow	Located in S section of Bedford County.
John Mountain	Mountain in S section of Cocke County, SW of Raven Branch.
John Sevier Station	Community in middle E section of Knox County. 6 mi E NE of Knoxville.
John Sevier Steamplant (U.S.-TVA)	Located on Holston River on S central section of Hawkins County.

Johnson City	City in NE section of Washington County. 6 mi NE of Jonesborough. Incorporated in 1869.
Johnson County JOHNSON COUNTY	County Seat: Mountain City. Zip Code 37683. Located in Northeast section of the State. Bounded by Carter and Sullivan Counties and the State of Virginia to the North and the State of North Carolina to the East. Named in honor of Thomas Johnson.
Johnson Hollow	Located in mmiddle N section of Davidson County, E of Germantown.
Johnson Hollow	Located in central S SE section of Humphreys County. 2 1/2 mi W of New Hope.
Johnson Hollow	Located in SW section of Stewart County, E of Lane Hollow.
Johnson Hollow	Located in S SW section of Williamson County, just N of Burwood.
Johnson Hollow	Located in SE section of Wilson County. 2 1/2 mi E NE of Greenvale.
Johnson Island	Island on the French Broad River in SE section of Knox County. N of Kimberlin Heights.
Johnson Lake	Lake in W section of Lauderdale County, SW of Ashport. Approx. 16 mi W of Ripley.
Johnsons Chapel	Community in E central section of DeKalb County.
Johnsons Crossroads	Community in W section of Sumner County. 11 mi W NW of Gallatin.
Johnsons Grove	Community in S SW section of Crockett County. 4 1/2 mi W SW of Alamo.
Johnsons Mill	Community on E SE border of Hickman County, S SE of Primm Springs.
Johnson Store	Community in NE corner of Hawkins County. NE of Valley View.
Johnsonville Steam Plant (U.S.-TVA)	Located on W border of Humphreys County. 9 1/2 mi W SW of Waverly.
Johnstown	Community in SW area of Coffee County.
Johnstown	Community in NW area of Franklin County.
Johntown	Community in E section of Trousdale County. 5 1/2 mi E SE of Hartsville, near county line.
Jones	Community in NE corner of Haywood County. 8 1/2 mi NE of Brownsville.
Jones Bend	Area in E section of Maury County, in a bend

Jones Bend, (Cont.)	of the Duck River.
Jones Bend Lake	Lake in W central section of Henry County. 3 mi W NW of Paris.
Jonesborough	County Seat of Washington County. Located near center of County. Incorporated in 1815. Oldest Town in the State.
Jones Chapel	Community in NW section of Pickett County. 3 1/2 mi NW of Byrdstown.
Jones Cove	Community in E section of Sevier County. 14 mi E SE of Sevierville.
Jones Hollow	Located in SE section of Houston County, S SW of Yellow Creek.
Jones Hollow	Located in E central section of Humphreys County. 2 1/2 mi W NW of New Hope.
Jones Mill	Community in NW corner of Henry County. 12 1/2 mi NW of Paris.
Jones Station	Community within the city limits of Chattanooga. 4 1/2 mi N NW of downtown at the foot of Signal Mountain. In Hamilton County.
Jonestown	Community in S area of Giles County.
Jones Valley	Community in E SE section of Hickman County. 12 mi E of Centerville.
Jonesville	Community in S area of Fentress County. 17 mi S of Jamestown.
Jonesville	Community in NE section of Roane County. Approx. 10 mi NE of Kingston.
Joppa	Community in W central section of Grainger County. 6 1/2 mi SW of Rutledge.
Joppa	Community in SW corner of White County. 12 mi SW of Sparta.
Jordonia	Community in central area of Davidson County, W of Nashville.
Joyce Kilmer-Slickrock Wilderness	Located in E NE section of Monroe County, E of Cowcamp Ridge.
J. Percy Priest Dam	Located in E area of Davidson County on Stone River E of Donelson.
J. Percy Priest Lake	Lake in E section of Davidson County on Stones River.
Jumbo	Community in SW area of Carroll County.
Jumpoff Falls	Located in W section of Marion County, W SW of

Jumpoff Falls, (Cont.)	Martin Springs.
Juno	Community in middle NW section of Henderson County. 8 mi W NW of Lexington.
Justice Hollow	Located in N NE section of Bedford County.
Justice Mountain	Mountain in E NE section of Morgan County, N of Bird Mountain.
Kagley	Community in SW area of Blount County. 2 1/2 mi SW of Christie Hill, 9 mi SW of Maryville.
Kansas	Community in middle E NE section of Jefferson County. 6 mi N NE of Dandridge.
Kansas	Community in middle E section of Sumner County. 6 mi NE of Gallatin.
Kappick Knob	Mountain in N central section of Jefferson County, S of Gravelly Hill.
Karns	Community in W section of Knox County. 10 1/2 mi W of Knoxville.
Kasserman	Community in Mid W area of Franklin County.
Kaufman Hollow	Located in middle N section of Davidson County, E of Whites Creek.
Kedron	Community in S area of Giles County. 10 mi S of Pulaski.
Kedron	Community in NE section of Maury County. 10 mi NE of Columbia.
Keebler Crossroads	Community in middle W NW section of Washington County. 7 mi W NW of Johnson City.
Keefe	Community in middle E section of Lake County. 3 1/2 mi SE of Tiptonville.
Keeling	Community in SW corner of Haywood County. 16 mi SW of Brownsville. 4 1/2 mi W SW of Stanton.
Keeling	Community in SE section of Tipton County. 13 mi SE of Covington.
Keenburg	Community in NW area of Carter County. 2 1/2 mi N of Elizabethton.
Keener Mountain	Mountain in NW section of Van Buren County, W of Spencer.
Keeton Pond	Pond near S border of Decatur County, S SE of Unity.
Keith Springs	Community in S central section of Franklin

Keith Springs, (Cont.)	County. 7 mi S of Winchester.
Kellertown	Community in E NE section of Bedford County. 10 mi E NE of Shelbyville.
Kelley Ridge	Ridge in N section of Marion County, S of Griffith Creek.
Kellum Gap	Community in central area of Giles County.
Kelly Knob	Mountain in W SW section of Cocke County, S of Wilton Springs.
Kelly Knob	Located in E SE section of McMinn County, N of Macedonia.
Kelly Town	Community in NE section of Roane County. S of Oliver Springs.
Kelso	Community in middle E SE section of Lincoln County. 6 mi E SE of Fayetteville.
Keltonburg	Community in SE area of DeKalb County. 6 1/2 mi S SE of Smithville.
Kempville	Community in NE section of Smith County. Approx. 8 mi N NE of Carthage.
Kennedy Hollow	Located in N central section of Humphreys County. 4 mi N NE of Waverly.
Kennedys Ridge	Ridge in NW section of McMinn County, W of Murray Store.
Kennerly Hollow	Located in middle NE section of Humphreys County. 2 mi N of Gorman.
Kenneytown	Community in N area of Greene County near Baileyton. 8 mi N NW of Greeneville.
Kennys Bend	Area in bend of Cumberland River, W NW section of Smith County. 7 mi W NW of Carthage.
Kenton	City in N area of Gibson County. 16 mi N NW of Trenton. Incorporated in 1899. Boundaries intend into Obion County.
Kentucky Lake	Kentucky Lake is formed in the S section of Kentucky where the Kentucky Dam backs up the Tennessee River.
Kenwood	Community in N section of Montgomery County. N of Clarksville.
Kepler	Community in middle S section of Hawkins County. 7 mi E of Rogersville.
Kerrville	Community in N section of Shelby County. 20 mi N NE of Memphis.

Ketchen	Community in NE section of Scott County. 15 mi NE of Huntsville.
Ketner Gap	Located in NE section of Marion County, E of Powells Crossroads.
Kettle Mills	Community in W NW section of Maury County. 13 mi W NW of Columbia.
Key	Community in N section of White County. 9 mi N of Sparta.
Key Corner	Community in N NE section of Lauderdale County. 13 mi N of Ripley.
Keyes Point	Community on W border of Lauderdale County. 21 1/2 mi W of Ripley, 3 mi W of Golddust.
Khotan	Community in W SW central section of Anderson County near Morgan County line. 2 mi N of Oliver Springs.
Kidwell	Community in NW area of Claiborne County.
Kiley Hollow	Located in E section of Humphreys County. 5 mi SE of McEwen.
Kill Buck Knob	Located in central W section of Sumner County. NE of Ocana.
Kilsyth	Community in Center of Campbell County. 5 mi NE of LaFollette.
Kimball	City in S SW section of Marion County. 4 mi W SW of Jasper. Incorporated in 1962.
Kimberlin Heights	Community in SE section of Knox County. 10 1/2 mi E SE of Knoxville.
Kimbro	Community in SE area of Davidson County. 13 mi SE of Courthouse.
Kimbrough Crossroad	Community in NE section of Jefferson County. 8 mi N NE of Dandridge.
Kimery	Community in SW section of Weakley County. 11 1/2 mi SW of Dresden near the county line.
Kimmons	Community on N NW border of Lewis County. 5 1/2 mi N of Hohenwald.
Kimsey	Community in E SE section of Polk County. 19 mi S SE of Benton.
Kincaid	Community in N section of Monroe County. Approx. 6 mi NE of Madisonville.
Kindaid Hollow	Located in S section of Bedford County.
Kinderhook	Community in N NW corner of Maury County. 15

Kinderhook, (Cont.)	mi NW of Columbia.
King Arthur Court	Community in Knox County. 10 1/2 mi W NW of downtown Knoxville.
Kingfield	Community in middle W section of Williamson County. 9 mi W of Franklin.
King Mountain	Mountain on E NE border of Overton County and W NW border of Fentress County, near Pickett County Line.
Kingsley Station	Community in S section of Knox County, S SW of Vestal. 2 1/2 mi S of downtown Knoxville.
Kingspoint	Community on Lake Chickamauga in Hamilton County. 8 mi E NE of downtown Chattanooga.
Kingsport	City in NW section of Sullivan County. 12 mi W of Blountville. Incorporated in 1822. Boundaries extend into Hawkins County.
Kingston	County Seat of Roane County. Located in N section of county. Incorporated in 1920.
Kingston Springs	City in SW area of Cheatham County. 12 mi S of Ashland City. Incorporation in 1965.
Kingston Steam Plant (U.S. - TVA)	Located in middle N section of Roane County. N of Kingston.
Kinneys	Community in W center section of Robertson County. 3 1/2 mi W of Springfield.
Kinzel Springs	Community in E Central section of Blount County. 10 mi SE of Maryville.
Kirby	Community in middle E SE section of Macon County. 7 mi E SE of Lafayette.
Kirk	Community in W SW section of Fayette County. 18 mi SW of Somerville.
Kirk Hill	Located in central W NW section of Sumner County. 1 1/2 mi E of Cottonwood.
Kirkland	Community in middle S SW section of Lincoln County. 7 mi S SW of Fayetteville.
Kirkland	Community in E SE section of Williamson County. 14 mi E SE of Franklin.
Kirkstall	Community in S Central area of Anderson County. 5 mi SW of Clinton.
Kirkwood	Community in NE section of Montgomery County. 9 mi E NE of Clarksville.
Kiser	Community in W section of Blount County near Marble Hill. 11 mi W of Maryville.

Kitchens
Community in S section of Lewis County. NE of Buffalo Valley.

Kitchens Creek
Creek in W area of Franklin County, flows into Elk River NE of Harmony.

Kite
Community in S section of Hawkins County. 5 mi S SE of Rogersville. 1 1/2 mi W of Needmore.

Kittrell
Community in E section of Rutherford County. 9 mi E SE of Murfreesboro.

Kitty Ray Mountain
Mountain in S section of Overton County. 12 mi S SE of Livingston.

Kleburne
Community in N NE section of Maury County. 9 mi N NE of Columbia, 2 mi N of Carters Creek.

Kline Hollow
Located in middle SE section of Humphreys County. 2 mi S of New Hope.

Klondike
Community in NW section of Hawkins County. 7 mi W NW of Rogersville.

Knapp
Community in N Central section of Anderson County. 3 mi S of Lake City.

Knight Hollow
Located in S SE section of Houston County, E of Silvertop.

Knight Hollow
Located in S central section of Humphreys County. 4 mi S of Waverly.

Knight Hollow
Located in SW section of Macon Hollow. 1 1/2 mi NW of Horsleys.

Knob Creek
Community in N section of Lauderdale County. 9 mi N of Ripley.

Knob Creek
Community in W SW section of Lawrence County. Approx. 3 mi SW of Spring Creek.

Knob Creek
Community in W section of Sevier County. 10 mi W SW of Sevierville.

Knob Creek
Community in NE section of Washington County. Approx. 5 mi NE of Jonesborough. W of Johnson City.

Knox County
County Seat: Knoxville. Zip Code 37902. Located in middle East section of the State. Bounded by Union, Grainger, Jefferson, Sevier, Blount, Loudon and Anderson Counties. Named in honor of Major General Henry Knox.

KNOX COUNTY

Knoxville
County Seat of Knox County. Located in S central section of County. Incorporated in 1815.

Kodak
Community in N NW section of Sevier County. 8

Kodak, (Cont.)	mi N NW of Sevierville.
Ko Ko	Community in S central section of Haywood County. 8 mi S of Brownsville. 7 1/2 mi E of Stanton.
Kyles Ford	Community in NE section of Hancock County. 10 mi E NE of Sneedville.
Kyle Valley	Located in N section of Hawkins County near Hancock County line, N of Frog Level.
Laager - Gruetli	Community in Central section of Grundy County. 5 mi SE of Altamont.
Lacassas	Community in middle NE section of Rutherford County. 8 mi NE of Murfreesboro.
Laconia	Community in E NE area of Fayette County. 6 1/2 mi E NE of Somerville.
Lacy	Community in SE section of Hardeman County. 12 1/2 mi SE of Bolivar. 13 mi E NE of of Saulsbury.
Ladds	Community in S SE section of Marion County. 6 1/2 mi SE of Jasper.
Lafayette	County Seat of Macon County. Located near center of the County. Incorporated in 1843.
Lafayette	Community in NW section of Putnam County. 12 mi W of Cookeville.
LaFollette	Community in Central section of Campbell County. 6 mi NE of Jacksboro. Incorporated in 1897.
LaGrange	City in SE area of Fayette County. 14 mi SE of Somerville. Incorporated in 1831.
Laguardo	Community in NW section of Wilson County. 10 mi W NW of Lebanon.
Lake Barkley	Lake in N NW section of Stewart County, W of Tobaccoport.
Lake Catherine	Lake in E central section of Cumberland County. W of Fairfield Glade. 8 mi E NE of Crossville.
Lake Cheston	Lake in E section of Franklin County. W of Sewanee.
Lake Chippewa	Lake in SW section of Davidson County. 12 mi W SW of downtown Nashville.
Lake City	City in N Central section of Anderson County. 3 mi from Campbell County line. Incorporated in 1939.

Lake County — County Seat: Tiptonville. Zip Code 38079. Located in the Northwest corner of the State. Bounded by Obion and Dyer Counties and he State of Kentucky to the North and the Mississippi River to the West. Named in honor of Reelfoot Lake.

Lake Drive — Community in middle E section of Lake County on Reelfoot Lake E SE of Tiptonville.

Lake Enoree — Lake in SW section of Davidson County, SW of Gower.

Lake Forest — Community within the city limits of Knoxville. 3 1/2 mi SE of downtown. In Knox County.

Lake Graham — Lake in middle E NE section of Madison County. 5 mi NE of Jackson.

Lake Harbor Estates — Community on Lake Chickamauga in Hamilton County. Approx. 11 mi NE of downtown Chattanooga. N of Booker T. Washington State Park.

Lake Hardeman — Lake in S center section of Hardeman County. 9 mi S SE of Bolivar. 9 mi SW of Hornsby.

Lake Hills — Community within the city limits of Chattanooga. 7 1/2 mi E NE of downtown in Highway 58 area of Hamilton County.

Lake Holiday — Lake in W central section of Cumberland County. 2 1/2 mi W of Crossville.

Lake in the Sky — Lake in near center of Blount County in Great Smoky Mountains near border.

Lake Isom — Lake in E section of Lake County in Lake Isom National Wildlife Refuge.

Lake Isom National Wildlife Refuge — Located on E SE border of Lake County, NE of Ridgely.

Lake Junior — Lake in S section of Hamilton County near Chickamauga Dam.

Lake Karen — Lake in middle E section of Warren County. 4 mi NE of McMinnville.

Lake Kyle — Lake in NE section of Stewart County on Fort Campbell Military Reservation.

Lake Ladd — Lake in SE corner of Overton County. 18 mi S SE of Livingston.

Lake LaJoie — Lake in NE section of Hardeman County in Chickasaw State Park. 4 1/2 mi W NW of Silerton.

Lakeland — City in middle section of Shelby County. 19 mi

Lakeland, (Cont.)	E NE of Memphis. Incorporated in 1977.
Lakeland Lake	Lake in E section of Shelby County. Within the city limits of Lakeland.
Lake Lindsey (Formerly David Crockett Lake)	Lake in David Crockett State Park, NW of Lawrenceburg. In Lawrence County. Named in honor of Edward M. Lindsey. Former mayor of Lawrenceburg and President of the International Association of Lions Clubs in 1966-67.
Lake Logan	Lake in SE section of Giles County. S of Baugh.
Lake Louise	Lake in NW section of Davidson County, W of Greenville.
Lake McKellar	Lake in SE section of Shelby County, off the Mississippi River.
Lakemont	Community in N Central area of Blount County. 5 mi N of Alcoa.
Lakemoore	Community in central section of Hamblen County N of Morristown.
Lakemoor Hills	Community in Knox County. 4 mi W SW of downtown Knoxville.
Lake O'Donnell	Lake in E section of Franklin County, E of Sewanee.
Lake Ocoee	Lake in central SW section of Polk County, S of Benton.
Lake Ogallala	Lake in NW area of Davidson County. 12 mi W SW of downtown Nashville.
Lake Placid	Lake in W area of Chester County in Chickasaw State Park.
Lake Rooney	Lake in middle N section of Fayette County, S of Moorman.
Lake Shosnana	Lake in middle E section of White County. 6 1/2 mi E of Sparta. S of Bon De Croft.
Lakeside	Community in N NW section of Monroe County. 8 mi N NE of Madisonville.
Lakesite	City in central section of Hamilton County. 15 mi NE of downtown Chattanooga on the Tennessee River. Incorporated in 1972.
Lake St. George	Lake in E central section of Cumberland County. 7 mi E NE of Crossville.
Lake Taal	Lake in NW section of Montgomery County. 2 1/2 mi N NE of Woodlawn.

Lake Tansi	Lake in SW section of Cumberland County. 6 mi S of Crossville.
Lake Tansi Village	Community in SW section of Cumberland County. 5 mi S of Crossville.
Lake Tio Khata	Lake in middle W section of Fayette County, S SE of Oakland.
Lake Tullahoma	Lake in SW area of Coffee County. N of Tullahoma.
Lake Tullahoma Estates	Community in SW section of Coffee County. N of Tullahoma.
Lakeview	Community in S SE section of Franklin County. 11 1/2 mi S SE of Winchester.
Lakeview	Community in central section of Gibson County. 4 mi NE of Trenton.
Lakeview	Community in central section of Hamblen County SW of Morristown.
Lakeview	Community in central NE section of Robertson County. 5 mi NW of Springfield.
Lakeview Lake	Lake in S section of Franklin County near Lakeview.
Lakeview Lake	Lake in central section of Giles County. N of Pulaski.
Lakeview Manor	Community in SE section of Henry County. 12 mi E SE of Paris.
Lake Waldensia	Community in SE section of Cumberland County. 6 mi of Crab Orchard.
Lake Weona	Lake in W section of Williamson County. 17 mi W of Franklin.
Lake Williams	Lake in center SE section of Madison County. 2 1/2 mi SE of Jackson.
Lake Windermere	Lake in middle W section of Shelby County. N of Raleigh.
Lake Womack	Lake in near center of Coffee County. 1 mi N of Ragsdale.
Lakewood	Community in Central Section of Carroll County SW of Huntingdon.
Lakewood	City in upper E area of Davidson County. 10 mi NE of Courthouse. Incorporated in 1959.
Lakewood	Community in Knox County. 7 1/2 mi W SW of downtown Knoxville.

Lake Woodhaven	Lake in SE central section of Dickson County in Montgomery Bell State Park.
Lakewood Village	Community on E NE border of Rhea County. Between Piney River and Watts Bar Lake. 18 mi N NE of Dayton.
Lamar	Community in middle S section of Washington County. 5 mi S of Jonesborough.
Lamb Bottoms	Area in NW section of Bedford County.
Lambert	Community in NW central section of Fayette County. 9 mi W NW of Somerville.
Lambert Lake	Lake in S central section of Blount County. 7 mi S of Maryville.
Lamb Gulf	Located in SE section of Cocke County, S of Laurel Mountain.
Lamont	Community in N NE section of Robertson County. 10 1/2 mi NE of Springfield.
Lamontville	Community in SW corner of McMinn County. 14 mi W SW of Athens.
Lancaster	Community in SE section of Smith County. 10 mi S SE of Carthage.
Lancaster Hill	Community in S SE section of Smith County. 2 mi W of Lancaster.
Lancelot Acres	Community in central W section of Giles County. Approx. 2 mi SW of Pulaski.
Lanceville	Community in E central section of Cocke County. 2 mi E NE of Wolf Creek.
Lancing	Community in central section of Morgan County. 3 mi W NW of Wartburg.
Land Between the Lakes	Located in NW section of Stewart County. Between the Tennessee River and the Cumberland River.
Landmark	Community within the city of Knoxville, W section of town. N of Crestwood Hills in Knox County.
Landrom Mountain	Mountain in NE section of Morgan County.
Lane	Community in N area of Dyer County. 11 mi N of Dyersburg.
Lane Hollow	Located in SW section of Stewart County, W of Johnson Hollow.
Langford Cove	Community in W NW section of Wilson County. 16 mi W of Lebanon.

Lanier	Community in SW section of Blount County. 11 mi SW of Maryville.
Lankford Town	Community in SE section of Grundy County, near White City.
Lantana	Community in SW area of Cumberland County. 6 1/2 mi S SW of Crossville.
Lapata	Community in Dyer County. 7 mi E NE of Dyersburg.
Largent Hollow	Located in SW section of Stewart County, W of Asbury.
Largo	Community in E section of Decatur County.
Lassiter Corner	Community in W section of Obion County. 18 mi W SW of Union City.
Latham	Community in middle N section of Weakley County. 9 mi N of Dresden.
Lathen Hill	Hill in E section of Benton County. Approx. 10 mi NE of Camden.
Lauderback Ridge	Ridge in SE section of Hamilton County.
Lauderdale County LAUDERDALE COUNTY	County Seat: Ripley. Zip Code 38063. Located in Western border of the State. Bounded by Dyer, Crockett, Haywood and Tipton Counties and the Mississippi River to the West. Named in honor of Col. James Lauderdale.
Laura Lake	Lake on N NE border of Maury County. 11 mi N NE of Columbia.
Laurel	Community near center of Anderson County. 3 mi SW of Clinton.
Laurel	Community in middle E section of Sevier County. Approx. 11 mi E SE of Sevierville.
Laurel Bloomery	Community in N NE section of Johnson County. 7 mi N NE of Mountain City.
Laurel Bluff	Community in middle S section of Roane County. 5 mi S of Kingston.
Laurel Bottom	Located in N NW section of Fayette County.
Laurel Brook	Community in SW corner of Rhea County. 5 1/2 mi W of Dayton.
Laurelburg	Community in W NW section of Van Buren County. 6 1/2 mi W SW of Spencer.
Laurel Fork	Community in SE section of Carter County near North Carolina border. 5 mi E of Roan Mountain.

Laurel Grove	Community near center of Anderson County, 8 mi NE of Oliver Springs.
Laurel Hill	Community in N section of DeKalb County. 10 mi N of Smithville.
Laurel Hill	Community on N NW border of Lawrence County. Approx. 6 mi W NW of Henryville.
Laurel Hill Lake	Lake in W NW section of Lawrence County. N of Ovilla.
Laurel Hill Wildlife Management Area	Located in NW section of Lawrence County.
Laurel Lake	Lake in E Central section of Blount County. 2 mi W of Townsend.
Laurel Lake	Lake in NW corner of Marion County, S of Monteagle.
Laurel Mountain	Mountain in SE corner of Cocke County, SE of Sandy Gap in Cherokee National Forest.
Laurel Mountain	Mountain in SE section of Cocke County, W of Boomer.
Laurel Mountain	Mountain in middle W NW section of Monroe County, S of Big Creek.
Laurel Spur	Community in SE section of Carter County.
Laurel Top	Mountain on SE border of Sevier County. In the Great Smoky Mountains. Ele. 5,907.
Lavendar	Community in middle W NW section of Morgan County. 11 mi W NW of Wartburg.
LaVergne	City on W NW border of Rutherford County. 13 mi NW of Murfreesboro. Incorporated in 1972.
Lavinia	Community in SW section of Carroll County. 8 mi S of Atwood.
Law	Community in W NW corner of Henderson County near Madison County line.
Law Chapel	Community in Central area of Blount County. 5 mi SE of Maryville.
Lawnville	Community in middle E section of Roane County. 3 1/2 mi E of Kingston.
Lawrence	Community on the NE border of the City of Jackson in Madison County.
Lawrenceburg	County Seat of Lawrence County. Located near center of county. Incorporated in 1825.
Lawrence County	County Seat: Lawrenceburg. Zip Code 38464.

Lawrence County, (Cont.) LAWRENCE COUNTY	Located in middle section of the State on the Southern border. Bounded by Wayne, Lewis, Maury and Giles Counties and the State of Alabama to the South. Names in honor of Captain James Lawrence.
Lawrence Knob	Located in S SE section of Wilson County. N of Fisher Knob.
Laws	Community in S central section of Cocke County.
Laws Hill	Community in central NE section of Marshall County. 8 mi NW of Lewisburg.
Lawson Crossroad	Community in E Central section of Blount County. 3 mi W SW of Townsend.
Lawson Mill	Community in middle SW section of Warren County. 5 mi S SW of McMinnville.
Laxion Lake	Lake in middle N section of Scott County. 6 1/2 mi N of Huntsville.
Lazy Acres	Community in Knox County. 8 mi W NW of downtown Knoxville.
Leach	Community in S Central area of Carroll County. 6 mi SW of Huntingdon.
Lead Mine Ridge	Ridge in SW section of Bradley County, E of Lebanon Ridge.
Leadville	Community in NE corner of Jefferson County. 10 1/2 mi N NW of Dandridge.
Leaf Lake	Lake in SW section of Tipton County. Approx. 2 mi N of Drummonds.
Lea Lake	Lake in SW section of Grainger County, W of Lea Springs.
Leanna	Community in middle N section of Rutherford County. 6 1/2 mi N NW of Murfreesboro.
Leapwood	Community in NE section of McNairy County. 12 mi NE of Selmer.
Lea Springs	Community in SW area of Grainger County. 11 1/2 mi SW of Rutledge.
Leathers Hollow	Located in W border of Macon County. 2 mi W of Eulia.
Leatherwood	Community in NW section of Wayne County. 7 mi NE of Waynesboro.
Leatherwood Creek	Creek in SW section of Stewart County, flows into the Tennessee River.

Leatherwood Island	Island in W NW section of Franklin County on Tims Ford Lake S of Tims Ford State Park.
Leaths Chapel Hollow	Located in E section of Sumner County, E of Bledsoe and Bransford.
Lebanon	Community in SW section of Bradley County. Approx. 9 mi S SW of Cleveland.
Lebanon	Community in NW section of Hardin County. 10 1/2 mi N NW of Savannah. 5 mi SW of Saltillo.
Lebanon	County seat of Wilson County. Located in near center of the county. Incorporated in 1819.
Lebanon Ridge	Ridge in SW section of Bradley County, W of Lead Mine Ridge.
Ledbetter	Community in E area of Gibson County.
Ledsfords Mill	Community in NE corner of Moore County. 10 mi N NE of Lynchburg.
Lee Knob	Located in NE section of Putnam County. 8 mi E of Cookeville. S of Barnes Hollow.
Leemans Corner	Community in middle S SE section of Wilson County. 5 mi S SE of Lebanon.
Leesburg	Community in middle W section of Washington County. 4 mi W of Jonesborough.
Lees Corner	Community in NE corner of Maury County. 12 1/2 mi E NE of Columbia.
Lees Station	Community in S Central section of Bledsoe County. 5 mi SW of Pikeville.
Lee Towhead	Located in SW section of Lake County.
Lee Valley	Community in NW section of Hawkins County. 8 mi NW of Rogersville.
Leeville	Community in middle W section of Wilson County. 7 mi W of Lebanon.
Leftwich	Community in E SE section of Maury County. 10 mi E SE of Columbia.
Legate	Community in middle NE section of Stewart County. 9 mi E NE of Dover.
Leighs	Community in N section of Tipton County. 3 mi N NW of Covington.
Leighton	Community on W SW border of Madison County. 14 mi W SW of Jackson.
Leinarts	Community near center of Anderson County. 3 mi E of Laurel Grove.

Leipers Fork	Community in middle W section of Williamson County. 7 1/2 mi W SW of Franklin.
Lenior City	City in middle N section of Loudon County. 5 mi NE of Loudon. Incorporated in 1907.
Lenow	Community in E section of Shelby County. 18 1/2 mi E NE of Memphis.
Lenox	Community in middle NW section of Dyer County. Approx. 7 mi W NW of Dyersburg.
Leoma	Community in middle S section of Lawrence County. 5 1/2 mi S of Lawrenceburg.
Leonardtown	Community in central N section of Sullivan County. 5 mi N NE of Blountville.
Leoni	Community in ES E section of Cannon County. 6 mi E SE of Woodbury.
Lesters	Community in S area of Giles County.
Lesters Lake	Lake in SE central area of Davidson County. 8 mi E SE of Courthouse.
Lever Lake	Lake in NW section of Williamson County, E of Brush Creek.
Lewisburg	County seat of Marshall County. Located in near center of county. Incorporated in 1837.
Lewisburg Lake	Lake in middle SW section of Marshall County. 4 1/2 mi SW of Lewisburg.
Lewis Chapel	Located in NE section of Sequatchie County on Walden Ridge, E of Dunlap near Hamilton County Line.
Lewis County LEWIS COUNTY	County Seat: Hohenwald. Zip Code 38462. Located in middle West section of the State. Bounded by Hickman, Maury, Lawrence, Wayne and Perry Counties. Named in honor of Meriwether Lewis.
Lewis Hollow	Loated in E SE section of Benton County.
Lewis Park	Community in central section of Lewis County. 4 1/2 mi E SE of Hohenwald.
Lewis State Forest	Located in W section of Lewis County. 4 mi SW of Hohenwald.
Lewis Store	Community in SW area of Coffee County. 10 1/2 mi N NW of Manchester.
Lexie	Community in W area of Franklin County. 11 mi W SW of Winchester.
Lexie Crossroads	Comunity in W section of Franklin County. 10

Lexie Crossroads, (Cont.)	1/2 mi W SW of Winchester.
Lexington	County Seat of Henderson County. Located near center of County. Incorporated in 1824.
Liberty	Community in Central area of Benton County. 2 mi N of Camden.
Liberty	Community in SW corner of Decatur County. 1 mi S SW of Decaturville.
Liberty	City in W area of DeKalb County. 10 mi W NW of Smithville. Incorporated in 1831.
Liberty	Community in S central section of Franklin County. 3 1/2 mi S of Winchester.
Liberty	Community in SE area of Giles County. 10 mi S SE of Pulaski.
Liberty	Community in NE corner of Henry County. 17 mi NE of Paris.
Liberty	Community in SW section of Jackson County. 8 mi SW of Gainesboro.
Liberty	Community in S central section of Lincoln County. 3 mi S SE of Fayetteville.
Liberty	Community in SE section of McNairy County. 14 mi SE of Selmer.
Liberty	Community in middle SE section of Morgan County. 2 1/2 mi E SE of Wartburg.
Liberty	Community in SW section of Sequatchie County. 8 1/2 mi SW of Dunlap.
Liberty	Community in NE section of Sumner County. 14 mi N NE of Gallatin.
Liberty	Community in central SW section of Sumner County. 4 mi W NW of Gallatin.
Liberty	Community in SW corner of Washington County. 14 mi S SW of Jonesborough.
Liberty	Community in middle S section of Weakley County. 5 1/2 mi S of Dresden.
Liberty Grove	Community in S section of Lawrence County. 14 mi S SW of Lawrenceburg. 4 mi E SE of Loretto.
Liberty Hill	Community in N area of Cocke County, 8 mi N of Newport.
Liberty Hill	Community in NE area of Fayette County. 6 mi NE of Somerville.

Liberty Hill	Community in NW area of Giles County. 13 mi NW of Pulaski.
Liberty Hill	Community in NW area of Grainger County. 6 mi W NW of Rutledge.
Liberty Hill	Community in NE area of Greene County. 13 mi NE of Greeneville.
Liberty Hill	Community in E SE section of McMinn County. 9 1/2 mi E SE of Athens.
Liberty Hill	Community in S section of Moore County. 9 mi S SE of Lynchburg.
Liberty Hill	Located in W section of Rhea County. 6 mi N of Dayton.
Liberty Hill	Community in W section of Williamson County. 18 mi W NW of Franklin.
Liberty Hill	Community in E SE section of Wilson County. 18 mi SE of Lebanon.
Lick Creek	Community in N area of Benton County. 18 mi N of Camden.
Lick Creek	Creek in NE section of Benton County, flows into Kentucky Lake.
Lick Creek	Creek in NE area of Decatur County.
Lick Creek	Creek in near center of Stewart County. 1 1/2 mi SE of Dover.
Lick Hollow	Located in SE section of Overton County, NW of Hanging Limb.
Licklog Ridge	Ridge in S section of Polk County.
Lickskillet	Community in E section of Union County. Approx. 3 mi N of Maynardville.
Lick Skillett	Community in SW section of Decatur County. 8 mi SW of Decaturville.
Lickton	Community in N section of Davidson County. 10 mi N NW of Courthouse.
Life	Community in central section of Henderson County. 5 mi SW of Lexington.
Lige Hollow	Located in SW corner of Wayne County. NE of Ransom Stand.
Lightfoot	Community in near center of Lauderdale County. 6 1/2 mi W of Ripley.
Light Mill	Community in SE corner of Hawkins County. 15 mi E of Rogersville.

Lillamay	Community in Central section of Cheatham County. 3 mi S of Ashland City.
Lillydale	Community in central N section of Unicoi County. E of Banner Hill.
Lily Grove	Community in Central area of Claiborne County. 8 mi W of Tazewell.
Limekin Hollow	Located in central section of Houston County. Approx. 3 mi W SW of Erin.
Limestone	Community in W SW section of Washington County. 10 mi SW of Jonesborough.
Limestone Cove	Community in NE section of Unicoi County. 9 mi N NW of Erwin.
Linary	Community in S central section of Cumerland County. 6 mi S SE of Crossville.
Lincoln	Community on S SE border of Lincoln County. 10 mi S SE of Fayetteville.
Lincoln County LINCOLN COUNTY	County Seat: Fayetteville Zip Code 37334 Located in South Central section of the State. Bounded by Bedford, Moore, Franklin, Giles and Marshall Counties and the State of Alabama to the South. Named in honor of Major General Benjamin Lincoln.
Lincoln Lake	Lake in E SE section of Lincoln County. 10 1/2 mi E SE of Fayetteville.
Lincoln Park	Community within the city limits of Knoxville, E of Lonsdale, 2 1/2 mi N of downtown. In Knox County.
Lincoya Hills	Community in central section of Davidson County, E of Nashville.
Linden	County seat of Perry County. Located in S section of county. Incorporated in 1849.
Linder Mountain	Mountain in middle NE section of Overton County. 3 mi NE of Livingston.
Lindsey Bend	Area in bend of the Cumberland River in W NW section of Wilson County.
Lindsey Hollow	Located in middle S section of Stewart County, SW of Bear Spring.
Lindsey Hollow	Located in S central section of Stewart County, S SW of Dover.
Liners	Community in SW corner of Montgomery County. W NW of Shiloh.
Line Spring	Community in W SW section of Sevier County.

Line Spring, (Cont.)	Approx. 12 mi S SW of Sevierville.
Linger Lake	Community in central section of Cumberland County. 4 1/2 mi N NE of Crossville.
Link	Community in S SW section of Rutherford County. SE of Versailles.
Linsdale	Community in NW section of Polk County. Approx. 4 1/2 mi N of Benton.
Linton	Community in SE corner of Davidson County, W SW of Pasquo.
Linwood	Community in middle E section of Wilson County. 7 mi E SE of Lebanon.
Lipe	Community in W section of Benton County.
Lisbon	Community in SE central section of Hardeman County. 11 mi S SE of Bolivar. 7 1/2 mi W NW of Pocahontas.
Littell Lake	Lake in SW section of Grundy County. 11 1/2 mi S SW of Altamont. 1 1/2 mi N NE of Summerfield.
Little Barren	Community in S area of Claiborne County. 10 mi SW of Tazewell.
Little Barren	Community in NE section of Union County. 8 mi N NW of Maynardville.
Little Brushy Mountain	Community in middle SE section of Morgan County. S of Petros.
Little Champion Lake	Lake in SW corner of Lauderdale County. Approx. 1 1/2 mi E of Fulton.
Little Cherokee	Community in middle SW section of Washington County. 4 1/2 mi S SE of Jonesborough.
Little Chestnut Mountain	Mountain in SE section of White County, SE of Lost Creek.
Little Cove	Community in middle W SW section of Sevier County. Approx. 7 mi S SW of Sevierville.
Little Crab	Community in W NW section of Fentress County. 7 mi W NW of Jamestown.
Little Creek	Community in NE area of Claiborne County. 7 mi N of Tazewell.
Little Creek	Community in N central area of Davidson County. 8 mi N of Courthouse. 6 mi SW of Goodlettsville.
Little Creek	Community in W NW section of Fentress County. 7 mi W NW of Jamestown.

Little Cumberland Mountain	Mountain in W Central section of Campbell County NW of Jacksboro.
Little Doe	Community in W central section of Johnson County. 4 mi W SW of Mountain City.
Little Dry Run Mountain	Mountain in SW section of Johnson County, SE of Doeville.
Little Duck River	River flowing through Manchester in Coffee County.
Little Emory	Community in N NE section of Roane County. 6 1/2 mi N NE of Kingston.
Little Frog Mountain	Mountain in middle SE section of Polk County.
Little Frog Mountain Wilderness	Located in middle SE section of Polk County. NW of the Copper Basin.
Little Goshen	Ridge in S SW section of Sevier County. 7 mi S of Gatlinburg, N of Goshen Ridge.
Little Hollow	Located in SE section of Humphreys County. 2 mi S SE of New Hope.
Little Hope	Community in middle W NW section of Rutherford County. 5 mi S of Smyrna.
Little Hope	Community in N section of Wayne County. 9 mi N of Waynesboro.
Little Hurricane Creek	Creek in W NW section of Franklin County, W of Winchester
Little John	Community in middle NW section of Shelby County. 12 mi N NE of Memphis.
Littlelot	Community in Middle E section of Hickman County. 8 mi E of Centerville.
Little Milligan	Community in E border of Carter County near Johnson County line. 10 mi E of Elizabethton.
Little Mountain	Mountain in W section of Bledsoe County, W of Sequatchie Valley.
Little Mountain	Mountain in SE section of Blount County, S of Townsend.
Little Mountain	Mountain in S SW section of Blount County, S of Chato, N of Chilhowee Mountain.
Little Mountain	Community in SE area of Carter County.
Little Mountain	Mountain in middle S section of Franklin County. Approx. 3 mi S of Winchester.
Little Mountain	Mountain in W SW section of Polk County, E of Parksville.

Little Mountain	Mountain in NE section of Sevier County. 9 mi E NE of Sevierville.
Little Mountain	Mountain in NE section of Unicoi County and SW section of Carter County.
Little Mountain	Mountain in S section of Unicoi County, S of Flag Pond.
Little Peavine Mountain	Mountain in E NE section of Cumberland County, NE of Peavine.
Little Pigeon River	River in N section of Sevier County, flows into the French Broad River.
Little Pilot Mountain	Mountain in middle SE section of Morgan County, E of Annadcl.
Little Possum Creek	Creek in N NW section of Hamilton County.
Little Richland Creek	Creek in NW section of Humphreys County. Begins 8 mi NW of Waverly.
Little Ridge	Ridge in E area of Claiborne County, N of Powell Mountain.
Little Ridge	Ridge in E section of Hancock County, E of Chestnut Grove.
Little River	Community in N Central area of Blount County near Knox County line. 5 mi N of Alcoa.
Little Rock Mills	Community in E NE section of Hickman County, E of Dogwood Flat.
Little Stone Mountain	Mountain in E section of Carter County, N of Poga.
Little Tennessee River	Flows from NC westward, forms boundary lines for Monroe & Blount Counties. N into Loudon County where it flows into the Tennessee River.
Little Texas	Community in middle SE section of Williamson County. 1 1/2 mi S SW of Peytonsville.
Littleton Hollow	Located in W NW section of Humphreys County. 3 mi SW of Trinity.
Little Turkey Creek	Creek in SW corner of Knox County, SW of Farragut.
Little Valley	Community in W section of Sevier County, S of Waldens Creek and Laurel Grove.
Little White Oak	Community in NE area of Campbell County, 4 mi S SE of Jellico.
Litton	Community in NE area of Bledsoe County. 13 mi NE of Pikeville.

Lively	Community in NW corner of Marshall County. 15 mi N of Lewisburg.
Liverworth	Community in S section of Montgomery County. 9 mi S SE of Clarksville.
Livesay Mill	Community in NE area of Hancock County. 10 mi E NE of Sneedville. 1 mi S of Kyles Ford.
Livingston	County Seat of Overton County. Located in near center of county. Incorporated in 1835.
Loafers Corner	Community in W NW section of Rutherford County. W of Smyrna.
Lobelville	City in N NE section of Perry County. 11 mi N NE of Linden. Incorporated in 1957.
Locke	Community in NW section of Shelby County. 13 1/2 mi N of Memphis.
Lockertsville	Community in N Central section of Cheatham County. 6 mi N NW of Ashland City.
Locust Gap	Located in S section of Johnson County near border. S of Mill Creek.
Locust Grove	Community in NE area of Dyer County. 12 mi NE of Dyersburg.
Locust Hill	Located in E section of Hamilton County.
Locust Knob	Located in S SE section of Rutherford County.
Locust Mount	Community in W NW section of Washington County. 6 1/2 mi W NW of Jonesborough.
Locust Springs	Community in N area of Greene County. 10 mi N of Greeneville.
Lodge	Community in S SW section of Marion County. 10 mi W of Jasper.
Lodi	Community on W border of Lawrence County. Approx. 6 mi W of Spring Creek.
Lofton	Community in NE section of Rutherford County. 8 mi NE of Murfreesboro.
Logans Hollow	Located in middle W section of Dickson County. 2 mi W of Taylors Crossroads.
Logans Lake	Lake in N NW section of McNairy County, SW of Finger.
Log Mountain	Mountain in NW section of Grainger County.
Lois	Community in middle SW section of Moore County. 3 1/2 mi S of Lynchburg.

Lomax Crossroads	Community in central section of Lewis County, W of Hohenwald.
London	Community in S central section of Cocke County. 12 mi E SE of Newport.
Lone Cove	Located in W section of Sequatchie County, NW of Cartwright.
Lone Mountain	Mountain in NE section of Anderson County, E of Norris.
Lone Mountain	Community in S central section Claiborne County. 5 mi S of Tazewell.
Lone Mountain	Mountain in S area of Claiborne County and E NE section of Union County.
Lone Mountain	Mountain in S SE section of Morgan County.
Lone Mountain	Mountain in S section of Rhea County, W SW of Dayton.
Lone Mountain	Community in S section of Scott County. 10 1/2 mi S of Huntsville.
Lone Mountain State Forest	Located in S SE section of Morgan County, NE of Deermont. S SE of Wartburg.
Lone Oak	Community in S section of Sequatchie County. 12 mi S of Dunlap.
Lone Star	Community in SW section of Sullivan County. 18 mi W SW of Blountville.
Lonewood	Community in NE section of Van Buren County. 10 mi E NE of Spencer.
Long Branch	Community in central SW section of Lawrence County. 8 mi SW of Lawrenceburg.
Long Creek	Community in E area of Cocke County. 9 mi E of Newport.
Long Creek	Community in W central section of Macon County. 4 1/2 mi W NW of Lafayette.
Long Hollow	Community in Central area of Campbell County near LaFollette.
Long Hollow	Located in NW section of Humphreys County. 2 mi W SW of Halls Creek.
Long Hollow	Located in E Section of Wayne County. E of Dick Cabin Ridge.
Long Hunter State Park	Located in E SE section of Davidson County. E of Percy Priest Lake.
Long Island	Island on Tennessee River, 3 mi S of Kingston

Long Island, (Cont.)	in Roane County.
Long Island	Community within the city of Kingsport, S section of town. In Sullivan County.
Long Lake	Lake in S SE section of Obion County. 11 1/2 mi S SW of Union City, N of Big Lake.
Long Mountain	Mountain in N section of Campbell County, SE of Newcomb.
Long Mountain	Mountain near E NE border of Warren County, S of Barnett Mountain.
Long Pond	Pond in SW central section of Franklin County. 5 mi SW of Winchester.
Long Pond	Pond in N NW section of Lauderdale County, E of Lake Chisholm.
Long Ridge	Ridge in SW section of Bledsoe County and N section of Sequatchie County.
Long Ridge	Ridge in NE corner of Jackson County, N of Carlock.
Long Ridge	Ridge in E SE section of Rutherford County. N of Big Springs.
Long Ridge	Ridge in N NE section of of Scott County, E of Pleasant Grove.
Long Rock	Community in N Central section of Carroll County. 4 mi N of Huntingdon.
Longs Bend	Community in E central section of Hawkins County. SE of Surgoinsville.
Longtown	Community in NW area of Fayette County. 11 1/2 mi NW of Somerville.
Longview	Community in NW area of Bedford County. 12 mi NW of Shelbyville.
Lonsdale	Community within city limits of Knoxville, E of West Haven. In Knox County.
Lookout Mountain	City in SW area of Hamilton County on top of Lookout Mountain. Incorporated in 1890.
Lookout Mountain	Mountain in SW section of Hamilton County near Chattanooga.
Lookout Valley	Formerly Tiftonia. Located in SW area of Hamilton County. 12 mi E of downtown Chattanooga.
Looney Islands	Community in middle S section of Knox County on the Tennessee River.

Loosahatchie Bar	Sand Bar on Mississippi River in Memphis, W of Mud Island. In Shelby County.
Loosahatchie Bottom	Located in middle N section of Fayette County.
Loosahatchie River Canal	Flows W from Hardeman County through middle N section of Fayette and Shelby Counties, where it flows into the Mississippi River.
Loretto	City in S SW section of Lawrence County. 13 mi S SW of Lawrenceburg. Incorporated in 1950.
Lorraine	Community in NE section of Rhea County. 19 mi N NE of Dayton.
Lost Creek	Creek in W section of Franklin County, SW of Brownington. Flows into Elk River.
Lost Creek	Community in middle SE section of White County. 6 1/2 mi E SE of Sparta.
Lost Creek Lake	Lake in SE section of Henderson County. 5 mi SE of Lexington. 6 1/2 mi NW of Scotts Hill.
Lost Lake	Lake in NW section of Lauderdale County, SE of Barr. Approx. 11 mi NW of Ripley.
Loudon	County seat of Loudon County. Located in central section of the County. Incorporated in 1860.
Loudon County LOUDON COUNTY	County Seat: Loudon. Zip Code 37774. Located in Southeastern section of the State. Bounded by Roane, Knox, Blount, Monroe and McMinn Counties. Named in honor of Fort Loudon.
Louise	Community in S SW section of Montgomery County. S of Cunningham.
Louis Hollow	Located in S section of Stewart County, N of Barnes Hollow.
Louisville	Community in NW section of Blount County. 5 mi NW of Alcoa.
Love Hollow	Located in SW section of Macon County. 1 1/2 mi N of Green Grove.
Lovejoy	Community in SE section of Overton County. 16 mi SE of Livingston.
Lovelace	Community in NE corner of Greene County. 20 mi NE of Greeneville.
Love Lady	Community in NW section of Pickett County. 2 mi W NW of Byrdstown.
Loveland	Community within the city limits of Knoxville. 5 1/2 mi N NE of downtown. In Knox County.

Lovell	Community in SW section of Knox County. 13 mi W SW of Knoxville.
Lovells Island	Island on Cumberland River, middle W NW section of Smith County. 2 mi SW of Riddleton.
Love Mountain	Located in middle E section of Morgan County.
Love Station	Community in N central section of Unicoi County. S of Banner Hill.
Lovetown	Community in W section of Maury County. Approx. 11 mi W of Columbia.
Lowe Mountain	Mountain in S SW section of Scott County, SW of Slick Rock.
Lower Holly Creek	Community in E SE section of Wayne County. Approx. 20 mi S SE of Waynesboro.
Lower Mill	Community in NE section of Hamilton County. 11 mi N NE of downtown Chattanooga near Valleybrook.
Lower Mocheson	Community in SE section of Lawrence County. Approx. 12 mi S SE of Lawrenceburg.
Lowland	Community in SE section of Hamblen County. 6 1/2 mi SE of Morristown.
Lowryville	Community in SE section of Hardin County, SE of Burnt Church.
Luciuda	Community in S SE section of Johnson County. 8 1/2 mi S of Mountain City.
Luckett	Community in central section of Lauderdale County. 8 mi W SW of Ripley.
Lucky	Community in N NW section of Warren County. 9 mi N NW of McMinnville.
Lucy	Community in middle N NW section of Shelby County. 13 mi N NE of Memphis.
Lulaville	Community in W section of Grainger County. 4 mi W SW of Rutledge.
Lumber Ridge	Ridge in SE section of Blount County. 4 mi E SE of Townsend.
Luminary	Community in NE section of Bledsoe County.
Luna	Community in middle SE section of Marshall County. 6 1/2 mi S SE of Lewisburg.
Lunns Store	Community in N section of Marshall County. 10 1/2 mi N of Oslin.
Luper Mountain	Mountain in E section of Cumberland County, N

Luper Mountain, (Cont.)	of Millstone.
Lupton City	Community within the city limits of Chattanooga. 5 1/2 mi N NE of downtown just E of Red Bank.
Luray	Community in W SW section of Henderson County. 11 mi W SW of Lexington. 8 mi W of Palestine.
Lusk	Community in SW area of Bledsoe County. 1 1/2 mi W of College Station.
Luskville	Community on S SW border of McMinn County. 12 1/2 mi S SW of Athens.
Luther	Community in S central section of Hancock County. 5 1/2 mi S SW of Sneedville. 2 1/2 mi N of Treadway.
Luther Lake	Lake in S central section of Dickson County. 7 1/2 mi S of Charlotte.
Luttrell	Community in SW section of Loudon County. 12 1/2 mi W SW of Loudon.
Luttrell	City in SE section of Union County. 4 mi SE of Maynardville. Incorporated in 1925.
Lutts	Community in W SW section of Wayne County. 15 mi SW of Waynesboro.
Lyles	Community in NE section of Hickman County. 12 mi N NE of Centerville.
Lyles Lake	Lake in NW section of Shelby County. NW of Locke.
Lynchburg	County Seat of Moore County. Located near center of county. Incorporated in 1833.
Lynn	Community in N NE section of Gibson County. 10 mi N NE of Trenton.
Lynn Garden	Community in N NW corner of Sullivan County. 14 mi W NW of Blountville. 2 mi N of Kingsport.
Lynn Mountain	Mountain in central NW section of Carter County, E of Elizabethton.
Lynnville	City in N area of Giles County. 12 1/2 mi N of Pulaski. Incorporated in 1838.
Lyons View	Community within the city limits of Knoxville. 4 mi W SW of downtown. In Knox County.
Lyonton	Community in E section of Knox County. 12 mi E NE of Knoxville.

Macedonia
Community in N area of Carroll County. 3 mi E of McKenzie.

Macedonia
Community in middle W section of Haywood County. 5 1/2 mi W of Brownsville.

Macedonia
Community in SE section of McMinn County. 9 1/2 mi SE of Athens.

Macedonia
Community in SE corner of Obion County. 14 1/2 mi S SE of Union City.

Macedonia
Community in middle NW section of White County. 8 1/2 mi N NW of Sparta.

Macey
Community in NW section of Smith County. 9 mi N NW of Carthage.

Mack Hollow
Located near W NW border of Macon County. 2 mi W of Rocky Mound.

Mackie Valley
Located in N section of Davidson County.

Mackins Hollow
Located in S central section of Humphreys County. 4 mi W of New Hope.

Maclellan Island
Island on Tennessee River near downtown Chattanooga in Hamilton County.

Macmillian
Community in Knox County. 9 1/2 mi NE of downtown Knoxville.

Macon
Community in W central section of Fayette County. 10 mi SW of Somerville.

Macon County
County Seat: Lafayette. Zip Code 37083. Located in North central border of the State. Bounded by Clay, Jackson, Smith, Trousdale and Sumner Counties and the State of Kentucky to the North. Named in honor of Nathaniel Macon.

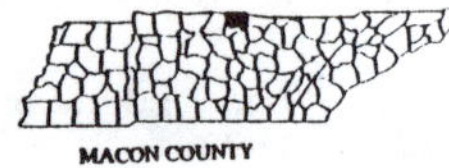
MACON COUNTY

Maddox
Community in central section of Hardin County. 4 1/2 mi S SE of Savannah.

Maddron Bald
Mountain in SE corner of Cocke County.

Madge
Community in NE corner of Shelby County. 27 mi NE of Memphis.

Madie
Community in S section of Lake County. 6 1/2 mi S of Tiptonville.

Madison
Community in N central section of Davidson County. 9 mi N NE of Courthouse.

Madison County
County Seat: Jackson. Zip Code 38301. Located in Southwest section of the State. Bounded by Gibson, Carroll, Henderson, Chester, Hardeman, Haywood and Crockett Counties. Named in honor of James Madison.

MADISON COUNTY

Madison Hall	Community in middle SW section of Madison County. 4 1/2 mi SW of Jackson.
Madisonville	County seat of Monroe County. Located in middle W NW section of the county. Incorporated in 1865.
Magahi Chapel	3 mi due E of Apison, 1 mi W of Bradley County Line. in Hamilton County.
Magnolia	Community in W section of Houston County. Approx. 10 1/2 mi W SW of Erin.
Magnolia Hollow	Located in S SW section of Houston County, S of Magnolia community.
Mahan Gap	Located in E section of Hamilton County off Highway 58.
Mahoney Mill	Community in NW section of Blount County. 7 mi W of Maryville.
Mailbox Hill	Located in W section of Hamilton County.
Major	Community in S SW section of Wilson County. 9 mi S SW of Lebanon.
Malesus	Community in S central section of Madison County. Approx. 5 mi S of Jackson.
Mallory	Community in central NE section of Williamson County. Approx. 4 mi NE of Franklin.
Malone	Community in SW section of Giles County.
Maloneyville	Community in middle N section of Knox County. 9 mi N NE of Knoxville.
Manchester	County Seat of Coffee County. Located in central section of Coffee County. Incorporated in 1838.
Manchester Park	Community within city limits of Chattanooga. 5 mi N of downtown off Hixson Pike in Hamilton County.
Manila	Community in middle E NE section of McMinn County. Approx. 7 mi E NE of Athens.
Mankinville	Community in S central section of Rutherford County. 5 mi S SE of Murfreesboro.
Manleyville	Community in SE section of Henry County. 10 mi E SE of Paris.
Mannings Hollow	Located in SW section of Davidson County.
Manring	Community in NW central area of Claiborne County. 1 1/2 mi S of Fork Ridge.

Mansfield	Community on S border of Henry County. 9 mi S SE of Paris.
Mansfield Gap	Community in middle NE section of Jefferson County. 7 mi N NE of Dandridge.
Mansfield Gulf	Valley in W NW section of Hamilton County.
Mansford	Community in middle W section of Franklin County.
Manson	Community in W area of Fentress County. 8 1/2 W SW of Jamestown.
Maple Creek Lake	In SE corner of Carroll County in Natchez Trace State Park.
Maple Grove	Community in NE area of Clay County.
Maple Grove	Community in middle N section of Macon County. 2 1/2 mi N NW of Lafayette.
Maple Grove	Community in middle E SE section of Madison County. Approx. 5 mi E SE of Jackson.
Maple Grove	Community in N border of Meigs County. 15 mi N NE of Decatur.
Maple Hill	Community in middle N section of Sullivan County. 4 mi NE of Blountville.
Maples	Community in N Central area of Anderson County. 2 mi E of Lake City.
Maple Springs	Community on S SE border of Hickman County. 10 mi SE of Centerville.
Maplewood	Community in central section of Davidson County. E of Nashville.
Marble City	Community within the city limits of Knoxville. 2 1/2 mi W of downtown. In Knox County.
Marbledale	Community in middle SE section of Knox County. 6 mi E SE of Knoxville.
Marble Hall	Community in W central section of Hawkins County. 4 1/2 mi W of Rogersville.
Marble Hill	Community in W Central section of Blount County. 8 mi W SW of Maryville.
Marble Hill	Community in middle S section of Moore County. 6 mi S SE of Lynchburg.
Marble Plains	Community in S NW section of Franklin County. 8 mi W NW of Winchester.
Marble Switch	Community in SW section of Bradley County. 6 mi SE of McDonald.

Marbleton Community in N section of Unicoi County. 8 1/2 mi NE of Erwin.

Marbuts Community in SW section of Giles County.

Marguerite Community in N NW section of Hamblen County. 3 mi N NW of Morristown.

Marion Community in NW corner of Claiborne County. 6 mi NW of Speedwell.

Marion Community in NW area of Dickson County.

Marion Community on S SW border of Montgomery County. 14 1/2 mi S SW of Clarksville.

Marion County County Seat: Jasper. Zip Code 37347. Located in Southeaster section of the State. Bounded by Franklin, Grundy, Sequatchie and Hamilton Counties and the States of Georgia and Alabama to the South. Named in honor of Brig. General Francis Marion.

MARION COUNTY

Marlborough Community in NE area of Carroll County. 11 mi NE of Huntingdon.

Marlow Community in W Central section of Anderson County. 5 mi E of Oliver Springs.

Marmor Community in W NW section of Blount County. 9 mi W NW of Maryville, near Ish Creek.

Marrowbone Community in E Central section of Cheatham County. 3 mi SE of Ashland City.

Marrowbone Lake Lake in W NW section of Davidson County, W of Greenville.

Marr Towhead Located in NW section of Lake County.

Marshall Community in NE corner of Hawkins County. N of Mt. Carmol.

Marshall County County Seat: Lewisburg. Zip Code 37091. Located in South Central section of the State. Bounded by Williamson, Rutherford, Bedford, Lincoln, Giles and Maury Counties. Named in honor of John Marshall.

MARSHALL COUNTY

Marshall Hill Community in N section of McMinn County. SE of Pond Hill.

Marshall Knob Located in middle S section of Rutherford County. 5 mi S of Murfreesboro.

Mars Hill Community in central NE section of Lawrence County. 3 mi NE of Lawrenceburg.

Mars Hill Community in NE section of Rhea County. 18 mi NE of Dayton.

Martel	Community in NE section of Loudon County. 9 mi NE of Loudon.
Martha	Community in middle NW section of Wilson County. 8 mi W NW of Lebanon.
Marthas Chapel	Community in S section of Montgomery County. 8 mi S of Clarksville.
Martin	City in middle W NW section of Weakley County. 8 1/2 mi W NW of Dresden. Incorporated in 1897.
Martin Camp	Community in middle E section of McNairy County. Approx. 5 mi E NE of Selmer.
Martins Mills	Community in W section of Wayne County. Approx. 13 mi SW of Waynesboro.
Martin Springs	Community in N NW section of Marion County. Approx. 10 mi W NW of Jasper.
Marvin	Community in NW section of Greene County. 11 mi NW of Greeneville, 1 1/2 mi S of Pilot Knob.
Marvin Chapel	Community in NW section of Grundy County. 8 mi W NW of Altamont.
Mary Chapel	Community in E area of Grainger County. 9 1/2 mi E of Rutledge.
Marys Grove	Community in S SW section of Lincoln County. 8 mi S SW of Fayetteville.
Maryville	County Seat of Blount County. Located in W Central section of county S of Alcoa. Incorporated in 1838.
Mascot	Community in NE section of Knox County. 12 mi E NE of Knoxville.
Mashburn	Community in middle E section of McMinn County. Approx. 4 mi E of Athens.
Mason	City in SE section of Tipton County. 12 mi S SE of Covington. Incorporated in 1869.
Mason Grove	Community in E area of Crockett County. 9 mi E of Alamo.
Mason Hall	Community on S SE border of Obion County. 15 mi S of Union City.
Mason Hollow	Community in SE section of Rutherford County.
Mason Knob	Located in S SW section of Wilson County. 4 mi W of Cainsville.
Mason Lake	Lake on N border of Henry County. 13 mi N of

Mason Lake, (Cont.) Paris.

Mason Springs — Community in Central section of Claiborne County.

Massengale Mountain — Mountain in W SW section of Campbell County, W of Caryville.

Massengill Lake — Lake in S SW section of Hamblen County. 4 mi SE of Morristown.

Massey Lake — Lake in SE section of Haywood County. Approx. 8 mi E SE of Brownsville.

Masseyville — Community in lower SW area of Chester County. 3 1/2 mi S of Hickory Corners.

Matlock Ford — Community in N central section of Hickman County. Approx. 7 mi N NW of Centerville.

Matlock Ridge — Ridge in W section of Loudon County, SE of Prospect.

Matthew — Community on SW border of Putnam County. 12 mi SW of Cookeville.

Matthews Lake — Lake in middle N section of Rutherford County. 6 mi N of Murfreesboro.

Maury City — City in W central section of Crockett County. 6 mi E NW of Alamo. Incorporated in 1911.

Maury County — County Seat: Columbia. Zip Code 38401. Located in South central section of the State. Bounded by Williamson, Marshall, Giles, Lawrence, Lewis and Hickman Counties. Named in honor of Abram Maury.

MAURY COUNTY

Maury Junction — Community in NW section of Crockett County. 8 mi NW of Alamo.

Maxey — Community in N NE area of Dyer County. 8 mi N NE of Dyersburg.

Maxwell — Community in SW area of Franklin County. 9 mi SW of Winchester.

Maxwell Chapel — Community on W border of Overton County. 8 1/2 mi W NW of Livingston.

Maxwell Mountain — Mountain in middle S SW section of Overton County, S SW of Okalona.

Mayday — Community in S SW section of Washington County. 6 mi S of Jonesborough.

Mayes Lake — Lake in S section of Hamblen County, S of Morristown.

Mayland — Community in W area of Cumberland County. 12

Mayland, (Cont.)	mi NW of Crossville.
Mayland Lake	Lake in W NW area of Cumberland County. N of Mayland.
Maymead	Community in middle S section of Johnson County. 4 1/2 mi S SW of Mountain City.
Maynardville	County Seat of Union County. Located in middle SE section of Union County. Incorporated in 1958.
Mayview Heights	Community in Knox County. 8 mi NW of downtown Knoxville.
McAllister Hill	Community in SE section of Polk County in the Copper Basin, E SE of Ducktown.
McAllisters Crossroads	Community in S section of Montgomery County. 12 mi S of Clarksville.
McAnnally Ridge	Ridge in NE section of Knox County, NE of Knoxville.
McBurg	Community on W border of Lincoln County. 14 mi W of Fayetteville.
McCains	Community in middle S section of Maury County. 7 mi S of Columbia.
McCampbell Knob	Located in S SE section of Blount County, near border. 7 mi S of Townsend.
McCarty	Community in S central section of Hamilton County. 5 mi E NE of downtown Chattanooga.
McCloud	Community in S section of Hawkins County. 4 mi SE of Rogersville. 1 mi NW of Strahl.
McClures Bend	Community in central E NE section of Smith County. 3 1/2 mi E NE of Carthage.
McCoin	Community in middle SE section of Jackson County. 3 1/2 mi SE of Gainesboro.
McCoinsville	Community in middle SE section of Jackson County. 3 mi S SE of Gainesboro.
McConnell	Community in NE section of Obion County. Approx. 10 mi E of Union City.
McCookville	Community in S center of Sevier County. 7 1/2 mi S SE of Sevierville.
McCord Hollow	Located in SW section of Davidson County, W of Robertson Island.
McCord Knob	Located in E SE section of Williamson County. 3 mi E of Kirkland.

McCormack Crossing	Community in N NE section of Maury County. 11 mi N NE of Columbia, S of Spring Hill.
McCrosky Island	Island on French Broad River in N NW section of Sevier County, E of Boyds Creek.
McCulley Mountain	Mountain in middle N NE section of Polk County.
McCutcheon Heights	Community in middle E section of Obion County. 4 mi S of Union City.
McDaniel	Community in E SE section of Williamson County. 11 1/2 mi E SE of Franklin.
McDonald	Community in SW section of Bradley County. 5 mi SW of Cleveland.
McDonald Hill	Community in Central section of Hawkins County. 2 mi SE of Rogersville.
McElroy	Community in NW corner of Van Buren County. 6 mi W NW of Spencer.
McEven	Community in NW central area of Carter County.
McEwen	City in middle E section of Humphreys County. 9 mi E NE of Waverly. Incorporated in 1907.
McGeetown	Community in SE section of Polk County in the Copper Basin, E of Isabella.
McGill Gulf	Valley in N NW section of Hamilton County.
McGlamerys Stand	Community in middle S section of Wayne County. 11 mi S of Waynesboro.
McHarg	Community in SE section of Polk County, W of Coletown.
McIllwain	Community in S Central section of Benton County. 3 1/2 mi E of Halladay.
McInturff	Community in NW section of Carter County.
McKellar Field	Located in middle W section of Madison County. 5 1/2 mi W SW of Jackson.
McKenzie	City in N area of Carroll County, 10 mi NW of Huntingdon. Incorporated in 1868. Boundaries also extend into Henry and Weakley Counties.
McKinley	Community in middle E section of Washington County. Approx. 3 mi E NE of Johnsborough.
McKinney Island	Island in NW corner of Jefferson County on the Holston River.
McKinnon	Community in W NW section of Houston County. 12 mi W of Erin.

McKnight — Community in NW corner of Maury County. Approx. 12 mi N NW of Columbia.

McLemoresville — City in W area of Carroll County. 9 mi W of Huntingdon. Incorporated in 1833.

McMahan — Community in middle E NE section of Williamson County. 7 mi E of Franklin.

McMahon — Community in NW section of Sevier County. 7 mi W NW of Sevierville.

McMillan — Community in middle E section of Knox County, SW of of Three Points.

McMinn County — County Seat: Athens. Zip Code 37303. Located in Southeastern section of the State. Bounded by Roane, Loudon, Monroe, Polk, Bradley and Meigs Counties. Named in honor of Joseph McMinn.

MCMINN COUNTY

McMinnville — County Seat of Warren County. Located near center of county. Incorporated in 1809.

McMullens — Community in W Central section of Blount County near Marble Hill.

McMullens — Community in E section of Loudon County. 9 mi E of Loudon, E of Centersville.

McNair Cut — Community in SE section of Dickson County.

McNairy — Community in NW section of McNairy County. 10 mi N NW of Selmer.

McNairy County — County Seat: Selmer. Zip Code 38375. Located in Southwest section of the State. Bounded by Hardeman, Chester and Hardin Counties and the State of Mississippi to the South. Named in honor of Judge John McNairy.

MCNAIRY COUNTY

McPheeters Bend — Community in E section of Hawkins County. 17 mi E NE of Rogersville.

Meacham — Community in N central section of Dyer County. 7 1/2 mi N of Dyersburg.

Meade Lake — Lake in S SW section of Tipton County. Approx. 2 1/2 mi S of Crosstown.

Meades Quarry — Community within the city limits of Knoxville. 3 mi E of downtown. In Knox County.

Meadorville — Community in S section of Macon County. 3 1/2 mi S SW of Lafayette.

Meadow — Community in SE section of Loudon County. 10 mi E SE of Loudon.

Meadow Branch — Community in E area of Grainger County. 14 mi

Meadow Branch, (Cont.)	E NE of Rutledge.
Meadowbrook	Community in middle N section of Blount County. 2 mi N of Maryville.
Meadowbrook	Community in S section of Knox County, S of Knoxville, N of Crenshaw.
Meadow Creek Mill	Community in SE area of Greene County near Cedar Creek.
Meadow Creek Mountain	Mountain in E central section of Cocke County, N of Del Rio in Cherokee National Forest.
Meadow Creek Mountain	Mountain in E section of Cocke County, S of Long Creek.
Meadow Creek Mountain	Mountain in S area of Greene County and E NE section of Cocke County. 10 mi S of Greeneville.
Meadow Mead	Community in central section of Henry County, E of Paris.
Meadow Park Lake	Lake in SW area of Cumberland County. 5 mi SW of Crossville.
Meadow View	Community in E area of Hamilton County. 13 mi E NE of downtown Chattanooga. NE of Snow Hill.
Means Hollow	Located in middle NE section of Overton County. 1 mi E NE of Oak Grove.
Mecca	Community on E SE border of McMinn County. Approx. 11 mi E SE of Athens. S of Prospect.
Medford	Community in N Central section of Anderson County. 3 mi S of Lake City.
Medford Station	Community in N Central section of Anderson County.
Medina	City in SE section of Gibson County. 15 mi SE of Trenton. Incorporated in 1907.
Medlock Hollow	Located in E section of Overton County. 7 mi E SE of Livingston. S of Alpine.
Medon	City in S section of Madison County. 11 mi S SW of Jackson. Incorporated in 1859.
Meeman-Shelby Forest and State Park	Located in NW corner of Shelby County. 13 mi N of Memphis.
Meigs County MEIGS COUNTY	County Seat: Decatur. Zip Code 37322. Located in Southeastern section of the State. Bounded by Rhea, Roane, McMinn, Bradley and Hamilton Counties. Named in honor of Johathon Meigs.

Meigs County Park	Located in N central section of Meigs County, NW of Peakland.
Meigs Mountain	Mountain in SW corner of Sevier County. 8 mi SW of Gatlinburg.
Melbourne	Community in NE area of Anderson County. 10 mi E NE of Clinton.
Melrose	Community in NE Central area of Blount County. 8 mi E of Maryville.
Melrose	Community within city limits of Nashville in Davidson County.
Melrose Park	Community in central section of Coffee County.
Melton Hill Dam	Dam on Tennessee River in N section of Loudon County.
Melton Hill Lake	Lake located in SE section of Anderson County on the Clinch River.
Melville	Community in central section of Hamilton County near Soddy Daisy.
Melvine	Community in NE Section of Bledsoe County. 11 mi NE of Pikeville.
Memphis	County Seat of Shelby County. Located in SW section of County. Incorporated in 1826.
Menglewood	Community in W central section of Dyer County. 9 mi W of Dyersburg.
Mentor	Community in N Central area of Blount County. 5 mi N of Maryville.
Mercer	Community in SW corner of Madison County. 16 mi SW of Jackson.
Meridian	Community in E central section of Cumberland County. 7 mi SE of Crossville.
Meriwether Lewis National Monument	Located in Lewis County, 5 mi E SE of Hohenwald.
Merry Mountain	Mountain in middle S SE section of Johnson County, N of Neva.
Merry Oaks	Community in central section of Davidson County, E of Nashville.
Michie	City in SE section of McNairy County. 12 mi SE of Selmer. Incorporated in 1961.
Middlebrook Heights	Community within the city limits of Knoxville. 4 mi W of downtown. In Knox County.
Middleburg	Community in SW central section of Hardeman

Middleburg, (Cont.)	County. 7 mi W SW of Bolivar. 4 mi NE of Hickory Valley.
Middleburg	Community in SE section of Henderson County. 9 mi E SE of Lexington.
Middle City	Community in central section of Dyer County. 3 mi W of Dyersburg.
Middle Creek	Community in middle N section of Sevier County. Approx. 3 mi S SE of Sevierville.
Middle Fork	Community in SW corner of Henderson County. 9 1/2 mi S SW of Lexington. 5 mi W of Center Hill.
Middle Ridge	Ridge in E SE section of Meigs County, E of Big Spring.
Middle Ridge	Ridge in S section of Unicoi County, SE of Flag Pond.
Middle Settlement	Community in NW section of Blount County. 3 mi W of Alcoa.
Middleton	City in SE section of Hardeman County. 15 mi S SE of Bolivar. 5 mi W of Pocahontas. Incorporated in 1856.
Middle Valley	Community in central section of Hamilton County. 12 mi N NE of downtown Chattanooga.
Midfields	Community in NW corner of Sullivan County. NW of Kingsport.
Midland	Community on S SW border of Rutherford County. 13 mi S SW of Murfreesboro.
Midnight Hollow	Located in central SE section of Montgomery County.
Midtown	Community in central NW section of Roane County. 3 1/2 mi W of Kingston.
Midtown	Community in NW section of Roane County. 5 mi E of Rockwood.
Midvale	Community within the city limits of Red Bank. In Hamilton County.
Midway	Community in SE section of Bedford County. 8 mi E SE of Shelbyville.
Midway	Community in NW area of Blount County. 2 mi E of Louisville.
Midway	Community in S area of Cannon County. 11 mi S of Woodbury.
Midway	Community in central area of Clay County. 5 mi

Midway, (Cont.)	W of Celina.
Midway	Community in SE area of Cocke County. 10 mi SE of Newport, 3 1/2 mi S of Del Rio.
Midway	Community in SE area of Crockett County. 8 mi SE of Alamo.
Midway	Community in SW area of Cumberland County. 11 1/2 mi SW of Crossville.
Midway	Community in E central area of DeKalb County. 3 mi E of Smithville.
Midway	Community in W SW area of Dyer County. 17 mi W SW of Dyersburg.
Midway	Community in E NE section of Franklin County. 13 mi E of Winchester.
Midway	Community in W central section of Greene County. 10 mi W of Greeneville.
Midway	Community in NW section of Henry County. 16 mi NW of Paris.
Midway	Community in W SW section of Henry County. Approx. 9 mi W SW of Paris.
Midway	Community in E SE section of Johnson County. 4 1/2 mi S SE of Mountain City.
Midway	Community in E NE section of Obion County. 6 mi E SE of Union City.
Midway	Community in SW section of Pickett County. Approx. 5 mi S SW of Byrdstown.
Midway	Community in NE section of Warren County. 9 1/2 mi N NE of McMinnville.
Midway	Community in middle NE section of Washington County. 3 mi SW of Johnson City.
Mifflin	Community in N area of Chester County. 8 1/2 mi N NE of Henderson.
Milan	City in E SE section of Gibson County. 11 mi E SE of Trenton. Incorporated in 1865.
Milan Arsenal and Wildlife Management Area	Located in SE section of Gibson County and in SW section of Carroll County.
Milburnton	Community in E NE section of Greene County. 15 mi NE of Greeneville.
Miles Crossroads	Community in SW section of Clay County. 13 mi W of Celina.

Mile Straight	Community on Highway 27 N of Red Bank near Soddy Daisy.
Milkly Way	Community in N central section of Giles County.
Milksick Mountain	Mountain in S section of White County. 4 mi S of Sparta.
Mill Brook	Community in W SW section of Washington County. 9 mi W SW of Jonesborough.
Mill Creek	Community in NE section of Anderson County, near Union County line. 12 mi N NE of Clinton.
Mill Creek	Community in NW section of Henry County between Jones Mill and Puryear.
Mill Creek	Community in S section of Johnson County. 7 mi S SW of Mountain City.
Mill Creek	Community in N section of Morgan County. 11 mi N of Wartburg.
Mill Creek	Community in middle SE section of Putnam County. 8 1/2 mi E SE of Cookeville.
Milldale	Community in middle N NE section of Robertson County. 8 1/2 mi NE of Springfield.
Milledgeville	City in NE corner of McNairy County. 19 mi NE of Selmer. Incorporated in 1961. Boundaries also extend into Hardin and Chester Counties.
Miller	Community in NE area of Fayette County. 7 1/2 mi N NE of Somerville.
Miller Cove	Located in middle E section of Blount County, SE of Walland.
Miller Cove	Located in S section of Sequatchie County, W of Lonc Oak.
Miller Cove Mountain	Mountain in E NE section of Blount County, E of Walland.
Miller Flats	Community in central section of Hawkins County. SW of Surgoinsville.
Miller Grove	Community in central section of Hamilton County. 15 mi N NE of downtown Chattanooga.
Miller Ridge	Ridge in E section of Monroe County in Cherokee National Forest.
Millers Cove	Mountain in middle N section of Overton County, S of Allons.
Millersville	City in W SW section of Sumner County. 14 mi W of Gallatin. Incorporated in 1981.

Millertown	Community in central NE section of Knox County. 7 mi NE of Knoxville.
Mill Hollow	Located in S section of Benton County.
Millican Grove	Community in N section of Sevier County. 4 mi NE of Sevierville.
Milligan College	In SW area of Carter County. 6 mi SW of Elizabethton.
Millington	City in N section of Shelby County. 18 mi N NE of Memphis. Incorporated in 1903.
Mill Pond	Community in N section of Sullivan County. 3 1/2 mi N NW of Blountville.
Mill Seat	Community in NW corner of Maury County. 17 mi NW of Columbia.
Millsfield	Community in N central section of Dyer County. 7 mi N of Dyersburg.
Mill Spring	Community in N NW section of Jefferson County. 11 1/2 mi N NW of Dandridge.
Millstone	Community in SE area of Cumberland County. 13 mi E SE of Crossville.
Millstone Knob	Located near N border of Trousdale County. 2 mi W NW of Halltown.
Millstone Mountain	Mountain in N section of Tipton County. Approx. 2 mi N of Mount Lebanon.
Milltown	Community in E SE section of Humphreys County. 12 1/2 mi E SE of Waverly.
Milltown	Community on W border of Jackson County. 8 1/2 mi W NW of Gainesboro.
Mill Town	Community in SE section of Macon County. 9 mi E SE of Lafayette.
Milltown	Community in N NW section of Marshall County. 9 mi N of Lewisburg.
Millview	Community in middle E section of Williamson County. 5 1/2 mi E SE of Franklin.
Millville	Community on W border of Lincoln County. Approx. 13 mi W of Fayetteville.
Milo	Community in NE section of Bledsoe County. 12 mi NE of Pikeville.
Milton	Community in NE corner of Rutherford County. 13 1/2 mi E NE of Murfreesboro.
Milton Hollow	Located in SW section of Stewart County, E of

Milton Hollow, (Cont.)	Mulbury Hill.
Mimosa	Community in central NE section of Lincoln County. 5 1/2 mi N NE of Fayetteville.
Mimosa Heights	Community in N Central section of Blount County. 6 mi N of Maryville.
Mine Lick Creek	Creek in NE area of DeKalb County, flows into the Caney Fork River.
Mine Lick Creek	Creek in SW section of Putnam County, off Caney Fork River.
Mineral Park	Community in SE area of Bradley County near McDonald.
Mineral Springs	Community in middle S SE section of Marion County. 5 mi E NE of Jasper.
Mineral Springs	Community on S SE border of Obion County. 17 mi S SE of Livingston.
Mine Ridge	Ridge in S SW section of Cocke County, SW of Raven Branch.
Minersville	Located in N section of Anderson County.
Mingo Mountains	Mountains in N NW section of Claiborne County, S and E of Bryson Mountain.
Mingo Swamp	Swamp in middle W section of Franklin County. NE of Taylortown.
Minnick	Community in SW section of Obion County. 20 mi SW of Union City.
Minnow Ford	Community in S SW section of Giles County. Approx. 10 mi S SW of Pulaski.
Minor Hill	City in SW section of Giles County. 12 1/2 mi SW of Pulaski. Incorporated in 1968.
Mint	Community in SW section of Blount County. 9 mi S SW of Maryville.
Mint Hollow	Located in SW corner of Montgomery County. 2 1/2 mi W SW of Shiloh.
Minton Hill	Located in N section of Claiborne County. 3 mi S SW of Arthur.
Miry Ridge	Ridge in SW section of Sevier County, near border. 8 mi S SW of Gatlinburg. N of Cold Spring Knob.
Miser Station	Community in NW area of Blount County. 5 mi W of Alcoa.

Missionary Ridge	Ridge in S section of Hamilton County, within the city limits of Chattanooga. Runs from the Georgia Line into East Chattanooga.
Missionary Ridge	Ridge in N NE section of Hickman County.
Miston	Community in NW area of Dyer County. 11 mi NW of Dyersburg.
Mitchell	Community in NE corner of Robertson County. 19 mi E NE of Springfield.
Mitchell	Community in NW corner of Sumner County. Approx. 4 mi N NW of Portland.
Mitchell Creek	Creek in E section of Clay County off Dale Hollow Lake. 6 mi E of Celina.
Mitchell Hollow	Located in near center of Humphreys County. 3 mi E of Waverly.
Mitchell Knob	Mountain in NW section of Van Buren County.
Mitchell Lake	Lake in SW area of Dyer County on Moss Island.
Mitchell Spring	Community in NW section of Washington County. 8 1/2 mi NW of Jonesborough.
Mitchellville	City in NW corner of Sumner County. 18 mi N NW of Gallatin. Incorporated in 1909.
Mixie	Community in N section of Carroll County. 9 mi NE of Huntingdon.
Mobra	Community in E SE section of White County. 12 mi E SE of Sparta.
Moccasin	Community in middle N section of Wayne County. 6 mi N of Waynesboro.
Moccasin Bend	Community within the city limits of Chattanooga at the foot of Lookout Mountain in Hamilton County.
Mockingbird Hill	Community in Knox County. 5 1/2 mi SW of Knoxville.
Mocking Crow Mountain	Mountain in SW section of Monroe County, SE of Jalapa.
Model	Community in N NW section of Stewart County. 13 mi NW of Dover.
Moffatt	Community in middle SE section of Obion County. Approx. 7 mi S of Union City.
Mohawk	Community in W area of Greene County. 13 mi W of Greeneville.
Mohawk Crossroad	Community in W NW area of Greene County. 12 mi

Mohawk Crossroad, (Cont.)	W NW of Greeneville.
Mole	Community in E section of Hawkins County. 15 mi E NE of Rogersville.
Molina	Community in middle SE section of Lincoln County. 6 1/2 mi SW of Fayetteville.
Mona	Community in N section of Rutherford County. 9 1/2 mi N NW of Murfreesboro.
Monoville	Community in middle NW section of Smith County. 4 mi N NW of Carthage.
Monroe	Community in middle NE section of Overton County. 5 1/2 mi NE of Livingston.
Monroe County MONROE COUNTY	County Seat: Madisonville. Zip Code 37354. Located in Southeastern section of the State. Bounded by Polk, McMinn, Loudon and Blount Counties and the State of North Carolina to the East. Named in honor of James Monroe.
Monsanto Lake	Lake in middle NW section of Maury County. 7 mi N NW of Columbia.
Montague	Community in E Nashville, Davidson County.
Montague	Community in SW corner of Rhea County. 5 1/2 mi SW of Dayton.
Monteagle	Community in SW section of Grundy County and N NW corner of Marion County. 14 mi S SE of Altamont. Incorporated in 1962.
Monteith Ridge	Ridge in S SW section of Sevier County, near border. 9 mi S of Gatlinburg.
Monterey	City in E section of Putnam County. 13 mi E of Cookeville. Incorporated in 1901.
Monterey Lake	Lake in E section of Putnam County. 2 mi S of Monterey.
Montery Lake	Lake in W SW area of Fayette County near Shelby County line W SW of Canadaville.
Montezuma	Community in W Central section of Chester County. 4 1/2 mi SW of Henderson.
Montgomery	Community in SW area of Decatur County.
Montgomery Bell State Park	Located in SE section of Dickson County. E of Dickson.
Montgomery County MONTGOMERY COUNTY	County Seat: Clarksville. Zip Code 37040. Located on the North Central border of the State. Bounded by Robertson, Cheatham, Dickson, Houston and Stewart Counties and the

Montgomery County, (Cont.) — State of Kentucky to the North. Named in honor of Col. John Montgomeny.

Montgomery Junction — Community in E SE section of Scott County. 9 mi SE of Huntsville.

Monticello — Located in central section of Williamson County. 2 mi N of Franklin.

Montlake — Mountain and community in W central section of Hamilton County W of Soddy Daisy. 14 mi N NE of downtown Chattanooga.

Mont Milner Lake — Lake in E area of Franklin County. 13 mi E of Winchester, S of Jackson Lake.

Montpier Farms — Community in middle N NW section of Williamson County. 6 mi N NW of Franklin.

Montvale — Community in Center of Blount County. 4 mi S of Maryville.

Moodyville — Community in middle S section of Pickett County. 3 1/2 mi SE of Byrdstown.

Moon — Community in NW area of Dyer County. 13 1/2 mi NW of Dyersburg.

Mooney — Community in NW section of Wayne County. Approx. 9 mi NW of Waynesboro.

Mooneyham — Community in E NE section of Van Buren County. 7 mi E of Spencer.

Mooney Hollow — Located in N NW section of Humphreys County. S SE of Warden Hollow. 9 mi N NW of Waverly.

Moon Island — Island on Tennessee River, NW of Big Spring. In Meigs County.

Moons — Community in E NE section of Henry County, near Big Sandy River. 13 mi E NE of Paris.

Moore County — County Seat: Lynchburg. Zip Code 37352. Located in South Central section of the State. Bounded by Bedford, Coffee, Franklin and Lincoln Counties. Named in honor of Major General William Moore.

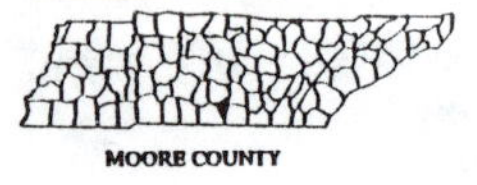

Moore Crossing — Located in S section of Marion County, E SE of New Hope.

Moorehead Hollow — Located in E NE section of Lincoln County, E of Douglas.

Moore Hollow — Located in central SW section of Dickson County. 4 mi SW of Dickson.

Moore Hollow — Located in NW section of Houston County, SE of Cotton Patch Crossroads.

Moore Hollow	Located in middle S section of Stewart County, S of Heddy Hollow.
Moore Hollow	Located in W SW section of Stewart County, S of Mulbury Hill.
Mooreland Heights	Community within the city limits of Knoxville. 3 mi S SE of downtown. In Knox County.
Mooresburg	Community in SW section of Hawkins County. 13 mi W SW of Rogersville.
Mooresburg Springs	Community in W section of Hawkins County. NW of Mooresburg.
Moores Camp	Community in NW Section of Anderson County, 8 mi NW of Oliver Springs.
Moores Chapel	Community in SE central section of Gibson County. 6 mi E SE of Trenton.
Moores College	Located in N section of Warren County. 10 mi N NE of McMinnville.
Mooresville	Community in W section of Marshall County. 7 mi W of Lewisburg.
Moore Switch	Community in central section of Hickman County. Approx. 2 mi N NW of Centerville.
Mooretown	Community in S Central section of Cannon County. 5 1/2 mi S of Woodbury.
Moor Hill	Located in W NW section of Rutherford County. 1 1/2 mi W SW of Hilltop.
Mooring	Community in SW section of Lake County. 5 mi S SW of Tiptonville.
Moorman	Community in N central section of Fayette County. 5 mi N NW of Somerville.
Morgan County MORGAN COUNTY	County Seat: Wartburg. Zip Code 37887. Located in middle East section of the State. Bounded by Scott, Anderson, Roane, Cumberland and Fentress Counties. Named in honor of Brig. General Daniel Morgan.
Morgan Hollow	Located in middle NW section of Humphreys County. 5 mi E of Trinity.
Morgan Ridge	Ridge in NW corner of Coffee County. N NW of Gossburg.
Morgan Springs	Community on W SW border of Rhea County. 7 1/2 mi NW of Dayton.
Morgansville	Community in Marion County located 6 mi N of Whitwell.

Morganton — Community in SE section of Loudon County. 9 1/2 mi SE of Loudon.

Morgantown — Community in SW section of Rhea County. W of Dayton.

Morley — Community in NE section of Campbell County. 5 mi E SE of Jellico.

Morningside Park — Park in middle E section of Knoxville. 1 1/2 mi NE of downtown. In Knox County.

Morny — Community in W NW section of Davidson County. 11 mi NW of Courthouse. 2 1/2 mi SW of Joelton.

Morris Chapel — Community in Central area of Benton County. 3 mi SE of Camden.

Morris Chapel — Community on NW border of Hardin County. 9 mi NW of Savannah. 2 1/2 mi NW of Right.

Morrison — City in SW section of Warren County. 10 mi SW of McMinnville. Incorporated in 1905.

Morrison City — Community on N NW border of Sullivan County. 14 mi W NW of Blountville.

Morrison Creek — Community in middle SE section of Jackson County. 4 mi E SE of Gainesboro.

Morristown — County Seat of Hamblen County. Located in central section of county. Incorporated in 1867.

Morrow Lake — Lake in central section of Maury County, S of Columbia.

Morton Hill — Community in middle S section of Haywood County, SW of Wallis.

Morton Knob — Located in E section of Williamson County. 11 mi E of Franklin, E of Potato Hill.

Morton Lake — Lake in middle NW section of Coffee County. NW of Manchester.

Moscow — City in S central section of Fayette County. 13 mi S of Somerville. Incorporated in 1860.

Mose Mountain — Mountain in central section of Monroe County, NE of Tellico Plains.

Mosheim — City in W central section of Greene County. 7 mi W NW of Greeneville. Incorporated in 1974.

Moshina Heights — Community in Knox County. 7 mi E NE of downtown Knoxville.

Mosquito Lake — Lake in W SW section of Shelby County, W of

Mosquito Lake, (Cont.)	Loosahatchie Bar.
Moss	Community in NW central section of Clay County. 7 mi NW of Celina.
Moss Bend	Area in bend of Caney Fork River in SE corner of Smith County. 2 mi E of Lancaster.
Moss Hollow	Located in N NW section of Humphreys County. 2 mi E of Halls Creek.
Moss Island	Located in SW section of Dyer County on Mississippi River.
Moss Island Wildlife Management Area	Located in SW section of Dyer County on Moss Island.
Motch	Community in N NW section of Claiborne County near border. N NE of Bryson Mountain.
Mountain City	County Seat of Johnson County. Located near center of County. Incorporated in 1905.
Mountain View	Community in middle W SW section of Scott County. 5 1/2 mi W SW of Huntsville.
Mount Airy	Community in Central section of Pickett County. Approx. 3 mi SE of Byrdstown.
Mount Airy	Community on NE border of Sequatchie County. 4 1/2 mi N NE of Dunlap.
Mount Ararat	Community in NE section of Cannon County near DeKalb County line. 9 mi NE of Woodbury.
Mount Belvoir	Community within the city limits of Chattanooga. 4 1/2 mi SE of downtown. In Hamilton County.
Mount Cammerer	Mountain in SW section of Cocke County on North Carolina line in the Great Smoky Mountains.
Mount Carmel	Community in SE area of Decatur County. 9 mi SE of Decaturville.
Mount Carmel	Community in SW area of Franklin County. 14 1/2 mi SW of Winchester.
Mount Carmel	Community in NW section of Greene County. 9 mi NW of Greeneville.
Mount Carmel	City in NE corner of Hawkins County. 22 mi NE of Rogersville. 4 mi NE of Church Hill. Incorporated in 1961.
Mount Carmel	Community in central E section of Tipton County. 4 1/2 mi S of Covington.

Mount Carmel	Community in S SW section of Washington County. 12 mi S SW of Jonesborough.
Mount Chapman	Mountain in SE corner of Sevier County. 8 mi SE of Pittman Center, S of Mount Guyot.
Mount Crest	Community in NW area of Bledsoe County. 5 mi NW of Pikeville.
Mount Davis	Mountain in SW corner of Sevier County. 12 mi S SW of Gatlinburg.
Mount Denson	Community in N central section of Robertson County. 2 1/2 mi N of Springfield.
Mount Gilead	Community in NW section of Henderson County. 10 mi NW of Lexington.
Mount Guyot	Mountain on E SE border of Sevier County. 14 mi E of Gatlinburg, in the Great Smoky Mountains. Ele. 6,621.
Mount Harmony	Community in N section of Bradley County. Approx. 10 mi N of Cleveland.
Mount Harmony	Community in E NE section of McMinn County. 6 mi NW of Athens.
Mount Harmony	Community in W SW section of Monroe County. 9 1/2 mi S of Madisonville. W of Tellico Plains.
Mount Helen	Community in E area of Fentress County. 12 1/2 mi E of Jamestown.
Mount Herman	Community in middle S SW section of Weakley County. 7 mi S SW of Dresden.
Mount Hope	Community in middle N section of Wayne County. 3 mi N of Waynesboro.
Mount Horeb	Community in middle section of Jefferson County. 5 mi N NW of Dandridge.
Mount Joy	Community on W SW border of Maury County. 14 mi SW of Columbia.
Mount Juliet	City in W section of Wilson County. 12 mi W of Lebanon. Incorporated in 1972.
Mount Lanier	Mountain in S section of Blount County.
Mount Lebanon	Community in E central section of Decatur County. 4 mi E SE of Decaturville.
Mount Lebanon	Community in middle W section of Lawrence County. Approx. 3 1/2 mi W NW of Gandy.
Mount Lebanon	Community in N section of Tipton County. 4 mi NW of Covington.

Mount LeConte	Mountain in S SE section of Sevier County. 3 mi SE of Gatlinburg, in the Great Smoky Mountains. Ele. 6,593.
Mount Mingus	Mountain in S section of Sevier County, S of Peregrine Peak. 7 mi S SE of Gatlinburg.
Mount Moriah	Community in SE area of Benton County. 7 mi SE of Camden.
Mount Moriah	Community in SW section of DeKalb County. 8 mi W SW of Smithville.
Mount Moriah	Community in NE area of Fayette County. 10 mi NE of Somerville.
Mount Nebo	Mountain in middle E section of Blount County, SE of Rocky Branch.
Mount Nebo	Community in SW section of Lawrence County. 18 mi SW of Lawrenceburg. 5 1/2 mi W SW of Loretto.
Mount Nebo	Community in W central section of Maury County. 8 mi W NW of Columbia.
Mount Olive	Community in N section of Grundy County. 6 mi N NE of Altamont.
Mount Olive	Community in S section of Knox County, S of Kingsley Station. 5 mi S of Knoxville.
Mount Olive	Community in NE central section of Marion County. 10 mi N NE of Jasper, W of Whitwell.
Mount Olive	Community in central NW section of Rutherford County. 3 mi NW of Murfreesboro.
Mount Orange	Community in W section of Gibson County. Approx. 4 mi W SW of Trenton.
Mount Pelia	Community in W section of Weakley County. 13 1/2 mi W of Dresden.
Mount Pisgah	Community in SW section of White County. 9 mi SW of Sparta. W of Doyle.
Mount Pleasant	Community in NW central section of Greene County near Mosheim. 4 mi W of Greeneville.
Mount Pleasant	Community on N border of Henry County. 13 1/2 mi N NE of Paris.
Mount Pleasant	City in middle SW section of Maury County. 11 mi W SW of Columbia. Incorporated in 1824.
Mount Pleasant	Community in middle S section of Scott County. 5 mi S SW of Huntsville.
Mount Roosevelt	Mountain on W border of Roane County.

Mount Roosevelt, (Cont.)	Elevation 2,036.
Mount Roosevelt State Forest	Located in SE area of Cumberland County on County line.
Mount Roosevelt State Forest	Located on NW border of Roane County.
Mount Roosevelt State Park	Located on S border of Morgan County.
Mount Sequoyah	Mountain on SE border of Sevier County. 12 mi E SE of Gatlinburg,in the Great Smoky Mountains. Ele. 5,945.
Mount Sinai	Community in S SW area of Dickson County. 12 1/2 mi S of Charlotte.
Mount Tabor	Community in middle NW area of Blount County. 3 mi W of Maryville.
Mount Tabor	Community in E central section of Decatur County.
Mount Tucker Addition	Community in N NE section of Sullivan County, S of Cross.
Mount Union	Community in SE section of Jackson County. 9 mi SE of Gainesboro.
Mount Union	Community in middle W section of Pickett. 2 1/2 mi S SE of Byrdstown.
Mount Vernon	Community in NW section of Blount County. 9 mi NW of Maryville.
Mount Vernon	Community in SW area of Coffee County. 6 mi SW of Manchester.
Mount Vernon	Community in SE area of Cumberland County. 16 mi E SE of Crossville.
Mount Vernon	Community in W SW section of Monroe County. 7 1/2 mi S of Madisonville.
Mount Vernon	Community in SW section of Rutherford County. 14 1/2 mi SW of Murfreesboro.
Mount Vernon	Community in middle NE section of Sumner County. 12 mi N NE of Gallatin.
Mount Vernon	Mountain in SE section of Wilson County. 2 mi S SW of Watertown.
Mount View	Community in SE section of Davidson County. 11 1/2 mi SE of Courthouse.
Mount View	Community in SW section of Grundy County. 12 mi SW of Altamont.

Mount Vinson	Community in middle E section of McNairy County. 11 mi E of Selmer.
Mount Zion	Community in NE area of Cheatham County. 7 mi NE of Ashland City.
Mount Zion	Community in SE area of Cumberland County.
Mount Zion	Community in SE section of Lawrence County. 13 mi S SE of Lawrenceburg.
Mount Zion	Community in NE corner of McNairy County. Approx. 17 mi NE of Selmer.
Mount Zion	Community in NE Section of Monroe County. Approx. 10 mi E of Madisonville.
Mount Zion	Community in S section of Montgomery County. S of Cunningham.
Mount Zion	Community in middle W section of Sevier County. 3 mi S of Sevierville.
Mount Zion	Community in S SW section of Warren County. 8 mi S SW of McMinnville.
Mount Zion Ridge	Ridge in W NW section of Bradley County, W of Eureka.
Mourbury	Community in E SE section of White County. 12 mi E SE of Sparta.
Mouse Creek Ridge	Ridge in NE section of Bradley County, E of Candies Creek Ridge and extends into SW section of McMinn County, W of Riceville.
Mousetail State Park	Located on W border of Perry County. On the Tennessee River near Perryville.
Mowbray	Community in W central section of Hamilton County on top of Mowbray Mountain. NW of Soddy Daisy. 17 mi N NE of downtown Chattanooga.
Mowbray Mountain	Mountain in W central section of Hamilton County. NW of Soddy Daisy.
Mud Bottom	Community in S SW section of Giles County. Approx. 14 mi S SW of Pulaski.
Mud Creek	Community in NE area of Coffee County. 9 1/2 mi N NE of Manchester.
Muddy Bottom	Located in NE section of Fayette County.
Muddy Creek Ridge	Ridge in E NE section of Rhea County, E of Spring City.
Muddy Creek Watershed Lake	Lake in SE corner of Hardeman County. 3 mi SE of Middleton.

Muddy Pond	Community in E SE section of Overton County. 17 mi SE of Livingston.
Mud Hollow	Located in W SW section of Sumner County. 2 mi SW of Two Chestnut.
Mud Island	Island on Mississippi River in Memphis, N of Downtown. In Shelby County.
Mud Lake	Lake in SW corner of Shelby County on the Mississippi State Line.
Mudsink	Community in middle E section of Williamson County. 3 1/2 mi E of Franklin.
Mudtavern	Community in E Nashville, Davidson County.
Mudville	Community in N NE section of Shelby County. E NE of Barretville.
Muex Corner	Community in SW corner of Haywood County. 13 mi SW of Brownsville. 1 1/2 mi S of Stanton.
Mulberry	Community NE section of Lincoln County. 7 1/2 mi NE of Fayetteville.
Mulberry Gap	Community in SE section of Cocke County.
Mulberry Hill	Community in W SW section of Stewart County. 8 mi W SW of Dover.
Mule Hollow	Community in central section of Knox County. SE border of Knoxville, NW of Ramsey.
Mule Lot Hollow	Located in N section of Humphreys County. 1 mi E SE of Woolworth.
Mullberry Gap	Community in N central section of Hancock County. 4 mi N NW of Sneedville. 1 mi from Virginia Border.
Mullens Cove	Located in E SE section of Marion County on the Tennessee River (Nickajack Lake). 8 mi E of Jasper.
Mulloy	Community on E NE border of Robertson County. 15 mi E NE of Springfield.
Mulloy	Community in W NW section of Sumner County. Approx. 6 mi W SW of Portland.
Munford	City in S SW section of Tipton County. 12 1/2 mi SW of Covington. Incorporated in 1905.
Mungers Pond	Lake on S border of Meigs County. 16 mi S SW of Decatur.
Murfreesboro	County Seat of Rutherford County. Located in near center of county. Incorporated in 1817.

Murphy Hills	Community in Knox County. 7 1/2 mi N of downtown Knoxville.
Murphys Chapel	Community in Sevier County, 5 mi SE of Sevierville.
Murray Hills	Community with city limits of Chattanooga. 7 1/2 mi E NE of downtown in Highway 58 area of Hamilton County.
Murray Store	Community in N section of McMinn County. 12 mi N NW of Athens.
Myatt Hollow	Located in SW section of Dickson County. 3 mi S of Tennessee City.
Myers	Community in middle N section of Franklin County, W of Decherd.
Naillon Town	Community in SW area of Cocke County.
Nameless	Community in S SW section of Jackson County. 7 1/2 mi S SW of Gainesboro.
Nance	Community in N Central section of Crockett County. 3 1/2 mi N of Alamo.
Nance Bend	Located in N NE section of Hardin County, NE of Havana.
Nance Ferry	Community in SW area of Grainger County on the Holston River.
Nances Grove	Community in NW section of Jefferson County. 12 1/2 mi NW of Dandridge.
Nankipoo	Community in NE section of Lauderdale County. 9 1/2 mi N NE of Ripley.
Napier	Community on S border of Lewis County. 9 mi S SE of Hohenwald.
Napier Lake	Lake in SE section of Lewis County. 7 1/2 mi S SE of Hohenwald.
Narrod Mountain	Mountain in SE section of Overton County, NW of Hanging Limb.
Narrows Knob	Mountain in S SW section of Johnson County, E NE of Dry Hill.
Narrows of the Harpeth State Park	Located in middle S section of Cheatham County, N of Kingston Springs.
Narrow Valley	Community in E central section of Grainger County. 5 mi E of Rutledge.
Nash	Community in S SW section of Putnam County. 11 mi SW of Cookeville.

Nashville	County seat of Davidson County and the State Capital. Located near center of county. Incorporated in 1806.
Natchez Trace State Park	Located in SW area of Benton County, extends into SE section of Carroll County and the NE corner of Henderson County.
Nathan Bedford Forrest State Park	Located on E Border of Benton County on Kentucky Lake. 7 mi NE of Camden
Natural Bridge	Community in N area of Cocke County. 8 mi NE of Newport.
Nauvoo	Community in central section of Dyer County. 4 mi N NW of Dyersburg.
Neapolis	Community in NE section of Maury County. 7 1/2 mi NE of Columbia.
Nebo Knobs	Located in S section of Rutherford County. N NW of Fosterville.
Neboville	Community in W area of Gibson County. 12 mi W NW of Trenton.
Neddy Mountain	Mountain in N NE section of Cocke County, SW of Baltimore.
Needmore	Community in NE section of Hamblen County. 9 1/2 mi NE of Morristown.
Needmore	Community on S border of Hawkins County. 5 1/2 mi SE of Rogersville.
Needmore	Community in central section of Marshall County. W of Lewisburg.
Needmore	Community in W SW section of Maury County. 12 1/2 mi W SW of Columbia.
Needmore	Community in SE section of McNairy County. Approx. 10 mi SE of Selmer.
Needmore	Community in NE section of Montgomery County. 4 1/2 mi N NE of Clarksville.
Needmore	Community in W SW section of Montgomery County. 12 1/2 mi W SW of Clarksville.
Needmore	Community in W NW section of Wilson County. 16 mi W of Lebanon.
Neely	Community in middle SW section of Madison County. 9 mi SW of Jackson.
Neely Crossroads	Community on S SE border of Clay County near Overton County line. 4 1/2 mi SE of Celina.
Neelys Bend	Located in E NE section of Davidson County, NW

Neelys Bend, (Cont.)	of Hermitage.
Negro Hollow	Located in S section of Houston County. Approx. 6 mi SW of Erin.
Negro Hollow	Located in N NW section of Macon County. 1 mi W of Haysville.
Neil Spring Hollow	Located in E NE section of Benton County.
Nenny	Community in E section of Hamblen County. 9 mi E NE of Morristown.
Neptune	Community in NW area of Cheatham County. 9 mi W NW of Ashland City.
Nero Hill	Located in SW section of Stewart County, E of Palmer Hollow.
Netherland	Community in S SW section of Overton County. 10 mi S SW of Livingston.
Neva	Community in S section of Johnson County. 6 mi S SW of Mountain City.
Neville Bay	Lake in N NW section of Stewart County. N of Tharpe.
Newbern	City in E NE area of Dyer County, 9 mi NE of Dyersburg. Incorporated in 1887.
New Bethel	Community in SW area of Fayette County.
New Bethel	Community in S SE section of McMinn County. Approx. 9 mi S SE of Athens. SW of Etowah.
New Bethel	Community in S SW section of Sullivan County. Approx. 6 mi SW of Bluff City.
New Boston	Community in W section of Henry County, SE of Cottage Grove.
Newburg Ridge	Ridge in S section of Lewis County, N of Oak Grove.
New Canton	Community in NE section of Hawkins County. 16 mi NE of Rogersville.
Newcastle	Community in W central section of Hardeman County near Fayette County border. 11 mi W SW of Bolivar. 5 mi W NW of Middleburg.
Newcomb	Community in NW section of Campbell County. 3 mi SW of Jellico.
New Corinth	Community in SW area of Grainger County. 8 mi SW of Rutledge.
New Deal	Community in W NW section of Sumner County. 11 mi NW of Gallatin.

New Dellrose	Community on W SW border of Lincoln County. 14 mi W SW of Fayetteville. (Dellrose P. O.)
Newell Station	Community in W NW section of Sevier County. 11 mi W of Sevierville.
New Enterprize	Community in SE central section of Gibson County. 7 1/2 mi SE of Trenton.
New Era	Community in S SW section of Cumberland County. 11 mi S of Crossville.
New Era	Community in middle NW section of Sevier County. Approx. 2 mi W SW of Sevierville.
New Era Ridge	Ridge in SW section of Perry County, NE of Peters Landing.
New Flys Village	Community in NW section of Maury County. 14 mi NW of Columbia.
Newfound Gap	Mountain in S SE section of Sevier County. 9 mi SE of Gatlinburg,in the Great Smoky Mountains. Ele. 5,046.
New Friendship	Community in N area of Chester County. 5 1/2 mi N of Henderson.
New Harmony	Community in E Central section of Bledsoe County. 6 mi SE of Pikeville near Rhea County Line.
New Harmony	Community in N central section of Hardin County, E NE of Cerro Gordo, NW of Crossroads.
New Harony	Community in middle SW section of Macon County. 4 1/2 mi SW of Lafayette.
New Haven	Community in NW section of Lawrence County. 13 mi W NW of Lawrenceburg.
New Haven	Community in middle NW section of Scott County. 7 mi N NW of Huntsville.
New Haven	Community in central NE section of Stewart County. 2 mi NW of Dover.
New Herman	Community in S Central area of Bedford County near Moore County line. 10 mi S of Shelbyville.
New Hope	Community in W NW section of Benton County. Approx. 4 mi N of Big Sandy.
New Hope	Community in NW area of Cheatham County near Montogomery County line. 6 mi W of Cheap Hill.
New Hope	Community in S central section of Hancock County. 4 1/2 mi SE of Sneedville. 3 1/2 mi E N NE of Luther.

New Hope	Community on W central border of Hardin County. 5 mi W SW of Savannah.
New Hope	Community in S section of Hawkins County. 8 mi E of Rogersville.
New Hope	Community in SE section of Henry County, NE of Mansfield.
New Hope	Community in W section of Houston County. Approx. 9 mi SW of Erin.
New Hope	Community in E section of Humphreys County. 9 mi E SE of Waverly.
New Hope	Community in E NE section of Jackson County. 8 1/2 mi E NE of Gainesboro.
New Hope	Community in S SE section of Lincoln County. 9 mi S SE of Fayetteville.
New Hope	City in S SW section of Marion County. 5 mi S SW of Jasper. Incorporated in 1974.
New Hope	Community in S SE section of McNairy County. Approx. 9 mi S SE of Selmer.
New Hope	Community in middle NE section of Montgomery County. 6 mi E NE of Clarksville.
New Hope	Community in middle W section of Roane County. 7 1/2 mi W SW of Kingston.
New Hope	Community on S border of Sequatchie County. 8 mi S of Dunlap.
New Hope	Community in W NW section of Williamson County. 17 mi W NW of Franklin.
New Hope Hollow	Located in S Sw section of Houston County, S of New Hope.
New Johnsonville	City on W SW border of Humphreys County. 10 mi W SW of Waverly. Incorporated in 1949.
New Lawton	Community in middle E NE section of McNairy County. 7 1/2 mi E NE of Selmer.
New Line R.R.	Located in central section of Hamblen County near Morristown.
New Loyston	Community in SW section of Union County. 7 mi S SW of Maynardville.
Newman Hollow	Located in W NW section of Dickson County. 3 1/2 mi N of Adams Crossroads.
Newman Ridge	Ridge in N NE section of Hancock County into the State of Virginia.

Newman Ridge	Ridge in W section of Hancock County. 7 mi W of Sneedville.
Newmansville	Community in NE central section of Greene County. 9 mi NE of Greeneville.
New Market	City in middle W NW section of Jefferson County. 10 mi NW of Dandridge. Incorporated in 1977.
New Markham	Community in NE section of Lake County. 7 mi NE of Tiptonville.
New Middleton	Community in middle SW section of Smith County. 6 mi S SW of Carthage.
New Midway	Community in middle E section of Roane County. 6 mi E SE of Kingston.
New Point	Community in NE section of Hamilton County. 24 mi NE of downtown Chattanooga. SW of Georgetown.
Newport	County Seat of Cocke County. Located in W central section of County. Incorporated in 1832.
Newport Camp	Community in NE section of Rhea County. 24 1/2 mi NE of Dayton.
New Prospect	Community in E section of Lawrence County. 5 mi S SE of Lawrenceburg.
New Providence	Community in middle NW section of Loudon County. 3 mi N NW of Loudon.
New Providence	Community within the City of Clarksville, S section. In Montgomery County.
New River	Community in SW central section of Scott County. 4 mi SW of Huntsville.
New Safford	Community on NE border of Henderson County. 12 1/2 mi E NE of Lexington.
New Salem	Community in central section of Hamilton County. 16 mi N NE of downtown Chattanooga.
New Salem	Community in middle S section of Jackson County. 3 mi S of Gainesboro.
New Salem	Community in E NE section of Scott County. 7 mi E NE of Huntsville.
Newsom	Community in SW area of Davidson County.
New Tazewell	City in central section of Claiborne County, W SW of Tazewell. Incorporated in 1915.
Newton	Community in SW area of Cumberland County. 15

Newton, (Cont.)	mi SW of Crossville.
Newton	Community in SE corner of Polk County. N of Copperhill.
Newtown	Community in NW area of Bedford County on Rutherford County line. 12 mi NW of Bell Buckle, 14 mi N of Shelbyville.
New Town	Community in N section of Savannah in Hardin County.
New Town	Community in S SW central section of Marshall County. 6 mi S SW of Lewisburg.
New Town	Community on N NE border of Maury County. E of Spring Hill.
Newtown	Community on S SW border of Rutherford County. 13 mi S SW of Murfreesboro.
New Town	Community on S border of Williamson County. Approx. 11 mi S of Franklin.
New Union	Community in Central section of Coffee County. 4 mi N of Manchester.
New Victory	Community in central S SW section of Washington County. 5 mi S SW of Jonesborough.
New Zion	Community in NW area of Carroll County. 6 mi NW of Huntingdon.
New Zion	Community in middle W NW section of Macon County. 9 mi W NW of Lafayette.
Nichols Hollow	Located on W NW border of Humphreys County, W of Brake Hollow. 7 mi W NW of Waverly.
Nichols Mountain	Mountain in SE section of Knox County near border, S of Shooks.
Nickajack Dam	Dam in S section of Marion County on the Tennessee River. 4 1/2 mi S of Jasper.
Nickajack Lake	Formed by the Nickajack Dam on the Tennessee River. Backs up to the Chickamauga Dam. Flows through downtown Chattanooga in Hamilton County.
Nickajack Lake	Lake formed by the Nickajack Dam on the Tennessee River. Backs up to the Chickamauga Dam in Chattanooga. Located in Marion County and Hamilton County.
Nickens Hollow	Located near W NW border of Davidson County. 2 mi N of Gower Island.
Nickletown	Community in S central section of Marion County. 2 mi E NE of Jasper.

Nicks Creek	Community in SW section of Campbell County. 14 mi W SW of LaFollette.
Nine Mile	Community in N Central section of Bledsoe County. 8 mi NE of Pikeville, 3 1/2 mi S of Melvine.
Nine Mile Ridge	Ridge in SE section of Hickman County.
Ninth Model	Community located 9 mi E NE of Manchester in Coffee County.
Niota	City in E NE section of McMinn County. 6 mi N NE of Athens. Incorporated in 1911.
Nixon	Community in SW section of Hardin County. 7 mi S of Savannah. 3 mi N of Pickwick Landing Dam.
Noah	Community in W area of Coffee County. 9 mi NW of Manchester.
Nobles	Community in NE central section of Henry County. 7 mi NE of Paris.
No Business Knob	Mountain in S section of Unicoi County, E of Ernestville.
Nolan Hollow	Located in E section of Humphreys County. 3 mi SE of McEwen.
Nolensville	Community in E NE section of Williamson County. 11 1/2 mi E NE of Franklin.
Nolichucky Dam	Dam on Nolichucky River in S section of Greene County. 8 mi S of Greeneville.
Nolichucky River	Flows from the State of North Carolina through Unicoi County, into Washington County, westward into Greene County, westward forming county lines for Hamblen, Cocke and Jefferson Counties and then flows into the French Broad River at Douglas Lake.
Nonaburg	Community in E section of McMinn County. 8 mi E SE of Athens.
Nonaville	Community in W NW section of Wilson County. 14 mi W NW of Lebanon.
No Pone Ridge	Ridge in E section of Meigs County, E of Goodfield.
Norene	Community in S section of Wilson County. 11 mi S SE of Lebanon.
Norma	Community in middle E SE section of Scott County. 7 1/2 mi SE of Huntsville.
Normandy	Town in SE section of Bedford County near Coffee County line. 11 mi E of Shelbyville.

Normandy, (Cont.)	Incpororated in 1921.
Normandy Lake	Lake on the Bedford County, Coffee County line. 12 mi E of Shelbyville.
Norris	City in NE area of Anderson County, 7 mi NE of Clinton. Incorporated in 1949.
Norris Dam	Dam on Clinch River on S border of Campbell County and N border of Anderson County.
Norris Dam State Park	Located in S section of Campbell County. 8 mi S SE of Jacksboro and extends into NE area of Anderson County.
Norris Lake	Lake across middle section of Union County (Clinch River).
Northbrook	Community in Knox County. 7 1/2 mi N NW of downtown Knoxville.
North Chattanooga	Community within the city limits of Chattanooga. 1 1/2 mi N of downtown. In Hamilton County.
North Chickamauga Creek	Creek in S central section of Hamilton County. Flows from Falling Water area into the Tennessee River S of Chickamauga Dam.
Northcott	Community in NW section of Sullivan County. Approx. 3 mi N of Kingsport.
North Cross Creek	Creek in middle E SE section of Stewart County. E of Bear Spring.
Northcutts Cove	Community in N section of Grundy County. 5 mi N of Altamont.
Northern Hills	Community within the city limits of Chattanooga on N border. Approx. 9 mi N NE of downtown. In Hamilton County.
North Etowah	Community in SE section of McMinn County. Approx. 7 mi SE of Athens. N of Etowah.
North Fork	Community in E SE section of Hawkins County. 4 mi SE of Surgoinsville.
North Hills	Community within the city limits of Knoxville. 3 1/2 mi N NE of downtown. In Knox County.
North Horn Lake	Lake in SW section of Shelby County near the State Line.
North Knoxville	Community within the city limits of Knoxville. 3 mi N of downtown. In Knox County.
Northpoint	Community in NW corner of Monroe County. N of Sweetwater.

North Riverside	Community in S SW section of Lewis County. 7 1/2 mi S SW of Hohenwald.
Northshore	Community within the city limits of Chattanooga near Lake Chickamauga. 8 mi NE of downtown. In Hamilton County.
Northshore Woods	Community in Knox County. 7 mi SW of Knoxville.
North Springs	Community in NW section of Jackson County. 9 mi NW of Gainesboro.
Norwood	Community in S SW section of Anderson County. 2 mi E of Oliver Springs.
Norwood	Community within city limits of Knoxville, NW of Lonsdale. In Knox County.
Norwood	Community with in the city limits of Knoxville. 4 mi NW of downtown. In Knox County.
Notchy Creek	Community in W section of Monroe County. 3 1/2 mi S of Madisonville.
Notchy Creek Knob	Located in W NW section of Monroe County, E of Notchy Creek.
Notchy Creek Knobs	Located in middle N section of Monroe County, SE of Hopewell Springs.
Nough	Community in SE section of Cocke County. 2 1/2 mi S SW of French Broad River. 11 1/2 mi SE of Newport.
Nubbin Ridge	Ridge in NW corner of Giles County.
Nubbin Ridge	Ridge in W section of Humphreys County. 2 mi N of Denver.
Nubia	Community in N section of Sumner County. 18 mi N NE of Gallatin.
Number One	Community in Sumner County.. Located approx. 6 mi E NE of Hendersonville.
Nunley Mountain	Mountain in S section of Warren County and N section of Grundy County.
Nunnelly	Community in N central section of Hickman County. 5 1/2 mi N of Centerville.
Nutbush	Community on middle NW border of Haywood County. 10 1/2 mi NW of Brownsville.
O'Neal Hollow	Located in central E section of Humphreys County. 1 1/2 mi S of Gorman.
O'Ryan Knob	Located in middle W section of Sumner County.

O'Ryan Knob, (Cont.)	E of Cottontown.
Oak City	Community in W NW section of Sevier County. 8 1/2 mi W NW of Sevierville.
Oakdale	Community in middle W NW section of Macon County. 6 mi W NW of Lafayette.
Oakdale	City in S SE section of Morgan County. 8 1/2 mi S SE of Wartburg. Incorporated in 1911.
Oak Dale	Community in middle NE section of Overton County. 7 mi E NE of Livingston.
Oakdale	Community in E SE section of Robertson County. 9 1/2 mi E SE of Springfield.
Oakdale	Community in central SW section of White County. 1 1/2 mi S SW of Sparta.
Oakfield	Community in N central section of Madison County. 7 mi N of Jackson.
Oak Grove	Community in S Central section of Campbell County near Anderson County Line. 5 mi SE of Jacksboro.
Oak Grove	Community in SW area of Carter County. 5 mi SW of Elizabethton.
Oak Grove	Community in S central section of Chester County. 4 mi SE of Henderson.
Oak Grove	Community in NE Section of Claiborne County. 8 mi NE of Tazewell.
Oak Grove	Community in NW area of Clay County. 11 1/2 mi W NW of Celina.
Oak Grove	Community in SW area of Dickson County, 14 1/2 mi SW of Charlotte.
Oak Grove	Community in NE section of Franklin County. 8 mi NE of Winchester.
Oak Grove	Community in SW area of Giles County. 8 1/2 mi S SE of Pulaski.
Oak Grove	Community in NW central section of Hardin County. 3 1/2 mi N of Savannah.
Oak Grove	Community in E central section of Henderson County. 3 1/2 mi E of Lexington.
Oak Grove	Community in NE central section of Henry County. 11 mi NE of Paris.
Oak Grove	Community in E section of Jefferson County. 3 mi E NE of Dandridge.

Oak Grove	Community in Knox County. 6 1/2 mi N NE of downtown Knoxville.
Oak Grove	Community in SW section of Lauderdale County. 18 mi W SW of Ripley.
Oak Grove	Community in S section of Lewis County. 6 1/2 mi S SE of Hohenwald.
Oak Grove	Community in N section of Loudon County. 4 1/2 mi N NE of Loudon.
Oak Grove	Community in W central section of Madison County. 4 1/2 mi W of Jackson.
Oak Grove	Community in middle E section of Marion County. 7 1/2 mi E NE of Jasper.
Oak Grove	Community in N NW section of Marion County. 12 mi N NW of Jasper.
Oak Grove	Community in N NW section of Monroe County. 5 mi N NE of Madisonville.
Oak Grove	Community in center E section of Overton County. 4 mi E of Livingston.
Oak Grove	Community in E section of Overton County. 7 1/2 mi E of Livingston.
Oak Grove	Community in SW section of Pickett County. 5 1/2 mi S SW of Byrdstown.
Oak Grove	Community in middle NW section of Polk County. 2 mi E NE of Benton.
Oak Grove	Community located in near center of Shelby County. 14 mi E NE of Memphis.
Oak Grove	Community in N section of Sumner County. 13 mi N NE of Gallatin.
Oak Grove	Community in middle N section of Union County. 7 mi N NW of Maynardville.
Oak Grove	Community in W section of Warren County. 10 1/2 mi W of McMinnville.
Oak Grove	Community in N section of Washington County. 9 mi N NE of Jonesborough.
Oak Grove Heights	Community in Knox County. 10 mi W of Knoxville.
Oak Grove Mountain	Mountain in E central section of Overton County. 3 mi E of Livingston.
Oak Hill	Community in SE area of Carter County. 8 mi S of Elizabethton.

Oak Hill	Community in E NE area of Cocke County.
Oak Hill	Community in central section of Cumberland County. 3 mi N NE of Crossville.
Oak Hill	City in S area of Davidson County, 6 mi S of Courthouse. Incorporated in 1952.
Oak Hill	Community in NE corner of Henry County. 16 mi NE of Paris.
Oak Hill	Community in central E SE section of Lawrence County. Approx. 6 mi SE of Lawrenceburg.
Oak Hill	Community in E section of Marshall County. Approx. 5 mi E of Lewisburg.
Oak Hill	Community in S SW section of Overton County. 8 mi S of Livingston.
Oak Hill	Community in NW corner of Pickett County. 5 mi W NW of Byrdstown.
Oak Hill	Community in SW section of Roane County. Approx. 11 mi S SW of Kingston.
Oak Hill	Community in NW section of Washington County. 8 mi W NW of Jonesborough.
Oakhurst	Community in N Central section of Blount County near Maryville.
Oakland	City in W central section of Fayette County. 9 1/2 mi W of Somerville. Incorporated in 1919.
Oakland	Community in S area of Grainger County. 7 mi S SE of Rutledge.
Oakland	Community in E central section of Henry County. 5 1/2 mi E SE of Paris.
Oakland	Community in central section of Jefferson County. 4 mi NW of Dandridge.
Oakland	Community within the City Limits of Knoxville, N central section W of Beverly in Knox County.
Oakland	Community in N NE section of Montgomery County. 7 mi NE of Clarksville.
Oakland	Community in central E SE section of Robertson County. 3 mi E SE of Springfield.
Oakland	Community in W central section of Warren County. 2 1/2 mi W of McMinnville.
Oakland	Community in W section of Washington County. 8 1/2 mi W SW of Jonesborough.
Oakland	Community in N NW section of Wilson County. 5

Oakland, (Cont.)	mi N NW of Lebanon.
Oaklawn	Community in W NW section of Shelby County. 10 mi N of Memphis.
Oakley	Community in N section of Overton County. 8 1/2 mi N of Livingston.
Oak Park	Community in SW area of Coffee County near Tullahoma.
Oak Park	Community in NW area of Franklin County.
Oak Plains	Community on E SE border of Montgomery County. 12 mi E SE of Clarksville.
Oak Ridge	City in SW area of Anderson County and NE area of Roane County. 4 mi SE of Oliver Springs. U.S. Energy Commission located here. Incorporated in 1959.
Oakridge	Community in SW section of Montgomery County. NE of Shiloh.
Oak View	Community in NE area of Blount County. 8 mi E NE of Maryville.
Oakview	Community in middle NW section of Haywood County. 5 mi NW of Brownsville.
Oakview	Community in N section of Sullivan County. 2 mi N NW of Blountville.
Oakville	Community within the city limits of Memphis. W of Parkway Village. In Shelby County.
Oakwood	Community in W NW section of Montgomery County. 12 mi W of Clarksville.
Oakwood Acres Lake	Lake in SE central section of Lincoln County. 3 mi SE of Fayetteville.
Oakwood Estates	Community in middle S section of Williamson County. 3 mi S of Franklin.
Obed River	Located in S central section of Morgan County, W SW of Wartburg and S of Lancing.
Obey City	Community in SE corner of Overton County. 17 mi SE of Livingston.
Obey River	Flows into Cumberland River NW of Celina. Dale Hollow Dam backs river up forming Dale Hollow Lake. Flows through Clay, Pickett, Overton and Fentress Counties.
Obion	City in middle S section of Obion County. 13 1/2 mi S SW of Union City. Incorporated in 1899.

Obion County

County Seat: Union City. Zip Code 38261. Located in Northwestern section of the State. Bounded by Weakley, Gibson, Dyer and Lake Counties and the State of Kentucky to the North. Named in honor of the Obion River.

Obion River — River flowing from NE border of Dyer County to the Mississippi River in SW of County.

Ocana — Community in SW section of Sumner County. 6 mi W of Gallatin.

Ocoee — Community on W border of Polk County. 5 mi S SW of Benton.

Ocoee Dam No. 1 — Dam in W SW section of Polk County. 5 mi S of Benton near Parksville on the Ocoee River.

Ocoee Dam No. 2 — Dam in middle S section of Polk County. 11 mi E SE of Benton on Ocoee River.

Ocoee Dam No. 3 — Dam in S SE section of Polk County. 14 mi SE of Benton on Ocoee River.

Ocoee River — Flows from North Georgia into Tennessee near Copperhill, thru Polk County into the Hiwassee River North of Benton.

Odd Fellows Hall — Community in NE area of Giles County.

Odle Hollow — Located in SE section of Benton County.

Odoms Bend — Located in S SE section of Sumner County. S SE of Gallatin.

Officer Orchard Ridge — Ridge in E section of Putnam County, E of Monterey.

Officers Chapel — Community in N NE section of Putnam County. 7 mi NE of Cookeville.

Offutt — Community in N Central section of Anderson County. 4 mi SE of Lake City.

Ogden — Community in SW section of Rhea County. 5 i W NW of Dayton.

Oglesby — Community in SE area of Davidson County.

Okeena Park — Community in central section of Dyer County near Dyersburg.

Okolona — Community in W area of Carter County. 7 mi SW of Elizabethton.

Okolona — Community in NE section of Hawkins County. 18 mi NE of Rogersville.

Okolona — Community in middle SW section of Overton County. 4 mi S of Livingston.

Okra	Community in N NW section of Pickett County. Approx. 3 mi N NW of Byrdstown.
Old Antoich	Community in NE section of Jackson County. 8 mi E NE of Gainesboro.
Old Black	Mountain in SW corner of Cocke County on Sevier County and North Carolina line in Great Smokey Mountains. Elev. 6370 ft.
Old Center	Community in NE area of Davidson County.
Old Chilhowee	Community in NE area of Blount County. 11 mi E of Maryville.
Old Cumberland	Community in W Central section of Bledsoe County. 10 mi W SW of Pikeville.
Olde Mill	Community in Hamilton County. 10 mi N NE of downtown Chattanooga.
Old Englewood	Community in E section of McMinn County, S of Englewood.
Oldfort	Community in W SW section of Polk County. 9 mi S SW of Benton.
Old Fremont	Community in middle W NW section of Obion County. 7 mi W of Union City.
Old Glory	Community in NW area of Blount County. 4 mi NW of Maryville.
Oldhams Creek - aka Boogertown	Community central section of Sevier County. 8 mi SE of Sevierville.
Old Hickory	Community in upper E section of Davidson County. 11 mi NE of Courthouse.
Old Hickory Dam	Located in NE section of Davidson County on Cumberland River.
Old Hickory Lake	Lake in NE area of Davidson County and S SW section of Sumner County, SE of Hendersonville (Cumberland River).
Old Hickory Wildlife Management Area	Located in SE section of Sumner County. Approx. 7 mi E SE of Gallatin.
Old Hollow Mill	Community in Mid W section of Franklin County.
Old Lawton	Community in middle E NE section of McNairy County. 7 1/2 mi E NE of Selmer.
Old Mill Hollow	Located in middle W section of Humphreys County. 1 mi E of Pursley.
Old Patty	Community in NW section of Polk County. Approx. 4 mi N of Benton.

Old River Lake	Lake in N NE section of Dyer County near Obion County line.
Old Salem	Community in SW section of Franklin County. 10 1/2 mi SW of Winchester.
Old Sam Hollow	Located in SW section of Dickson County. 2 mi W of Oak Grove.
Old Springville	Community in E section of Henry County. 10 mi E of Paris.
Old Stone Fort State Park	Located in SW area of Manchester in Coffee County.
Old Sweetwater	Community in NW corner of Monroe County. N NE of Sweetwater.
Oldtown	Community in W NW section of Cocke County. 2 1/2 mi N NE of Newport.
Old Washington	Community in SE section of Rhea County. 7 mi E NE of Dayton.
Old Winesap	Community in SW area of Cumberland County. 13 mi S SW of Crossville.
Old Zion	Community in middle W NW section of White County. 6 1/2 mi W NW of Sparta.
Olivehill	Community in E NE section of Hardin County. 12 1/2 mi N NE of Savannah.
Oliver Springs	City located in W Central section of Anderson County on Morgan County line. 3 mi W NW of Oak Ridge. Incorporated in 1905. Boundaries also extend into Morgan and Roane Counties.
Olivet	Community in N central section of Giles County.
Olivet	Community in center of Hardin County. 2 1/2 mi E of Savannah.
Oneida	City in middle N section of Scott County. 6 mi N NW of Huntsville. Incorporated in 1913.
Only	Community in NW section of Hickman County. 13 1/2 mi W NW of Centerville, S of Bucksnort.
Ooltewah	Community in SE section of Hamilton County. 15 mi E of downtown Chattanooga, N of Collegedale.
Open Lake	Lake in W NW section of Lauderdale County. 9 1/2 mi W NW of Ripley.
Open Pond	Pond in SE corner of Decatur County on Clifton Bend.

Opossum Hollow	Located in SW section of Stewart County, N of Leatherwood Creek.
Opossum Island	Island on Dale Hollow Lake. 8 mi E NE of Celina in Clay County.
Oppossum	Community in SE section of Lauderdale County. 3 mi S SW of Ripley.
Oral	Community on E border of Roane County. 9 1/2 mi E SE of Kingston.
Orchard Hollow	Located in middle S section of Stewart County, E of Bluegrass Ridge.
Orchard Knob	Community in N NE section of Roane County. 1 mi NE of Kingston.
Orebank	Community in middle N NW section of Sullivan County. 7 1/2 mi W NW of Blountville.
Ore Springs	Community in E section of Weakley County. Approx. 7 mi E of Dresden.
Orgains Crossroads	Community in middle S section of Montgomery County. 6 mi S of Clarksville.
Orlinda	City in middle NE section of Robertson County. 11 mi NE of Springfield. Incorporated in 1965.
Orme	City in SW corner of Marion County. 11 mi S SW of Jasper. Incorporated in 1935.
Orphan Home Lake	Lake in N NE border of Maury County. 11 mi N NE of Columbia, E SE of Spring Hill.
Orysa	Community in SE corner of Lauderdale County. 9 mi S SE of Ripley.
Osage	Community in NW central section of Henry County. 6 mi W NW of Paris.
Osemont Chapel	Community in E area of Cannon County. 7 mi E of Woodbury.
Oslin	Community in middle N section of Marshall County. 4 1/2 mi SW of Rich Creek.
Ostella	Community in S section of Marshall County. 9 mi S of Lewisburg.
Oswego	Community in N section of Campbell County. 2 mi SW of Jellico.
Otes	Community in S section of Hawkins County. 7 mi S of Rogersville. 2 mi SE of Summitt.
Otter Creek Junction	Community in middle E SE section of Cumberland County. 5 mi E SE of Crossville.

Otter Pond — Pond in SW section of Lauderdale County, in the Anderson-Tully Wildlife Area.

Ottinger — Community in N NE section of Cocke County. 4 mi NE of Parrottsville.

Ottway — Community in N central section of Greene County. 8 mi N NW of Greeneville.

Overall — Community in middle SW section of Rutherford County. 5 mi SW of Murfreesboro.

Overton — Community within the city limits of Memphis, N section. S of Woodstock in Shelby County.

Overton County — County Seat: Livingston. Zip Code 38570. Located in the Northern middle area of the State. Bounded by Pickett, Fentress, Cumberland, Putnam, Jackson, and Clay Counties. Named in honor of John Overton.

OVERTON COUNTY

Ovilla — Community in W NW section of Lawrence County. Approx. 8 mi S of Red Hill.

Ovoca — Community in SW section of Coffee County. 8 1/2 mi SW of Manchester.

Ovoca Lake — Lake in SW area of Coffee County near Ovoca.

Owens Chapel — Community in middle E section of Robertson County. 6 1/2 mi E of Springfield.

Owl City — Community in NE section of Haywood County. 10 mi N NE of Brownsville.

Owl City — Community in E section of Lake County, E of Wynnburg, SE of Tiptonville.

Owl Hollow — Located in NE section of Dickson County. 3 mi N of White Oak Flat.

Owl Hollow — Located in SE section of Hamilton County.

Owl Hollow — Located in central section of Houston County, S of Erin.

Owl Hollow — Located in SW section of Montgomery County. 1 1/2 mi W NW of Shiloh.

Owl Hollow — Located in S central section of Wayne County. N NW of Collinwood.

Owl Hoot — Community in S section of Lake County. 13 mi S SW of Tiptonville.

Oxmoor Hills — Community in Knox County. 10 mi W NW of downtown Knoxville.

Ozone — Community in SE area of Cumberland County. 13 mi E SE of Crossville.

Ozone	Community in N section of Overton County. 8 mi N NE of Livingston.
Pace Point	Located in E NE section of Henry County, on N tip of Tennessee National Wildlife Refuge.
Pactolus	Community in SW section of Sullivan County. Approx. 2 mi W NW of Colonial Heights.
Pailo	Community in SW area of Bledsoe County. 12 mi SE of Pikeville, 6 mi W of Smithtown.
Paines Chapel	Community in NE area of Cheatham County. 7 mi NE of Ashland City.
Painter Spring	Community in SW corner of Washington County, S of Mt. Carmel.
Paint Mountain	Mountain in S section of Greene County.
Paint Rock	Community in S section of Roane County. 8 1/2 mi S of Kingston.
Paint Rock Ridge	Ridge in S SE section of Roane County.
Palestine	Community in W SW section of Chester County. 14 mi SW of Henderson.
Palestine	Community in SW central section of Henderson County. 4 1/2 mi SW of Lexington.
Palestine	Community in SW central section of Henry County. 5 1/2 mi W SW of Paris.
Palestine Mountain	Mountain in N section of Overton County. N of Allons.
Palisades	Community on Signal Mountain in Hamilton County. 5 mi N NW of Chattanooga.
Pall Mall	Community in NW area of Fentress County. 8 1/2 mi N NW of Jamestown.
Palmer	City in SE corner of Grundy County. 10 mi SE of Altamont. Incorporated in 1925.
Palmer Hollow	Located in W SW section of Stewart County, E of Taylor Hollow.
Palmer Shelter	Community in SW area of Carroll County.
Palmersville	Community in NE section of Weakley County. 10 1/2 mi NE of Dresden.
Palmetto	Community in SW Section of Bedford County.
Palmetto	Community on E NE border of Marshall County. Approx. 8 mi E NE of Lewisburg.
Palmyra	Community in middle W SW section of Montgomery

Palmyra, (Cont.)	County. 9 1/2 mi SW of Clarksville.
Pals Lake	Lake in NW area of Davidson County, SW of Forest Grove.
Pandora	Community in W SW section of Johnson County. 8 1/2 mi W SW of Mountain City.
Pan Gap	Community within the city limits of Chattanooga. 3 1/2 mi W of downtown near Lookout Valley in Hamilton County.
Pannell Ridge	Ridge in central NE section of Bedford County. 4 mi E NE of Shelbyville.
Panther Bay	Lake in W section of Stewart County, inlet off the Tennessee River. N of Fort Henry.
Panther Creek State Park	Located in W section of Hamblen County. 6 mi W of Morristown on the Holston River.
Panther Knob	Mountain in SE section of Johnson County, N of Trade.
Papaw	Community in SW section of Hancock County. 7 mi W of Treadway. 2 mi W of Bray.
Papaw Ridge	Community in S SW area of Dyer County. 8 1/2 mi SW of Dyersburg.
Paperville	Community in N NE section of Sullivan County. 3 mi E of Bristol.
Paperville Knobs	Mountain in N NE section of Sullivan County, E of Bristol.
Paradise Lake	Lake in central SW section of Marshall County. 3 1/2 SW of Lewisburg.
Paradise Lake	Lake in E section of Shelby County, E of Lakeland.
Paragon Mill	Community in NE section of Davidson County.
Paris	County Seat of Henry County. Located near center of County. Incorporated in 1823.
Paris Landing State Park	Park in NE corner of Henry County on Tennessee River. 18 mi NE of Paris.
Park City	Located in SW section of Hamilton County.
Park City	Community within the city limits of Knoxville. 2 1/2 mi NE of downtown. In Knox County.
Park City	Community in S central section of Lincoln County. 5 mi S of Fayetteville.
Parker	Community in SE area of Dyer County. 6 mi E SE of Dyersburg.

Parker	Community in middle N section of Pickett County. 2 mi N NE of Byrdstown.
Parker Gap	Located in S SE section of Hamilton County.
Parker Hollow	Located in middle S section of Stewart County, NE of Asbury.
Parker Hollow	Located in SW section of Stewart County, NW of Asbury.
Parkers Crossroads	City on N border of Henderson County. 10 mi N of Lexington. Incorporated in 1981.
Parkers Island	Island on Cumberland River, middle W NW section of Smith County. 2 mi N NW of Rock City.
Parker Swamp	Swamp in N NW section of Hardeman County, W of Cloverport.
Park Grove	Community in N central section of Lawrence County. 5 1/2 mi N NW of of Lawrenceburg.
Parksburg	Community on S border of Madison County. 10 mi S of Jackson. 4 mi E NE of Medon.
Parks Store	Community in SW area of Bradley County. 3 mi SE of McDonald.
Park Station	Community in SE section of Maury County. 9 mi SE of Columbia.
Parksville	Community in W SW section of Polk County. 5 mi S of Benton.
Parksville Lake	Lake in near center of Polk County, NE of section of Lake Ocoee.
Parkway Village	Community within the city limits of Memphis. SE section, E of Oakville. In Shelby County.
Parragon	Community in NE section of Putnam County. 5 1/2 mi N NE of Cookeville.
Parrotsville	City in NE area of Cocke County. 6 mi NE of Newport. Incorporated in 1923.
Parry	Community in middle S section of Williamson County. Approx. 2 1/2 mi S of Franklin.
Parsons	City in N central section of Decatur County. 5 mi N of Decaturville. Incorporated in 1913.
Pasgah	Community in E area of Giles County.
Pasquo	Community in SW area of Davidson County. 13 mi NW of Courthouse.
Pate Hill	Community in W SW section of Greene County. 13

Pate Hill, (Cont.)	mi SW of Greeneville.
Patmos Chapel	Community in N area of Coffee County. 9 mi of Manchester.
Patten Island	John A. Patten Island on Lake Chickamauga, located 13 1/2 mi N NE of downtown Chattanooga at Harrison Bay in Hamilton County.
Patterson	Community in W SW section of Rutherford County. 12 mi W SW of Murfreesboro.
Patterson Crossroads	Community in N central section of Claiborne County. 9 mi NW of Tazewell.
Patterson Mountain	Mountain in NW section of Anderson County.
Pattersonville	Community in SE section of Fayette County. 9 mi S SE of Somerville.
Patton Hollow	Located in SE section of Wilson County. 2 mi S of Watertown.
Patty	Community in NW section of Polk County. 4 1/2 mi N of Benton.
Patty Hollow	Located in SE section of Humphreys County. 1 mi S of New Hope.
Paulette	Community in SW section of Union County. 6 1/2 mi SW of Maynardville.
Pawpaw Plains	Community in E section of Roane County. Approx. 10 mi S of Kingston.
Payne Cove	Community in SW section of Grundy County. 9 mi SW of Altamont.
Paynes Bend	Area in bend of Cumberland River, W NW section of Smith County. 4 mi W NW of Carthage.
Paynes Store	Community in W section of Trousdale County. Approx. 5 mi W of Hartsville.
Peabody	Community in Central area of Campbell County. 6 mi N NE of LaFollette.
Peach	Community in SW section of Giles County.
Peach	Community on E SE border of Lawrence County. Approx. 14 mi SE of Lawrenceburg.
Peak	Community in S Central section of Anderson County. 3 mi SE of Clinton.
Peakland	Community in N central section of Meigs County. 8 mi N NE of Decatur.
Peak Ridge	Ridge in middle S section of Johnson County, W of Neva.

Peaks Hill	Located in E section of Rutherford County. E of Kittrell.
Peaky Mountain	Mountain in E section of Morgan County, E of Sunbright.
Pea Ridge	Ridge in SW section of DeKalb County, near the border. S of Mt. Moriah.
Pea Ridge	Community in W central section of Lawrence County. 8 mi W SW of Lawrenceburg.
Pearl City	Community in W SW section of Lincoln County. 7 mi W SW of Fayetteville.
Pearson Hollow	Located in E section of Sumner County. 2 mi E of Bledsoe.
Peavine	Community in NE central section of Cumberland County.
Peavine Mountain	Mountain in E NE section of Cumberland County, E NE of Fairfield Glade.
Peavine Mountain	Mountian in S section of Polk County, NW of Licklog Ridge.
Pebble Hill	Community in E SE section of McNairy County. 10 1/2 mi E SE of Selmer.
Peckerwood Hollow	Located in middle S SW section of Williamson County. 2 mi E NE of Boston.
Peckerwood Point	Community in SW section of Tipton County. 15 mi SW of Covington.
Peddlers Ridge	Ridge in middle W NW section of Macon County. 2 mi SE of Gap of the Ridge.
Pedigo	Community in NW section of Knox County. 9 1/2 mi N NW of Knoxville.
Peeled Chestnut	Community in W section of White County. 11 mi W NW of Sparta.
Peewee	Community in NW area of Campbell County.
Pegram	City in S Central section of Cheatham County. 12 mi S of Ashland City. Incorporated in 1974.
Pelham	Community in SW area of Grundy County. 12 mi SW of Altamont.
Penile Hill	Community in NW central section of Franklin County. 7 mi N NW of Winchester.
Pennine	Community in middle N section of Rhea County. 11 1/2 mi N NE of Dayton.
Pennington Bend	Located in middle E NE section of Davidson

Pennington Bend, (Cont.) County, E of Inglewood.

Pennington Chapel Community in E section of Union County. 7 1/2 mi NW of Maynardville.

Peppertown Community on S SW border of Lawrence County. Approx. 5 mmi S SE of Loretto.

Percy Priest Dam Dam in E area of Davidson County on Stones River E of Donelson.

Percy Priest Lake Lake in E area of Davidson County on Stones River.

Peregrine Peak Mountain in S section of Sevier County. 6 mi SE of Gatlinburg.

Perrin Hollow Community in SW area of Grainger County. 12 mi SW of Rutledge.

Perry County County Seat: Linden. Zip Code 37096. Located in middle West section of the State. Bounded by Humphreys, Hickman, Lewis, Wayne, Decatur and Benton Counties. Named in honor of Commodore Oliver Hazard Perry.

PERRY COUNTY

Perry Hollow Located in N section of Humphreys County. 2 mi S of Woolworth.

Perryville Community in E central section of Decatur County. 5 mi E NE of Decaturville.

Persia Community in S central section of Hawkins County. 4 mi S of Rogersville.

Peter Cave Cove Located in N section of Marion County, W of Pine Hill.

Peterman Bend Area in bend of Obey River. 2 mi E SE of Celina in Clay County.

Petersburg Community in Central section of Hawkins County. 2 1/2 mi E of Rogersville.

Petersburg City in N NW border of Lincoln County, partly in Marshall County. 12 mi N NW of Fayetteville. Incorporated in 1837. Boundaries also extend into Marshall County.

Peters Landing Community in SW corner of Perry County. 13 mi SW of Linden.

Peters Mill Community in E SE section of Knox County. 12 1/2 mi E of Knoxville.

Petros Community in E section of Morgan County. 8 1/2 mi E of Wartburg.

Petway Community in W Central section of Cheatham

Petway, (Cont.) County. 6 mi SW of Ashland City.

Peytona
Community in middle W SW section of Sumner County. Approx. 7 mi NE of Hendersonville.

Peytonsville
Community in SE section of Williamson County. 9 mi SE of Franklin.

Phiferes
Community in central section of Van Buren County. Approx. 6 mi S SE of Spencer.

Phifer Hollow
Located in E NE section of Benton County.

Phifer Mountain
Mountain in S SE section of Putnam County. 7 mi SE of Cookeville.

Philadelphia
City in S SW section of Loudon County. 6 mi SW of Loudon. Incorporated in 1968.

Philadelphia
Community in E SE section of Maury County. Approx. 7 mi SE of Columbia.

Philadelphia
Community in SW section of Washington County. 12 1/2 mi SW of Jonesborough.

Phillippi
Community in central section of DeKalb County. 3 mi E NE of Smithville.

Phillippy
Community in NE section of Lake County. 9 mi NE of Tiptonville.

Phillips
Community in NE section of Savannah in Hardin County.

Phillips
Community in N NW section of Monroe County. 5 mi NW of Madisonville.

Phillips Bend
Community in E central section of Hawkins County on the Holston River, SE of Stony Point.

Phillips Hollow
Located in E NE section of Sumner County and into the W NW section of Macon County.

Phillips Ridge
Ridge in N NE section of Fentress County. 2 mi N NW of Sharp Place.

Phillips Ridge
Ridge in N section of Scott County, N of Oneida.

Pickel Island
Island in the French Broad River. 4 1/2 mi E of downtown Knoxville.

Pickett County
County Seat: Byrdstown. Zip Code 38549. Located on North Central border of the State. Bounded by Fentress, Overton and Clay Counties, and the State of Kentucky to the North. Named in honor of Howell L. Pickett.

PICKETT COUNTY

Pickett Gulf
Valley in W section of Hamilton County.

Pickett Lake	Lake in E section of Pickett County in Pickett State Park and Forest.
Pickett State Park and Forest	Located in E section of Pickett County.
Pickwick Landing Dam	Located in SW section of Hardin County on Pickwick Lake, 11 mi S of Savannah.
Pickwick Landing Reservation (U.S.-TVA)	In SW section of Hardin County on Pickwick Lake.
Pickwick Landing State Park	State Park located in SW section of Hardin County. 11 mi S of Savannah.
Pickwick Village	Community in SW section of Hardin County on Pickwick Lake.
Piedmont	Community in SW section of Grundy County. 13 1/2 mi SW of Altamont.
Piedmont	Community in SW central section of Jefferson County. 6 1/2 mi W NW of Dandridge.
Pierce	Community on E border of Carter County. 8 mi E of Elizabethton.
Pierce Station	Community in NE section of Obion County. Approx. 8 mi E NE of Union City.
Piersol Lake	Lake in NW section of Shelby County. N of Giles Town.
Pies Fuqua Hollow	Located in central SE section of Humphreys County. 2 mi E of New Hope.
Pigeon Forge	City in middle W section of Sevier County. 5 mi S of Sevierville. Incorporated in 1961.
Pigeon River	River in Cocke County that flows from North Carolina into the French Broad River.
Pigeon Roost	Community in NW central section of Humphreys County. 1 1/2 mi NW of Waverly.
Pikeville	County Seat of Bledsoe County located near center of county. Incorporated in 1830.
Pillowville	Community in S section of Weakley County. 10 mi S SE of Dresden.
Pilot Island	Island on Norris Lake in W section of Union County.
Pilot Knob	Community in NW area of Greene County. 12 mi NW of Greeneville.
Pilot Knob	Located in middle S section of Putnam County, S of Cookeville.

Pilot Knob	Located in E section of Rutherford County. E of Kittrell.
Pilot Knob	Located in SE section of Rutherford County. 1 1/2 mi S of Big Springs.
Pilot Knob	Located in SW section of Smith County near county line. 1 1/2 mi W NW of Brush Creek.
Pilot Knob	Located in S SW section of Sumner County. Approx. 6 mi E NE of Hendersonville.
Pilot Knob	Located in middle S section of Wilson County. 2 1/2 mi SE of Holloway.
Pilot Mountain	Mountain in NE area of Anderson County.
Pilot Mountain	Mountain in middle N NE section of Morgan County.
Pilot Mountain	Community in N central section of Morgan County. 7 1/2 mi N NW of Wartburg.
Pine Creek	Creek in SE Central section of DeKalb County, flows into the Caney Fork River.
Pine Creek	Community in SE section of Van Buren County. Approx. 8 mi S SE of Spencer.
Pine Crest	Community in S Central section of Campbell County. 6 mi S of LaFollette.
Pine Crest	Community in W section of Carter County.
Pine Grove	Community in N NE section of Greene County. 15 mi N NE of Greeneville.
Pine Grove	Community in NW section of Loudon County. 4 1/2 mi N NW of Loudon.
Pine Grove	Communtiy in N section of McMinn County. 10 mi N NW of Athens.
Pine Grove	Community within the city of Pigeon Forge, N of Welcome Center. In Sevier County.
Pine Grove	Community in middle NW section of Sevier County. 3 mi S of Sevierville.
Pine Grove	Community in middle E section of Van Buren County. 3 1/2 mi N of Spencer.
Pine Haven	Community in N central section of Fentress County. 1 1/2 mi N of Jamestown.
Pine Hill	Community in SW area of Bradley County. 3 mi S of McDonald.
Pine Hill	Community in W central section of Clay County. 8 mi W of Celina.

Pine Hill	Community in NE section of Henry County, NE of Buchanan.
Pine Hill	Community in N NE section of Marion County. 12 1/2 mi N NE of Jasper.
Pine Hill	Community in middle N section of Scott County. 7 mi N NE of Huntsville.
Pine Hill Lake	Lake in S SW section of Williamson County. 10 mi SW of Franklin.
Pine Hill Ridge	Ridge in E SE section of Hamilton County.
Pine Hollow	Located in central section of Hamilton County.
Pine Knob	Mountain in S section of Johnson County, E of Buntontown.
Pine Lake	Lake in W Central section of Bledsoe County near Fall Creek Falls State Park. 5 mi W of Pikeville.
Pine Lake	Lake in S central section of Henderson County. 6 mi S SW of Lexington, W of Center Hill.
Pineland	Community in middle SW section of Meigs County. 7 mi SW of Decatur.
Pine Mountain	Mountain in S section of Blount County. E SE of Happy Valley.
Pine Mountain	Mountain in NW section of Campbell County along Interstate 75.
Pine Mountain	Mountain in SE section of Johnson County, S of Sandy.
Pine Mountain	Mountain in E SE section of Johnson County, near border. E of Walnut Grove.
Pine Mountain	Mountain in SW section of Monroe County, N of Holly Springs.
Pine Mountain	Mountain in E NE section of Sevier County. 12 mi E of Sevierville.
Pine Mountain	Mountain in middle W section of Sevier County, W of Pigeon Forge.
Pine Mountain	Mountain in middle SE section of White County, N of Dodson.
Pine Orchard	Community in S SW section of Morgan County. 10 mi S SW of Wartburg.
Pine Ridge	Ridge along SE section of Anderson County and into Union County.
Pine Ridge	Ridge in N section of Hawkins County, near

Pine Ridge, (Cont.)	Hancock County line, W of Frog Level.
Pine Ridge	Ridge in E section of Monroe County, W of Big Fodderstack.
Pine Ridge	Community on E border of Polk County. 19 mi E SE of Benton.
Pine Ridge	Ridge in N section of Roane County.
Pine Spring	Community in S area of Greene County. 13 mi S of Greeneville in Cherokee National Forest.
Pine Top	Community in E NE section of Hardeman County. 3 mi S of Silerton.
Pine Top	Community in N section of Loudon County. 6 mi N NE of Loudon.
Pineview	Community in W NW section of Perry County. 9 1/2 mi NW of Linden.
Pineview Heights	Community in SW area of Tullahoma in Coffee County.
Pineville	Community in Central section of Hamblen County. 3 mi E of Morristown.
Pinewood	Community in N NW section of Hickman County. 9 mi N of Centerville.
Piney	Community in S central section of Loudon County. 3 mi SE of Loudon.
Piney Bay	Lake in W section of Stewart County, inlet off the Tennessee River. S of Fort Henry.
Piney Flats	Community in S section of Sullivan County. 8 mi S SE of Blountville.
Piney Grove	Community in SW area of Carter County. 9 mi S of Elizabethton.
Piney Grove	Community in E NE section of Hardeman County. 3 mi SW of Silerton.
Piney Grove	Community in E NE section of Hardin County. Approx. 9 mi E NE of Savannah.
Piney Grove	Community in N NE section of Hawkins County. 15 mi NE of Rogersville.
Piney Grove	Community in S section of McMinn County. 5 1/2 mi S of Athens.
Piney Grove	Community in NE section of Washington County. Approx. 9 mi E NE of Jonesborough. E of Johnson City.
Piney Mountain	Mountain in W central section of Cocke County,

Piney Mountain, (Cont.)	E of Edwina.
Piney Mountain	Mountain in S section of Sevier County. 3 mi SE of Gatlinburg, E of Mount Le Conte.
Piney Woods	Community within the city limits of Chattanooga. 4 mi S of downtown. In Hamilton County.
Pinhook	Community in E section of Putnam County, W of Monterey.
Pinhook	Community near center of Union County. 2 mi N NW of Maynardville.
Pinkney	Community in W SW section of Lawrence County. W SW of Knob Creek.
Pinnacle	Community in NE area of Cheatham County. 6 1/2 mi NE of Sycamore.
Pinnacle	Community in middle E SE section of Sevier County. Approx. 11 mi SE of Sevierville.
Pinnacle Mountain	Mountain in N section of Unicoi County, N of Unicoi.
Pin Oak Lake	Lake in middle section of Henderson County. 6 1/2 mi E NE of Lexington.
Pins Mountain	Mountain in N NW section of Hawkins County. 5 mi NW of Rogersville.
Pinson	Community on E SE border of Madison County. 10 mi S SE of Jackson.
Pinson Mounds State Archaeological Area	Located in SE corner of Madison County. 10 mi SE of Jackson.
Pinson Mounds State Park	Pocated in SE corner of Madison County. 10 mi S SE of Jaokson.
Pioneer	Community in W Central section of Campbell County near Scott County Line. 8 mi NW of Jacksboro.
Pipers Chapel	Community in middle NW section of Sumner County. 13 mi N NW of Gallatin.
Piperton	City in SW area of Fayette County. 20 mi SW of Somerville. Incorporated in 1974.
Pisgah	Community in S SW area of DeKalb County. 6 mi SW of Smithville.
Pisgah	Community in E SE section of Shelby County. 19 1/2 mi E of Memphis.
Pisgah	Community in middle N section of Weakley

Pisgah, (Cont.)	County. 6 mi N of Dresden.
Pitcher Ridge	Ridge in S section of Franklin County. W of Lakeview.
Pitt Hill	Located in middle W NW section of Sumner County. 2 mi SW of Cottonwood.
Pittman Center	City in middle E SE section of Sevier County. 12 mi SE of Sevierville. Incorporated in 1974.
Pittsburg Landing	Community in middle SW section of Hardin County. 6 mi SW of Savannah. 6 1/2 mi NW of Pickwick Landing Dam.
Plainfield	Community in N Central section of Blount County near Maryville. S of Alcoa.
Plain Grove	Community in W SW section of Pickett County. 6 1/2 mi SW of Byrdstown.
Plainview	Community in E central section of Chester County.
Plainview	Community in S section of Rutherford County. 11 mi S SE of Murfreesboro.
Plainview Heights	Community in SW area of Tullahoma in Coffee County.
Plant	Community in W SW section of Humphreys County. 8 1/2 mi SW of Waverly.
Plantation Hills	Community within the city limits of Knoxville. 3 1/2 mi N NE of downtown. In Knox County.
Plateau	Community in NW central section of Cumberland County.
Platts Pond	Pond on W border of Henry County. 11 mi W of Paris, just N of Como.
Pleasant Gap	Community in N NW section of Knox County. 10 1/2 mi N NW of Knoxville.
Pleasant Green	Community in W section of Morgan County. 13 mi W NW of Wartburg.
Pleasant Grove	Community in SW section of Bedford County. 6 mi SW of Shelbyville, 4 mi NE of Richmond.
Pleasant Grove	Community in W area of Cocke County. 5 mi S of Newport.
Pleasant Grove	Community in S SW section of Decatur County, E of Thurman.
Pleasant Grove	Community in W section of Jefferson County. 12 1/2 mi W of Dandridge.

Pleasant Grove	Community in S section of Lincoln County. 6 1/2 mi S of Fayetteville.
Pleasant Grove	Community in SE section of Maury County. N of Culleoka.
Pleasant Grove	Community in N NE section of Scott County. 12 1/2 mi N NE of Huntsville.
Pleasant Grove	Community in NE section of Sumner County. 19 mi NE of Gallatin.
Pleasant Grove	Community in S section of Union County. 4 mi S SW of Maynardville.
Pleasant Hill	Community in SW section of Benton County. Approx. 6 mi NW of Camden.
Pleasant Hill	Community in SW section of Benton County. Approx. 7 mi W SW of Chalklevel.
Pleasant Hill	Community in E area of Chester County.
Pleasant Hill	Community in SW corner of Claiborne County. 2 mi E NE of Speedwell.
Pleasant Hill	City in W area of Cumberland County. 10 mi W NW of Crossville. Incorporated in 1903.
Pleasant Hill	Community in S SW section of Decatur County, N of Montgomery.
Pleasant Hill	Community in E area of Greene County. 11 mi E of Greeneville.
Pleasant Hill	Community in S section of Hawkins County. 8 mi S SW of Rogersville.
Pleasant Hill	Community in central section of Henderson County. 4 mi E NE of Lexington.
Pleasant Hill	Community in SE section of Henry County, S SE of Spring Creek.
Pleasant Hill	Community in S section of Lauderdale County. 8 1/2 mi SW of Ripley.
Pleasant Hill	Community in central N NW section of Macon County. 4 mi NW of Lafayette.
Pleasant Hill	Community in N section of Meigs County. 11 mi N NE of Decatur.
Pleasant Hill	Community in central section of Moore County. 3 mi E NE of Lynchburg.
Pleasant Hill	Community in central E section of Obion County. 4 1/2 mi S SE of Union City.
Pleasant Hill	Community in SW section of Rutherford County.

Pleasant Hill, (Cont.)	12 mi SW of Murfreesboro.
Pleasant Hill	Community in middle W NW section of Sevier County. 3 1/2 mi W SW of Sevierville.
Pleasant Hill Knob	Located in middle E NE section of Williamson County. 9 mi E of Franklin.
Pleasant Hills	Community in central W SW section of Maury County. 4 mi SW of Columbia.
Pleasant Point	Community in S central section of Lawrence County. 8 mi S SW of Lawrenceburg.
Pleasant Ridge	Community in N Central section of Cannon County. 4 mi NW of Woodbury.
Pleasant Ridge	Community in SW section of Franklin County. 12 mi NW of Winchester.
Pleasant Ridge	Community within the city limits of Knoxville. 5 1/2 mi W NW of downtown. In Knox County.
Pleasant Ridge	Community in S SE section of Putnam County. 8 1/2 mi SE of Cookeville.
Pleasant Shade	Community in N section of Smith County. 9 mi N of Carthage.
Pleasant Vale	Community in NE central section of Greene County. 10 mi NE of Greeneville.
Pleasant Valley	Community in N central section of Giles County.
Pleasant Valley	Community on E border of Lawrence County. Approx. 6 mi N NE of Lawrenceburg.
Pleasant Valley	Community near S SW border of Macon County. 6 1/2 mi SW of Lafayette.
Pleasant Valley	Community in W section of Sumner County. 12 mi W NW of Gallatin.
Pleasant Valley	Community in middle NW section of Washington County. 4 mi N NW of Jonesborough.
Pleasant View	Community in SE section of Cannon County near Warren County line. 6 mi SE of Woodbury.
Pleasant View	Community on N Border of Cheatham County near Robertson County line. 5 mi N of Sycamore.
Pleasant View	Community in E central section of Claiborne County. 3 1/2 mi E of Tazewell.
Pleasant View	Community in W section of Hamblen County. 8 mi W SW of Morristown.

Pleasantville	Community in SW corner of Hickman County. 15 mi SW of Centerville.
Plum Grove	Community in N NE section of Hawkins County. 17 1/2 mi NE of Rogersville.
Plum Orchard Hollow	Located in W SW section of Dickson County. 2 mi N of Tennessee City.
Plum Point Bar	Located on W border of Lauderdale County, S of Keys Point.
Pocahontas	Community in N area of Coffee County. 11 mi N of Manchester.
Pocahontas	Community in SE corner of Hardeman County. 17 1/2 mi SE of Bolivar. 2 1/2 mi N of Essary Springs.
Pocahontas Lake	Lake in SW section of McNairy County. W NW of Big Hill Pond State Park.
Poga	Community in SE area of Carter County on North Carolina border. 8 mi NE of Roan Mountain.
Point Park	Located in SW section of Hamilton County on Lookout Mountain.
Point Pleasant	Community in NW area of Cocke County. 10 mi N of Newport.
Point Pleasant	Community on S SW border of Decatur County.
Polecat	Community in SW section of Humphreys County, NW of Bakerville.
Polk	Community in middle S section of Obion County. 9 mi S SW of Union City.
Polk County POLK COUNTY	County Seat: Benton. Zip Code 37307. Located in Southeastern corner of the State. Bounded by Bradley, McMinn and Monroe Counties and the State of North Carolina to the East and the State of Georgia to the South. Named in honor of James Knox Polk.
Polk Lake	Lake in W SW section of Sumner County. 9 mi W of Gallatin.
Pollard	Community in S central section of Houston County. 3 1/2 mi S SE of Erin.
Pollards Mill	Community in SE section of Hardin County, W of Walnut Grove.
Pomona	Community in W section of Cumberland County. 5 mi W of Crossville.
Pomona	Community in S central section of Dickson County. 10 mi S of Charlotte.

Pomona Road	Community in W NW central section of Cumberland County. 7 1/2 mi NW of Crossville.
Pond	Community in SW central section of Dickson County. 7 mi SW of Charlotte.
Ponderosa Hills	Community in Knox County. 8 1/2 mi NW of downtown Knoxville.
Ponders	Community in middle W section of Roane County. 10 mi SE of Ponders.
Pond Hill	Community in middle N section of McMinn County. 7 1/2 mi N NW of Athens.
Pond Mountain	Mountain in E central section of Carter County, E of Hampton.
Pond Mountain	Mountain in N NE section of Polk County.
Pond Mountain Wilderness	Located in central section of Carter County, SE of Braemer.
Pondville	Community in N NE section of Sumner County. 14 1/2 mi N NE of Gallatin.
Pontotac Hill	Located in E NE section of Fayette County, W of Laconia.
Poor	Community in SE corner of Hardeman County. S of Middleton.
Poor Valley	Located in N NW section of Claiborne County, N of Red Hill.
Poor Valley Ridge	Ridge across middle NE section of Grainger County.
Pope	Community in W section of Perry County. 8 1/2 mi W of Linden.
Poplar	Community in W SW section of Anderson County. 1 mi E of Oliver Springs.
Poplar Bridge	Community in N Central Section of Cheatham County.
Poplar Corner	Community in NE corner of Haywood County. 10 mi E NE of Brownsville.
Poplar Creek	Community in W NW section of Maury County. 11 mi W NW of Columbia.
Poplar Grove	Community in Claiborne County. 7 1/2 mi N NE of Tazewell.
Poplar Grove	Community in N central section of Gibson County. 5 1/2 mi N of Trenton.
Poplar Grove	Community in E SE section of Humphreys County.

Poplar Grove, (Cont.)	2 mi S of Milltown.
Poplar Grove	Community in NE corner of Lauderdale County. 14 mi N NE of Ripley.
Poplar Grove	Community in SW section of Sullivan County. 16 mi W SW of Blountville.
Poplar Hill	Community in S SE section of Giles County. 12 mi S SE of Pulaski.
Poplar Hill	Community in central SW section of McMinn County. 3 1/2 mi SW of Athens.
Poplar Hill	Community in W SW section of Overton County. Approx. 9 mi W SW of Livingston.
Poplar Hollow	Located in W section of Davidson County.
Poplar Hollow	Located in central W NW section of Sumner County. 2 mi N NE of Cottonwood.
Poplar Ridge	Community in NE area of Dyer County. 14 mi N NE of Dyersburg.
Poplar Spring	Community in SW area of Carroll County.
Poplar Spring Hollow	Located in W SW section of Montgomery County. 2 mi W of Stringtown.
Poplar Springs	Community in W NW section of Henderson County. 11 1/2 mi W NW of Lexington. 1 mi N of Blue Goose.
Poplar Springs	Community located near center of Loudon County. 3 mi E of Loudon.
Poplar Springs	Community in middle E section of Roane County. 6 mi E of Kingston.
Poplar Top	Community in middle W section of Maury County. 6 mi W of Columbia.
Poplar Tree Lake	Lake in W NW section of Shelby County. NW of Ramsey.
Poplins Crossroads	Community in W NW section of Bedford County on Old Columbia Road. 9 mi W NW of Shelbyville.
Pork Hill	Located in E section of Williamson County near border. 12 mi E of Franklin.
Porter	Community in SE area of Dickson County. 14 mi S SE of Charlotte.
Porter Court	Community in center of Henry County, just N of Paris.
Porterfield	Community near W NW border of Cannon County at

Porterfield, (Cont.)	Rutherford County line. 6 mi NW of Woodbury.
Porter Gap	Community in N section of Lauderdale County. 11 mi N of Ripley.
Porter Lake	Lake in E section of Rhea County. 13 mi NE of Dayton.
Porters Chapel	Community in middle SW section of Maury County. 9 mi SW of Columbia.
Porters Creek	Community in E SE section of Hardeman County. 11 mi SE of Bolivar. 4 mi W of McNairy County line.
Porters Mountain	Mountain in SE section of Sevier County. 6 mi S of Pittman Center.
Portland	City in NW section of Sumner County. 14 mi N NW of Gallatin. Incorporated in 1905.
Port Royal	Community on E NE border of Montgomery County. 12 mi E of Clarksville.
Port Royal State Park	Located in E NE section of Montgomery County, near the Robertson County line.
Port Serena	Community on Lake Chickamauga in Dallas Bay area of Hamilton County. 13 mi N NE of downtown Chattanooga.
Posey Hill	Located in W SW section of Wilson County. 3 mi S of Silver Springs.
Possum Creek	Creek in N area of Hamilton County. Flows into Tennessee River E of Bakewell.
Possumpaw Hollow	Located in NW corner of Coffee County, N of Gossburg.
Possumtrott Hollow	Located in S section of Bedford County.
Postelle	Community in middle SE section of Polk County. 17 mi SE of Benton.
Post Oak	Community in W Central area of Benton County.
Post Oak	Community in middle N section of Putnam County. 4 mi N of Cookeville.
Post Oak	Community in W NW section of Roane County. 6 1/2 mi W of Kingston.
Post Oak	Community in W NW section of Sevier County, near Knob Creek.
Potato Hill	Located in E section of Williamson County. 9 mi E of Franklin.
Potatopatch Hallow	Located in middle E section of Stewart County,

Potatopatch Hallow, (Cont.)	S of Bear Spring.
Potato Ridge	Ridge in SE section of Sevier County. 6 mi E SE of Gatlinburg.
Pottsville	Community on E border of Maury County. 12 mi E of Columbia.
Powder Springs	Community in W area of Grainger County. 9 mi W SW of Rutledge.
Powell	Community in W NW section of Knox County. 8 1/2 mi W NW of Knoxville.
Powell Chapel	Community in central section of Giles County. 4 mi NE of Pulaski.
Powell Heights	Community in Knox County. 8 mi NW of downtown Knoxville.
Powell Lake	Lake in SE section of Haywood County, N of Hillville.
Powell Mountain	Mountain in E area of Claiborne County between Pleasant View and Howard Quarter extends into W NW section of Hancock County into Virginia.
Powell River	Flows through Claiborne, Union and into Campbell County where it flows into the Clinch River.
Powells Chapel	Community on SE central border of Hardeman County. 13 1/2 mi E SE of Bolivar near McNairy County Line.
Powells Crossroads	City in central NE section of Marion County. 11 mi NE of Jasper. Incorporated in 1976.
Powell Valley	Community in W central section of Claiborne County. 13 mi W NW of Tazewell.
Powers	Community in Central area of Fayette County. 3 1/2 mi W of Somerville.
Prairie Creek	Community in central section of Hamilton County near Soddy Daisy.
Prairie Peninsula	Community on Lake Chickamauga in Dallas Bay area of Hamilton County.
Prairie Plains	Community in SE section of Coffee County. 11 mi SE of Manchester.
Prater	Community in E Central section of Cannon County. 4 1/2 mi E of Woodbury.
Prater Hill	Located in SE section of Rutherford County. E of Big Springs.

Prentice Cooper State Forest	Located in SW section of Hamilton County on Walden's Ridge and the E SE section of Marion County.
Presidents Island No. 45	Island in SW section of Shelby County. On the Mississippi River.
Presley Lake	Lake in NW area of Carroll County. 2 1/2 mi NE of McLemoresville.
Preston Ridge	Ridge in SE section of Moore County.
Preston Woods	Community in N NW section of Sullivan County, 3 mi E of Kingsport.
Price Hollow	Located in S section of Houston County, E of Reuben Hollow.
Price Lake	Lake in S section of Cheatham County, near the border.
Price Mountain	Mountain in NW section of Sequatchie County, SW of Cagle.
Price Ridge	Ridge in W SW section of Marion County, N of Lodge.
Priests Spur	Community in E NE section of Carroll County, N of Bruceton.
Primm Springs	Community in E section of Hickman County. 12 mi E NE of Centerville.
Princeton	Community in NE section of Washington County. Approx. 7 mi NE of Jonesborough. N of Johnson City.
Privet Mountain	Mountain in NE central section of Scott County. NE of Shug Mountain.
Probst	Community in N central section of Polk County. Approx. 8 mi E of Benton.
Prock Hollow	Located in N section of Davidson County, SW of Lickton.
Proctor City	Community in N central section of Lake County. 3 1/2 mi N NE of Tiptonville.
Promise	Community in middle N NE section of Dickson County. 2 mi N of Charlotte.
Prophet Ridge	Ridge in W SW section of Hawkins County, S of Mooresburg.
Prospect	Community in W Central section of Benton County.
Prospect	Community in NE section of Blount County. 10 mi E NE of Maryville, 2 mi W of Ellejoy.

Prospect	Community in W Central section of Bradley County. 2 mi W of Cleveland.
Prospect	Community in S area of Giles County. 11 1/2 mi S SE of Pulaski.
Prospect	Community in S section of Lincoln County. 5 mi S of Fayetteville.
Prospect	Community in W section of Loudon County. 5 mi W of Loudon.
Prospect	Community on SE border of McMinn County. 10 1/2 mi E SE of Athens.
Prosperity	Community in E SE section of Macon County. 9 mi E SE of Lafayette.
Prosperity	Community in middle N section of Shelby County. 13 1/2 mi NE of Memphis.
Prosperity	Community in SE corner of Wilson County. 20 mi SE of Lebanon.
Protemus	Community in middle NW section of Obion County. 10 mi W SW of Union City.
Providence	Community in NE area of Blount County. 10 mi NE of Alcoa.
Providence	Community in SE area of Davidson County.
Providence	Community in SW area of Grundy County. 14 mi SW of Altamont.
Providence	Community in S section of Lewis County. S of Riverside.
Providence	Community on W NW border of Madison County. 14 mi W NW of Jackson.
Providence	Community in NE section of Sumner County. 16 mi N NE of Gallatin. NW of Westmoreland.
Providence	Community in S section of Trousdale County. 4 mi S SE of Hartsville.
Prowell Lake	Lake in middle NW section of Wilson County. 6 mi W NW of Lebanon.
Pruden	Community in NW area of Claiborne County on Kentucky Line. 9 mi N of Speedwell.
Pruett	Community in N Central Section of Anderson County. 1 mi E of Lake City.
Pruette Spring	Community on S border of Humphreys County, S of Buffalo.
Puckett Store	Community in SW corner of Rutherford County. S

Puckett Store, (Cont.)	of Pleasant Hill.
Pulaski	County Seat of Giles County. Located in central section of county. Incorporated in 1849.
Pull Tight	Community in E SE section of Williamson County.
Pulltight Hill	Located in middle S section of Wilson County. 2 mi E of Bairds Mill.
Pulltight Hollow	Located in W SW section of Hamilton County.
Pumpkin Center	Community in NW section of Blount County. 3 mi SW of Louisville.
Pumpkin Center	Communtiy in SE area of Bradley County. 7 mi SE of Cleveland.
Pumpkin Center	Community on NE border of Monroe County. 15 1/2 mi E NE of Madisonville.
Pumpkin Ridge	Ridge in central W section of Stewart County, S of Fair View.
Pumpkintown	Community in NE section of Macon County. 8 mi NE of Lafayette.
Pumpkin Valley	Located in N section of Hawkins County, NW of Eidson.
Punch Bowl Mountain	Mountain in E section of Cocke County, S of Harmony Grove.
Puncheon Camp	Community in N central section of Grainger County. 3 mi N NW of Rutledge.
Purdy	Community in N central section of McNairy County. 5 mi NE of Selmer.
Pursley	Community in W NW section of Humphreys County, NE of Denver.
Puryear	City in N central section of Henry County. 10 mi N of Paris. Incorporated in 1909.
Puryears Bend	Area in bend of Cumberland River, S section of Trousdale County. 4 mi S SW of Hartsville.
Push	Community on W SW border of Obion County. 20 1/2 mi W SW of Union City.
Putman Well	Community in NW section of Bedford County. 13 mi N of Shelbyville, 1/2 mi N of Cater Crossroads.
Putnam County	County Seat: Cookeville. Zip Code 38501. Located in North Central section of the the

Putnam County,	State. Bounded by Jackson, Overton, Cumberland, White, DeKalb and Smith Counties. Named in honor of Isreal Putnam.
Pyburn	Community in SW section of Hardin County. 3 mi N of Pickwick Landing Dam. 9 mi S of Savannah.
Quebeck	Community in S SW section of White County. 9 1/2 mi S SW of Sparta.
Quercus	Community in NW corner of Lawrence County. Approx. 4 mi N NW of Henryville.
Quincy	Community in N central section of Crockett County. 4 mi N NE of Alamo.
Quito	Community in SW corner of Tipton County. 19 mi SW of Covington.
Rabbit Valley	Located in S SE section of Hamilton County.
Raccoon Mountain	Mountain in SW section of Hamilton County and extends into the SE corner Marion County.
Raccoon Mountain Pumped Storage Dam and Reservoir	Located in SE corner of Marion County on the Tennessee River.
Racoon Valley	Community in S section of Union County. Approx. 3 mi W SW of Maynardville.
Rader	Community in Central section of Greene County. 5 1/2 mi W of Greeneville.
Radmoor	Community within the city limits of Chattanooga. 8 mi E SE of downtown. In Hamilton County.
Radnor	Community in S central section of Davidson County. 3 mi S SE of Courthouse.
Radnor Lake	Lake in S area of Davidson County. S of Oak Hill.
Radnor Lake State Natural Area	Located in S area of Davidson County, S of Oak Hill.
Rafter	Community in central SE section of Monroe County. 13 1/2 mi SE of Madisonville.
Raft Hollow	Located in E NE section of Denton County.
Ragsdale	Community in Central section of Coffee County. 4 mi E of Manchester.
Rainbow Lake	Lake on Signal Mountain in Hamilton County near Prentice Cooper State Forest.
Rainbow Lake	Located in NE section of Wayne County. 8 1/2 mi NE of Waynesboro.

Raines Knob	Mountain in W SW section of Cocke County, N of Denton.
Rains Ridge	Ridge in middle S section of Cannon County. 6 mi S SW of Woodbury. 1 1/2 mi E of Burgen.
Raleigh	Community in middle section of Shelby County. Within the city limits of Memphis. 8 mi from downtown.
Rally Hill	Community on E NE border of Maury County. 12 mi E NE of Columbia.
Ralston	Community in middle W NW section of Weakley County. 5 1/2 mi W NW of Dresden.
Ramah	Community in S SE section of Lawrence County. 11 mi S of Lawrenceburg. 6 mi E of Loretto.
Ramer	City in S SW section of McNairy County. 7 mi S SW of Selmer. Incorporated in 1958.
Ramsey	Community in middle SE section of Knox County, SE of Knoxville.
Ramsey	Community in W NW section of Shelby County. 11 mi N of Memphis.
Ramsey Hollow	Located in E section of Hamilton County.
Ramsey Lake	Lake in SW central section of Grundy County. SW of Coalmont.
Randolph	Community in W section of Tipton County. 13 1/2 mi W SW of Covington.
Randolph Hollow	Located in W NW section of Dickson County. 2 mi N NW of Adams Crossroads.
Range (Turkeytown)	Community in NW area of Carter County. 2 mi E of Watagua.
Rankin	Community in NW area of Cocke County. 6 mi N NW of Newport.
Rankin Cove	Community in S section of Marion County. 3 1/2 mi SE of Jasper.
Ransom Stand	Community in SW corner of Wayne County. 23 mi S SW of Waynesboro, near the county line.
Rascal Town	Community on S SW border of Lawrence County. 18 mi S SW of Lawrenceburg. 5 mi S of Loretto.
Rattlesnake Hollow	Located in N NW section of Hamilton County.
Rattlesnake Hollow	Located in N section of Polk County.
Raus	Community in SE Section of Bedford County. 9 mi SE of Shelbyville.

Raven Branch	Community in S central section of Cocke County. 9 1/2 mi SE of Newport.
Raven Hill	Community in SE corner of Claiborne County. 6 1/2 mi SE of Tazewell.
Raven Mountain	Mountain in S section of Cocke County, S of Click Mill.
Ravenscroft	Community in NE section of White County. 10 mi E NE of Sparta.
Ray Bluff Knob	Located in W section of Jackson County. 2 mi E NE of Rough Point.
Ray Chapel	Community in NE section of Bedford County on Old Columbia Road. 12 mi W NW of Shelbyville.
Ray Creek	Creek in E area of Grainger County, N of Heltonville.
Ray Mountain	Mountain in S SE section of Cocke County, SE of Grassy Fork.
Rayon City	Community in NE section of Davidson County, N of Old Hickory.
Raysville	Community in middle NE section of Moore County. 4 1/2 mi NE of Lynchburg.
Read Lake	Lake in W section of Hamilton County, N of Red Bank.
Read Lakes	Lake in S SW section of Tipton County. Approx. 2 mi E of Wilkinsville.
Readyville	Community near W Border of Cannon County. 6 mi W of Woodbury.
Reagan	Community in SE section of Henderson County. 10 1/2 mi S SE of Lexington. 4 1/2 mi W of Scotts Hill.
Reagan	Community in E NE border of McMinn County. 9 mi N NE of Athens.
Reagantown	Community in N NW section of Sevier County, S of Sevierville.
Rebecca Lake	Lake in S SW section of Lincoln County. Approx. 6 mi S of Fayetteville.
Rebecca Lake	Lake in W NW section of Shelby County. NE of Locke.
Red Ash	Community in SW area of Campbell County NW of Caryville.
Red Bank	Community in E Central area of Blount County near Kinzel Springs. 2 1/2 mi S SW of

Red Bank, (Cont.)	Townsend.
Red Bank	City in S central section of Hamilton County. Surrounded by the City of Chattanooga, located about 5 mi N of downtown Chattanooga. Incorporated in 1955.
Redbank Hill	Hill in S SW section of Stewart County, near border, E of Bradley Hollow.
Red Boiling Springs	City in E section of Macon County. 10 mi E of Lafayette. Incorporated in 1953.
Redbud Lake	Lake in E NE section of Henderson County. 8 mi E NE of Lexington.
Red Clay State Park	On SW Border of Bradley County on Georgia Line. 12 mi S of Cleveland.
Red Cliff	Community in N tip of Morgan County. 18 mi N NW of Wartburg.
Red Fox Ridge	Ridge in NE section of Johnson County, NE of Cold Spring.
Red Hill	Community in S Central area of Bradley County. Apporx. 6 mi S of Cleveland.
Red Hill	Community in N Central section of Claiborne County. 9 mi NW of Tazewell.
Red Hill	Community in NE area of Claiborne County. 1 1/2 mi E of Big Spring Union. 10 1/2 mi NE of Tazewell.
Red Hill	Community in NW area of Fentress County. 10 mi NW of Jamestown.
Red Hill	Community in N NW central section of Lawrence County. 6 1/2 mi NW of Lawrenceburg.
Red Hill	Community in NE section of Marion County. 12 1/2 mi N NE of Jasper.
Red Hill	Community in N section of Pickett County. 3 1/2 mi N NE of Byrdstown.
Red Hill	Community in central section of Weakley County. 1 1/2 mi N of Dresden.
Red Hills	Community located in NE corner of Bradley County near McMinn County Line.
Red Hills	Located in middle SW section of McMinn County, S of Cedar Springs.
Red House	Community in SW section of Grainger County. 9 1/2 mi SW of Rutledge.
Red Knobs	Located in SE section of Loudon County and W

Red Knobs, (Cont.)	section of Blount County.
Red Knobs	Located in W section of Monroe County, E of Mount Vernon.
Redman Point Bar	Sand Bar on Mississippi River in Memphis, W of Frayser. In Shelby County.
Red Mountain	Mountain in S SE section of Knox County. S of Sevier Home.
Red Mountain	Mountain in W NW section of Monroe County, W of Belltown.
Red Oak	Community in W NW section of Lincoln County. 15 mi W NW of Fayetteville.
Red Oak Knobs	Mountain in N NE section of Sevier County. 6 mi NE of Sevierville.
Red Oak Mountain	Mountain in SW area of Campbell County on Anderson County Line.
Red Row	Community in middle SW section of Maury County. 11 mi SW of Columbia.
Red Sulphur Springs	Community on S border of Hardin County. 16 mi S of Savannah. 5 1/2 mi S of Pickwick Dam.
Red Walnut	Community in SW section of Decatur County, W of Montgomery.
Redwine	Community in NW area of Cocke County. 9 mi N of Newport, 1 1/2 mi SE of Point Pleasant.
Reeders Crossing	Community in SE section of Dickson County. 9 mi SE of Charlotte.
Reedtown	(Reidtown) Community on W border of Cocke County. 4 mi W of Newport.
Reedy	Community in NW corner of Sullivan County. 13 1/2 mi W of Blountville.
Reelfoot	Community in middle E section of Lake County. 2 1/2 mi E SE of Tiptonville.
Reelfoot Lake	Lake in NE section of Lake County and NW section of Obion County.
Reelfoot Lake State Park	Located in middle E section of Lake County on Reelfoot Lake E of Tiptonville and extends into the W area of Obion County.
Reelfoot National Wildlife Refuge	Located in NW section of Obion County. 15 mi W of Union City.
Reelfoot Wildlife Management Area	Located in NE section of Lake County.

Reese Mountain	Mountain in SE section of Polk County, N of McGeetown.
Reesetown	Community in SE section of Polk County in the Copper Basin, E of Dogtown.
Reeves	Community in central E NE section of Washington County. 3 mi E NE of Jonesborough.
Reeves Hollow	Located in S section of Benton County.
Rega	Community in W Central section of Blount County near Marble Hill.
Rehoboth	Community in E section of Dyer County. 7 1/2 mi E of Dyersburg.
Reid Hill	Located in central section of Williamson County. 2 mi E NE of Franklin.
Reliance	Community in NW section of Claiborne County. 1 mi SW of Fork Ridge.
Reliance	Community in middle N section of Polk County. 9 mi W of Benton.
Remy	Community in Central area of Campbell County near LaFollette.
Reneger Hollow	Located in SW section of Bedford County.
Reuben Hollow	Located near S border of Houston County. Approx. 5 mi S SW of Erin.
Reubensville	Community on middle E NE border of Robertson County. 17 1/2 mi E NE of Springfield.
Reubensville	Community in NW section of Sumner County, on Robertson County border. W of Scattersville.
Reverie	Community in W section of Tipton County. NE of Richardsons.
Revilo	Community in E SE section of Lawrence County. 8 mi S SE of Lawrenceburg.
Rexton Hollow	Located in S SW section of Marion County, E of Orme.
Reynolds Mountain	Mountain in middle N section of Overton County, W of Allons.
Rhea County RHEA COUNTY	County Seat: Dayton. Zip Code 37321. Located in Southeastern section of the State. Bounded by Cumberland, Roane, Meigs, Hamilton and Bledsoe Counties. Named in honor of John Rhea.
Rheatown	Community in E area of Greene County. 9 mi E NE of Greeneville.

Rhinehard Valley	Located in S SE section of Hamilton County.
Rhodes Lake	Lake in SW area of Dyer County on Moss Island.
Rhyan Springs	Community in middle NE section of Overton County. 7 mi NE of Livingston.
Rialto	Community on N NE border of Tipton County. 5 mi N NE of Covington.
Rice Bend	Community in S tip of Unicoi County. 14 mi S SW of Erwin.
Riceville	Community in middle SW section of McMinn County. 7 mi SW of Athens.
Rich	Community in NW section of Giles County. 14 mi N NW of Pulaski.
Richard City	City on S SW border of Marion County. 8 mi SW of Jasper. 2 mi SW of South Pittsburg. Incorporated in 1907.
Richardsons	Community on W border of Tipton County. 17 mi W SW of Covington.
Richardsons Cove	Community in central E NE section of Sevier County. 8 mi E SE of Sevierville.
Rich Creek	Community in N section of Marshall County. Approx. 5 mi S of Chapel Hill.
Richland	Community in SW section of Grainger County. 13 mi SW of Rutledge.
Richland Knob	Mountain Range across middle S section of Grainger County.
Richmond	Community in SW Section of Bedford County. 10 mi SW of Shelbyville.
Richmond Roads	Community in NW section of Hickman County. Approx. 9 mi W NW of Centerville.
Rich Mountain	Mountain in SE section of Blount County, S of Lawson Crossroads.
Rich Mountain	Mountain in NE area of Campbell County S of White Oak.
Rich Mountain	Mountain in S section of Cocke County, SW of Grassy Fork.
Rich Mountain	Mountain in E SE section of Greene County near Unicoi County line.
Rich Mountain	Mountain in S section of Greene County, N of Buzzard Point Mountain.
Rich Mountain	Mountain in E NE section of Sevier County and

Rich Mountain, (Cont.)	W NW section of Cocke County.
Rich Mountain	Mountain in S central section of Unicoi County, N of Ernestville.
Richville	Community in central section of Clay County. 6 mi W of Celina, N of Midway.
Richwoods	Community in SW area of Dyer County. 7 mi W SW of Dyersburg.
Ricker Mountain	Mountain in S section of Greene County, E of Paint Mountain.
Rickman	Community in SW section of Overton County. 9 mi S SW of Livingston.
Riddles Store	Community in N section of McMinn County. 12 mi N NE of Athens.
Riddleton	Community in NW section of Smith County. 6 mi NW of Carthage.
Ridenour	Community in W SW section of Union County. 9 mi W SW of Maynardville.
Ridgedale	Community in W area of Cumberland County. 1 mi W of Crossville.
Ridgedale	Community within the city limits of Chattanooga. 3 mi S SE of downtown. In Hamilton County.
Ridgedale	Community within the city limits of Knoxville. 6 mi W NW of downtown. In Knox County.
Ridgefields	Community in NW corner of Sullivan County. W of Kingsport.
Ridgely	City in S section of Lake County. 8 mi S of Tiptonville. Incorporated in 1909.
Ridgeside	City within the limits of Chattanooga in Hamilton County. 3 1/2 mi E SE of downtown. Incorporated in 1931.
Ridgetop	Community in E NE section of Lewis County. 11 1/2 mi E NE of Hohenwald.
Ridgetop	City in SE section of Robertson County. 10 mi SE of Springfield. Incorporated in 1935, boundaries also extend into Davidson County.
Ridgetop Lake	Lake in SE section of Robertson County. 2 mi SE of Greenbrier.
Ridgeview	Community in W section of Hamblen County. 3 mi W of Morristown.
Ridgeview Heights	Community in middle NE section of Knox County.

Ridgeview Heights, (Cont.)	1 mi N of Maloneyville.
Ridgeville	Community in E central section of Moore County. 4 mi E of Lynchburg.
Ridley	Community in W SW section of Maury County. Approx. 9 mi W SW of Columbia.
Ridley Hollow	Located in S SW section of Williamson County, NW of Thompson Station.
Riggs Crossroads	Community in SE corner of Williamson County on Rutherford County line. 18 mi SE of Franklin.
Right	Community in NW section of Hardin County. 7 mi NW of Savannah. 3 1/2 mi N NE of Bethlehem.
Right Hand Arm Lake	Lake in W section of Lauderdale County, E of Open Lake. Approx. 8 mi W NW of Ripley.
Riley	Community in NE section of Claiborne County. 2 mi S SE of Hopewell.
Riley Creek	Community in SW area of Coffee County.
Ringgold	Community in N section of Montgomery County. N of Clarksville.
Rinnie	Community in N area of Cumberland County. 14 mi N of Crossville.
Riovista	Community in W area of Carter County. 3 mi W SW of Elizabethton.
Ripley	County seat of Lauderdale County. Located in middle E section of the County. Incorporated in 1838.
Ripshin Lake	Lake in S area of Carter County W of Roan Mountain State Park.
Ripshin Ridge	Ridge in SE section of Carter County, S of Whitehead Hill.
Ritchie	Community in E central section of Claiborne County. 6 mi NE of Tazewell.
Ritchie Ridge	Ridge in NW section of Hamilton County.
Ritta	Community in N central section of Knox County. 6 1/2 mi N NE of Knoxville.
Riverdale	Community in E section of Knox County. 9 mi E of Knoxville.
River Heights	Community in middle W section of Hardin County. 4 mi W of Savannah.
River Heights	Community in central section of Maury County.

River Heights, (Cont.)	2 mi N of Columbia.
River Hill	Community in central section of Unicoi County. 4 mi SE of Erwin.
River Hill	Community in S section of White County. Approx. 7 mi S of Sparta, near Van Buren County Line.
River Knob	Mountain in W SW section of Hawkins County. 7 mi W SW of Rogersville.
River Knobs	Located in E section of Rhea County. 7 mi E of Evensville.
River Ridge	Ridge in S SE section of Claiborne County, S of Springdale.
River Ridge	Ridge in E section of Hancock County, SW of Kyles Ford.
River Ridge	Ridge in central section of Hancock County, SW of Sneedville.
River Ridge	Ridge in middle W section of Roane County.
Riversburg	Community in N central section of Giles County.
Riverside	Community in NE area of Claiborne County. 7 mi NE of Tazewell.
Riverside	Community in S section of Lewis County. W of Voorhies.
Riverside	Community within the City of Columbia, NE section. In Maury County.
Riverside	Community in middle N section of Monroe County. 7 1/2 mi E of Madisonville.
Riverside	Communitiy in middle SE section of Sullivan County. 8 mi E SE of Blountville.
Riverton	Community in W NW section of Fentress County.
River View	Community in N central section of Claiborne County. 7 mi NW of Tazewell.
Riverview	Community in E area of Grainger County. 8 mi E of Rutledge.
Riverview	Community in Central section of Hamblen County near Morristown.
Riverview	Community within the city limits of Chattanooga. 2 mi N of downtown in Hamilton County.
Riverview	Community in central section of Unicoi County.

Riverview, (Cont.)	2 1/2 mi SW of Erwin.
Riverview	Community in W section of Van Buren County. 7 1/2 mi SW of Spencer.
Rives	City in middle E section of Obion County. 5 mi S of Union City. Incorporated in 1905.
R. M. Steelman Lake	Lake in SE section of Lincoln County. W of Flintville.
Roan Creek	Creek in SW section of Johnson County, flows into the Watauga River.
73 Roane County ROANE COUNTY	County Seat: Kingston. Zip Code 37763. Located in Southeastern section of the State. Bounded by Morgan, Anderson, Knox, Loudon, McMinn, Meigs, Rhea and Cumberland Counties. Named in honor of Archibold Roane.
Roane County Park	Located in NW section of Roane County. 1 mi E of Postoak.
Roan Mountain	Community in SE area of Carter County. 12 mi SE of Elizabethton.
Roan Mountain	Mountain near S border of Carter County on North Carolina Line S of Cove Creek.
Roan Mountain State Park	In SE area of Carter County at Roan Mountain.
Roaring Springs	Community in N area of Greene County near Baileyton. 9 mi N NE of Greeneville.
Robbins	Community in middle SW section of Scott County. 7 mi SW of Huntsvile.
Robco Lake	Lake in SW corner of Shelby County. S of Cord Lake.
Roberts	Community in W NW section of Madison County. Approx. 9 mi W NW of Jackson.
Roberts	Community in SW section of Putnam County. 11 mi W SW of Cookeville.
Roberts Gap	Located in W section of Hamilton County.
Roberts Hollow	Located in middle S section of Humphreys County. 5 mi S of Waverly.
Robertson	Community in SW area of Chester County. 5 1/2 mi S of Hickory Corner.
74 Robertson County ROBERTSON COUNTY	County Seat: Springfield. Zip Code 37172. Located on North Central Border of the State. Bounded by Sumner, Davidson, Cheatham and Montgomery and the State of Kentucky to the North. Named in honor of James Robertson.

Robertson Fork	Community on W SW border of Marshall County. 9 mi SW of Lewisburg.
Robertson Lake	Lake in W section of Shelby County. N of Frayser.
Roberts Ridge	Ridge in W section of Coffee County. 2 mi S of Baucom.
Robinson Crossroads	Community in W SW section of Knox County. 13 1/2 mi W of Knoxville.
Robinson Crusoe Island	Island in the W SW section of Shelby County on the Mississippi River.
Robinson Lake	Community in central E section of Williamson County. 3 mi SE of Franklin.
Robinson Mill	Community in central section of Loudon County. 1 1/2 mi SE of Loudon.
Robinson Ridge	Ridge in NW section of Putnam County, S of Gentry.
Robison	Community in SE area of Carroll County.
Roby	Community in E area of Chester County near Henderson County Line. 13 1/2 mi E of Henderson.
Rock Bridge	Community in central NE section of Sumner County. 9 1/2 mi N NE of Gallatin.
Rock City	Community in central section of Giles County.
Rock City	Community in W section of Smith County. 6 mi W of Carthage.
Rock City	Community in N NW section of Sullivan County. Approx. 6 mi E NE of Kingsport.
Rock Creek	Community in N NE section of Unicoi County. Approx. 3 mi E of Erwin.
Rockdale	Community in SW corner of Maury County. S of Sandy Hook.
Rockdale	Community in N NW section of Rutherford County.
Rockford	City in N Central section of Blount County. 3 mi NE of Alcoa. Incorporated in 1970.
Rock Haven	Community in NE area of Grainger County. 8 mi E NE of Rutledge.
Rock Hill	Community in NE central section of Hancock County. 5 1/2 mi E NE of Sneedville. 4 mi SW of Kyles Ford.

Rock Hill	Community in middle E section of Henderson County. 4 1/2 mi E SE of Lexington. 3 mi W SW of Chesterfield.
Rock Hill	Community in S section of Sullivan County. 9 mi S SE of Blountville.
Rock House	Community in E section of Trousdale County. Approx. 3 mi E SE of Hartsville.
Rockhouse	Community in SE central section of White County. 3 mi E of Sparta.
Rockhouse Hollow	Located in E section of Sumner County, E SE of Withamtown.
Rock Island	Community in NE corner of Warren County. 12 mi NE of McMinnville.
Rock Island State Rustic Park	Located in N NE section of Warren County. E of Berea and N of Campaign.
Rockland	Community within the city limits of Hendersonville, SW section. In Sumner County.
Rockport	Community in SE section of Benton County. Approx. 4 mi SE of Chalklevel.
Rock Springs	Community in N NE section of Dickson County. 10 mi N NE of Charlotte.
Rock Springs	Community in E central section of Dyer County.
Rock Springs	Community in N NW section of Henderson County. 10 1/2 mi N NW of Lexington.
Rock Springs	Community in middle E section of Maury County. 6 1/2 mi E of Columbia.
Rock Springs	Community in W NW section of Rutherford County. W SW of Smyrna.
Rock Springs	Community in W SW section of Rutherford County. 11 mi S SW of Murfreesboro.
Rock Springs	Community in SW section of Sullivan County. 13 1/2 mi W SW of Blountville.
Rock Station	Community in E NE section of Warren County. 9 mi E SE of McMinnville.
Rockvale	Community in middle SW section of Rutherford County. 9 1/2 mi SW of Murfreesboro.
Rockville	Community in NW section of Monroe County. 5 1/2 mi N of Madisonville.
Rockwood	City in W section of Roane County. 12 mi W of Kingston. Incorporated in 1895.

Rockwood Hill	Community in central section of Greene County. 3 mi S SW of Greeneville.
Rocky Branch	Community in E Central area of Blount County. 6 mi E of Maryville.
Rocky Flats	Community in E SE section of Sevier County bordering Cocke County and the Great Smoky Mountain National Park.
Rocky Fork	Community in W NW section of Rutherford County. SW of Smyrna.
Rocky Fork	Community in S section of Unicoi County. 10 1/2 mi SW of Erwin.
Rocky Grove	Community on E border of Sevier County. 17 mi E SE of Sevierville.
Rocky Hill	Community within city limits of Knoxville, SW of Bearden. In Knox County.
Rocky Hill	Located in E SE section of Williamson County. 14 mi E SE of Franklin, 1 mi E of Triune.
Rocky Hollow	Located in central section of Houston County, SW of Erin.
Rocky Knob	Located in SE section of Blount County, S of Townsend.
Rocky Mound	Community in NW corner of Macon County. 9 1/2 mi NW of Lafayette.
Rocky Mountain	Mountain in E section of Blount County. SE of Bates Mountain.
Rocky Point	Community in E section of Hamblen County. 6 1/2 mi E of Morristown.
Rocky Point	Community in middle E SE section of Putnam County. 7 mi E SE of Cookeville.
Rocky Ridge	Community in NE section of Overton County. 7 mi NE of Livingston.
Rocky Ridge	Ridge in W SW section of Sevier County. 2 1/2 mi S SE of Wears Valley.
Rocky Spring	Community in middle W section of Monroe County. N NE of Mount Vernon.
Rocky Springs	Community in S SW section of Sullivan County. 6 1/2 mi S SW of Blountville.
Rocky Valley	Community in middle section of Jefferson County. 8 mi W NW of Dandridge.
Roddy	Community in NE section of Rhea County. 24 i NE of Dayton.

Roddy Springs	Community in SE section of Grundy County near Tracy City.
Rodemer	Community in N central section of Hickman County. Approx. 8 mi N NE of Centerville.
Roe	Community in S section of Hamblen County. 2 mi S of Morristown.
Roe Junction	Community in S central section of Hamblen County. 3 mi S of Morristown.
Ro Ellen	Community in E SE section of Dyer County. 6 mi E of Dyersburg.
Rogana	Community in E section of Sumner County. Approx. 7 mi E NE of Gallatin.
Rogers	Community in E central section of Cumberland County. 15 mi E NE of Crossville.
Rogers Creek	Community in W NW section of McMinn County. 3 mmi W of Clearwater.
Rogers Creek Ridge	Ridge in W NW section of McMinn County between Rogers Creek and Clearwater.
Rogers Hollow	Located in S section of Warren County. 9 mi S of McMinnville.
Rogers Ridge	Ridge in NE section of Johnson County, E of Laurel Bloomery.
Rogers Spring	Community in S central section of Hardeman County. 14 mi S of Bolivar. 12 mi E of Grand Junction.
Rogers Springs	Springs located in S section of Hardeman County, W SW of Middleton.
Rogersville	County seat of Hawkins County. Located in center of County. Incorporated in 1835.
Rolling Fields	Community within the city of Columbia, W section of town. In Maury County.
Rolling Hills	Community in central section of Hamblen County near Morristown.
Rolling Hills	Located in central section of Marshall County, SW of Lewisburg.
Rome	Community in W section of Smith County. 6 1/2 mi W of Carthage.
Rome Island	Island on Cumberland River. W section of Smith County, 2 mi W of Rock City.
Romeo	Community in N area of Greene County. 10 1/2 mi N NW of Greeneville.

Roneys Store	Community in W section of Obion County. Approx. 4 mi N of Hornbeak.
Ropers Knob	Located in middle N section of Williamson County. 2 mi N of Franklin.
Rose Bailey Lake	Lake in central E section of Roane County. SE of Kingston.
Rose Creek	Community in middle W NW section of McNairy County. 6 mi W NW of Selmer.
Rosedale	Community in NW area of Anderson County. 8 mi N of Oliver Springs.
Rose Hill	Community in E central section of Madison County. 4 mi E of Jackson.
Rose Hill	Community in middle E section of Union County. 5 mi N NE of Maynardville.
Rosemark	Community in N NE section of Shelby County. 22 mi NE of Memphis.
Roseville	Community in SE section of Bedford County. 9 mi E of Shelbyville, 2 1/2 mi W of Normandy.
Roslin	Community in S area of Fentress County. 14 mi S of Jamestown.
Rosser	Community in E Central section of Carroll County. 5 mi E NE of Huntingdon.
Ross Mountain	Mountain in S SE corner of Grundy County, W of Palmer.
Rossview	Community in middle NE section of Montgomery County. 7 1/2 mi N NE of Clarksville.
Rossville	City in SW section of Fayette County. 17 1/2 mi SW of Somerville. Incorporated in 1903.
Rossville	Community within the city limits of Chattanooga and North Georgia.
Rossville Junction	Community in SW section of Fayette County, S of Rossville.
Rotherwoods Heights	Community in NW corner of Hawkins County.
Rough Hollow	Located in middle N section of Benton County.
Rough Point	Community in middle W section of Jackson County. 3 1/2 mi W of Gainesboro.
Rough Ridge	Located on SE border of Monroe County.
Round Cove	Located in SE section of Putnam County. 10 mi SE of Cookeville. W SW of Calfkiller.

Round Hill	Community in NE section of Giles County. Approx. 14 mi N NE of Pulaski.
Round Knob	Mountain in E section of Carter County, SW of Poga.
Round Lake	Lake in NE area of Dyer County near Obion County line.
Round Mountain	Mountain in W NW section of Cocke County, NW of Carson Springs.
Round Mountain	Mountain in SE section of Cocke County, W of Wasp.
Round Mountain	Mountain in SW section of Cocke County in Great Smoky Mountains. SW of Catons Grove.
Round Mountain	Mountain in N NE section of Scott County, S of Chitwood Mountain.
Round Pond	Community in S section of Montgomery County. 5 mi S of Clarksville.
Round Rock	Community in SW area of Campbell County. 3 mi SE of Caryville.
Round Top	Community in E SE section of Wilson County. Approx. 22 mi SE of Lebanon.
Round Top Knob	Located near E SE border of Wilson County, S of Liberty Hill.
Round Top Mountain	Mountain in middle SE section of Overton County. 12 mi S SE of Livingston.
Routon	Community in SW section of Henry County. 6 mi S SW of Paris.
Rover	Community in NW area of Bedford County. 15 mi NW of Shelbyville, 3 1/2 mi N of Unionville.
Rowark Cove	Community in NE area of Franklin County. 11 mi E NE of Winchester.
Rowe Gap	Community in S central section of Franklin County. 6 mi S of Winchester.
Rowland Hollow	Located in W SW section of Sumner County. 1 1/2 mi W SW of White Hill.
Rowland Station	Community in middle NE section of Warren County. 7 mi NE of McMinnville.
Roy	Community in S SE central section of Madison County. Approx. 7 mi S SE of Jackson.
Royal	Community in Bedford County near Shelbyville.
Royal Blue	Community in W Central section of Campbell

Royal Blue, (Cont.) County. 6 mi NW of Jacksboro.

Royal Oaks Community in Central section of Coffee County. 1 mi S of Manchester.

Royal Oaks Community within the city limits of Chattanooga. Approx. 9 mi E SE of downtown, near East Brainerd.

Royal Oaks Community in central section of Maury County. 3 mi N of Columbia, N of Bel Air.

Rozells Mill Community in S SE section of Lincoln County. 9 1/2 mi S SE of Fayetteville.

Rucker Community in middle S section of Rutherford County. 7 mi S of Murfreesboro.

Rucker Knob Located in N NE section of Rutherford County. 2 mi N of Lascassas.

Rudderville Community in E SE section of Williamson County. 9 mi E SE of Franklin.

Rudolph Community in N section of Haywood County. 7 1/2 mi N of Brownsville.

Rugby Community in N tip of Morgan County. 18 mi N NW of Wartburg.

Ruppertown Community in S section of Lewis County. SW of Voorhies.

Rural Hill Community in SE section of Davidson County. 1 1/2 mi N NW of Mount View.

Rural Vale Community in SW section of Monroe County. 14 mi S of Madisonville.

Rushing Bay Lake in NW section of Stewart County, inlet off the Tennesee River. N of Ginger Bay.

Rushing Hollow Located in NW section of Humphreys County, S of Bull Hollow. 10 mi NW of Waverly.

Rushy Springs Community in NE section of Jefferson County. 8 mi N NE of Dandridge.

Ruskin Community in W area of Dickson County. 10 mi W of Charlotte.

Russell Chapel Community in W section of Sullivan County. 13 1/2 mi W of Blountville.

Russell Crossroad Community in SW central area of Greene County. 7 mi SW of Greeneville.

Russell Crossroads Community in W SW section of Henderson County. 10 mi W SW of Lexington.

Russell Fork — Community in NE central section of Campbell County. 6 mi N NE of LaFollette.

Russell Hill — Community in S SE section of Macon County. 9 1/2 mi SE of Lafayette.

Russell Mill — Community in SW corner of Claiborne County. 1 mi SE of Speedwell.

Russellville — Community in mid NE section of Hamblen County. 6 mi NE of Morristown.

Rutherford — City in N area of Gibson County. 10 1/2 mi N NW of Trenton. Incorporated in 1859.

Rutherford County — County Seat: Murfreesboro. Zip Code 37130. Located in central section of the State. Bounded by Wilson, Cannon, Coffee, Bedford, Marshall, Williamson and Davidson Counties. Named in honor of Major General Griffith Rutherford.

RUTHERFORD COUNTY

Ruthton — Community in central NE section of Sullivan County. 11 mi E of Blountville.

Ruthville — Community in N NW section of Weakley County. 11 mi N NW of Dresden. W SW of Chestnut Glade.

Rutledge — County Seat of Grainger County. Located in W section of County. Incorporated in 1927.

Rutledge Falls — Community in S central section of Coffee County. 5 mi S SW of Manchester.

Rutledge Hill — Community in SE corner of Coffee County. 15 mi SE of Manchester.

Ryall Springs — Community in SE area of Hamilton County. 12 mi E SE of Chattanooga.

Rye Hollow — Located in middle E section of Houston County, E of Pollard.

Sadie — Community in NE area of Carter County. 9 mi NE of Elizabethton.

Sadler — Community in NW section of Putnam County. 14 mi W NW of Cookeville.

Sadlersville — Community in NW section of Robertson County. 14 1/2 mi W NW of Springfield.

Safley — Community in middle SE section of Warren County. 6 mi SE of McMinnville.

Sage Hollow — Located in middle E SE section of Houston County, E of Pollard.

Sailors Rest — Community in SW section of Montgomery County. 16 mi SW of Clarksville.

Sainville	Community in E area of Coffee County. 10 mi E NE of Manchester.
Sale Creek	Community in N area of Hamilton County. 26 mi N NE of Chattanooga. N of Bakewell.
Sale Creek	Rises in S area of Rhea County W of Dayton and then flows S through the N section of Hamilton County into the Tennessee River.
Salem	Community in NE area of Cocke County. 3 mi E of Parrottsville.
Salem	Community on S border of Hickman County. Approx. 10 mi S of Centerville.
Salem	Community in N section of Lewis County. 7 mi NE of Hohenwald.
Salem	Community in central SE section of Montgomery County. 5 mi S SE of Clarksville.
Salem	Community in S section of Tipton County. 10 mi S SW of Covington.
Saltillo	City on middle N border of Hardin County. 12 mi N of Savannah. 9 mi NE of Right. Incorporated in 1951.
Salt Lick Creek	Creek in SW section of Jackson County, off Cumberland River.
Salt Spring Mountain	Mountain in E NE section of Monroe County, N of Cowcamp Ridge.
Samburg	City on W border of Obion County near Reelfoot Lake. 17 mi S SW of Union City. Incorporated in 1907.
Sam Hart Hollow	Located in S section of Bedford County.
Sampson	Community in NW section of Bledsoe County. 6 mi W NW of Pikeville.
Sampson Mountain Wilderness	Mountain in SE corner of Greene County. E of Greystone.
Sampson Ridge	Ridge in E section of Dickson County, W of Harpeth Valley.
Sams Ridge	Ridge in E SE corner of Blount County. E of Defeated Ridge.
Sand Banks Ridge	Ridge in SW section of Stewart County, S of Mulbury Hill.
Sanders Crossing	Community in S section of Grundy County. 10 S of Altamont.
Sanders Lake	Lake in N central section of Giles County. N

Sanders Lake, (Cont.)	of Wales.
Sanderson Hollow	Located in N section of Humphreys County. 2 mi N of Gorman.
Sandhill	Community in central SE section of Weakley County. Approx. 5 mi SE of Dresden.
Sandlick	Community in S central section of Claiborne County. 7 1/2 mi SW of Tazewell.
Sand Mountain	Mountain in SW section of Polk County.
Sand Mountain	Mountain in N central section of Sevier County, N of Caton.
Sand Ridge	Community in W central section of Henderson County. 5 1/2 mi W NW of Lexington.
Sand Springs	Community in middle E SE section of Putnam County. 9 mi E SE of Cookeville.
Sandstone Knob	Located in N section of Trousdale County. 2 mi W of Halltown.
Sand Switch	Community in E NE area of Franklin County. 13 1/2 mi E NE of Winchester.
Sandy	Community in W SW area of Fentress County. 12 1/2 mi SW of Jamestown.
Sandy	Community in SE section of Johnson County, E of Crackers Neck.
Sandy Gap	Community in SE area of Cocke County. 5 mi S of Del Rio, 12 mi SE of Newport.
Sandy Hook	Community in SW corner of Maury County. 14 mi SW of Columbia.
Sandy Lane	Community in S SW section of Monroe County. 5 1/2 mi S SE of Tellico Plains.
Sandy Point	Community in W Central section of Benton County. 2 mi W of Camden.
Sandy Ridge	Community in SE section of Jefferson County. 4 1/2 mi S SE of Dandridge.
Sandy Springs	Community in SW section of Robertson County. 0 1/2 mi SW of Springfield.
Sandy Valley	Located in W SW section of Sumner County. 3 mi W NW of Ocana.
Sanford	Community in SW section of McMinn County. 10 mi SW of Athens.
Sanford Hill	Community in W central section of Chester

Sanford Hill, (Cont.)	County.
Sanford Knob	Located in W NW section of Rutherford County. 2 mi N of Rock Springs.
Sango	Community in middle E section of Montgomery County. 8 mi E SE of Clarksville.
Sante Fe	Community in middle NW section of Maury County. 10 mi N NW of Columbia.
Saratoga Springs	Community in NW Section of county in Bledsoe State Forest. 8 mi NW of Pikeville.
Sardis	Community in W central section of Cocke County. 5 mi S of Newport and 2 mi E of Pleasant Grove.
Sardis	City in SE corner of Henderson County. 15 mi S SE of Lexington. Incorporated in 1949.
Sartain Hollow	Located in W section of Coffee County, S of Baucom.
Sassafras Mountain	Mountain located in NW Section of Anderson County.
Sassafras Ridge	Ridge in E SE section of Monroe County, SE of Flats Mountain.
Sassafrass Stand Ridge	Ridge in SE section of Perry County.
Saulsbury	City in SW central section of Hardeman County. 15 1/2 mi S SW of Bolivar. 5 1/2 mi E of Grand Junction. Incorporated in 1901.
Saundersville	Community in S SW section of Sumner County. Approx. 4 mi E NE of Hendersonville.
Savage Point	Located in N central section of Sequatchie County, W of Brush Creek.
Savannah	County Seat of Hardin County. Located in middle W section of the County. Incorporated in 1833.
Savannah Creek	Creek in E area of Hamilton County. Flows into Wolftever Creek.
Sawdust	Community in middle W NW section of Maury County. 9 1/2 mi W NW of Columbia.
Sawmill Hollow	Located in middle SE section of Montgomery County.
Sawmill Ridge	Ridge in N section of Fentress County. 3 mi E of Fairview.

Sawyer	Community in W section of Hamilton County on Walden's Ridge. W of Falling Water.
Sawyer Mountain	Mountain in E section of Cocke County, E of French Broad.
Sawyers Mill	Community on W Border of Benton County. 4 mi W of Camden.
Sayre Hollow	Located in W section of Humphreys County. 2 mi W NW of Pursley.
Scales Mountain	Mountain in W SW section of Rutherford County. 3 mi S of Almaville.
Scandlyn	Community in NE corner of Roane County. 12 mi NE of Kingston.
Scarboro	Community in SE area of Anderson County.
Scarbrough	Community in N NW corner of Madison County. 11 mi N NW of Jackson.
Scattersville	Community in W NW section of Sumner County. 16 mi NW of Gallatin on Robertson County border.
Scenic Lake	Lake in W SW area of Fayette County near Shelby County line W of Canadaville.
Schelley Knob	Located in SW section of Jackson County, W of Gainesboro.
Schoolhouse Mountain	Mountain in central N section of Overton County, E of Livingston.
Scott	Community in NW section of Meigs County, S of Fooshee Pass.
Scott County SCOTT COUNTY	County Seat: Huntsville. Zip Code 37756. Located in North Central section of the State. Bounded by Campbell, Anderson, Morgan, Fentress and Pickett Counties and the State of Kentucky to the North. Named in honor of General Winfield Scott.
Scott Hill	Community in middle S SW section of Carroll County, S of Leach.
Scott Lake	Lake in NW area of Cheatham County. 9 mi W of Henderson.
Scott Mill	Community on W border of Greene County. 17 mi W of Greeneville, E of Beulah.
Scott Pinnacle	Located in SE corner of White County.
Scott Pond	Pond in N NE section of Cocke County, N of Baltimore.
Scottsboro	Community in W section of Davidson County. 2

Scottsboro, (Cont.)	mi W of Jordonia.
Scotts Hill	City in SE section of Henderson County. 12 1/2 mi SE of Lexington. 6 mi N NE of Sardia. Incorporated in 1917. Boundaries also extend into Decatur County.
Scotts Hollow	Located in E section of Davidson County.
Scott State Forest	Located in W NW section of Scott County. 12 mi N NW of Huntsville.
Scratch Ankle Hollow	Located in SE corner of Marion County near Whiteside.
Screamer	Community on S SW border of Maury County. S of Spencer Hill.
Scroggins Hollow	Located in SE section of Hamilton County.
Scruggs Hollow	Located in W SW section of Macon County. S of Fairview.
Seal Hollow	Located in middle NE section of Cannon County. 4 mi E NE of Woodbury.
Seaton Springs	Community in middle N section of Sevier County, S of Jay Ell Road.
Seaton Top	Mountain in central section of Sevier County in Shields Mountain Range, N NE of McCookville.
Second Creek	Community in S SE section of Lawrence County. Approx. 15 mi S of Lawrenceburg.
Second Creek Island	Island on the Cumberland River in S SW section of Trousdale County. 1 mi SE of Walnut Grove.
Seeber Flats	Community in middle NW section of Anderson County. 6 mi NW of Clinton.
Seehorn	Community in E section of Jefferson County near French Broad.
Seehorn Creek	Creek in E section of Jefferson County, flows into the French Broad River near French Broad.
Selmer	County Seat of McNairy County. Located near center of County. Incorporated in 1901.
Sengtown	Community in N section of Sumner County. 15 mi N of Gallatin.
Sentertown	Community in Knox County. 8 1/2 mi NE of downtown Knoxville.
Sequatchie	Community located in near center of Marion County. 3 1/2 mi N NE of Jasper.

Sequatchie County

SEQUATCHIE COUNTY

County Seat: Dunlap. Zip Code 37327. Located in Southeastern section of the State. Bounded by Van Buren, Bledsoe, Hamilton, Marion, Grundy and Warren Counties. Named in honor of the Sequatchie Valley.

Sequatchie River

Begins in S section of Cumberland County, flows S SW through Bledsoe, Sequatchie and Marion Counties where it flows into the Tennessee River.

Sequoia Grove

Community in E Central section of Bradley County near Cleveland.

Sequoyah Hills

Community in central section of Hamilton County. Approx. 13 mi NE of downtown Chattanooga. E of Middle Valley.

Sequoyah Hills

Community within city limits of Knoxville, NE of Bearden. In Knox County.

Sequoyah Nuclear Plant

TVA Nuclear Plant on the Tennessee River E of Soddy Daisy. 18 mi NE of downtown Chattanooga in Hamilton County.

Serles

Community in E central section of Hardeman County. 10 mi E SE of Bolivar. 4 mi S of Hornsby.

Seth

Community near W SW border of Maury County. 14 mi W SW of Columbia, 3 mi S of Hampshire.

Settling Baskins

Community located on N border of Bradley County on McMinn County Line.

Seven Islands

Islands on the French Broad River, E SE section of Knox County. S of Peter Mill.

Sevier County

SEVIER COUNTY

County Seat: Sevierville. Zip Code 37862. Located in on Eastern Border of the State. Bounded by Blount, Knox, Jefferson and Cocke Counties and the State of North Carolina to the East. Named in honor of John Sevier.

Sevier County Park

Located in NE section of Sevier County, SE of Union Grove.

Sevier Home

Community in S section of Knox County. W SW of Shooks.

Sevierville

County Seat of Sevier County. Located in NW section of county. Incorporated in 1887.

Sewanee

Community in E area of Franklin County. 11 mi E of Winchester.

Sewee

Community in NE section of Meigs County near border, S of Boggess Crossroads.

Sewell Creek

Creek in NW section of Pickett County, flows

Sewell Creek, (Cont.)	into the Wolf River.
Sexton	Community in SW area of Giles County.
Sexton Mountain	Mountain in NW area of Campbell County W of Zeb Mountain.
Seymour	Community in NE corner of Blount County on county line.
Seymour	Community in W NW section of Sevier County. Approx. 12 mi W of Sevierville.
Seymour Heights	Community in W NW section of Sevier County. 11 mi W of Sevierville.
Sgt. Alvin York Mill State Historic Area	Located in NW section of Fentress County.
Shackle Island	Community in SW section of Sumner County. 9 1/2 mi W SW of Gallatin, N of Hendersonville.
Shacklett	Community in S area of Cheatham County. 10 mi S of Ashland City.
Shaddy Grove Hollow	Located in NE section of Hamilton County.
Shadtown	Community in N section of Unicoi County. Approx. 8 mi NE of Erwin.
Shady Acres	Community in central section of Coffee County.
Shady Grove	Community in NE section of Coffee County. 11 1/2 mi N NE of Manchester.
Shady Grove	Community in N NE area of Franklin County. 11 mi NE of Winchester.
Shady Grove	Community in N central section of Hamilton County. 18 mi N NE of downtown Chattanooga.
Shady Grove	Community in NW section of Hardin County, W of Saltillo.
Shady Grove	Community in S section of Jackson County. 7 1/2 mi S of Gainesboro.
Shady Grove	Community in S section of Jefferson County. 5 mi SW of Dandridge.
Shady Grove	Community in SE section of Knox County. 18 mi SE of Knoxville.
Shady Grove	Community on E SE border of Lincoln County. 13 mi E SE of Fayetteville.
Shady Grove	Community in E section of Montgomery County. 10 1/2 mi E SE of Clarksville.

Shady Grove	Community in E NE section of Putnam County. 10 mi E NE of Cookeville.
Shady Grove	Community in middle SE section of Sevier County. 8 1/2 mi SE of Sevierville.
Shady Grove	Community in SE section of Trousdale County. Approx. 2 mi SE of Hartsville.
Shady Grove	Community in middle W SW section of White County. 6 1/2 mi W SW of Sparta.
Shady Grove (Duck River P.O.)	Community in SE corner of Hickman County. 11 1/2 mi E SE of Centerville.
Shady Hill	Community in middle SE section of Henderson County. 7 mi SE of Lexington. 5 1/2 mi NW of Scotts Hill.
Shady Rest	Community in central NE section of Warren County. 3 1/2 mi NW of McMinnville.
Shady Valley	Community in W NW section of Johnson County. 7 1/2 mi W NW of Mountain City.
Shaffner	Community in E NE border of Obion County. Approx. 4 mi E SE of Union City.
Shakerag Ridge	Ridge in W SW section of Lawrence County near border.
Shallow Bluff Island	Island on the Tennessee River on S SW border of Decatur County.
Shallowford	Community in S central section of Unicoi County. 4 1/2 mi SW of Erwin.
Shallow Ford Hill	Located in W SW section of Sumner County. Approx. 5 mi N of Hendersonville.
Shallowford Hills	Community within the city limits of Chattanooga. 8 mi E of downtown. In Hamilton County.
Shandy	Community in N central section of Hardeman County. 3 mi N NE of Bolivar.
Shanghai	Community in S SW section of Hardin County. 14 mi S of Savannah. 4 mi S of Pickwick Dam.
Shannondale	Community within the city limits of Knoxville. 7 mi N of downtown. In Knox County.
Shannon Hills	Community in central section of Hamilton County. Approx. 10 mi N NE of downtown Chattanooga. Approx. 3 mi N of Hixson.
Sharon	City in middle SW section of Weakley County. 8 mi W SW of Dresden. Incorporated in 1901.

Sharon Park	Community within the city of Columbia, middle S section of town. In Maury County.
Sharpe Place	Community in NE section of Fentress County. 8 mi NE of Jamestown.
Sharp Gap	Community within the city limits of Knoxville. 3 1/2 mi N NW of downtown. In Knox County.
Sharp Place	Community in N NW section of Fentress County. 8 mi E SE of Pall Mall.
Sharps Chapel	Community in N central section of Union County. 6 1/2 mi N NW of Maynardville.
Sharps Ferry	Community in S SW section of Obion County. Approx. 3 mi E SE of Cloverdale.
Sharps Ridge Park	Park in N central section of Knoxville. 3 1/2 mi N NW of downtown. In Knox County.
Sharpsville	Community in middle E section of Rutherford County. 7 mi E NE of Murfreesboro.
Shaver Mill	Community in S central section of Sullivan County. 4 1/2 mi S SW of Blountville.
Shaver Town	Community in W SW section of Smith County. 7 mi S SW of Carthage.
Shaw	Community in middle NW section of Haywood County. 9 1/2 mi N NW of Brownsville.
Shawanee	Community in upper N central section of Claiborne County. 9 mi N NW of Tazewell.
Shaw Lake	Lake in SE section of Haywood County. 7 mi SE of Brownsville. 3 mi W of Brickyard Pond.
Shawnette	Community in middle E SE section of Wayne County. 11 mi S SE of Waynesboro.
Shawtown	Community in W NW section of Obion County. 13 1/2 mi W SW of Union City.
Shea	Community in SW corner of Campbell County. 7 mi SW of Caryville.
Sheep Rock Mountain	Mountain in central section of Scott County, SE of New River.
Shelby County SHELBY COUNTY	County Seat: Memphis. Zip Code 38103. Located in Southwest corner of the State. Bounded by Tipton and Fayette Counties and the State of Mississippi to the South and the Mississippi River to the West. Named in honor of Isaac Shelby.
Shelby Forest	Located in NW section of Shelby County.

Shelbyville — County Seat of Bedford County located in center of county. Incorporated in 1819.

Shelbyville Mills — Community in Central area of Bedford County. 2 mi SW of Shelbyville.

Shell Creek — Community in SE area of Carter County. 2 mi E of Roan Mountain.

Shellmound — Community on S border of Marion County. 5 1/2 mi S SE of Jasper on Nickajack Lake.

Shell Mountain — Mountain in NE section of Sevier County. 9 mi E of Sevierville.

Shellsford — Community in middle E section of Warren County. 3 1/2 mi E of McMinnville.

Shelton Hollow — Located in middle S section of Cannon County. 5 1/2 mi S of Woodbury, S of Carrick Hollow.

Shepherd — Community within the city limits of Chattanooga, in the Airport area of town. In Hamilton County.

Shepherd Forest — Community on Signal Mountain in Hamilton County. 6 mi N NW of Chattanooga.

Shepp — Community in middle SW section of Haywood County. 8 mi S Sw of Brownsville. 4 mi NE of Stanton.

Sherrell Hollow — Located in W SW section of Davidson County, N of Dozier Hollow.

Sherrilltown — Community in middle S SE section of Wilson County. Approx. 11 mi S SE of Lebanon.

Sherwood — Community in E SE section of Franklin County. 13 mi SE of Winchester.

Sheybogan — Community in S Central section of Cannon County. 5 mi S SE of Woodbury.

Shields Mountain — Mountain in central section of Sevier County, N NE of McCookville.

Shields Ridge — Ridge in middle SW section of Jefferson County. 5 mi W NW of Dandridge.

Shiloh — Community in E Central section of Bedford County on Coffee County line. 5 mi E of Wartrace.

Shiloh — Community in SE corner of Carroll County near Decatur County line. 11 mi E of Clarksburg.

Shiloh — Community in S area of Grainger County. 5 1/2 mi S of Rutledge.

Shiloh	Community on W SW border of Hardin County. 10 mi SW of Savannah, SW of Shiloh National Military Park.
Shiloh	Community in NW section of Hawkins County. 7 mi NW of Rogersville.
Shiloh	Community in SE corner of Jackson County. 8 1/2 mi SE of Gainesboro. 1 1/2 mi SE of Center Grove.
Shiloh	Community in SW section of Montgomery County. 14 mi S SW of Clarksville.
Shiloh	Community in middle E SE section of Overton County. 9 mi E SE of Livingston.
Shiloh	Community in middle E section of Rutherford County. 2 mi E of Murfreesboro.
Shiloh Church	Community in middle E section of Sumner County. 6 1/2 mi NE of Gallatin.
Shiloh National Military Park	Located on E SE border of Hardin County. 7 mi SW of Savannah. 6 mi NW of Pickwick Dam.
Shiloh Ridge	Ridge in E SE section of Meigs County, E of Big Spring.
Shingle Hollow	Located in E NE section of Hamilton County.
Shingle Mill Hollow	Located in N NW section of Hamilton County.
Shingletown	Community in middle NE section of Johnson County. 5 mi N NE of Mountain City.
Shining Rock	Community in S central section of DeKalb County. 3 1/2 mi S of Smithville.
Shipetown	Community in NE section of Knox County. 10 mi NE of Knoxville. 2 mi NE of Three Points.
Shipp Hollow	Located in middle W SW section of Sumner County. 3 mi N NE of Millersville.
Shipps Bend	Community in center of Hickman County. 2 mi W of Centerville.
Shirley	Community in E area of Fentress County. 10 1/2 mi SE of Jamestown.
Shirley Hollow	Located in N NW section of Cannon County. 6 mi N of Woodbury.
Shirleyton	Community in NE section of Marion County. 3 mi N of Whitwell.
Shooks	Community in SE section of Knox County. 7 mi SE of Knoxville.

Shooks Gap	Community in NE area of Blount County.
Shooks Gap	Community on W NW border of Sevier County. 12 1/2 mi W of Sevierville.
Shop Hollow	Located in SW section of Stewart County, SE of Mulbury Hill.
Shop Springs	Community in central SE section of Wilson County. 7 mi SE of Lebanon.
Shore	Community in W SW section of Giles County. Approx. 9 mi SW of Pulaski.
Short Creek	Community in S section of Rutherford County. Approx. 12 mi S SE of Murfreesboro.
Shortfoots Pond	Pond in W SW section of Monroe County, NW of Tellico Plains.
Short Hollow	Ridge in W section of Wayne County of the county line.
Short Mountain	Community in Central NE section of Cannon County. 7 mi NE of Woodbury.
Short Mountain	Mountain in NE area of Cannon County. 6 mi NE of Woodbury.
Short Mountain	Mountain in W section of Cocke County, NW of Allan Grove.
Short Mountain	Mountain in W section of Hancock County, W of Sneedville.
Short Mountain	Mountain in W section of Hawkins County, ranges between Mooresburg and Altonville.
Short Mountain	Mountain in NE central section of Sevier County, E of Richardsons Cove.
Short Mountian	Mountain in middle W section of Campbell County, W of Ivydell.
Short Tail Springs	Located in middle SE section of Hamilton County. Approx. 14 mi NE of downtown Chattanooga, NE of Harrison.
Shoulder Hollow	Located in middle S section of Stewart County, W of Carlisle.
Shouns	Community in S SE section of Johnson County, S of Mountain City.
Shrum Hollow	Located in S SE section of Macon County. 2 mi E of Beech Bottom.
Shubert	Community in central section of Lewis County. S SW of Hohenwald.

Shug Mountain	Mountain in NE central section of Scott County. SW of Privet Mountain.
Siam	Community in N central section of Carter County. 3 mi E of Elizabethton.
Sibley	Community in NW section of Hardin County, E NE of Right.
Sidonia	Community in W SW section of Weakley County. 11 1/2 mi W SW of Dresden.
Signal Hills	Community within the city limits of Chattanooga. 4 mi N NW of downtown in Hamilton County.
Signal Mountain	Mountain in SW area of Hamilton County, part of Walden's Ridge .
Signal Mountain	Town on Signal Mountain located on Walden's Ridge in Hamilton County. 6 mi N NW of downtown Chattanooga. Incorporated in 1919.
Signal Point	Located in SW section of Hamilton County.
Silers Bald	Mountain on S border of Sevier County. In the Great Smoky Mountains. Ele. 5,607.
Silerton	City on NE border of Hardeman County. 12 mi E NE of Bolivar. Small portion of city is in Chester County. Incorporated in 1923.
Silica	Community in Central section of Campbell County, 3 mi W SW of Jacksboro.
Siloam	Community on W border of Macon County. 10 1/2 mi W of Lafayette.
Siloam (Dog Hill)	Community in W area of Crockett County. 1 mi W NW of Alamo.
Silvacola	Community in middle N NW section of Sullivan County. 4 mi NW of Blountville.
Silver City	Community in E section of Hamblen County. 7 1/2 mi E of Morristown.
Silver Creek	Community in W NW section of Marshall County. 5 1/2 mi W SW of Cowden.
Silverdale	Community within the city limits of Chattanooga. 10 mi E of downtown in Hamilton County.
Silver Grove	Community in middle E section of Sullivan County. 7 mi E SE of Blountville.
Silver Hill	Community in N section of Rutherford County. 11 mi N of Rutherford.
Silver Lake	Community in N NE section of Johnson County,

Silver Lake, (Cont.)	NE of Wills.
Silver Moon Lake	Lake in SW corner of Madison County. 18 mi SW of Jackson.
Silver Point	Community in SW section of Putnam County, 14 mi W SW of Cookeville.
Silver Springs	Community in W section of Wilson County. 9 mi W of Lebanon.
Silverton	Community on W border of Chester County. 1 mi SW of Henderson.
Silvertop	Community on S SE border of Houston County. 8 mi S SE of Erin.
Simmons Ridge	Ridge in N section of Claiborne County, E of Forge Ridge.
Sims Hollow	Located in E section of Hamilton County.
Sims Neck	Located in NW section of Hamilton County.
Sims Ridge	Community in W section of Lawrence County. 12 1/2 mi W SW of Lawrenceburg.
Sims Spring	Community in W Central section of Bedford County.
Sims Spring	Community in W section of Bedford County. 3 1/2 mi S SW of Halls Mill.
Sinclair Lake	Lake in W SW section of Rhea County. 7 mi N NW of Dayton.
Singleton	Community in SE area of Bedford County. 6 mi SE of Shelbyville.
Singleton	Community in N Central section of Blount County on Knox County line. 7 mi N of Maryville.
Sink Creek	Creek in SE area of DeKalb County off Caney Fork River.
Sinkhole Mountain	Mountain in W section of Sevier County, W of Cove Creek Cascades.
Sinking Cove	Community in SE area of Franklin County. 13 mi SE of Winchester.
Sinking Creek Lake	Lake in SW section of Knox County, NE of Blue Grass.
Sink Mountain	Mountain in SW section of Johnson County, S of Doeville.
Sisco Mountain	Mountain in middle S section of Overton County. 10 mi SE of Livingston.

Sissom Hollow	Located in S SW section of Cannon County. 9 1/2 mi S SW of Woodbury.
Sitka	Community in SE section of Gibson County. 13 mi SE of Trenton.
Sixmile	Community in Central area of Blount County. 6 mi S of Maryville.
Sixteenth Model	Community in W area of Coffee County. 8 1/2 mi W NW of Manchester.
Skaggston	Community in NE section of Knox County. 12 mi NE of Knoxville.
Skinem	Community in S SW section of Lincoln County. 4 1/2 mi S of Fayetteville.
Skinner Crossroad	Community in W section of Greene County. 14 mi W of Greeneville.
Skinner Hill	Located in S SE section of Williamson County, S of Cross Keys. 13 mi S SE of Franklin.
Skinner Mountain	Mountain in W section of Fentress County, W of Glenobey.
Skullbone	Community in NE area of Gibson County. 12 1/2 mi NE of Trenton.
Skull Island	Island on Tennessee River, approx. 3 mi N NE of Harrison Bay State Park in Hamilton County.
Skunk Ridge	Ridge in S section of Blount County
Sky Lake	Lake within the city limits of Memphis, W of Lake Windemere. In Shelby County.
Skyline Park	Community on Signal Mountain in Hamilton County. 7 mi N NW of Chattanooga.
Skymont	Boy Scout Camp in NW section of Grundy County. 8 mi W of Altamont.
Sladestone	Community in N Central section of Anderson County. 6 mi N NW of Clinton.
Slaughter Hollow	Located in middle E section of Humphreys County. 3 mi S of McEwen.
Slayden	City in NW section of Dickson County. 10 1/2 mi NW of Charlotte. Incorporated in 1913.
Slick Rock	Community in middle S section of Scott County. 7 1/2 mi S of Huntsville.
Slide	Community in middle S section of Hawkins County. 5 mi E SE of Rogersville.
Slide Hollow	Located in E SE section of Carter County, N of

Slide Hollow, (Cont.)	Laurel Fork.
Sliders Knob	Located in middle N NE section of Williamson County. 2 mi S of Brentwood.
Sloan Ridge	Ridge in W SW section of Sevier County. 3 mi SE of Cove Creek Cascades.
Sloanville	Community in N NW section of Shelby County. Approx. 3 mi W of Millington.
Smarden	Community in S SE section of Williamson County. Approx. 12 mi SE of Franklin.
Smart Mountain	Mountain in S section of Van Buren County, S of Pine Creek.
Smartt	Community in middle SW section of Warren County. 4 1/2 mi SW of McMinnville.
Smith Bend	Area in bend of Cumberland River, SE of Gladdice in Jackson County.
Smith County SMITH COUNTY	County Seat: Carthage. Zip Code 37030. Located in North central section of the State. Bounded by Macon, Jackson, Putnam, DeKalb, Wilson and Trousdale Counties. Named in honor of Daniel Smith.
Smithfield	Community in S section of Monroe County. NE of Coker Creek.
Smith Hollow	Located in W NW section of Dickson County. 1 1/2 mi N of Adams Crossroads.
Smith Hollow	Located in middle N NW section of Humphreys County. 2 mi W SW of Woolworth.
Smith Hollow	Located in N section of Smith County. 2 mi W of Cartwright.
Smith Hollow	Located in SE section of Wilson County. 3 mi E of Sherrilltown.
Smith Island	Island on Holston River, S of Church Hill.
Smith Lake	There are two Smith Lakes in Henry County, located approx. 4 mi N of Paris.
Smithland	Community in E SE section of Lincoln County. 11 mi E SE of Fayetteville.
Smith Mountain	Mountain in middle E section of Polk County.
Smith Pond	Pond in SW section of Chester County, NW of Masseyville.
Smithtown	Community in SE section of Bledsoe County. 9 mi S of Pikeville, 2 1/2 mi W of Brayton.

Smithtown	Community in middle W section of Marion County. Approx. 6 mi W of Jasper.
Smithville	County Seat of DeKalb County. Located near center of the County. Incorporated in 1843.
Smithwood	Community within the city limits of Knoxville. 4 1/2 mi N of downtown. In Knox County.
Smokey Junction	Community in E SE section of Scott County. 1 mi SE of Huntsville.
Smoky Mountain	Mountain along SE border of Scott County.
Smothers	Community in SE area of Benton County near Carroll County line. 9 mi SW of Camden.
Smyrna	Community in E central area of Carroll County. 6 mi E SE of Huntingdon.
Smyrna	Community in E NE section of Marshall County. 10 1/2 mi N NE of Lewisburg.
Smyrna	Community in middle W section of Pickett County. 2 mi S SW of Byrdstown.
Smyrna	City in NW section of Rutherford County. 10 mi NW of Murfreesboro. Incorporated in 1869.
Smyrna	Community in middle SE section of Warren County. 5 mi SE of McMinnville.
Snaggy Island	Island in NW corner of Jefferson County on the Holston River.
Snag Mountain	Mountain along E SE border of Sevier County, S of Rocky Grove.
Snake Den Mountain	Mountain in SW corner of Cocke County.
Snake Hollow	Located in W NW section of Hancock County. 7 mi W of Sneedville.
Sneedville	County Seat of Hancock County. Located in central section of the county. 4 1/2 mi S of Virginia Border. Incorporated in 1953.
Snodgrass	Community in S central section of Claiborne County.
Snowbird Mountain	Mountain on S border of Cocke County on the North Carolina line in Cherokee National Forest.
Snow Hill	Community in E area of Hamilton County. 17 mi E NE of downtown Chattanooga.
Snows Hill	Community in W central section of DeKalb County. 4 mi W NW of Smithville.

Soapstone Hill	Located in S section of Rutherford County. E of Forterville.
Soddy Creek	Creek in N central area of Hamilton County. Flows in Tennessee River N of Soddy Daisy.
Soddy Daisy	City in N central section of Hamilton County. 16 mi N NE of Chattanooga. Incorporated in 1969.
Soddy Lake	Inlett off the Tennessee River in the middle N section of Hamilton County, in Soddy Daisy area.
Soffell Island	Island on French Broad River in N section of Sevier County, N of Catlettsburg.
Sol Messer Mountain	Mountain in S SW section of Cocke County, S of Click Mill.
Solo	Community in NE section of Tipton County. 3 mi E NE of Covington.
Solway	Community in W section of Knox County. 14 mi W of Knoxville, NW of Robinson Crossroads.
Somerville	County Seat of Fayette County. Located in E central section of county. Incorporated in 1826.
Sorrell Chapel	Community in SE area of Dyer County.
Southall	Community in S central section of Williamson County. 4 mi SW of Franklin.
South Berlin	Community on middle W border of Marshall County. 4 1/2 mi NW of Lewisburg.
South Carthage	City in near center of Smith County. S & W of Carthage. Incorporated in 1963.
South Chickamauga Creek	Creek in E section of Hamilton County. Flows from N Georgia through East Ridge and Chattanooga into the Tennessee River approx. 2 mi S of Chickamauga Dam.
South Cleveland	Community in SE Section of Bradley County near Cleveland.
South Clinton	Community in SE central area of Anderson County, 1 mi SE of Clinton.
South Covington	Community in central E section of Tipton County. 2 1/2 mi S SW of Covington.
South Cumberland State Park	Located in S SW section of Grundy County, N of Summerfield.
South Cumberland State Park (Savage	Located in middle NE section of Grundy County, E of Altamont.

South Cumberland State Park (Savage Gulf Natural Area), (Cont.)	
South Dyersburg	Community in central section of Dyer County near Dyersburg.
Southern Hills	Community within the city of Columbia, S section of town. In Maury County.
South Fork	Community in S area of Dyer County. 7 mi S of Dyersburg.
South Fulton	City in NE corner of Obion County. 11 mi E NE of Union City. Incorporated in 1909.
South Hall	Community in N Central section of Blount County near Maryville.
South Harriman	Community in W NW section of Roane County, S of Harriman.
South Holston Lake	Lake (Holston River) in E section of Sullivan County.
South Knoxville	Community within the city limits of Knoxville. 1 mi SE of downtown. In Knox County.
South Liberty	Community in middle SW section of McMinn County. 6 mi S SW of Athens.
South Pittsburg	City on S SW border of Marion County. 6 mi SW of Jasper. Incorporated in 1899.
Southport	Community in middle S SW section of Maury County. 10 1/2 mi S SW of Columbia.
Southside	Community in SW corner of Hardin County. 13 mi S SW of Savannah. 6 mi W SW of Pickwick Landing Dam.
Southside	Community in S SE section of Montgomery County. 11 mi S SE of Clarksville.
South Tunnel	Community in central section of Sumner County. 6 mi N NW of Gallatin.
Spain Hollow	Located in W SW section of Humphreys County. 1 mi SE of New Johnsonville.
Spanish Needle Knob	Located near E NE border of Wilson County. 10 mi NE of Lebanon.
Spanish Trails	Community within the city of Knoxville, W section of town. N of Cedar Bluff in Knox County.
Sparkman	Community in N NW section of Van Buren County. 5 mi N NW of Spencer.

Sparta	County seat of White County. Located in near center of county. Incorporated in 1833.
Speakman Hollow	Located in N section of Macon County. 2 mi E SE of Green Valley.
Speedwell	Community in W area of Claiborne County. 17 mi W of Tazewell.
Spence Hollow	Located in near center of Humphreys County. 1 1/2 mi S of Waverly.
Spencer	County Seat of Van Buren County. Located in N central section of the County. Incorporated in 1909.
Spencer Hill	Community in S SW section of Maury County. 13 1/2 mi S SW of Columbia.
Spencers Mill	Community in SE area of Dickson County. 14 1/2 mi SE of Charlotte.
Spivey	Community in NE corner of Macon County. 12 mi E NE of Lafayette.
Sportsmans Lake	Lake in NW section of Sumner County. E NE of Portland.
Spot	Community in NW section of Hickman County. 10 mi SW of Centerville.
Spout Springs	Community in W NW section of Obion County. Approx. 6 mi N of Hornbeak.
Springbrook	Community in NE corner of Madison County. 12 mi NE of Jackson.
Springbrook Lake	Lake in NE section of Madison County. Approx. 11 mi NE of Jackson.
Spring City	City in middle N section of Rhea County. 16 mi N NE of Dayton. Incorporated in 1895.
Spring Creek	Community in E SE section of Henry County, W SW of Manleyville.
Spring Creek	Community in W central section of Lawrence County. N of Crewstown. Approx. 9 mi N of Loretto.
Spring Creek	Community in NE corner of Madison County. 13 mi NE of Jackson.
Spring Creek	Community in middle W SW section of McMinn County. Approx. 7 mi W SW of Athens.
Spring Creek	Community in W section of Perry County. 8 1/2 mi W NW of Linden.
Spring Creek	Community in SE corner of Warren County.

Spring Creek Ridge	Ridge in N section of McMinn County, N of Clearwater.
Springdale	Community in SE central section of Claiborne County. 3 mi SE of Tazewell.
Springdale	Community in NW section of Sullivan County. Just S of Kingsport.
Springers Station	Community in SW section of Lawrence County. Approx. 5 mi N NE of Loretto, just N of Pleasant Point.
Springfield	County Seat of Robertson County. Located near center of county. Incorporated in 1819.
Spring Hill	Community in S Central section of Anderson County, near Knox County line. 3 mi S of Clinton.
Spring Hill	Community in S section of Haywood County. 10 mi S of Brownsville. 7 mi E SE of Stanton.
Spring Hill	Community on W border of Henderson County. 10 mi W NW of Lexington.
Spring Hill	Community in NE section of Houston County. Approx. 4 1/2 mi E NE of Erin.
Spring Hill	City on N NE border of Maury County. 11 1/2 mi N NE of Columbia. Boundaries also extend into Williamson County. Incorporated in 1838. Home of Saturn Automobile Plant.
Spring Hill	Community in NE Section of White County. 7 mi NE of Sparta.
Spring Hollow	Located on E border of Houston County, E NE of Yellow Creek.
Spring Lake	Community in central section of Shelby County. N of Bartlett.
Spring Place	Community in Knox County. 6 mi N NE of downtown Knoxville.
Springs Chapel	Community in S area of Fentress County. 13 mi S of Jamestown.
Springtown	Community in N NE section of Polk County. 11 1/2 mi E NE of Benton.
Springvale	Community in SE section of Hamblen County. 5 mi E SE of Morristown.
Springview	Community in W Central section of Blount County. 6 mi SW of Maryville.
Springville	Community in SE section of Henry County. 10 1/2 mi S SE of Paris.

Spruce Pine	Community in W section of Hawkins County. 11 1/2 mi W of Rogersville.
Spurgeon	Community in N section of Washington County. 9 1/2 mi N of Jonesborough.
Squawberry	Community in SE section of Carter County near North Carolina border. 5 mi S of Roan Mountain.
Squirrel Flat	Community in NW section of Fentress County. 5 mi NW of Jamestown.
Squirrel Hollow	Located in E SE section of Benton County.
Stacy	Community in SE section of Hawkins County. 12 mi E NE of Rogersville.
Staffords Store	Community in S section of Weakley County. 13 1/2 mi S of Dresden, near the county line.
Staffordtown	Community on S SW border of Polk County. 19 mi SE of Benton.
Stainville	Community in NW Section of Anderson County on Campbell County line. 12 mi N of Oliver Springs.
Stakely Mill	Community in Middle W section of Monroe County. 5 1/2 mi S of Madisonville.
Stamp Creek Ridge	Ridge in middle S section of Roane County. S of Bacon Ridge.
Stamps Hollow	Located in E section of Putnam County. 12 mi E SE of Cookeville. S SE of Pinhook.
Standing Rock	Community in W NW section of Perry County. Approx. 11 mi W NW of Linden.
Standing Rock Creek	Creek in S SW section of Stewart County, flows into the Tennessee River. W of Mulbury Hill.
Standing Rock Hollow	Located in middle W SW section of Dickson County. 4 mi NW of Dickson.
Standing Stone Lake	Lake in NW section of Overton County, S of Timothy.
Standing Stone State Park and Forest	Located in SE section of Clay County and extends into NW corner of Overton County.
St. Andrews	Community in E NE section of Franklin County. 13 mi E of Winchester.
St. Andrews Lake	Lake in E NE section of Franklin County. S of Sand Switch near Grundy County Line.
Stanfield Hollow	Located in SE section of Houston County. Approx. 4 mi SW of Yellow Creek.

Stanfill	Community in NW section of Campbell County near Pioneer.
Stanley Junction	Community in middle N section of Scott County. Approx. 3 mi S SE of Oneida.
Stansbury Mountain	Mountain in E SE section of Polk County.
Stanton	City in SW corner of Haywood County. 12 mi SW of Brownsville. Incorporated in 1927.
Stantonville	City on E border of McNairy County. 9 1/2 mi E of Selmer. Incorporated in 1966.
Starkeytown	Community in middle W SW section of Sevier County. 3mi S SW of Pigeon Forge.
Star Point	Community in NW section of Pickett County. 6 mi W of Byrdstown.
Starr Mountain	Mountain located in the SW corner of Monroe County and extends into the N section of Polk County.
Statehouse Ridge	Ridge in N NE section of Fentress County. 4 mi E SE of Pall Mall.
State Line	Community on S border of Lincoln County. 11 mi S of Fayetteville.
Statem Gap	Community in central section of Hamblen County near Morristown.
Statesville	Community in SE section of Wilson County. 16 mi SE of Lebanon.
Static	Community on middle N border of Pickett County. 4 1/2 mi N NE of Byrdstown.
Station Camp Creek	Creek in SW section of Gallatin, flows into Old Hickory Lake.
Staunton Mill	Community in central section of Greene County. 3 mi S of Greeneville.
Stave Hollow	Located in W section of Humphreys County. 2 mi N of New Johnsonville.
Stavely Hollow	Located in W SW section of Stewart County, S of Mulbury Hill.
Stayton	Community in N area of Dickson County. 7 mi N of Charlotte.
St. Bethlehem	Community in middle N section of Montgomery County. 3 1/2 mi NE of Clarksville.
St. Clair	Community in S SW section of Hawkins County. 7 mi SW of Rogersville.

St. Clair	Community in NE section of Rhea County. 20 mi NE of Dayton.
Steadman Ridge	Ridge in SE section of Lawrence County. E of Idaho.
Steel Tram Ridge	Ridge in E SE section of Overton County, E of Hanging Limb.
Stella	Community in S SW section of Giles County. 11 1/2 mi S SW of Pulaski.
St. Elmo	Community within the city limits of Chattanooga. 4 mi S of downtown at the foot of Lookout Mountain.
Stephany Ridge	Ridge in N central section of Humphreys County. 2 mi N of Waverly.
Stephens	Community in SE section of Morgan County. W of Tupper Town.
Stephens Lake	Lake in middle W section of Williamson County. 8 mi W of Franklin.
Stephenson	Community in SE area of Coffee County. 10 SE of Manchester.
Stephens Ridge	Ridge on N border of Clay County into Kentucky. 4 1/2 mi N NW of Celina.
Steppsville	Community in S section of Warren County. 10 mi S SE of McMinnville.
Sterling Park	Community in central section of Hamilton County. Approx. 11 mi N NE of downtown Chattanooga. NE of Hixson.
Steward Hills	Located in middle NE section of Williamson County. 3 mi S of Brentwood.
Stewart	Community in NW central section of Houston County. 8 1/2 mi W of Erin.
Stewart Chapel	Community in SE section of Lincoln County. 11 mi SE of Fayetteville.
Stewart Chapel	Community in NW section of Warren County. 10 1/2 mi NW of McMinnville.
Stewart County STEWART COUNTY	County Seat: Dover. Zip Code 37058. Located in Northwest section of the State. Bounded by Montgomery, Houston, Benton and Henry Counties and the State of Kentucky to the North. Named in honor of Duncan Stewart.
Stewart Hill	Community in middle W section of Washington County. 2 mi NW of Jonesborough.
Stewart Hollow	Located in SW section of Dickson County. 2 1/2

Stewart Hollow, (Cont.)	mi W of Oak Grove.
Stewarts Lake	Lake in W central section of Dickson County. 4 mi N of Dickson.
Stewart State Forest	Located in S SE section of Stewart County. 8 mi S SE of Dover.
Stillhouse Hollow	Located in E SE section of Benton County.
Stinger	Community in SW section of Dyer County, N of Tiger Tail
Stinking Creek	Community in N Central section of Campbell County. 5 mi S of Jellico.
Stinson Hollow	Located in SE section of Benton County.
Stiversville	Community on S border of Maury County. 12 mi S of Columbia.
St. James	Community in S area of Greene County. 11 1/2 mi S SW of Greeneville, 3 mi W of Cedar Creek.
St. John	Community in NE section of Clay County. 11 mi E NE of Celina.
St. Joseph	City in Lawrence County, 17 1/2 mi S SW of Lawrenceburg. Incorporated in 1919. Home of Terry Roberson.
St. Marys	Community in E area of Franklin County. 10 mi E of Winchester.
St. Marys	Community in SW area of Lawrence County. Approx. 3 mi S SE of Loretto.
Stock Creek	Located in S Section of Knox County. 7 1/2 mi S SE of Knoxville.
Stockton	Community in E central section of Fentress County. 6 mi E SE of Jamestown.
Stockton Valley	Community in W section of Loudon County. 7 1/2 mi W of Loudon.
Stokes	Community in SE section of Dyer County. 10 1/2 mi E SE of Dyersburg.
Stone	Community in middle N section of Jackson County. 2 1/2 mi N of Gainesboro.
Stone Mountain	Mountain in S central section of Cocke County, SE of Pleasant Grove in Cherokee National Forest.
Stone Mountain	Mountain along N border of Greene County, NE of Baileyton into S section of Hawkins County.

Stone Mountain	Mountain in NW central section of Hawkins County.
Stone Mountain	Mountain in N central section of Hawkins County, N of Striggersville.
Stone Mountain	Mountain on S border of Johnson County on North Carolina Line.
Stone Mountain	Mountain in NE section of Unicoi County and SW section of Carter County.
Stonewall	Community in middle SE section of Smith County. 5 mi SE of Carthage.
Stoney Point	Community in W NW section of Dickson County. 11 mi W NW of Charlotte.
Stony Flat	Area in W SW section of Anderson County.
Stony Gap	Community in Mid E section of Hancock County. 4 mi E SE of Sneedville.
Stony Point	Community in middle NE section of Hawkins County. 12 mi NE of Rogersville.
Stony Point	Community in E section of Knox County. 11 mi E of Knoxville.
Storey Hollow	Located im middle W section of Humphreys County. 1 mi S of Pursley.
Stout Hill	Located in E section of Carter County, N NW of Poga.
Stovall Gap	Located in W NW section of Trousdale County. 1 mi N of Templow.
Stowers	Community in W section of Morgan County. NW of Deer Lodge.
St. Paul	Community in W SW section of Tipton County. 17 mi W SW of Covington.
St. Petersburg	Community in middle W section of Haywood County. 7 mi W NW of Brownsville.
Strahl	Community in S section of Hawkins County. 4 1/2 mi SE of Rogersville. 1 mi NW of Needmore.
Straight Fork	Community in E SE section of Scott County. 8 mi E SE of Huntsville.
Strambler Knob	Located in N NW section of Williamson County. 4 mi N of Franklin.
Strauss Mill	Community in N central section of Coffee County.
Strawberry Plains	Community on W border of Jefferson County. 15

Strawberry Plains, (Cont.)	mi W NW of Dandridge.
Striggersville	Community in central section of Hawkins County. 2 1/2 mi N NE of Rogersville.
Stringers Ridge	Ridge in SW section of Hamilton County between Chattanooga and Red Bank.
Stringtown	Community in NE section of Cannon County. 4 mi E of Auburntown.
Stringtown	Community in NW area of Gibson County. 14 mi N NW of Trenton.
Stringtown	Community in N section of Hardin County, SE of Saltillo.
Stringtown	Community in central section of Henderson County. 2 mi S of Lexington.
Stringtown	Community in W SW section of Montgomery County. W of Dotsonville.
Stringtown	Community in E SE section of White County. Approx. 9 mi E SE of Sparta.
Stroudville	Community in W SW section of Robertson County. 12 1/2 mi W SW of Springfield.
Stuart Heights	Community within the city limits of Chattanooga. 4 mi N of downtown off Hixson Pike in Hamilton County.
Sturdivant Crossing	Community in SW corner of Madison County. 17 mi SW of Jackson.
Suburban Hills	Community in middle SW section of McMinn County. Approx. 5 mi W SW of Athens.
Suck Creek	Community in NE section of Marion County. 13 1/2 mi E NE of Jasper.
Sugar Camp Hill	Located in W SW section of Sumner County. Approx. 6 mi N of Hendersonville.
Sugar Camp Knob	Mountain in middle W section of Sevier County, SE of Pigeon Forge.
Sugar Creek	Community in N central section of Jackson County. 6 mi N NE of Gainesboro.
Sugar Creek	Community on N NE border of Johnson County. 10 mi N NE of Mountain City.
Sugar Grove	Community in SE section of Bradley County. 6 mi SE of Cleveland.
Sugar Grove	Community in middle NE section of Roane County. 4 mi NE of Kingston.

Sugar Grove	Community in NE corner of Sumner County. 5 mi N NW of Westmoreland.
Sugar Hill	Community in W central section of Hardeman County. 3 1/2 mi SW of Bolivar. 3 1/2 mi NE of Middleburg.
Sugar Hill	Community in S section of Perry County. Approx. 4 mi S SE of Linden.
Sugar Hollow	Located at S SE border of Montgomery County. S of McAllister Crossroads.
Sugarland Mountain	Mountain in S SW section of Sevier County. 5 mi S of Gatlinburg.
Sugarlands	Area in Great Smoky Mountains where Park Headquarters is now located. 2 mi SW of Gatlinburg.
Sugarlimb	Community in central section of Loudon County, N NE of Loudon.
Sugarloaf	Community at the foot of Sugarloaf Mountain in W section of Sevier County.
Sugarloaf Mountain	Mountain in SW section of Polk County near Parksville.
Sugarloaf Mountain	Mountain in W section of Sevier County, N of DuPont Springs.
Sugar Mountain	Mountain in S SE section of Monroe County, E of Chinquapin Ridge.
Sugartown Ridge	Ridge in middle SE section of Jackson County, SW of Morrison Creek.
Sugar Tree	Community in NE section of Decatur County. Approx. 17 mi N NE of Decaturville.
Sugartree Knob	Located in middle NE section of Cannon County. 5 mi NE of Woodbury.
Suggs Creek	Community in SW section of Wilson County. 13 mi SW of Lebanon.
Sullivan County SULLIVAN COUNTY	County Seat: Blountville. Zip Code 37617. Located in Northeast corner of the State. Bounded by Johnson, Carter, Washington and Hawkins Counties and the State of Virginia to the North. Named in honor of Major General John Sullivan.
Sullivan Gardens	Community in W SW section of Sullivan County. 16 mi W SW of Blountville.
Sulphur	Community in SW section of Overton County. Approx. 6 mi S SW of Livingston.

Sulphura	Community in middle N section of Sumner County. 10 1/2 mi N of Gallatin.
Sulphur Hollow	Located in W NW section of Hancock County. 9 mi W of Sneedville.
Sulphur Spring	Community in section section of Hamblen County. 3 1/2 mi S of Morristown.
Sulphur Springs	Community in Central section of Anderson County. W of Leinerts.
Sulphur Springs	Community in S Central area of Cheatham County.
Sulphur Springs	Communty in central NW section of Lincoln County. 7 mi W NW of Fayetteville.
Sulphur Springs	Community in middle S SW section of McNairy County. 5 1/2 mi W SE of Selmer.
Sulphur Springs	Community in Central section of Pickett County. Approx. 4 mi E SE of Byrdstown.
Sulphur Springs	Community in middle NW section of Washington County. 5 mi NW of Jonesborough.
Sumac	Community in E NE central section of Giles County. 6 mi NE of Pulaski.
Summer City	Community in E section of Bledsoe County. 5 mi E SE of Pikeville near Rhea County line.
Summerfield	Community in S section of Grundy County E of Monteagle. 13 mi S SW of Altamont.
Summers Hollow	Located in S SW section of Houston County, N of New Hope.
Summersville	Community in SW section of Sullivan County. Approx. 2 mi SW of Colonial Heights.
Summertown	Community in W area of Hamilton County on Walden's Ridge. 8 mi N of downtown Chattanooga. 3 mi NE of Signal Mountain.
Summertown	Community on N border of Lawrence County. 13 1/2 mi N of Lawrenceburg.
Summitt	Community in SE section of Hamilton County. 12 mi E of downtown Chattanooga.
Summitt	Community in S section of Hawkins County. 8 1/2 mi S SW of Rogersville. 3 1/2 mi NE of Bulls Gap.
Summmitville	Community in NE area of Coffee County. 8 mi NE of Manchester.
Sumner County	County Seat: Gallatin. Zip Code 37066. Located

Sumner County, (Cont.)	in North Central section of the State. Bounded by Macon, Trusdale, Wilson, Davidson and Robertson Counties and the State of Kentucky to the North. Named in honor of Major General Jethro Sumner.
SUMNER COUNTY	
Sumner County Park	Located in S section of Sumner County. On Old Hickory Lake.
Sumner Knob	Located near E border of Williamson County. 14 mi E SE of Franklin.
Sunbright	Community in N central section of Morgan County. 10 mi N NW of Wartburg.
Sunkist Beach	Community located near center of Lake County. 2 1/2 mi S of Tiptonville.
Sunk Lake	Lake in middle W section of Lauderdale County. 12 mi E of Ripley.
Sunnyhill	Community in S central section of Haywood County. 4 mi S of Brownsville.
Sunnyside	Community in Central section of Greene County. 3 mi S SE of Greeneville.
Sunny Side	Community in E section of Henry County, N of West Sandy Creek Wildlife Area.
Sunnyside	Community in S section of of Loudon County. 6 mi S SW of Loudon.
Sunnyside	Community in central SW section of Maury County. 3 1/2 mi S SW of Columbia.
Sunnyside	Community in E NE section of Obion County. 5 mi E SE of Union City.
Sunnyside	Community in N NW section of Sullivan County. Approx. 5 mi E of Kingsport.
Sunrise	Community in S central section of Hickman County. 7 mi S SE of Centerville.
Sunrise	Community in middle NE section of Knox County. 10 mi NE of Knoxville.
Sunrise	Community in NE section of Macon County. Approx. 7 mi NE of Lafayette.
Sunrise Towhead	Located in SW section of Lauderdale County, W of Mississippi River.
Sunset	Community in W central section of Grainger County. 4 1/2 mi S SW of Rutledge.
Sunset	Community in SW section of Pickett County. 3 1/2 mi S SW of Byrdstown.

Sunset Gap	Community on SW border of Cocke County on Sevier County line. 9 1/2 mi SW of Newport.
Sunset Gap	Community on E NE border of Sevier County. 15 mi E of Sevierville.
Sunset Hills	Community in SW central section of Hamblen County 3 mi W NW of Morristown.
Sunshine Lake	Lake in E Central area of Carroll County E of Smyrna.
Surgoinsville	City in middle section of Hawkins County. 8 mi NE of Rogersville. Incorporated in 1815.
Susong	Community in N tip of Cocke County, near Hamblen County line. 5 mi N NW of Briar Thicket.
Susong	Community in SE area of Hamblen County near Springvale.
Sutherland	Community in N NW section of Johnson County. 9 mi N of Mountain City.
Swafford Knob	Located in SW section of McMinn County, W of Claxton.
Swafford Pond	Pond in central section of Bledsoe County. 1 mi NE of Pikeville.
Swanagan Mountain	Mountain in NE corner of Sullivan County.
Swan Bluff	Community in SE section of Hickman County. Approx. 4 1/2 mi S SE of Centerville.
Swan Lake	Lake in NW section of Lauderdale County, NW of Chisholm Lake.
Swann	Community in middle E section of Jefferson County. 3 mi E of Dandridge.
Swannsylvania	Community in E section of Jefferson County. 6 mi E of Dandridge.
Sweeten Cove	Located in SW section of Marion County, W of Kimball.
Sweetgum	Community in N section of Van Buren County. 4 mmi N NE of Spencer.
Sweetgum Hollow	Located in middle W section of Houston County, S of Barnes Hollow.
Sweet Lips	Community in SE section of Chester County. 7 mi E SE of Henderson.
Sweeton Hill	Community in SE section of Grundy County, near Tracy City.

Sweet Ridge	Ridge in S SW section of Sevier County. 6 mi S SE of Gatlinburg, S of Sugarland Mountain.
Sweetwater	Community in SW section of Lewis County. 6 mi SW of Hohenwald.
Sweetwater	Community in NW corner of Monroe County. 7 mi NW of Madisonville. Incorporated in 1897.
Swift	Community in N central section of Hardin County. 10 1/2 mi NE of Savannah. 3 1/2 mi NE of Cerro Gordo.
Sycamore	Community in N Central section of Cheatham County. 3 mi N of Ashland City.
Sycamore	Community in S SW section of Williamson County. Approx. 10 mi S SW of Franklin.
Sycamore Hall	Community in E section of Claiborne County. 4 mi E of Tazewell.
Sycamore Lake	Community in S central section of Henderson County. 5 1/2 mi S of Lexington. 8 mi N NW of Scotts Hill.
Sycamore Landing	Community in S SW section of Humphreys County. 12 mi S SW of Waverly.
Sycamore Swamp	Located in E SE section of Lincoln County, SE of Gum Springs.
Sycamore Valley	Community in middle E section of Macon County. 5 mi E of Lafayette.
Sykes	Community in S SW section of Smith County. 9 mi S of Carthage.
Sykes Hollow	Located in NW section of Houston County, E NE of McKinnon.
Sykes Hollow	Located in W section of Stewart County. Approx. 2 mi N of Mulbury Hill.
Sylco	Community in middle S SW section of Polk County. Approx. 10 mi S SE of Benton.
Sylco Ridge	Ridge in SW section of Polk County.
Sylvia	Community in W Central section of Dickson County. 4 1/2 mi W of Charlotte.
Tabernacle	Community in middle E section of Tipton County. 5 mi E SE of Covington.
Tab Hollow	Located in middle E section of Houston County, E SE of Erin.
Table Rock Mountain	Mountain in S section of Overton County, near border. 13 mi S SE of Livingston.

Tabor	Community in N central section of Cumberland County. 6 mi N NW of Crossville.
Tackett Creek	Community in NE section of Campbell County near Claiborne County line. 7 mi E SE of Jellico.
Taft	Community on S SW border of Lincoln County. 12 1/2 mi SW of Fayetteville.
Talbott	Community in N NE section of Jefferson County. 9 1/2 mi N of Dandridge.
Tallassee	Community in SW corner of Blount County on Chilhowee Lake. 15 mi S SW of Maryville.
Talley	Community in SE section of Marshall County. 8 1/2 mi SE of Lewisburg.
Talley Hill	Located in middle SE section of Williamson County. 3 mi E of Callie.
Tampico	Community in S SW area of Grainger County. 6 mi S SW of Rutledge.
Tanglewood	Community in central NW section of Smith County. 2 1/2 mi NW of Carthage.
Tansi	Community in SW section of Cumberland County on Lake Tansi. 5 mi S of Crossville.
Tantallon	Community in E SE section of Franklin County. Approx. 10 mi E SE of Winchester, N of Sherwood.
Tanyard Hollow	Located in E section of Benton County. Approx. 9 mi NE of Camden.
Tappy Top	Located in SW section of Franklin County. SE of Huntland.
Tariffville	Community in middle E NE section of Monroe County. E of Union Hall.
Tarkiln Ridge	Ridge in S section of Blount County. 13 mi S of Maryville.
Tarlton	Community in N NE section of Grundy County. 6 mi NW of Altamont.
Tarpley	Community in SE central area of Giles County. 4 1/2 mi S SE of Pulaski.
Tarsus	Community in S SW section of Montgomery County. 12 mi SW of Clarksville.
Tasso	Community in E Central section of Bradley County. 3 mi N NE of Cleveland.
Tate	Community in Central section of Carroll

Tate, (Cont.)	County. 3 1/2 mi SW of Huntingdon.
Tate	Community in SE section of Coffee County. 12 1/2 mi SE of Manchester.
Tater Hill	Located in N section of Fentress County, NE of Pall Mall.
Tate Springs	Community in NE section of Grainger County. 10 1/2 mi E NE of Rutledge.
Tatesville	Community in E section of Grundy County, S of Barkertown. 10 mi E SE of Altamont.
Tatlock Lake	Lake in NE section of Tipton County. Approx. 2 mi SW of Covington.
Tattletown	Community in W section of Sevier County between Waldens Creek and Goose Gap at foot of Chilhowee Mountain.
Tatumville	Community in E area of Dyer County. 11 mi E of Dyersburg.
Tayes Hollow	Located in E section of Putnam County. 11 mi S SE of Cookeville. S of Pinhook.
Taylor Chapel	Community in NE area of Fayette County. 7 mi N NE of Somerville.
Taylor Chapel	Community in central SW section of Stewart County. 5 mi SW of Dover.
Taylor Creek	Creek in NW central section of Franklin County. Runs N to S through Estill Springs.
Taylor Crossroads	Community in NW area of Bedford County. 12 mi NW of Shelbyville, 13 mi W of Bell Buckle.
Taylor Crossroads	Community in NW central area of Dickson County. 5 1/2 mi W NW of Charlotte.
Taylor Hollow	Located in W SW section of Stewart County, S SW of Mulbury Hill.
Taylor Hollow	Located in E section of Sumner County. 2 mi E of Bledsoe, E of Pearson Hollow.
Taylor Mill	Community in W NW section of Washington County. 5 1/2 mi W of Jonesborough.
Taylor Ridge	Ridge in NW section of Hamilton County.
Taylors	Community in E Central area of Bradley County near Cleveland.
Taylors	Community in NE section of White County. 8 1/2 mi NE of Sparta.
Taylors Chapel	Community in middle N NE section of Stewart

Taylors Chapel, (Cont.)	County. 6 mi N of Dover.
Taylors Crossing	Community in SE section of Henderson County. 11 mi SE of Lexington.
Taylors Crossing	Communtiy in N NE section of Overton County. 10 mi N NE of Livingston.
Taylorsville	Community in W section of Maury County. Approx. 13 mi W of Columbia.
Taylortown	Town in Mid W Section of Franklin County.
Taylortown	Community in S SE section of Humphreys County. 11 mi S SE of Waverly.
Taylortown	Community in W NW section of Lincoln County. 11 mi W NW of Fayetteville.
Taylorville	Community in NE section of Wilson County. 7 mi NE of Lebanon.
Tazewell	County Seat of Claiborne County. Located in SE central section of county. Incorporated in 1830.
Teague	Community in N NE section of Hardeman County. 11 1/2 mi N of Bolivar. 8 mi NW of Silerton.
Teasley Hollow	Located in middle N section of Cheatham County. 1 mi E of Lockertsville.
Tekoa	Community in W central section of Knox County. 6 1/2 mi W of Knoxville.
Telford	Community in middle SW section of Washington County. 5 mi SW of Jonesborough.
Tell	Community in NE section of Anderson County. 6 mi NE of Clinton.
Tellico Dam	Located in central NE section of Loudon County, on the Little Tennessee River (Tellico Lake).
Tellico Lake	Lake in Monroe County located S SE of Tellico Plains.
Tellico Lake (Little Tennessee River)	Located in Monroe County NE of Madisonville.
Tellico Mountain	Mountain in SE section of Monroe County, E of Mocking Crow Mountain, S of Tellico Plains.
Tellico Plains	City in central SW section of Monroe County. 12 mi S SE of Madisonville. Incorporated in 1911.
Temperance Hall	Community in N section of DeKalb County. 9 mi

Temperance Hall, (Cont.)	N NW of Smithville.
Templeton	Community in NE section of Dyer County. 12 1/2 mi NE of Dyersburg.
Templow	Community in W NW section of Trousdale County. 5 mi W NW of Hartsville.
Tench	Community in S section of Fentress County. 6 mi S of Jamestown.
Ten Mile	Community in NE section of Meigs County. 13 mi N NE of Decatur.
Ten Mile Knob	Located in N section of Meigs County, N NE of Ten Mile.
Tennemo	Community in NW area of Dyer County. 13 1/2 mi NW of Dyersburg.
Tennessee Aquarium	A Fresh Water Aquarium on the banks of the Tennessee River in downtown Chattanooga. In Hamilton County.
Tennessee City	Community in SW area of Dickson County. 11 1/2 mi SW of Charlotte.
Tennessee National Wildlife Refuge (Big Sandy Unit)	Located in NW section of Benton County, W SW of Lick Creek and extends N into E NE section of Henry County. S of Paris Landing State Park.
Tennessee National Wildlife Refuse	Duck River Unit located on W SW border of Humphreys County, SW of Waverly.
Tennessee Ridge	Ridge in central section of Houston County, S of Erin.
Tennessee Ridge	City in N central section of Houston County. 4 mi W of Erin. Incorporated in 1960.
Tennessee River	The Tennessee River begins where the Holston and French Broad Rivers join in Knoxville. It flows along the Knox and Blount County lines into Loudon County where the Little Tennessee River flows into it, flows into Roane County, South into Rhea and Meigs Counties where it forms county lines and is backed up by the Watts Bar Dam. Flows southward into Hamilton County where it is backed up by the Chickamauga Dam forming Lake Chickamauga, flows into Marion County where it is backed up by the Nickajack Dam forming the Nickajack Lake. Flows through the Northern portion of the States of Alabama and Mississippi and re-enters Tennessee in Hardin County where it is backed up by the Pickwick Dam. Flows Northward forming county lines for Decatur and Perry Counties, Humphrey and Benton Counties and for

Tennessee River, (Cont.)	Stewart and Henry Counties and then flows into Kentucky where it flows into the Ohio River. Total length of the Tennessee River is 652 miles.
Tennga	Community in SW corner of Polk County. 13 1/2 mi S SW of Benton.
Tenpenny Hollow	Located in central section of Cannon County. 2 mi S of Woodbury, W of Davenport Hollow.
Terra Atra Lake	Lake in E section of Fayette County, E SE of Somerville.
Terrell	Community in W NW section of Weakley County. 14 mi W NW of Dresden.
Terry	Community in SW section of Carroll County. 1 mi SW of Huntingdon.
Terry Creek	Community in W Central section of Campbell County. 2 mi N of Pioneer.
Terry Estates	Community in central section of Giles County. Approx. 2 mi S of Pulaski.
Texas Knobs	Located in S section of Meigs County, S of Brittsville.
Tharpe	Community in middle NW section of Stewart County. 8 mi NW of Dover.
The Barrens	Located in N section of Marion County, N NE of Lynchburg.
The Big Bottom	Swamp in Hardeman County. 5 mi SE of Bolivar.
The Boulevard	Mountain in S SE section of Sevier County. 7 mi E SE of Gatlinburg, S of Brushy Mountain.
The Camp Hollow	Located in E NE section of Benton County.
The Chimneys	Area in the Great Smoky Mountains in the S section of Sevier County.
The Hogback	Mountain near W SW border of Sevier County. 4 mi W of Hatchertown, near Park Settlement.
The Knobs	Located in middle S section of McMinn County, S of Athens.
The Knobs	Located in W NW section of Monroe County, S of Christianburg.
The Knobs	Mountain in E section of Johnson County, E of Vinegar Hill
The Mountain	Mountain in middle N section of Fayette County, N NW of Somerville.

The Narrows	Located in S SW section of Cheatham County. 2 mi NW of Shacklett.
Theodore	Community in central section of Lewis County, 1 mi N NE of Hohenwald.
The Pinnacle	Mountain in NE section of Sevier County, N of Rich Mountain.
The Swamps	Located in middle N section of Robertson County, 3 mi N NE of Springfield.
Theta	Community in N section of Maury County. 11 mi N of Columbia.
The Wye	Community in N Central section of Anderson County. 1 mi S of Lake City.
Thick	Community in N section of Marshall County. 14 1/2 mi N NE of Lewisburg.
Thief Neck Island	Island on Tennessee River. 9 mi W SW of Kingston in Roane County.
Third Creek	Community within the city limits of Knoxville. 4 1/2 mi W NW of downtown. In Knox County.
Thomas	Community in S SW section of Putnam County. 9 1/2 mi SW of Cookeville.
Thomas Bridge	Community in central section of Sullivan County. 3 1/2 mi E SE of Blountville.
Thomas Ridge	Located in N section of Smith County. 2 mi N of Pleasant Shade.
Thomas Spring	Community in SW section of Cumberland County. 13 mi W SW of Crossville.
Thomaston Hollow	Located in W SW section of Montgomery County. 1 1/2 mi from Needmore.
Thomasville	Community in NW corner of Cheatham County. 8 mi NW of Sycamore.
Thompson's Store	Community in NE area of Clay County. 6 mi NE of Celina.
Thompson Crossroad	Community in NE section of Hardin County, SSW of Olive Hill.
Thompson Hollow	Located in S SW section of Houston County, SW of New Hope.
Thompson Hollow	Located in S SW section of Macon County and NE section of Trousdale County.
Thompson Hollow	Located in middle SE section of Stewart County, N of Carlisle.

Thompson Lake	Lake in S SE section of Williamson County. 11 mi S SE of Franklin.
Thompson Ridge	Ridge in N NW section of Putnam County, N of Baxter.
Thompsons Crossroads	Community in W section of Dickson County. 1 1/2 mi S of Adams Crossroads.
Thompsons Station	Community in S section of Williamson County. 9 mi S of Franklin.
Thorne Hollow	Located on S SW border of Montgomery County. 2 mi S SW of Shiloh.
Thorne Store	Community in S SW section of Giles County. Approx. 14 mi S SW of Pulaski.
Thorn Grove	Community in E section of Knox County. 13 mi E of Knoxville.
Thorn Hill	Community in N NE section of Grainger County. 9 mi NE of Rutledge.
Thornton	Community in SW section of Knox County. 13 mi W SW of Knoxville. NE of Farragut.
Thornton Ridge	Ridge in middle W section of Wayne County. E of Arnold Hollow.
Three Mountains	In SE area of Carter County. 8 mi S SE of Elizabethton.
Three Oaks	Community in NE section of Lawrence County. 9 mi N NE of Lawrenceburg.
Three Point	Community in middle SW section of Lauderdale County. 10 1/2 mi W SW of Ripley.
Three Points	Community in middle NE section of Knox County. 10 mi NE of Knoxville.
Three Points	Community in central N section of Monroe County. 9 Mi E of Madisonville.
Throck-Morton	Community in SE section of Stewart County. 12 mi E SE of Dover.
Thula	Community in W area of Greene County. 14 mi W of Greeneville.
Thunderhead Mountain	Mountain in SE corner of Blount County on North Carolina Line. Elev. 5,530 ft.
Thurman	Community in SW section of Decatur County, S SE of Liberty.
Tibbs	Community in NW section of Haywood County. 8 1/2 mi NW of Brownsville.

Tick Ridge	Ridge in E section of Jackson County, N of Burristown.
Tidwell	Community in S SE section of Dickson County. 11 mi S of Charlotte.
Tidwell	Community in NE corner of Hickman County. 18 mi NE of Centerville.
Tidwell Hollow	Located in W section of Davidson County.
Tiftonia	Now called Lookout Valley. Located in SW area of Hamilton County. 5 mi W of Chattanooga.
Tiger Tail	Community in S SW section of Dyer County, E of Moss Island.
Tigertown	Community in central section of Hamblen County near Morristown.
Tiger Valley	Community in S central section of Carter County. 8 mi S of Elizabethton.
Tigrett	Community in SE area of Dyer County. 10 mi SE of Dyersburg.
Tigrett Wildlife Management Area	Located on E border of Dyer County, E of Dyersburg.
Tilda High Top	Mountain in W section of Sevier County, E SE of Cove Creek Cascades.
Tilda Ridge	Ridge in W section of Sevier County, E of Cove Creek Cascades.
Tilghman	Community in NW area of Gibson County. 14 mi NW of Trenton.
Tillman Hollow	Located in W NW section of Coffee County, N NW of Noah.
Timbercrest	Community within the city limits of Knoxville. 4 1/2 mi W of downtown. In Knox County.
Timberlake	Community in N central section of Henderson County. 4 mi N of Lexington.
Timberlake	Community in Knox County. 3 mi SW of Knoxville.
Timber Lake Lake	Lake in central section of Lincoln County. 1 1/2 mi SE of Fayetteville.
Timberlink	Community on Signal Mountain in Hamilton County. 6 1/2 mi N NW of Chattanooga.
Timber Ridge	Ridge in E section of Cocke County, E of Harmony Grove.
Timber Ridge	Community in SW central section of Greene

Timber Ridge, (Cont.)	County. 7 mi SW of Greeneville.
Timber Ridge	Ridge in SW corner of Sevier County, S of Meigs Mountain.
Timothy	Community in NW corner of Overton County. 8 1/2 mi NW of Livingston.
Tims Ford Dam	Dam on the Elk River in W section of Franklin County. Forms Tims Ford Lake.
Tims Ford Lake	Lake in Mid W area of Franklin County on Elk River.
Tims Ford State Park	Park in W section of Franklin County. S & E of Marble Plains. 8 mi E of Winchester.
Tin Cup	Community in Central area of Benton County. S of Camden.
Tin Cup	Community in central section of Benton County.
Tinesville	Community on Walden's Ridge in Hamilton County near Fairmont.
Tioga	Community in NW area of Anderson County.
Tip Gap	Community in SE section of Claiborne County.
Tiprell	Community in N central section of Claiborne County. In Cumberland Gap National Park. 11 mi NW of Tazewell.
Tipton	Community in S SW section of Tipton County. 14 mi SW of Covington.
Tipton County TIPTON COUNTY	County Seat: Covington. Zip Code 38019. Located Southwest section of the State. Bounded by Lauderdale, Haywood, Fayette and Shelby Counties and the Mississippi River to the West. Named in honor or Jack Tipton.
Tiptonville	County Seat of Lake County. Located in middle N section of County.Incorporated in 1900.
Tiptop	Community in NW Section of Bledsoe County. 3 mi NW of Pikeville.
Titus	Community in NW area of Campbell County near Pioneer.
Tobaccoport	Community in N section of Stewart County. 11 mi N NW of Dover.
Todd Hollow	Located in S central section of Cannon County. 2 1/2 mi S of Woodbury.
Todds Lake	Lake in SE section of Murfreesboro, in Rutherford County.

Todd Town	Community in W SW section of Cumberland County. 12 mi W SW of Crossville.
T.O. Fuller State Park	Located in SW corner of Shelby County.
Tolbert Hollow	Located in SW section of Cannon County. 10 mi S SW of Woodbury.
Toliveer Lake	Lake in middle SW section of Coffee County. 2 mi S SW of Manchester.
Tollett Lake	Lake in N Central section of Bledsoe County S of Ninemile.
Tolley Town	Community in SE corner of Carter County. 11 mi S of Elizabethton.
Tomahawk Knob	Located in W SW section of Smith County. 2 mi W of New Middleton.
Tompkins Lake	Lake in NW section of Shelby County. N NW of Cuba.
Tom Redford Ridge	Ridge in W section of of Williamson County, N of Kingfield.
Tom Town	Community in S central section of Cocke County. 12 mi SE of Newport.
Toone	City in N central section of Hardeman County. 7 mi N NE of Bolivar. 8 1/2 mi W of Silerton. Incorporated in 1903.
Toper Ridge	Ridge in S SW section of Cocke County, S of Raven Branch.
Top of the World Estates	Community in S section of Blount County. 9 mi S SE of Maryville.
Topside	Community in S section of Knox County. 7 mi S of Knoxville.
Topsy	Community in NE section of Wayne County. 8 1/2 mi N NE of Waynesboro.
Toqua	Community in N section of Monroe County near Tellico Lake. 10 mi E NE of Madisonville.
Torbet	Community in SE section of Grundy County, near Tracy City.
Tottys Bend	Community in Middle E section of Hickman County. 5 1/2 mi E of Centerville.
Toulon	Community in NW corner of Haywood County. 13 mi NW of Brownsville.
Towee	Community in N NE section of Polk County. 12 1/2 mi E NE of Benton.

Towee Mountain	Mountain in N NE section of Polk County.
Town Acres	Community in central section of Greene County near Greeneville.
Town Creek	Community in N central section of Claiborne County. 10 1/2 mi NE of Tazewell.
Town Knob	Mountain in central section of Hawkins County, N and W of Rogersville.
Townsend	Town in E central section of Blount County. 13 mi E SE of Maryville. Incorporated in 1921.
Trace Creek	Creek in W section of Humphreys County. Begins W NW of Denver.
Tracy City	City in S section of Grundy County. 12 mi S of Altamont. Incorporated in 1915.
Trade	Community in SE corner of Johnson County. 9 mi S SE of Mountain City.
Trail of Tears State Scenic Route	Located in SW section of Bradley County, N of Red Clay State Park.
Trails West	Community in Knox County. 8 mi W SW of downtown Knoxville.
Tranquillity	Community on NW border of McMinn County. 9 mi NW of Athens.
Travis McNatt Lake	Lake in SW section of McNairy County. In Big Hill Pond State Park.
Travisville	Community in middle section of Pickett County. 7 1/2 mi E of Byrdstown.
Treadville Bottom	Located in middle NW section of Fayette County, E of Griffin.
Treadway	Community in S central section of Hancock County. 7 1/2 mi S of Sneedville. 1 mi from Hawkins County line.
Treasure Island	Island on Lake McKellar in SW section of Shelby County.
Treet Mountain	Mountain in E section of Overton County, S of Ivyton.
Tremont	Community in E SE section of Blount County. 5 mi SE of Townsend.
Trent Island	Island on W border of Jefferson County on the Holston River.
Trenton	County Seat of Gibson County. Located in S central section of county. Incorporated in 1826.

Trent Valley — Community in central section of Hancock County. 2 1/2 mi SE of Sneedville.

Trentville — Community in E section of Knox County. 11 mi E NE of Knoxville.

Trezevant — City in W area of Carroll County. 3 mi NE of Atwood. Incorporated in 1911.

Trigg — Community in NE area of Giles County and SW border of Marshall County.

Trigonia — Community in S SE section of Loudon County. 12 mi SE of Loudon.

Trimble — City in NE area of Dyer County. 16 mi NE of Dyersburg. Incorporated in 1905. Boundaries also extend into Obion County.

Trinity — Community in NW section of Humphreys County, 6 mi NW of Waverly.

Trinity — Community in middle NE section of Williamson County. 7 mi E of Franklin.

Triplett Hollow — Located in middle W section of Houston County, N of Magnolia.

Triune — Community in E section of Williamson County. 13 mi E SE of Franklin.

Trooper Island — Island on Dale Hollow Lake. 14 mi NE of Celina in Clay County.

Trousdale — Community in middle SE section of Sumner County. Approx. 2 mi E of Gallatin.

Trousdale — Community in W section of Warren County. Approx. 9 mi W of McMinnville.

Trousdale County — County Seat: Hartsville. Zip Code 37074. Located in North Central section of the State. Bounded by Macon, Smith, Wilson and Sumner Counties. Named in honor of Governor William Trousdale.

TROUSDALE COUNTY

Trousdale Hollow — Located in E SE section of Smith County, SE of Stonewall.

Troy — City in near center of Obion County. 8 1/2 mi SW of Union City. Incorporated in 1831.

Trundle Crossroads — Community in W NW section of Sevier County. 10 mi W of Sevierville.

Tubbs Hollow — Located in SE corner of Houston County.

Tucker Gap — Located in middle W section of Wilson County. 5 mi W SW of Lebanon.

Tuckers Corner	Community in NE section of Gibson County. 5 1/2 mi E NE of Trenton.
Tuckers Crossroads	Community in E section of Wilson County. 6 1/2 mi E of Lebanon.
Tucker Springs	Community in SW area of Bradley County E of McDonald.
Tullahoma	City in SW corner of Coffee County. 10 mi SW of Manchester. Incorporated in 1903. Boundaries also extend into Franklin County.
Tullahoma Lake	Lake in SW area of Coffee County. N of Tullahoma.
Tulu	Community on E SE border of McNairy County. Approx. 13 mi E SE of Selmer.
Tumbling	Community in E SE section of Weakley County. 10 mi E SE of Dresden. E of Gleason.
Tupper Town	Community in W Central section of Anderson County.
Tupper Town	Community in SE corner of Morgan County.
Turkey Creek	Creek in NW corner of Humphreys County. 10 1/2 mi NW of Waverly.
Turkey Creek	Community in E NE section of Moore County. 5 mi E NE of Lynchburg.
Turkey Creek Mountain	Mountain in central S SE section of Monroe County, S of Waucheesi.
Turkey Foot	Community in Hamilton County. 9 mi E NE of downtown Chattanooga, near Booker T. Washington State Park.
Turkey Knob	Mountain in S SW section of Cocke County, S of Hartford.
Turkey Mountain	Mountain in S SW section of Overton County, near border. 2 mi SE of Rickman.
Turkeypen Ridge	Ridge in SE section of Blount County. 3 mi S of Townsend.
Turkey Pen Ridge	Ridge in S central section of Stewart County, SE of Dover.
Turkeyscratch Mountain	Mountain in E NE section of Warren County, N of Goodbars.
Turkeytown (Range)	Community in W area of Carter County. 3 mi W SW of Elizabethton.
Turkeytown Ridge	Ridge in S section of Clay County, S of Baptist Ridge.

Turkey Track	Located in W NW corner of Lawrence County.
Turley	Community in W Central section of Campbell County. 5 mi NW of Jacksboro.
Turley Mountain	Mountain in W section of Campbell County, W of Royal Blue.
Turner Lake	Lake in S SW section of McNairy County. 12 mi S SW of Selmer.
Turners Station	Community in NE corner of Sumner County. 3 1/2 mi N NW of Westmoreland.
Turnersville	Community in middle W SW section of Robertson County. 9 mi W SW of Springfield.
Turney	Community in S central area of Giles County. 4 mi S SW of Pulaski.
Turney Center for Youthful Offenders	Prison Camp for Youth located in W section of Hickman County. 13 mi W NW of Centerville. S of Only.
Turney Knob	Located in S SE section of Wilson County. E SE of Greenvale.
Turnpike	Community on middle W border of Haywood County. 11 mi W of Brownsville. 8 mi S SE of Stanton.
Turpin Hollow	Located near W SW border of Sumner County. 3 mi W of White Hill.
Turtletown	Community in E section of Polk County. 17 mi E SE of Benton.
Tusculum	City in E central section of Greene County. 4 mi E of Greeneville. Incorporated in 1959.
Twin Lake	Lake in middle E section of Dickson County. 3 mi E NE of Dickson.
Twin Lake	Community in S section of Williamson County. 9 mi S of Franklin.
Twin Lakes	Lake in middle SW section of Carroll County, NE of Howley.
Twin Oak	Community in S SW section of Putnam County. 9 mi SW of Cookeville.
Twin Oaks	Community in NE section of Sullivan County on the Virginia Border. N NE of Friendship.
Twinton	Community on E SE border of Overton County. 13 mi E SE of Livingston.
Two Chestnut	Community in W SW section of Sumner County. 10 mi W NW of Gallatin, E of Whitehouse.

Twomey	Community near center of Hickman County, S of Centerville.
Tyler Mountain	Mountain in E central section of Monroe County in Cherokee National Forest.
Tylersville	Community in SW area of Dyer County. 9 mi W SW of Dyersburg.
Tyner	Community within the city limits of Chattanooga. 10 mi E of downtown in Hamilton County.
Tyner Hills	Community within the city limits of Chattanooga. 9 mi E of downtown. In Hamilton County.
Tyree Lake	Lake in E section of Gibson County, N of Concord.
Tyson Store	Community in NW area of Gibson County. 13 mi NW of Trenton.
Una	Community in SE section of Davidson County. 2 1/2 mi N NW of Rural Hill.
Unaka	Community in N section of Carter County. 2 mi NW of Winner.
Unaka Mountain	Mountain along NE border of Unicoi County, SE of Erwin.
Unaka Mountain Wilderness	Located in NE section of Unicoi County, S of Davis Springs. 7 mi E of Erwin.
Unaka Springs	Community in S central section of Unicoi County. 3 1/2 mi S SW of Erwin.
Unaka View	Community in W SW section of Washington County. 3 mi W SW of Jonesborough.
Underwood	Community in N section of Macon County. 6 1/2 mi N NE of Lafayette.
Underwood	Community in N NW section of Sevier County. 10 mi N NW of Sevierville.
Unicoi	Community in N section of Unicoi County. 5 mi NE of Erwin.
Unicoi County UNICOI COUNTY	County Seat: Erwin. Zip Code 37650. Located in Northeast section of the State. Bounded by Greene, Washington and Carter Counties and the State of North Carolina to the East. Named for the Indian tribal name, Unaka, which means
Unicoi Mountain	Mountain in NE section of Polk County.
Unicoi Wildlife Management Area	Located in middle W section of Unicoi County.

Unicoi Wildlife Management Area (State), (Cont.)	
Union	Community in SE Corner of Bradley County. 9 mi SE of Cleveland.
Union	Community in NW section of Hardin County. 6 1/2 mi N of Savannah. 1 1/2 mi W of Hookers Bend.
Union	Community on E border of Haywood County. 8 mi E of Brownsville.
Union	Community in central SE section of Morgan County. 6 mi E SE of Wartburg.
Union	Community in middle NE section of Raone County. Approx. 5 mi E NE of Kingston.
Union	Community in middle N section of Union County. Approx. 6 mi N NW of Maynardville.
Union	Community in NE section of Union County. 7 mi N of Maynardville.
Union	Community in middle E section of Warren County. 5 mi E NE of McMinnville.
Union Camp	Community in middle SE section of Macon County. 6 mi E SE of Lafayette.
Union Central	Community in E central section of Gibson County.
Union City	County seat of Obion County. Located in middle N NE section of county. Incorporated in 1867.
Union County UNION COUNTY	County Seat: Maynardville. Zip Code 37807. Located in Northeast section of the State. Bounded by Claiborne, Grainger, Knox, Anderson and Campbell Counties. Named because of the strong sentiment of the people in the region for the preservation of the Federal Union.
Union Cross	Community in N section of Henderson County. 8 1/2 mi N NW of Lexington.
Union Fork	Community in middle N section of Hamilton County, just N of Soddy Lake off Highway 27.
Union Grove	Community in W NW section of Blount County. 5 mi W of Maryville.
Union Grove	Community in SW area of Blount County. 14 mi SW of Maryville.
Union Grove	Community in SE area of Bradley County. 6 mi E SE of Cleveland.

Union Grove	Community in middle E section of Maury County. 4 1/2 mi E SE of Columbia.
Union Grove	Community in N section of McMinn County. 11 mi N of Athens.
Union Grove	Community in E central section of Meigs County. 1 1/2 mi E SE of Decatur.
Union Grove	Community in N NW section of Sevier County. 5 mi N of Sevierville.
Union Hall	Community on central N border of Monroe County. 6 mi E NE of Madisonville.
Union Heights	Community in S central section of Hamblen County. 3 mi SE of Morristown.
Union Hill	Community in W central section of Clay County. 10 mi W of Celina.
Union Hill	Community in NE section of Davidson County. 3 mi W NW of Goodlettsville.
Union Hill	Community on S SE border of Jackson County. 8 1/2 mi S SE of Gainesboro.
Union Hill	Community in SE section of Lawrence County. 10 1/2 mi S of Lawrenceburg.
Union Hill	Community in middle S section of Overton County. 6 mi S of Livingston.
Union Hill	Community in middle N NW section of Sevier County. 1 1/2 mi N NE of Sevierville.
Union Hill	Community in near center of Sumner County. 4 1/2 mi N of Gallatin.
Union Hollow	Located in W section of Dickson County. 2 mi E of Thompsons Crossroads.
Union Ridge	Community in E Central section of Bedford County. 3 1/2 mi E of Wartrace.
Union Temple	Community in NE area of Greene County. 11 mi N NE of Greeneville.
Union Valley	Community on NW border of Sevier County. 12 mi NW of Sevierville.
Unionville	Community in W NW area of Bedford County. 11 mi NW of Shelbyville, 13 mi W of Bell Buckle.
Unionville	Community in S area of Dyer County. 6 1/2 mi S SW of Dyersburg.
Unita	Community in E section of Loudon County. 9 mi E of Loudon.

Unity	Community in S section of Decatur County, S of Pleasant Grove.
Unity	Community in N section of Overton County. Approx. 6 mi N of Livingston.
University of Tennessee Space Institute	Located in the N section of Franklin County on the N bank of Woods Reservoir.
Upchurch	Community in N central section of Greene County. 6 1/2 mi N NE of Greeneville.
Upper Holly Creek	Community in E SE section of Wayne County. Approx. 16 mi S SE of Waynesboro.
Upper Mockeson	Community n SE section of Lawrence County. Approx. 12 mi S SE of Lawrenceburg.
Upper Shell Creek	Community in SE section of Carter County. 3 mi SE of Roan Mountain.
Upper Sinking	Community in SW corner of Hickman County. 12 1/2 mi SW of Centerville.
Upper Windrock	Community in W Central section of Anderson County. 12 mi W of Clinton.
Uptonville	Community in S SW section of Madison County. 14 mi S SW of Jackson.
U. S. Atomic Energy Commission in Oak Ridge	Located in E section of Roane County. 10 mi E NE of Kingston.
Ussery Hollow	Located in central NW section of Humphreys County. 3 mi N of Waverly.
Utah	Community in SE section of Decatur County. Approx. 4 mi E of Decaturville.
Valdeau	Community within the city limits of Red Bank, S section. In Hamilton County.
Vale	Community in NE area of Carroll County. 12 mi NE of Huntingdon.
Valleybrook	Golf Course community with the city limits of Chattanooga. 10 mi N NE of downtown near Hixson in Hamilton County.
Valley Creek	Community in NW area of Claiborne County near Kentucky Line. 8 1/2 mi N NW of Speedwell.
Valley Forge	Community in Central section of Carter County. 3 mi S of Elizabethton.
Valley Grove	Community in S SE section of Knox County. 9 mi SE of Knoxville.

Valley Home Community in SW section of Hamblen County. 5 mi S SW of Morristown.

Valley Ridge Ridge in W NW section of Sequatchie County, W of Fredonia.

Valley View Community in S Central section of Anderson County. 4 mi S of Clinton.

Valley View Community in NE section of Hawkins County. 18 mi NE of Rogersville.

Valleyview Community in N NE section of Rutherford County. 9 1/2 mi N NE of Murfreesboro.

Van Buren Community in SW section of Hardeman County. 10 mi S SW of Bolivar. 3 1/2 mi SE of Hickory Valley.

Van Buren County County Seat: Spencer. Zip Code 38585. Located in South Central section of the State. Bounded by White, Cumberland, Bledsoe, Sequatchoe, Grundy and Warren Counties. Names in honor of Martin Van Buren.

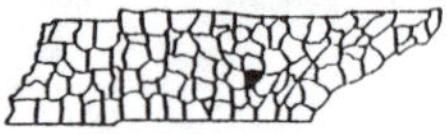

VAN BUREN COUNTY

Vance Community in E central section of Sullivan County. 6 1/2 mi E of Blountville.

Vandever Community in SW area of Cumberland County. 9 mi S SW of Crossville.

Van Dyke Community in S section of Henry County. 5 1/2 mi S of Paris.

Van Hill Community in Middle SE section of Hawkins County. 11 mi E of Rogersville.

Vanleer City in NW section of Dickson County. 7 mi W NW of Charlottte. Incorporated in 1915.

Vannata Community in N Central section of Bedford County. 9 mi N of Shelbyville, 7 mi W of Bell Buckle.

Vanntown Community on S SE border of Lincoln County. 12 mi SE of Fayetteville.

Vardy Community in N central section of Hancock County. 4 mi N NE of Sneedville. 1 mi from Virginia Line.

Vasper Community in SE area of Campbell County. 2 mi SE of Caryville.

Vaughn Gap Located in S SE section of Johnson County, S of Crackers Neck.

Vaughn Pond Pond in Hardeman County N NE of Bolivar near Shandy.

Vaughns Gap	Located in SW section of Davidson County.
Vaughns Grove	Community in E central section of Gibson County. 5 mi E NW of Trenton.
Verbie Knob	Located in E section of Putnam County, SE of Monterey.
Verble	Community in E SE section of Putnam County. 11 mi E SE of Cookeville.
Verdun	Community in N NW section of Scott County. 6 1/2 mi N NW of Huntsville.
Vernon	Community in NW section of Hickman County. 6 1/2 mi N NW of Centerville.
Vernon Heights	Community in SW section of Sullivan County. Approx. 4 mi W of Colonial Heights.
Verona	Community in N central section of Marshall County. 4 mi N NE of Lewisburg.
Versailles	Community in S SW section of Rutherford County. 11 1/2 mi S SW of Murfreesboro.
Versailles Knob	Located in S SW section of Rutherford County. S of Versailles.
Vervilla	Community in SW section of Warren County. 8 mi S SW of McMinnville.
Vesta	Community in S SW section of Wilson County. 12 mi S SW of Lebanon.
Vestal	Community on western edge of South Knoxville in Knox County. 1 1/2 mi S of downtown Knoxville.
Veto	Community in S area of Giles County. 14 mi S SE of Pulaski.
VFW Lake	Lake in middle W NW section of Lawrence County. W of Center.
Viar	Community in E SE section of Dyer County.
Vice Presidents Island	Island on Mississippi River, in SW section of Shelby County.
Vick Hollow	Located in central section of Benton County.
Victoria	Community in center NE section of Marion County. 7 mi NE of Jasper.
Victory	Community in Central area of Campbell County near LaFollette.
Vildo	Community in NW section of Hardeman County. 12 mi NW of Bolivar. 6 mi N NE of Whiteville.

Village Green	Community in SW section of Knox County. 15 mi SW of Knoxville, W of Farragut.
Vine	Community in S SW section of Wilson County. 13 mi S SW of Lebanon.
Vinegar Hill	Located in middle section of Stewart County, W of Bear Spring.
Vinegar Hill	Community in NE section of Sullivan County. 13 mi E of Blountville.
Vine Ridge	Community on E SE border of Overton County. 14 mi E SE of Livingston.
Vinson Cross Roads	Community in NW section of Warren County. 10 mi NW of McMinnville.
Viola	City in S SW section of Warren County. 11 mi S SW of McMinnville. Incorporated in 1901.
Virtue	Community in SW section of Knox County, SW of Farragot. 17 mi SW of Knoxville.
Volunteer Heights	Community in W central section of Cumberland County.
Volunteer Ordinance Works	Federal Property within the city limits of Chattanooga. 9 mi E NE of downtown in Hamilton County.
Vonore	City in N section of Monroe County. 8 mi NE of Madisonville. Incorporated in 1965.
Voorhies	Community in S section of Lewis County. E of Riverside.
Vose	Community in N Central area of Blount County. 2 mi N of Maryville.
Vowell Mountain	Mountain in N NW section of Anderson County, W of Lake City.
Waco	Community in N area of Giles County. 12 1/2 mi N of Pulaski.
Waconda Point	Community in central section of Hamilton County near Harrison.
Waddell Hollow	Located in central W section of Williamson County. N of Bingham.
Wade	Community in NW section of Rutherford County. Approx. 9 mi NW of Murfreesboro.
Walden	City on Walden's Ridge in Hamilton County. 9 mi N of downtown Chattanooga. 4 mi N of Signal Mountain. Incorporated in 1975.
Walden Ridge	Ridge in middle W section of Anderson County.

Walden Ridge	Ridge in NE section of of Bledsoe County. 14 mi NE of Pikeville.
Walden Ridge	Ridge in W section of Coffee County. SE of Baucom.
Walden Ridge	Mountain range in W section of Hamilton County and E section of Sequatchie County, runs in a Northerly direction through Rhea County.
Waldens Creek	Community in middle W section of Sevier County. 6 1/2 mi S SW of Sevierville.
Waldensia	Community in E section of Cumberland County, S of Millstone. 14 mi E SE of Crossville.
Wales	Community in W central section of Giles County. 4 1/2 mi NW of Pulaski.
Walker Bend	Area in bend of Obey River. 2 mi E of Celina in Clay County.
Walker Mountain	Mountain in middle NW section of White County, NW of Sparta.
Walker Pond	Pond in S SW section of Tipton County. Approx. 1 mi S of Crosstown.
Walkertown	Community in NE central section of Greene County. 8 mi N NE of Greeneville.
Walkertown	Community in W center section of Hardin County. 2 1/2 mi S of Savannah.
Walland	Community in E Central section of Blount County. 9 mi E of Maryville.
Wallen Ridge	Ridge in S area of Claiborne County. N of Lone Mountain.
Wallen Ridge	Ridge in NW corner of Hancock County.
Waller Pond	Pond in SW area of Lauderdale County, in the Anderson-Tully Wildlife Area.
Walling	Community in SW section of White County. 11 mi SW of Sparta.
Walnut Grove	Community in NW section of Bedford County. 1 mi SW of Newtown.
Walnut Grove	Community in SE corner of Campbell County, 9 mi SE of LaFollette.
Walnut Grove	Community in SW area of Franklin County. 9 mi S SE of Winchester.
Walnut Grove	Community in N area of Gibson County. 13 mi N of Trenton.

Walnut Grove	Community in SE corner of Hardin County. 17 mi SE of Savannah. 11 1/2 mi E SE of Pickwick Dam.
Walnut Grove	Community in E SE section of Johnson County, SE of Mountain City.
Walnut Grove	Community in central section of Meigs County. 3 mi E NE of Decatur.
Walnut Grove	Community in W section of Robertson County. 13 mi W NW of Springfield.
Walnut Grove	Community in N section of Sevier County. 5 mi E NE of Sevierville.
Walnut Grove	Community in S SE section of Sullivan County. 8 mi SE of Blountville.
Walnut Grove	Community in W section of Sumner County. 11 mi W NW of Gallatin.
Walnut Grove	Community in N NW section of Tipton County. 7 1/2 mi W NW of Covington.
Walnut Grove	Community in W section of Trousdale County. 4 mi W of Hartsville.
Walnut Grove	Community in N NW section of White County. 7 1/2 mi N NW of Sparta.
Walnut Grove Lake	Lake in middle SE section of Shelby County. S of Cordovia.
Walnut Hill	Community in SE area of Crockett County. 6 mi SE of Alamo.
Walnut Hill	Community in N NE section of Sullivan County. SW of Bristol.
Walnut Knob	Located in SW section of Smith County. 2 mi NW of Brush Creek.
Walnut Log	Community in NW section of Obion County. 14 1/2 mi W NW of Untion City.
Walnut Mountain	Mountain in W Central section of Campbell County, 7 mi N of Jacksboro.
Walnut Shade	Community in NE section of Macon County. 11 1/2 mi E NE of Lafayette.
Walter Crossroad	Community in W central section of Greene County. 8 mi SW of Greeneville.
Walterhill	Community in middle N section of Rutherford County. Approx. 6 mi N of Murfreesboro.
Wa-Ni Village	Village in S area of Grainger County. 5 mi SE of Rutledge.

Ward Chapel	Community in W area of Coffee County. 5 1/2 mi W of Manchester.
Warden Hollow	Located in N NW section of Humphreys County near Houston County line. Approx. 10 mi N NW of Waverly.
Ward Hollow	Located in S section of Bedford County.
Wardlow Pocket	Lake in NW section of Lauderdale County, SE of Barr.
Ware Branch	Inlet of Tennessee River, N of Skull Island across the river from Shady Grove in Hamilton County.
Warren	Community in Central section of Fayette County. 5 1/2 mi W of Somerville.
Warren County WARREN COUNTY	County Seat; McMinnville. Zip Code 37110. Located in South Central section of the State. Bounded by DeKalb, White, Van Buren, Sequatchie, Grundy, Coffee and Cannon Counties. Named in honor of General Joseph Warren.
Warren Hollow	Located in E section of Williamson County. 9 mi E of Franklin, SW of Potato Hill.
Warrens Bluff	Community in SE central section of Henderson County. 5 mi S SE of Lexington.
Warrensburg	Community in W area of Greene County. 15 mi W of Greeneville. 3 1/2 mi S of Skinner Crossroad.
War Ridge	Ridge in SW corner of Hancock County.
Warriors Path State Park	Located in W SW section of Sullivan County, NE of Colonial Heights.
Wartburg	County Seat of Morgan County. Located in central section of the County. Incorporated in 1968.
Wartrace	Town in E Central section of Bedford County. 7 mi NE of Shelbyville, 4 mi S of Bell Buckle. Incorporated in 1903.
Wartrace Lake	Lake in center of Robertson County.
Warwicktown	Community in middle S section of Union County. 5 mi W SW of Maynardville.
Washburn	Community in W area of Grainger County. 4 1/2 mi W NW of Rutledge.
Washington College	Community in SW section of Washington County. 8 mi SW of Jonesborough.
Washington County	County Seat: Jonesborough. Zip Code 37659.

Washington County, (Cont.) WASHINGTON COUNTY	Located in Northeast section of the State. Bounded by Sullivan, Carter, Unicoi, Greene and Hawkins Counties. Named in honor of George Washington.
Washington Ferry	Ferry in E SE section of Rhea County. Crosses the Tennessee River to Decatur.
Washington Heights Estates	Community in Knox County. 9 mi W NW of downtown Knoxville.
Wasp	Community in SE section of Cocke County. 4 mi SE of French Broad.
Watauga Dam (TVA)	In E central section of Carter Carter on Watauga River.
Watauga Flats	Community in E NE section of Washington County. 11 mi NE of Jonesborough.
Watauga Lake	Lake in middle N section of Carter County, S of Horseshoe.
Watauga Point	Community in W section of Carter County. 3 mi SW of Elizabethton.
Watauga River	In E central area of Carter County on Watauga Lake. 5 mi S SE of Elizabethton.
Water Hollow	Located in middle W section of Houston County, N NE of New Hope.
Water River	River in NE section of Rhea County, off Watts Bar Lake at Spring City.
Watertown	Community in E section of Blount County. 3 mi E of Rocky Branch.
Watertown	City in E SE section of Wilson County. 11 mi SE of Lebanon. Incorporated in 1905.
Water Valley	Community in NW section of Maury County. 12 1/2 mi NW of Columbia.
Waterville	Community in SE section of Bradley County.
Watkins	Community in SW central section of DeKalb County. 3 mi SW of Smithville.
Watson	Community in E central section of Cumberland County. 12 mi E NE of Crossville.
Watson	Community in S central section of Hickman County. Approx. 5 mi S SW of Centerville.
Watson	Community in W central section of Rutherford County. 3 mi W of Murfreesboro.
Watson	Community in SE section of Williamson County. 14 1/2 mi SE of Franklin. E of Cross Keys.

Watson Hollow — Located in S section of Stewart County, S of Moore Hollow.

Watts Bar — Located in NW corner of Meigs County.

Watts Bar Dam — Dam on the Tennessee River, located in the NW section of Meigs County. Half of dam is in Meigs the other half in Rhea County.

Watuaga — Community in NW corner of Carter County near Washington County line. Incorporated in 1960.

Waucheesi — Community in middle SE section of Monroe County. 15 mi SE of Madisonville.

Waucheesi Mountain — Mountain on S border of Monroe County, E of Smithfield.

Wauhatchie — Community SW area of Hamilton County. 5 mi SW of downtown Chattanooga.

Waverly — County Seat of Humphreys County near center of County. Incorporated in 1837.

Waverly Hollow — Located in N NW section of Humphreys County. 3 mi S SW of Concord.

Way — Community in Central section of Benton County.

Wayland Springs — Community in SW corner of Lawrence County. 18 mi SW of Lawrenceburg. 4 1/2 mi W NW of St. Joseph.

Wayne County — County Seat: Waynesboro. Zip Code 38485. Located in South Central section of the State. Bounded by Hardin, Decatur, Perry, Lewis and Lawrence Counties and the State of Alabama to the South. Named in honor of Major General Anthony Wayne.

WAYNE COUNTY

Waynesboro — County seat of Wayne County. Located in central section of the county. Incorporated in 1827.

Wayside — Community in E central section of Coffee County. 5 mi NE of Manchester.

Wayside — Community in central N section of Warren County. 4 mi N of McMinnville.

Weakley — Community in W NW section of Giles County. 10 mi W NW of Pulaski.

Weakley County — County Seat: Dresden. Zip Code 38225. Located in the Northwest section of the State. Bounded by Henry, Carroll, Gibson and Obion Counties and the State of Kentucky to the North. Named in honor of Robert Weakley.

WEAKLEY COUNTY

Wears Cove — Located in W SW section of Sevier County, S of

Wears Cove, (Cont.)	Hatchertown. 8 mi W of Gatlinburg.
Wears Valley	Community in SW section of Sevier County. 11 mi S SW of Sevierville.
Weatherly Switch	Community in SW section of Bradley County. 9 mi SW of Cleveland.
Weaver	Community in middle E section of Sullivan County. 8 mi E of Blountville. 4 mi S of Bristol.
Webb Chapel	Community on W border of Obion County. 19 mi W SW of Union City.
Webber City	Community in middle NE section of Lawrence County. 8 mi N NE of Lawrenceburg.
Webb Lake	Lake in N central section of McMinn County. 3 mi NW of Athens.
Webbs Creek	Creek in middle E section of Sevier County. E of Laurel.
Webbs Jungle	Community in NE section of Bedford County. 12 mi NE of Shelbyville.
Webbs Mountain	Mountain in E section of Sevier County.
Webbtown	Community in E central section of Macon County. 3 1/2 mi E SE of Lafayette.
Welch	Community in NW section of Cumberland County.
Welch Crossroad	Community in middle N section of Union County. 8 mi N NW of Maynardville.
Welch Hollow	Located in E section of Putnam County. 9 mi E of Cookeville. S of Bilbrey.
Welchland	Community in middle SW section of Van Buren County. 7 1/2 mi S SW of Spencer.
Well Hollow	Located in N NW section of Humphreys County. 2 mi E NE of Hall Creek.
Wells	Community in SE area of Hamilton County near Ooltewah.
Wells Creek	Creek in SE section of Stewart County near Cumberland City Steam Plant.
Wells Hole Gap	Located in middle NE section of Monroe County in Cherokee National Forest.
Well Spring	Community in E Central section of Campbell County near Claiborne County line. 10 mi NE of LaFollette.
Wells Switch	Community 2 mi due north of Weatherly Station

Wells Switch, (Cont.)	in Bradley County.
Wellsville	Community in SW section of Blount County. 12 mi SW of Maryville, 6 mi W of Christie Hill.
Wellwood	Community on E border of Haywood County. 9 mi E NE of Brownsville.
Welsh Camp	Community in SW corner of Campbell County. 6 mi SW of Caryville.
Wesleyanna	Community in middle S section of McMinn County. 6 mi S SE of Athens.
West	Community in SE section of Gibson County. 14 1/2 mi SE of Trenton.
West	Community in Knox County. 11 mi W SW of Knoxville.
Westavia Woods	Community within the city limits of Knoxville. 6 mi W of downtown. In Knox County.
Westbourne	Town in Central section of Campbell County, 9 mi NE of LaFollette.
West Cyruston	Community in W SW section of Lincoln County. 10 mi W SW of Fayetteville.
Westel	Community in SE section of Cumberland County. 17 mi E SE of Crossville.
West Emory	Community in SW section of Knox County. 11 1/2 mi SW of Knoxville.
West End	Community in W central section of Bledsoe County. 1 mi NW of Pikeville.
West End	Community in Cocke County within the city limits of Newport.
West Forest	Community within the city limits of Knoxville. 7 mi W of downtown. In Knox County.
West Harpeth	Community in S section of Williamson County. 6 mi S SW of Franklin.
West Haven	Community within the city limits of Knoxville. 3 1/2 mi W NW of downtown. In Knox County.
West Haven	Community in central W section of Maury County. 2 mi W of Columbia, N of Field Crest.
West Hills	Community within the city limits of Knoxville. 6 mi W SW of downtown. In Knox County.
West Hollow	Located in W SW section of Giles County. W of Anthony Hill.

West Junction	Community in SW section of Memphis. E of T. O. Fuller State Park in Shelby County.
West Knoxville	Community within the city limits of Knoxville. 2 1/2 mi W SW of downtown.
Westlyn	Community within the city limits of Knoxville. 6 1/2 mi W SW of downtown. In Knox County.
West Maryville	Community in W central section of Blount County near Maryville.
West Meade	Community in central section of Coffee County.
West Meade	Community in SW section of Davidson County. 2 mi W NW of Belle Meade.
West Meade	Community within the city of Columbia, W SW section of town. In Maury County.
West Mill	Community in W area of Cumberland County. 8 mi W of Crossville.
West Miller Cove	In E Central section of Blount County. 9 mi E SE of Maryville.
Westmoreland	City in E NE section of Sumner County. 17 mi NE of Gallatin. Incorporated in 1901.
Westmoreland Heights	Community within the city limits of Knoxville. 5 mi W SW of downtown. In Knox County.
West Myers	Community in W central section of Cocke County. 6 mi E SE of Newport.
Westover	Community in W center section of Madison County. 3 mi W of Jackson.
West Point	Community in W SW section of Lawrence County. 13 mi SW of Lawrenceburg. 6 1/2 mi W NW of Loretto.
Westport	Community in SE area of Carroll County. 4 1/2 mi E NE of Clarksburg.
West Robbins	Community in middle W SW section of Scott County. 7 1/1 mi SW of Huntsville.
West Sandy	Community in E section of Henry County, W of Old Springville.
West Sandy Creek Wildlife Management Area	Located in E section of Henry County, S of Sunny Side.
West Shiloh	Community on E SE border of McNairy County. 11 1/2 mi E SE of Selmer.
Westside	Community in W area of Giles County.

Westside Heights	Community in SW area of Coffee County.
West Springbrook	Community in N Central section of Blount County near Maryville.
West Union	Community in NW section of Shelby County. N NE of Cuba.
West Union	Community in middle E section of Weakley County. 4 mi E of Dresden.
West View	Community in SE area of Hamilton County near Ryall Springs.
West View	Community within the city limits of Knoxville. 2 mi W NW of downtown. In Knox County.
Westwood	Community in SW section of Coffee County.
Westwood	Community in central W SW section of Maury County. 3 1/2 mi S SW of Columbia, N of Pleasant Hill.
Westwood Gardens	Community on the W border of the City of Jackson in Madison County.
Westwood Hills	Community in W central section of Blount County. 4 mi S SW of Maryville.
Westwood Homes	Community in Central section of Coffee County. 2 mi N NE of Manchester.
Wetmore	Community on N NW border of Polk County. 8 mi NW of Benton.
Whale Pond	Pond in SW section of Lauderdale County, in the Anderson-Tully Wildlife Area.
Wheel	Community in W SW area of Bedford County. 9 mi W of Shelbyville, 2 mi from Marshall County line.
Wheeler Hollow	Located in N section of Humphreys County. 3 mi S of Woolworth.
Wheelerton	Community in E SE section of Giles County. 13 mi E SE of Pulaski.
Whetstone Mountain	Mountain in S section of Morgan County, S of Little Brushy Mountain.
Whigg Ridge	Located in SE section of Monroe County. N of Rough Ridge.
Whispering Hills	Community in Knox County. 7 1/2 mi N NW of downtown Knoxville.
Whispering Pine	Community in N section of Unicoi County. 9 1/2 mi NE of Erwin.

Whitaker	Community in SW section of Bedford County. 2 1/2 mi S of Wheel.
White Bluff	City in E area of Dickson County. 8 mi S SE of Charlotte. Incorporated in 1869.
White Chapel	Community in S section of Warren County. 5 mi S of McMinnville.
White City	Community in S section of Grundy County. 12 mi S of Altamont.
White County WHITE COUNTY	County Seat: Sparta. Zip Code 38583. Located in middle East Central section of the State. Bounded by Putnam, Cumberland, Bledsoe, Van Buren, Warren and DeKalb Counties. Named in honor of John White.
Whitedirt Hollow	Located in middle S section of Stewart County, S of Carlisle.
White Fern	Community on W border of Henderson County. 12 mi W of Lexington.
Whitehaven	Community within the city limits of Memphis, SW section. In Shelby County.
Whitehead	Community in central section of Marshall County. 2 mi N of Lewisburg.
Whitehead Hill	Community in S central section of Carter County. 8 mi S of Elizabethton.
White Hill	Community in W section of Sumner County. Approx. 8 mi N NW of Hendersonville.
White Hill	Community in W section of Van Buren County. 8 1/2 mi SW of Spencer.
White Hollow	Located in W central section of Humphreys County. 3 mi SW of Waverly.
White Hollow	Located in middle W SW section of Macon County. 1 1/2 mi S SW of Gap of the Ridge.
White Hollow	Located in S section of Stewart County, near Houston County Line.
White Hollow	Community in NW section of Union County in Chuck Swan State Forest.
White Horn	Community in S section of Hawkins County. 9 mi S SW of Rogersville. 2 1/2 mi NE of Bulls Gap.
Whitehouse	Community in NW corner of Hickman County. Approx. 12 mi NW of Centerville.
White House	Community in W section of Sumner County. Approx. 11 mi N of Hendersonville. Incorporated in 1971. Boundaries also extend into

White House, (Cont.)	Robertson County.
White Oak	Community in NE area of Campbell County. 6 mi SE of Jellico.
White Oak	Community within the city limits of Red Bank in Hamilton County.
White Oak	Community in NW section of Hardin County, 9 mi N NW of Savannah, SE of Lebanon.
White Oak	Communty in N section of Macon County. 6 mi N NE of Lafayette.
White Oak	Community in S section of Morgan County. 6 1/2 mi S of Wartburg.
Whiteoak	Community near S SW border of Williamson County. 1 1/2 mi W SW of Greenbrier.
Whiteoak Creek	Creek in SW corner of Houston County, off Tennessee River.
Whiteoak Crossing	Community in SW corner of Perry County. 11 1/2 mi S SW of Linden.
White Oak Flat	Community in NE central section of Dickson County. 5 mi E NE of Charlotte.
Whiteoak Lake	Lake in E NE section of Roane County. 11 mi E NE of Kingston in Oak Ridge.
White Oak Mountain	Mountain along the Western Border of Bradley County and the E section of Hamilton County and into the State of Georgia.
White Oak Mountain	Mountain in N central section of Polk County, E SE of Probst.
White Oaks	Community in Central section of Coffee County.
White Oak Wildlife Management Area	Located in W NW section of Hardin County, S of Lebanon.
White Pine	City in NE corner of Jefferson County. 9 mi NE of Dandridge. Incorporated in 1893.
White Ridge	Ridge in SW corner of Giles County.
White Rock	Community in S Central area of Carter County. 8 mi SE of Elizabethton.
White Rock Mountain	Mountain in SE area of Carter County, E of Blevins.
Whites	Community in W section of Sevier County, W of Sevierville between Highway 441 and Chilhowee Mountain.
Whitesand	Community in S central section of Greene

Whitesand, (Cont.)	County. 8 mi S of Greeneville.
Whites Bend	Located in W section of Davidson County. 6 mi W of Bordeaux.
Whites Bend	Area in bend of Cumberland River, SW of Rough Point in Jackson County.
Whitesburg	Community in NE section of Hamblen County. 10 E NE of Morristown.
Whites Chapel	Community in SW corner of Shelby County. 7 1/2 mi S SW of Memphis.
Whites Creek	Community in middle N section of Davidson County. 4 mi N of Bordeaux.
Whites Hollow	Located in SE section of Benton County.
Whiteside	Community on S SE border of Marion County. 9 mi SE of Jasper.
Whites Lake	Lake in NW section of Dyer County. 10 mi W NW of Dyersburg
White Station	Community within the city limits of Memphis, E of Germantown. In Shelby County.
Whitetop Knob	Mountain Range in N NE section of Sullivan County, SW of Bristol.
Whiteville	City in NW section of Hardeman County. 10 mi NW of Bolivar. 7 1/2 mi N of Newcastle. Incorporated in 1901.
Whiteville Lake	Lake in W central section of Hardeman County. 8 mi W NW of Bolivar. 6 mi N NE of Newcastle.
Whitfield	Community in W central section of Hickman County. Approx. 8 mi W of Centerville.
Whithorne	Community in W section of Carroll County. 14 mi SW of Huntingdon.
Whitleyville	Community in N section of Jackson County. 6 1/2 mi N NW of Gainesboro.
Whitlock	Community in N central section of Henry County. 5 mi N NW of Paris.
Whittaker Cove	Located near S SE border of Putnam County. 8 mi S SE of Cookeville.
Whittle Springs	Community within the city limits of Knoxville. 4 mi N of downtown. In Knox County.
Whitway	Community in E area of Gibson County. 1 mi E of Trenton.
Whitwell	City in central NE section of Marion County.

Whitwell, (Cont.)	11 mi N NE of Jasper. Incorporated in 1956.
Wilber Lake	Lake (Watauga River) in N central section of Carter County, NE of Dogtown.
Wilbur Dam	In N central area of Carter County on Watauga River.
Wilcox	Community in N area of Crockett County. 10 1/2 mi N NW of Alamo.
Wilcox Hollow	Located in W SW section of Hamilton County.
Wildcat Hollow	Located in W section of Coffee County. 2 mi W SW of Busy Corner.
Wilder	Community in SW section of Fentress County. 14 mi SW of Jamestown.
Wilder Chapel	Community in NE area of Franklin County. 11 1/2 mi NE of Winchester.
Wilder Point	Located in SW section of Hamilton County.
Wildersville	Community on N border of Henderson County. 9 1/2 mi N of Lexington.
Wild Plum	Community in S central section of Cumberland County. 4 1/2 mi S SE of Crossville.
Wildwood	Community in NE area of Blount County. 6 mi NE of Maryville.
Wildwood Lake	Lake in S Central area of Bradley County. Just SE of Cleveland.
Wilhite	Community in S central section of Putnam County. 3 mi S of Cookeville.
Wilhite	Community in E NE section of Sevier County, E of Jones Cove.
Wilkerson Corner	Community in S section of Haywood County, E NE of Asbury.
Wilkersonville	Community in S SW section of Tipton County. 18 mi SW of Covington.
Wilkinstown	Community in W section of Decatur County. Approx. 3 mi N NW of Decaturville.
Willard	Community in NW section of Trousdale County. 4 mi N NW of Hartsville.
Willardtown	Community in SW section of Jefferson County. 9 mi W of Dandridge.
Willet Mountain	Mountain in E NE section of Putnam County. 6 mi E of Cookeville. S of Brotherton.

Willette
Community in SE corner of Macon County. 11 mi E SE of Lafayette.

Williams
Community in middle N section of Macon County. 2 mi N of Lafayette.

Williamsburg
Community in SE section of McMinn County. 7 mi S SE of Athens. N of Etowah.

Williamsburg
Community in near center of Sevier County. 6 1/2 mi S SE of Sevierville.

Williams Chapel
Community in N section of Shelby County. 19 mi N NE of Memphis.

Williams Creek
Community in middle NW section of Scott County. 10 mi NW of Huntsville.

Williams Crossroads
Community in NE area of DeKalb County. 8 mi NE of Smithville.

Williams Hollow
Located in NE corner of Humphreys County. 5 mi N NE of McEwen.

Williams Hollow
Located in middle N section of Humphreys County. 4 mi N NE of Waverly.

Williams Island
Island on Tennessee River within the city limits of Chattanooga in Hamilton County.

Williams Lake
Lake in W NW section of Shelby County. W SW of Ramsey.

Williams Mountain
Mountain in W section of Roane County, SW of Rockwood.

Williamson County
County Seat: Franklin. Zip Code 37064. Located in middle W central section of the State. Bounded by Cheatham, Davidson, Rutherford, Marshall, Maury, Hickman and Dickson Counties. Named in honor of Dr. Hugh Williamson.

WILLIAMSON COUNTY

Williamsport
Community in W NW section of Maury County. 11 1/2 mi W NW of Columbia.

William Springs
Community in N NW section of Grainger County. 6 mi NW of Rutledge.

Williams Store
Community on E SE border of Lawrence County. Approx. 10 mi SE of Lawrenceburg.

Willis
Community in NE section of Hancock County on Virginia Border. 12 mi E NE of Sneedville. 1 1/2 mi NE of Kyles Ford.

Willis
Community in S section of Haywood County, W of KoKo.

Willis Hollow
Located in central section of Benton County.

Willis Springs	Community in SW corner of Polk County, E of Conasauga.
Williston	City in central section of Fayette County. 6 mi S of Somerville. Incorporated in 1970.
Willow Grove	Community in SE area of Bedford County. 9 mi E SE of Shelbyville.
Willow Grove	Community in NE corner of Clay County.
Willow Grove	Community in E central section of Haywood County. 5 mi E of Brownsville.
Willow Lake	Lake in middle NW section of Sumner County. S of Fountain Head.
Wills	Community in middle NE section of Johnson County. 4 mi N NE of Mountain City.
Wilmore Hollow	Located in SE section of Macon County. E of Gum Springs.
Wilson County WILSON COUNTY	County Seat: Lebanon. Zip Code 37087. Located in middle central section of the State. Bounded by Sumner, Trousdale, Smith, DeKalb, Cannon, Rutherford and Davidson Counties. Named in honor of David Wilson.
Wilson Hill	Community in W SW section of Marshall County. Approx. 5 mi W SW of Lewisburg.
Wilson Hollow	Located in E NE section of Benton County. Approx. 2 mi SE of Faxon.
Wilson Knob	Located in E section of McMinn County. 2 mi SE of Englewood.
Wilson Mountain	Mountain in NW section of Overton County. 6 mi NW of Livingston.
Wilson Station	Community on W border of Monroe County. 7 1/2 mi S SW of Madisonville.
Wilsonville	Community in W area of Cocke County. 3 mi W of Newport.
Wilton Springs	Community in W central section of Cocke County. 6 mi S of Newport.
Winchester	County Seat of Franklin County. Located in central area of county. Incorporated in 1821.
Winchester Springs	Community in NW central section of Franklin County. 5 1/2 mi NW of Winchester.
Windle	Community in middle W SW section of Overton County. 5 mi SW of Livingston.
Windletown	Community in E SE section of Overton County.

Windletown, (Cont.)	13 mi E SE of Livingston.
Windrock	Community in W Central Section of Anderson County. 3 mi N of Oliver Springs.
Windrock Mountain	Mountain in SW section of Anderson County, N of Oliver Springs.
Windrow	Community in central SW section of Rutherford County. 9 1/2 mi W SW of Murfreesboro.
Windy City	Community in N NW section of Madison County. 10 mi N NW of Jackson.
Winesap	Community in SW section of Cumberland County.
Winfield	City in N section of Scott County. 10 mi N NE of Huntsville. Incorporated in 1983.
Winfree Knob	Located in S SW section of Smith County. 7 mi S of Carthage.
Wingo	Community in NW area of Carroll County. 4 mi N of McLemoresville.
Winklers Crossroads	Community in NE corner of Macon County. 12 mi NE of Lafayette.
Winn Crossing	Community in N section of Marshall County. 2 mi N NW of Chapel Hill.
Winner	Community in central section of Carter County. 5 mi NE of Elizabethton.
Winn Springs	Community on S border of Hardin County. 4 mi S SE of Pickwick Dam.
Winona	Community in central section of Putnam County. 2 1/2 mi E SE of Cookeville.
Winona	Community in SE central section of Scott County. 3 1/2 mi SE of Huntsville.
Winsap	Community in NW area of Bledsoe County. 11 mi N NE of Pikeville.
Winslow	Community in S SE section of Morgan County, SE of Coal Hill.
Winton Town	Community in E area of Coffee County. 9 1/2 mi E of Manchester.
Wirmingham	Community on NE border of Overton County. 10 mi NE of Livingston.
Wise Hill	Comunity within the city limits of Knoxville. 2 1/2 mi S SE of downtown.
Wiseman Branch	Stream in W area of Franklin County on he Elk River.

Withamtown	Community in NE section of Sumner County. 13 1/2 mi N NE of Gallatin. SW of Westmoreland.
Witt	Community in S section of Hamblen County. 5 mi S of Morristown.
Wixtown	Community in middle W section of Macon County, NW of Gap of the Ridge.
Wolf Creek	Community in W area of Cocke County. 13 mi E SE of Newport.
Wolf Creek	Community in SW corner of Lawrence County. S of Mount Nebo.
Wolf Creek	Creek in E NE section of of Rhea County. 14 mi NE of Dayton.
Wolf Creek	Community in E NE section of Rhea County. 14 mi NE of Dayton.
Wolf Hill	Community on E border of Sumner County. 12 1/2 mi E NE of Gallatin.
Wolf Island	In middle W section of Hardin County on Tennessee River, W of Savannah.
Wolf Pond	Pond in E NE section of Hamilton County, E of Grasshopper.
Wolf River	Community in NW area of Fentress County. 8 mi N NW of Jamestown.
Wolf River	River in N NW section of Pickett County (Dale Hollow Lake).
Wolf River	Begins in the State of Mississippi and flows N into Fayette County and then W through Fayette and Shelby Counties where it flows into the Mississippi River.
Wolftever Creek	Creek in E area of Hamilton County (Harrison Bay Area), flows into the Tennessee River.
Wolverine	Community in middle S SW section of Obion County. N NE of Obion.
Womack	Community in middle N section of Warren County. 5 1/2 mi N NW of McMinnville.
Wood	Community in W NW section of Monroe County. Approx. 2 mi S of Sweetwater.
Woodbine	Community in S SE section of Davidson County.
Woodbury	County Seat of Cannon County. Located near center of county. 8 mi S of Auburntown. Incorporated in 1843.
Woodby Hill	Community in SW area of Carter County. 9 mi S

Woodby Hill, (Cont.)	of Elizabethton.
Wooddale	Community in E section of Knox County. 9 1/2 mi E NE of Knoxville.
Wood Duck Island	Island on Norris Lake in W section of Union County.
Wooded Oaks	Community within the city limits of Knoxville. 6 mi W NW of downtown.
Woodfield Park	Community in Knox County. 6 mi E SE of downtown Knoxville.
Woodland	Community on middle E border of Haywood County. 9 1/2 mi E of Brownsville.
Woodland Acres	Community in central E section of Henry County. Approx. 4 mi NE of Paris.
Woodland Acres	Community in Knox County. 7 1/2 mi W SW of Knoxville.
Woodland Heights	Community within city limits of Savannah, in N section of city. In Hardin County.
Woodland Heights	Community in S central section of Hickman County. Approx. 2 mi S SW of Centerville.
Woodland Mills	City on N border of Obion County. 5 1/2 mi NW of Union City. Incorporated in 1968.
Woodlawn	Community in central section of Cumberland County. 2 1/2 mi N of Crossville.
Woodlawn	Community in N central section of Greene County. 10 mi N NW of Greeneville.
Woodlawn	Community in N section of Loudon County. 9 1/2 mi N of Loudon.
Woodlawn	Community in middle NW section of Montgomery County. 8 1/2 mi W of Clarksville.
Woodlawn	Community in central SE section of Washington County. 1 1/2 mi S SE of Jonesborough.
Woodlawn	Community in middle S section of Wayne County. 10 1/2 mi S SE of Waynesboro.
Woodmore	Community within the city limits of Chattanooga. 5 mi E of downtown in Hamilton County.
Woodrow	Community in E area of Giles County.
Woodrow	Community in NW section of Sullivan County. Approx. 4 mi SE of Kingsport.
Woods Hollow	Located in E SE section of Benton County.

Woodson Chapel	Community in S SE section of Davidson County.
Woods Reservoir	Lake in N section of Franklin County part of Elk River, backed up by the Elk River Dam.
Woodstock	Community in middle W NW section of Shelby County. 10 1/2 mi N NE of Memphis.
Woods Valley	Community in N NW section Dickson County. 9 mi N NW of Charlotte.
Woodville	Community in Lower SW section of Chester County near McNairy County line. 6 1/2 mi S of Hickory Corners.
Woodville	Community in NW corner of Haywood County. 15 1/2 mi NW of Brownsville.
Woody	Community in NW Central section of Cumberland County. 8 mi N NW of Crossville.
Woolly Top Mountain	Mountain in SE corner of Sevier County. 7 mi SE of Pittman Center. E of Portners Mountain.
Woolridge	Community in NW section of Campbell County near Kentucky line. 3 mi W of Jellico.
Woolworth	Community in N NE section of Humphreys County. 11 mi N NE of Waverly.
Work	Community in NE section of Hamilton County. 23 mi N NE of downtown Chattanooga. W of New Point at Dividing Ridge.
Wrencoe	Community in S SE section of Davidson County.
Wright	Community in middle S SW section of Knox County. 9 mi S SW of Knoxville.
Wright	Community in N NE section of Lake County, NE of Proctor City.
Wright Hollow	Located in S SW section of Macon Hollow. 2 mi E of Beech Hill.
Wright Mountain	Mountain in S SW section of Scott County near border, S SW of Lone Mountain.
Wrigley	Community in NE section of Hickman County. 10 1/1 mi NE of Centerville.
Wyatts Chapel	Community in middle NE section of Stewart County. 7 mi NE of Dover.
Wyatt Village	Community in E SE section of Grainger County. 13 mi E NE of Rutledge.
Wyly	Community in NW section of Benton County.
Wyly Hollow	Located in central section of Humphreys

Wyly Hollow, (Cont.)	County. 3 mi S SE of Waverly.
Wynn	Community in Central section of Campbell County near LaFollette.
Wynnburg	Community in center of Lake County. 3 1/2 mi S of Tiptonville.
Wyricktown	Community in E NE section of Knox County, SE of Mascot.
Yager	Community in central NW section of Warren County. Approx. 3 mi NW of McMinnville.
Yaller Breeches Holler	Located in E section of Sevier County, between Jones Cove and Cocke County line.
Yankeetown	Community in middle N section of White County. 5 mi N NE of Sparta.
Yateston	Community in W SW section of White County. 7 1/2 mi W SW of Sparta.
Yell	Community in middle S section of Marshall County. 5 1/2 mi S of Lewisburg.
Yellow Creek	Community in W area of Dickson County. 9 mi W SW of Charlotte.
Yellow Creek	Community in E section of Houston County. Approx. 6 1/2 mi E SE of Erin.
Yellow Knob	Mountain in W section of Sevier County. 4 mi W of Waldens Creek.
Yellow Mountain	Mountain in SE section of Carter County, on border of North Carolina.
Yellow Springs	Community in NW section of Decatur County. Approx. 15 mi N of Decaturville.
Yettland Park	Community in middle N NW section of Sevier County. Approx. 2 mi NW of Sevierville.
Yoakum Crossroad	Community in NW section of Claiborne County. 11 mi W NW of Tazewell.
Yokley	Community in N NW section of Giles County. 16 mi N NW of Pulaski.
Yorkville	CIty in NW area of Gibson County. 13 mi NW of Trenton. Incorporated in 1964.
Young Bend	Community in E Central section of DeKalb County. 5 1/2 mi E SE of Smithville.
Youngs Crossing	Community in NW central section of Madison County. 8 1/2 mi N NW of Jackson.
Youngville	Community in middle N NE section of Robertson

Youngville, (Cont.)	County. Approx. 6 mi N NE of Springfield.
Yount Town	Community in central section of Hancock County S of Luther.
Yukon	Community in S SW section of Lincoln County. 7 1/2 mi SW of Fayetteville.
Yuma	Community in SE area of Carroll County near Henderson County line. 4 mi SE of Clarksburg.
Yum Yum	Community in N central section of Fayette County. 7 mi N of Somerville.
Zacharytown	Community in NE corner of Knox County. 14 mi NE of Knoxville.
Zeb Mountain	Mountain in NW area of Campbell County E of Sexton Mountain.
Zenith	Community in E NE section of Fentress County.
Zion	Community in middle W section of Maury County. 6 mi S SW of Columbia.
Zion Grove	Community in central SE section of Sevier County. 9 1/2 mi SE of Sevierville.
Zion Hill	Community in E central section of Hawkins County, W NW of Surgoinsville.
Zion Hill	Community in middle SE section of McMinn County. Approx. 5 mi SE of Athens.
Zollers P. O.	Old Post Office in the W section of Sevier County, now known as Sugarloaf.
Zu Zu	Community in N area of Fayette County. 10 mi N of Somerville.

SECTION TWO:

Lakes, Rivers and Streams of Tennessee

Pages 358-382

LAKES, RIVERS AND STREAMS OF TENNESSEE

Abernathy Lake	Lake in near center of Giles County. N of Pulaski.
Akers Lake	Lake in NW section of Wilson County. 11 mi NW of Lebanon.
Apple Lake	Lake is S section of Davidson County near Williamson County line.
Arrow Lake	Lake in SW section of Maury County. 12 mi SW of Columbia.
Ashburn Creek	Creek in E section of Clay County near Pickett County border.
Ault Lake	Lake in W section of Jefferson County. 5 mi SW of Jefferson City.
Badger Spring Lake	Lake in S SW section of Maury County. 11 1/2 mi S SW of Columbia. S of Southport.
Bards Creek	Creek in middle NW section of Stewart County. 7 mi NW of Dover. E of Tharpe.
Bards Lake	Lake in middle NW section of Stewart County. SE of Tharpe.
Bartons Creek	Creek in N NW section of Wilson County, flows into Cumberland River.
Bass Bay	Inlet off Kentucky Lake (Tennessee River) in E NE section of Benton County. Approx. 17 mi N NE of Camden.
Baylor Lake	Lake in SW section of Hamilton County on Baylor School Campus in Chattanooga.
Bear Creek	Creek in middle NW section of Stewart County. 4 mi NW of Dover.
Bedford Lake	A small body of water located on the E border of Bedford County. 5 mi E SE of Wartrace.
Beech Creek	Creek in SE area of Decatur County on Wayne County line.
Beech Lake	Lake in center of Henderson County, NW of Lexington.
Beech River	River in central section of Decatur County. Flows across the county.
Ben Henry Lake	Lake in NE corner of Hardeman County.
Benjamin Franklin Lake	Lake in W SW section of of Wilson County. 2 mi S SW of Silver Springs.
Bennett Lake	Lake in W central section of Lawrence County.

Bennett Lake, (Cont.)	N of Gandy.
Big Creek	Body of water in S section of Campbell County (Norris Lake).
Big Creek Lake	Lake in central section of Grundy County, N of Coalmont. 4 mi S of Altamont.
Big Eagle Creek	Creek on NE border of Overton County (Dale Hollow Lake).
Big Elk Creek	Creek in SE section of Stewart County. 3 mi E of Carlisle.
Big Hill Pond	Pond in SW corner of McNairy County. 11 mi SW of Selmer, in Big Hill Pond State Park.
Big Hurricane Creek	Creek in N central section of DeKalb County off Center Hill Lake.
Big Lake	Lake in S SE section of Obion County. 12 mi S SW of Union City, S of Long Lake.
Big Oak Lake	Lake in middle NE section of Maury County. 8 mi NE of Columbia.
Big Richland Creek	Creek in NW section of Humphreys County. 8 mi NW of Waverly.
Big Ridge Lake	Lake in W SW section of Union County in Big Ridge State Park.
Big Sandy River	River in NE section of Henry County. S of Paris Landing State Park.
Big Spring Lake	Lake in S SE corner of Humphreys County near Perry County Line.
Bikerstaff Lake	Lake in SW area of Bledsoe County S of Fall Creek Falls State Park.
Birdsong Creek	Creek in SE section of Benton, W of Mt. Moriah. Flows into Tennessee River.
Blair Lake	Lake in NE corner of Madison County. Approx. 11 mi NE of Jackson.
B Lakes	Lake within the city limits of Coalmont in Grundy County. 6 mi S of Altamont.
Bledsoe Creek	Creek in SE section of Sumner County. Flows into Cumberland River (Old Hickory Lake).
Blooming Grove Creek	Creek in W section of Montgomery County, flows into Cumberland River. Runs E and N of Stringtown.

Blue Creek	Creek in S SW section of Humphreys County, flows into Tennessee River.
Blue Pond	Pond in SW section of Lauderdale County, in the Anderson-Tully Wildlife Area.
Blue Water Lake	Located in E NE section of Williamson County. 14 mi E NE of Franklin.
Boiling Fork Creek	Creek in central section of Franklin County, flows NW to SE through Winchester.
Bomer Lake	Lake in central section of Haywood County, NW of Brownsville.
Boone Lake	Lake in S SW section of Sullivan County, S of Holston.
Boston Branch Lake	Lake in W section of Hamilton County on Waldens Ridge. Approx. 5 mi N NE of Fairmount, Approx. 5 mi W of Daisy.
Brackens Lake	Lake in SW area of Dyer County on Moss Island.
Briarpatch Lake	Lake in W central section of Henry County. 7 mi W of Paris.
Brickyard Pond	Pond in SE section of Haywood County. 9 mi E SE of Brownsville. 6 1/2 NE of Eurekaton.
Brown Lake	Lake in E SE section of Lawrence County. NW of Gum Springs.
Browns Creek Lake	Lake in NE section of Henderson County. 8 mi NE of Lexington.
Browns Lake	Lake in N NW section of Davidson County on Robertson County line.
Browns Lake	Lake on S SE border of Robertson County. SW of Ridgetop.
Buck Creek Lake	Lake in E NE section of White County near Putnam County Line. 11 mi E NE of Sparta.
Buffalo River	Flows from Lawrence County through Lewis, Wayne, Perry and Humphreys Counties, where it flows into the Duck River.
Burgess Falls Lake	Lake in NW corner of White County. 3 mi W of Macedonia.
Byrd Bay	Lake in W NW section of Stewart County, inlet off the Tennessee River. S of Clay Bay.
Byrd Lake	Lake in SW central section of Cumberland County. S of Cumberland Mountain State Park.

Calfkiller River	Begins in Putnam County near the town of Calfkiller. Flows S into and through White County where it flows into the Caney Fork River.
Campbell Cove Lake	Lake in middle SE section of Polk County, NE of Dogtown.
Camps Lakes	Lakes in W NW section of Shelby County, S SE of Ramsey.
Cane Creek	Flows from SW section of Bledsoe County, N through Van Buren County where it flows into the Caney Fork River.
Cane Creek	Creek on W border of Houston County, flows into Tennessee River.
Caney Fork River	Begins in SE corner of White County, flows W where it is joined by the Cane Creek and forms the boundary lines for White and Van Buren Counties. N into Dekalb County where it is backed up by the Center Hill Dam forming the Center Hill Lake. NW into Smith County where it flows into the Cumberland River.
Cantrells Lake	Lake in central section of Davidson County. 2 1/2 mi NE of Bordeaux.
Carol Lake	Lake in central section of Grundy County. S of Cumberland Heights. 2 1/2 mi SE of Altamont.
Carroll Creek	Creek in SW section of Coffee County, flows into Duck River.
Casper Lake	Lake in N section of Shelby County, E SE of Kerrville.
Cates Pond	Pond in W section of Jefferson County. 1 mi S SE of Strawberry Plains.
Catfish Lake	Lake in SW section of Fayette County near Shelby County line, SW of Canadaville.
Cedar Creek	Creek in SE section of Campbell County (Norris Lake).
Cedar Lake	Lake in NE central section of Henderson County. 4 1/2 mi E NE of Lexington.
Center Hill Lake	Lake in N Central section of DeKalb County on the Caney Fork River.
Champion Lake	Lake in SW section of Lauderdale County. Approx. 1 1/2 mi SE of Fulton.
Cheatham Lake	Lake in NW area of Cheatham County on Cumberland River.

Cheek Lake	Lake in middle NE section of Davidson County, SE of Montague.
Cherokee Lake	Lake (Holston River) in NW section of Jefferson County, SE section of Grainger County, NW section of Hamblin County and SW section of Hawkins County.
Chickamauga Lake	Formed by the Chickamauga Dam in the Tennessee River backs up to the Watts Bar Dam in Rhea County. Chickamauga Dam is located in the City of Chattanooga, County of Hamilton.
Chilhowee Lake	Lake in the SW corner of Blount County on the Monroe County line.
Chilhowee Lake (Little Tennessee River)	Located on E NE border of Monroe County.
Chisholm Lake	Lake in NW section of Lauderdale County. Approx. 8 mi N NW of Ripley.
Circle H Ranch Lake	Lake in S section of Lincoln Couonty. 9 mi S of Fayetteville.
City Lake	Lake in central SW section of Overton County. S of Livingston.
City Lake	Lake in middle E section of Putnam County. 5 mi SE of Cookeville.
City Lake	Lake in NW section of Sumner County. NE of Portland.
Clarksville Lake	Lake in middle W section of Montgomery County. 9 mi W SW of Clarksville.
Clay Bay	Lake in W NW section of Stewart County, inlet off the Tennessee River. S of Ginger Bay.
Clear Creek Lake	Lake in N NE central section of Giles County. SE of Bufords.
Clement Lake	Lake in W NW section of Williamson County. 1 mi N NW of Fairview.
Clinch River	Flows from the State of Virginia into Hawkins and Hancock Counties, forms boundary for Claiborne and Grainger Counties, flows through Union County forms boundary for Campbell and Anderson Counties, flows into Roane County where in flows into the Tennessee River.
Clovercroft Lake	Lake in middle E NE section of Williamson County. 6 1/2 mi E of Franklin.
Coffee Lake	Lake in S section of Haywood County, E of Ko

Coffee Lake, (Cont.)	Ko.
Collier Lake	Lake in center E section of Madison County, between Jackson and Lake Graham.
Collins River	Begins in the NE section of Warren County and flows NE into the Caney Fork River. SW of Walling.
Colverts Lake	Lake in center of DeKalb County, E of Smithville.
Conservation League Lake	Lake in middle NW section of Scott County. 8 1/2 mi N NW of Huntsville.
Convict Lake	Lake in SW section of Lauderdale County, E of Anderson-Tully Wildlife Area at the Ft. Pillow State Prison Farm.
Cooper Lake	Lake in middle NW section of Scott County. 7 mi NW of Huntsville.
Cora Lake	Lake in SW corner of Shelby County. N of Robco Lake.
Corbin Lake	Lake in W area of Grainger County. 4 1/2 mi W SW of Rutledge.
Cordell Hull Lake	Lake in central E section of Smith County (Cumberland River).
Cove Creek	Creek in S area Campbell County (Norris Lake).
Craig Lake	Lake in S section of Cheatham County, near the border.
Crocker Springs Lake	Lake in NW area of Davidson County, E of Joelton.
Crockett Bay	Lake in N NW section of Stewart County near the Kentucky border. NW of Tobaccopart.
Crow Pond	Pond in NW section of Hamilton County.
Crutcher Lake	Lake in SW section of Lauderdale County, W of Anderson-Tully Wildlife Area.
Crutcher Lake	Lake in SW section of Sumner County. 7 mi W of Gallatin.
Crystal Springs Lake	Lake in SE section of Lincoln County. E of Crystal Springs.
Cub Creek	Creek in NE central section of Decatur County.
Cub Creek Lake	Lake in NE corner of Henderson County. 13 mi NE of Lexington.

Cub Creek	Creek in middle E section of Stewart County. SW of Atkins.
Cumberland River	Flows from Kentucky into Clay County, South into Jackson County, Southwest into Smith County where it is backed up by the Cordell Hull Dam. Flows Westward into Trousdale, Wilson and Sumner Counties where it forms county lines, into Davidson County, thru Cheatham, Montgomery and Stewart Counties and into Kentucky where it flows into the Ohio River.
Cummings Creek	Creek in middle W section of Montgomery County, flows into Cumberland River, E of Dotsonville.
Cunningham Broadbent Lake	Lake in middle W NW section of Montgomery County. 2 mi S of Woodlawn.
Curry Pond	Pond in E NE section of Hamilton County. W of Highway 58 and Dolly Pond Road. Approx. 1 1/2 mi SE of Skull Island.
Daddys Creek	Flows from S section of Cumberland County in NE direction into Morgan County where it flows into the Obed River.
Dale Hallow Lake	Located in the E central section of Clay County (Obey River).
Davis Lake	Lake in S Central section of Bedford County. 6 mi S of Shelbyville.
Davy Crockett Lake	Lake in S central section of Greene County on Nolichucky River.
Day Lake	Lake in E area of Franklin County. 13 mi E of Winchester, S of Jackson Lake.
Day Lake	Lake on N NW border of Marion County. 16 mi W NW of Jasper partly in Franklin County.
Dillon Pond	Pond in N section of the city of Livingston. In Overton County.
Doe Creek	Creek in SW section of Decatur County on Harden County line.
Doe Creek Lake	Lake in E NE section of White County. 9 1/2 mi E NE of Sparta, N of DeRossett.
Dogwood Lake	Lake in E NE section of Henderson County. 9 mi E NE of Lexington.
Dogwood Lakes	Lake in SW section of Cumberland County. Between Midway and New Era. 12 mi S SW of Crossville.

Dorton Lake	Lake in SW area of Cumberland County. N of Tansi Lake.
Douglas Lake	Lake in NW area of Cocke County and the S SE section of Jefferson County. (French Broad River)
Drakes Creek	Creek in S SW corner of Sumner County. Flows into Cumberland River.
Drane Lake	Lake in W NW section of Shelby County. N of Frayser.
Dry Creek	Creek in central area of Franklin County, W of Winchester.
Dry Fork Bay	Lake in W section of Stewart County, inlet off the Tennessee River. N of Fort Henry.
Duck River	Flows from Coffee County where it is backed up by the Normandy Dam forming Normandy Lake, into Bedford, Marshall, Maury, Hickman and Humphreys Counties where it flows into the Tennessee River.
Dunbar Lake	Lake in middle NE section of Montgomery County. 3 1/2 mi E NE of Clarksville.
Duncan Lake	Lake in central area of Franklin County. 6 mi N of Winchester.
Dunham Lake	Lake in SW section of Dyer County, SE of Bradleytown.
Eagle Bluff Lake	Lake in S Central area of Campbell County N of Jacksboro.
Eagle Creek	Creek in SE section of Benton County, flows into Tennessee River. E of Eagle Creek community.
Eagle Creek	Creek in W section of DeKalb County, flows into Caney Fork River. E of Philippi.
Eagle Creek	Inlet off Kentucky Lake (Tennessee River) in NE section of Henry County, SW of Paris Landing State Park.
Eagle Lake	Lake in W NW section of Shelby County. SW of Poplar Tree Lake.
East Camp Creek	Creek S of Gallatin, flows into Old Hickory Lake. In Sumner County.
Echo Lake	Lake in central area of Giles County. NW of Pulaski.
Edwards Lake	Lake in NW section of Shelby County. E NE of

Edwards Lake, (Cont.)	Locke.
Elaine lake	Lake located in SE area of Bedford County near Hilltop. 8 mi SE of Shelbyville.
Elk River	Flows from Grundy County near Elkhead into Coffee County where it is backed up of the Elk River Dam forming Woods Reservoir and by the Tims Ford Dam forming the Tims Ford Lake, into Moore, Lincoln and Giles Counties where it flows into the State of Mississippi.
Emory River	River in N section of Roane County, N of Kingston, off Tennessee River.
Englewood Lake	Lake in NW center of Obion County. 7 mi W SW of Union City.
Estes Pond	Located on N border of Lake County, N of Proctor City.
Eva Lake	Lake in E section of Franklin County. 12 mi E of Winchester, SW of Jackson Lake.
Everett Lake	Lake in W section of Dyer County, W SW of Ayers.
Fall Creek	Creek in E central section of DeKalb County, flows into Caney Fork River.
Fall Creek Lake	Lake in Fall Creek Falls State Park.
Falling Water River	River in E area of DeKalb County, flows into Caney Fork River.
Falling Water River	River on S SW border of Putnam County.
Ferguson Creek	Creek in E area of DeKalb County, flows into Caney Fork Creek.
Fern Lake	Lake in N central border of Claiborne County on Kentucky Line. 3 mi W of Harrogate.
Flat Creek	Creek in N section of Sevier County (Douglas Lake).
Fletcher Lake	Lake in SW section of Lauderdale County, W of Anderson-Tully Wildlife Area.
Forked Deer River	River on SW border of Dyer County. Flows into Obion River.
Fort Loudoun Lake	Lake in E NE section of Loudon County, E of Lenoir City (Tennessee River).
Fort Patrick Henry Lake	Lake in W NW section of Sullivan County, SE of Kingsport.

Fox Creek Lake	Lake in middle N section of Cumberland County. 4 mi N NE of Crossville.
Frances Lake	Lake in N central section of Cumberland County. 7 mi N NE of Crossville.
French Broad River	Flows from the State of North Carolina into Cocke County, where the Nolichucky River flows into it. Flows into Jefferson County where it is backed up by the Douglas Dam, forming Douglas Lake, and into Sevier County, westward into Knox County where it joins the Holston River forming the Tennessee River.
Frese Pond	Pond in S central section of Hardeman County. W of Roger Springs. 14 mi S of Bolivar.
Garrett Lake	Lake in E NE section of Weakley County, E of Jewell.
German Creek	Creek in E area of Grainger County. S of Tate Springs.
Gibson Pond	Pond in Hardeman County E NE of Bolivar.
Ginger Bay	Lake in NW section of Stewart County, inlet off the Tennessee River. S of Rushing Bay.
Gin House Lake	Lake in SW section of Tipton County. Approx. 2 mi N of Munford.
Glengary Lake	Lake in central section of Fayette County. 4 mi W of Somerville.
Glenview Lake	Lake in SW section of Tipton County. Approx. 2 mi NW of Munford.
Goose Lake	Lake in NE section of Dyer County near Obion County line.
Goose Pond	Pond in SE section of Coffee County, on Arnold Engineering Development Center.
Goose Pond	Lake in SW section of Grundy County, S of Mt. View.
Goose Pond	Pond in W section of Lauderdale County, S of Right Hand Arm Lake. Approx. 8 mi W NW of Ripley.
Grand Valley Lake	Lake in Hardeman County. 8 mi S of Bolivar. 4 mi E NE of Van Buren.
Grasshopper Creek	Creek in NE section of Hamilton County, N of Grasshopper, flows into Chickamauga Lake.
Greenbriar Lake	Lake in middle N section of Wilson County. 4 mi N NW of Lebanon.

Greenbrier Lake	Lake in SE section of Robertson County, E of Greenbrier.
Green Lake	Lake in S central section of Claiborne County W of Chittum and S of Tazewell.
Grices Creek	Creek in SE corner of Stewart County. N of Cumberland City.
Gross Lake	Lake in SW section of Cumberland County. SE of Midway. 12 mi SW of Crossville.
Gum Pond	Pond in NW section of Lauderdale County, SE of Lake Chisholm.
Guntersville Lake	Lake in S SW section of Marion County, E of South Pittsburg (Tennessee River).
Harmon Creek	Creek in E NE section of Benton County. Approx. 11 mi E NE of Camden. Flows into Tennessee River.
Harpeth River	River on W border of Cheatham County. Flows into Cumberland River.
Hava Lakotu Lakes	Lakes in E section of Dickson County. 1 mi NW of Claylick.
Herb Parsons Lake	Lake in W SW section of Fayette County near Shelby County line SW of Canadaville.
Hidden Cove Lake	Lake in W section of Wilson County. 12 mi W SW of Lebanon.
Hil-A-Wa Lake	Lake in central SW section of Marshall County. 2 mi W SW of Lewisburg.
Hitch Pond	Pond in NW section of Blount County. 9 mi W NW of Maryville. N of Mt. Vernon.
Hiwassee River	Flows from Hiwassee Lake in North Carolina into Polk County, forms county lines for Bradley and McMinn Counties, into Meigs County where it flows into the Tennessee River.
Hodges Lake	Lake in W section of Jefferson County, SW of Hodges.
Holland Pond	Pond in N central section of Franklin County. 5 1/2 mi N NE of Winchester.
Holmes Creek	Creek in N central section of DeKalb County, flows into Center Hill Lake.
Holston River	Flows from the State of Virginia, southward into Sullivan County forming South Holston Lake, west into Hawkins County, southwest into Grainger, Hamblen and Jefferson Counties

Holston River, (Cont.)	forming Cherokee Lake, flows southwest into Knox County where it joins the French Broad River forming the Tennessee River.
Hood Lakes	Lakes in S central section of Lawrence County. S of Lawrenceburg.
Hoopers Lake	Located in SW area of Carroll County, between Howley and Hickory Flat.
Horn Lake	Lake in SW corner of Shelby County. S of Robco Lake.
Horseshoe Lake	Lake in NE section of Dyer County, S of Poplar Ridge.
Howard H. Baker, Sr. Lake	Lake in middle N section of Scott County. 7 mi N NW of Huntsville.
Huckleberry Lake	Lake in SW section of Dickson County. 2 mi S SE of Tennessee City.
Hughes Bay	Lake in W NW section of Stewart County, inlet off the Tennessee River. S of Byrd Bay.
Humbolt Lake	Lake in NE area of Crockett County. 8 mi E NE of Alamo on Gibson County line.
Hunter Lake	Lake in NE section of Maury County. 7 mi N NE of Columbia.
Hurricane Creek	Creek in NW section of Franklin County, flows into Elk River.
Hurricane Creek	Creek in NW corner of Houston County, flows into the Tennessee River.
Hurricane Creek	Creek in SW section of Putnam County off Center Hill Lake, SW of Silver Point.
Indian Boundary Lake	Lake in middle E section of Monroe County in Cherokee National Forest.
Indian Creek	Creek in N central area of DeKalb County, flows into the Caney Fork River.
Indian Creek	Creek on W SW border of Humphreys County. 12 mi W SW of Waverly.
Indian Rock Lake	Lake in SW area of Cumberland County. E of Newton. 12 mi S SW of Crossville.
Ingram Lake	Lake in middle N section of Maury County. 6 mi N NE of Columbia, W of Neapolis.
Irons Creek	Creek in E section of Clay County, off Dale Hollow Lake.

Ish Creek	Creek in W NW section of Blount County, flows into the Tennessee River. S of Mt. Vernon.
Jackson Lake	Lake in E area of Franklin County. 13 mi E of Winchester, E of Sewanee.
Jackson Lake	Located in middle N section of Williamson County. 3 mi N NE of Franklin.
Jennings Pond	Pond in NW section of Lauderdale County, E of Lake Chisholm.
Johnson Lake	Lake in W section of Lauderdale County, SW of Ashport. Approx. 16 mi W of Ripley.
Jones Bend Lake	Lake in W central section of Henry County. 3 mi W NW of Paris.
J. Percy Priest Lake	Lake in E section of Davidson County on Stones River.
Keeton Pond	Pond near S border of Decatur County, S SE of Unity.
Kentucky Lake	Kentucky Lake is formed in the S section of Kentucky where the Kentucky Dam backs up the Tennessee River.
Kitchens Creek	Creek in W area of Franklin County, flows into Elk River NE of Harmony.
Lake Barkley	Lake in N NW section of Stewart County, W of Tobaccoport.
Lake Catherine	Lake in E central section of Cumberland County. W of Fairfield Glade. 8 mi E NE of Crossville.
Lake Cheston	Lake in E section of Franklin County. W of Sewanee.
Lake Chippewa	Lake in SW section of Davidson County. 12 mi W SW of downtown Nashville.
Lake Enoree	Lake in SW section of Davidson County, SW of Gower.
Lake Graham	Lake in middle E NE section of Madison County. 5 mi NE of Jackson.
Lake Hardeman	Lake in S center section of Hardeman County. 9 mi S SE of Bolivar. 9 mi SW of Hornsby.
Lake Holiday	Lake in W central section of Cumberland County. 2 1/2 mi W of Crossville.
Lake in the Sky	Lake in near center of Blount County in Great Smoky Mountains near border.

Lake Isom	Lake in E section of Lake County in Lake Isom National Wildlife Refuge.
Lake Junior	Lake in S section of Hamilton County near Chickamauga Dam.
Lake Karen	Lake in middle E section of Warren County. 4 mi NE of McMinnville.
Lake Kyle	Lake in NE section of Stewart County on Fort Campbell Military Reservation.
Lake Ladd	Lake in SE corner of Overton County. 18 mi S SE of Livingston.
Lake LaJoie	Lake in NE section of Hardeman County in Chickasaw State Park. 4 1/2 mi W NW of Silerton.
Lakeland Lake	Lake in E section of Shelby County. Within the city limits of Lakeland.
Lake Lindsey (Formerly David Crockett La	Lake in David Crockett State Park, NW of Lawrenceburg. In Lawrence County. Named in honor of Edward M. Lindsey. Former mayor of Lawrenceburg and President of the International Association of Lions Clubs in 1966-67.
Lake Logan	Lake in SE section of Giles County. S of Baugh.
Lake Louise	Lake in NW section of Davidson County, W of Greenville.
Lake McKellar	Lake in SE section of Shelby County, off the Mississippi River.
Lake O'Donnell	Lake in E section of Franklin County, E of Sewanee.
Lake Ocoee	Lake in central SW section of Polk County, S of Benton.
Lake Ogallala	Lake in NW area of Davidson County. 12 mi W SW of downtown Nashville.
Lake Placid	Lake in W area of Chester County in Chickasaw State Park.
Lake Rooney	Lake in middle N section of Fayette County, S of Moorman.
Lake Shosnana	Lake in middle E section of White County. 6 1/2 mi E of Sparta. S of Bon De Croft.
Lake St. George	Lake in E central section of Cumberland County. 7 mi E NE of Crossville.

Lake Taal	Lake in NW section of Montgomery County. 2 1/2 mi N NE of Woodlawn.
Lake Tansi	Lake in SW section of Cumberland County. 6 mi S of Crossville.
Lake Tio Khata	Lake in middle W section of Fayette County, S SE of Oakland.
Lake Tullahoma	Lake in SW area of Coffee County. N of Tullahoma.
Lakeview Lake	Lake in S section of Franklin County near Lakeview.
Lakeview Lake	Lake in central section of Giles County. N of Pulaski.
Lake Weona	Lake in W section of Williamson County. 17 mi W of Franklin.
Lake Williams	Lake in center SE section of Madison County. 2 1/2 mi SE of Jackson.
Lake Windermere	Lake in middle W section of Shelby County. N of Raleigh.
Lake Womack	Lake in near center of Coffee County. 1 mi N of Ragsdale.
Lake Woodhaven	Lake in SE central section of Dickson County in Montgomery Bell State Park.
Lambert Lake	Lake in S central section of Blount County. 7 mi S of Maryville.
Laura Lake	Lake on N NE border of Maury County. 11 mi N NE of Columbia.
Laurel Hill Lake	Lake in W NW section of Lawrence County. N of Ovilla.
Laurel Lake	Lake in E Central section of Blount County. 2 mi W of Townsend.
Laurel Lake	Lake in NW corner of Marion County, S of Monteagle.
Laxion Lake	Lake in middle N section of Scott County. 6 1/2 mi N of Huntsville.
Leaf Lake	Lake in SW section of Tipton County. Approx. 2 mi N of Drummonds.
Lea Lake	Lake in SW section of Grainger County, W of Lea Springs.
Leatherwood Creek	Creek in SW section of Stewart County, flows

Leatherwood Creek, (Cont.)	into the Tennessee River.
Lesters Lake	Lake in SE central area of Davidson County. 8 mi E SE of Courthouse.
Lever Lake	Lake in NW section of Williamson County, E of Brush Creek.
Lewisburg Lake	Lake in middle SW section of Marshall County. 4 1/2 mi SW of Lewisburg.
Lick Creek	Creek in NE section of Benton County, flows into Kentucky Lake.
Lick Creek	Creek in NE area of Decatur County.
Lick Creek	Creek in near center of Stewart County. 1 1/2 mi SE of Dover.
Lincoln Lake	Lake in E SE section of Lincoln County. 10 1/2 mi E SE of Fayetteville.
Littell Lake	Lake in SW section of Grundy County. 11 1/2 mi S SW of Altamont. 1 1/2 mi N NE of Summerfield.
Little Champion Lake	Lake in SW corner of Lauderdale County. Approx. 1 1/2 mi E of Fulton.
Little Duck River	River flowing through Manchester in Coffee County.
Little Hurricane Creek	Creek in W NW section of Franklin County, W of Winchester
Little Pigeon River	River in N section of Sevier County, flows into the French Broad River.
Little Possum Creek	Creek in N NW section of Hamilton County.
Little Richland Creek	Creek in NW section of Humphreys County. Begins 8 mi NW of Waverly.
Little Tennessee River	Flows from NC westward, forms boundary lines for Monroe & Blount Counties. N into Loudon County where it flows into the Tennessee River.
Little Turkey Creek	Creek in SW corner of Knox County, SW of Farragut.
Logans Lake	Lake in N NW section of McNairy County, SW of Finger.
Long Lake	Lake in S SE section of Obion County. 11 1/2 mi S SW of Union City, N of Big Lake.

Long Pond	Pond in SW central section of Franklin County. 5 mi SW of Winchester.
Long Pond	Pond in N NW section of Lauderdale County, E of Lake Chisholm.
Loosahatchie River Canal	Flows W from Hardeman County through middle N section of Fayette and Shelby Counties, where it flows into the Mississippi River.
Lost Creek	Creek in W section of Franklin County, SW of Brownington. Flows into Elk River.
Lost Creek Lake	Lake in SE section of Henderson County. 5 mi SE of Lexington. 6 1/2 mi NW of Scotts Hill.
Lost Lake	Lake in NW section of Lauderdale County, SE of Barr. Approx. 11 mi NW of Ripley.
Luther Lake	Lake in S central section of Dickson County. 7 1/2 mi S of Charlotte.
Lyles Lake	Lake in NW section of Shelby County. NW of Locke.
Maple Creek Lake	In SE corner of Carroll County in Natchez Trace State Park.
Marrowbone Lake	Lake in W NW section of Davidson County, W of Greenville.
Mason Lake	Lake on N border of Henry County. 13 mi N of Paris.
Massengill Lake	Lake in S SW section of Hamblen County. 4 mi SE of Morristown.
Massey Lake	Lake in SE section of Haywood County. Approx. 8 mi E SE of Brownsville.
Matthews Lake	Lake in middle N section of Rutherford County. 6 mi N of Murfreesboro.
Mayes Lake	Lake in S section of Hamblen County, S of Morristown.
Mayland Lake	Lake in W NW area of Cumberland County. N of Mayland.
Meade Lake	Lake in S SW section of Tipton County. Approx. 2 1/2 mi S of Crosstown.
Meadow Park Lake	Lake in SW area of Cumberland County. 5 mi SW of Crossville.
Melton Hill Lake	Lake located in SE section of Anderson County on the Clinch River.

Mine Lick Creek	Creek in NE area of DeKalb County, flows into the Caney Fork River.
Mine Lick Creek	Creek in SW section of Putnam County, off Caney Fork River.
Mitchell Creek	Creek in E section of Clay County off Dale Hollow Lake. 6 mi E of Celina.
Mitchell Lake	Lake in SW area of Dyer County on Moss Island.
Monsanto Lake	Lake in middle NW section of Maury County. 7 mi N NW of Columbia.
Monterey Lake	Lake in E section of Putnam County. 2 mi S of Monterey.
Montery Lake	Lake in W SW area of Fayette County near Shelby County line W SW of Canadaville.
Mont Milner Lake	Lake in E area of Franklin County. 13 mi E of Winchester, S of Jackson Lake.
Morrow Lake	Lake in central section of Maury County, S of Columbia.
Morton Lake	Lake in middle NW section of Coffee County. NW of Manchester.
Mosquito Lake	Lake in W SW section of Shelby County, W of Loosahatchie Bar.
Muddy Creek Watershed Lake	Lake in SE corner of Hardeman County. 3 mi SE of Middleton.
Mud Lake	Lake in SW corner of Shelby County on the Mississippi State Line.
Mungers Pond	Lake on S border of Meigs County. 16 mi S SW of Decatur.
Napier Lake	Lake in SE section of Lewis County. 7 1/2 mi S SE of Hohenwald.
Neville Bay	Lake in N NW section of Stewart County. N of Tharpe.
Nickajack Lake	Formed by the Nickajack Dam on the Tennessee River. Backs up to the Chickamauga Dam. Flows through downtown Chattanooga in Hamilton County.
Nickajack Lake	Lake formed by the Nickajack Dam on the Tennessee River. Backs up to the Chickamauga Dam in Chattanooga. Located in Marion County and Hamilton County.
Nolichucky River	Flows from the State of North Carolina through

Nolichucky River, (Cont.)	Unicoi County, into Washington County, westward into Greene County, westward forming county lines for Hamblen, Cocke and Jefferson Counties and then flows into the French Broad River at Douglas Lake.
Normandy Lake	Lake on the Bedford County, Coffee County line. 12 mi E of Shelbyville.
Norris Lake	Lake across middle section of Union County (Clinch River).
North Chickamauga Creek	Creek in S central section of Hamilton County. Flows from Falling Water area into the Tennessee River S of Chickamauga Dam.
North Cross Creek	Creek in middle E SE section of Stewart County. E of Bear Spring.
North Horn Lake	Lake in SW section of Shelby County near the State Line.
Oakwood Acres Lake	Lake in SE central section of Lincoln County. 3 mi SE of Fayetteville.
Obed River	Located in S central section of Morgan County, W SW of Wartburg and S of Lancing.
Obey River	Flows into Cumberland River NW of Celina. Dale Hollow Dam backs river up forming Dale Hollow Lake. Flows through Clay, Pickett, Overton and Fentress Counties.
Obion River	River flowing from NE border of Dyer County to the Mississippi River in SW of County.
Ocoee River	Flows from North Georgia into Tennessee near Copperhill, thru Polk County into the Hiwassee River North of Benton.
Old Hickory Lake	Lake in NE area of Davidson County and S SW section of Sumner County, SE of Hendersonville (Cumberland River).
Old River Lake	Lake in N NE section of Dyer County near Obion County line.
Open Lake	Lake in W NW section of Lauderdale County. 9 1/2 mi W NW of Ripley.
Open Pond	Pond in SE corner of Decatur County on Clifton Bend.
Orphan Home Lake	Lake in N NE border of Maury County. 11 mi N NE of Columbia, E SE of Spring Hill.
Otter Pond	Pond in SW section of Lauderdale County, in the Anderson-Tully Wildlife Area.

Ovoca Lake	Lake in SW area of Coffee County near Ovoca.
Pals Lake	Lake in NW area of Davidson County, SW of Forest Grove.
Panther Bay	Lake in W section of Stewart County, inlet off the Tennessee River. N of Fort Henry.
Paradise Lake	Lake in central SW section of Marshall County. 3 1/2 SW of Lewisburg.
Paradise Lake	Lake in E section of Shelby County, E of Lakeland.
Parksville Lake	Lake in near center of Polk County, NE of section of Lake Ocoee.
Percy Priest Lake	Lake in E area of Davidson County on Stones River.
Pickett Lake	Lake in E section of Pickett County in Pickett State Park and Forest.
Piersol Lake	Lake in NW section of Shelby County. N of Giles Town.
Pigeon River	River in Cocke County that flows from North Carolina into the French Broad River.
Pine Creek	Creek in SE Central section of DeKalb County, flows into the Caney Fork River.
Pine Hill Lake	Lake in S SW section of Williamson County. 10 mi SW of Franklin.
Pine Lake	Lake in W Central section of Bledsoe County near Fall Creek Falls State Park. 5 mi W of Pikeville.
Pine Lake	Lake in S central section of Henderson County. 6 mi S SW of Lexington, W of Center Hill.
Piney Bay	Lake in W section of Stewart County, inlet off the Tennessee River. S of Fort Henry.
Pin Oak Lake	Lake in middle section of Henderson County. 6 1/2 mi E NE of Lexington.
Platts Pond	Pond on W border of Henry County. 11 mi W of Paris, just N of Como.
Pocahontas Lake	Lake in SW section of McNairy County. W NW of Big Hill Pond State Park.
Polk Lake	Lake in W SW section of Sumner County. 9 mi W of Gallatin.
Poplar Tree Lake	Lake in W NW section of Shelby County. NW of

Poplar Tree Lake, (Cont.)	Ramsey.
Porter Lake	Lake in E section of Rhea County. 13 mi NE of Dayton.
Possum Creek	Creek in N area of Hamilton County. Flows into Tennessee River E of Bakewell.
Powell Lake	Lake in SE section of Haywood County, N of Hillville.
Powell River	Flows through Claiborne, Union and into Campbell County where it flows into the Clinch River.
Presley Lake	Lake in NW area of Carroll County. 2 1/2 mi NE of McLemoresville.
Price Lake	Lake in S section of Cheatham County, near the border.
Prowell Lake	Lake in middle NW section of Wilson County. 6 mi W NW of Lebanon.
Radnor Lake	Lake in S area of Davidson County. S of Oak Hill.
Rainbow Lake	Lake on Signal Mountain in Hamilton County near Prentice Cooper State Forest.
Rainbow Lake	Located in NE section of Wayne County. 8 1/2 mi NE of Waynesboro.
Ramsey Lake	Lake in SW central section of Grundy County. SW of Coalmont.
Ray Creek	Creek in E area of Grainger County, N of Heltonville.
Read Lake	Lake in W section of Hamilton County, N of Red Bank.
Read Lakes	Lake in S SW section of Tipton County. Approx. 2 mi E of Wilkinsville.
Rebecca Lake	Lake in S SW section of Lincoln County. Approx. 6 mi S of Fayetteville.
Rebecca Lake	Lake in W NW section of Shelby County. NE of Locke.
Redbud Lake	Lake in E NE section of Henderson County. 8 mi E NE of Lexington.
Reelfoot Lake	Lake in NE section of Lake County and NW section of Obion County.

Rhodes Lake	Lake in SW area of Dyer County on Moss Island.
Ridgetop Lake	Lake in SE section of Robertson County. 2 mi SE of Greenbrier.
Right Hand Arm Lake	Lake in W section of Lauderdale County, E of Open Lake. Approx. 8 mi W NW of Ripley.
Ripshin Lake	Lake in S area of Carter County W of Roan Mountain State Park.
R. M. Steelman Lake	Lake in SE section of Lincoln County. W of Flintville.
Roan Creek	Creek in SW section of Johnson County, flows into the Watauga River.
Robco Lake	Lake in SW corner of Shelby County. S of Cord Lake.
Robertson Lake	Lake in W section of Shelby County. N of Frayser.
Rose Bailey Lake	Lake in central E section of Roane County. SE of Kingston.
Round Lake	Lake in NE area of Dyer County near Obion County line.
Rushing Bay	Lake in NW section of Stewart County, inlet off the Tennesee River. N of Ginger Bay.
Sale Creek	Rises in S area of Rhea County W of Dayton and then flows S through the N section of Hamilton County into the Tennessee River.
Salt Lick Creek	Creek in SW section of Jackson County, off Cumberland River.
Sanders Lake	Lake in N central section of Giles County. N of Wales.
Savannah Creek	Creek in E area of Hamilton County. Flows into Wolftever Creek.
Scenic Lake	Lake in W SW area of Fayette County near Shelby County line W of Canadaville.
Scott Lake	Lake in NW area of Cheatham County. 9 mi W of Henderson.
Seehorn Creek	Creek in E section of Jefferson County, flows into the French Broad River near French Broad.
Sequatchie River	Begins in S section of Cumberland County, flows S SW through Bledsoe, Sequatchie and Marion Counties where it flows into the Tennessee River.

Sewell Creek	Creek in NW section of Pickett County, flows into the Wolf River.
Shaw Lake	Lake in SE section of Haywood County. 7 mi SE of Brownsville. 3 mi W of Brickyard Pond.
Shortfoots Pond	Pond in W SW section of Monroe County, NW of Tellico Plains.
Silver Moon Lake	Lake in SW corner of Madison County. 18 mi SW of Jackson.
Sinclair Lake	Lake in W SW section of Rhea County. 7 mi N NW of Dayton.
Sink Creek	Creek in SE area of DeKalb County off Caney Fork River.
Sinking Creek Lake	Lake in SW section of Knox County, NE of Blue Grass.
Sky Lake	Lake within the city limits of Memphis, W of Lake Windemere. In Shelby County.
Smith Lake	There are two Smith Lakes in Henry County, located approx. 4 mi N of Paris.
Smith Pond	Pond in SW section of Chester County, NW of Masseyville.
Soddy Creek	Creek in N central area of Hamilton County. Flows in Tennessee River N of Soddy Daisy.
Soddy Lake	Inlett off the Tennessee River in the middle N section of Hamilton County, in Soddy Daisy area.
South Chickamauga Creek	Creek in S section of Hamilton County. Flows from N Georgia through East Ridge and Chattanooga into the Tennessee River approx. 2 mi S of Chickamauga Dam.
South Holston Lake	Lake (Holston River) in E section of Sullivan County.
Sportsmans Lake	Lake in NW section of Sumner County. E NE of Portland.
Springbrook Lake	Lake in NE section of Madison County. Approx. 11 mi NE of Jackson.
Standing Rock Creek	Creek in S SW section of Stewart County, flows into the Tennessee River. W of Mulbury Hill.
Standing Stone Lake	Lake in NW section of Overton County, S of Timothy.
St. Andrews Lake	Lake in E NE section of Franklin County. S of

St. Andrews Lake, (Cont.)	Sand Switch near Grundy County Line.
Station Camp Creek	Creek in SW section of Gallatin, flows into Old Hickory Lake.
Stephens Lake	Lake in middle W section of Williamson County. 8 mi W of Franklin.
Stewarts Lake	Lake in W central section of Dickson County. 4 mi N of Dickson.
Sunk Lake	Lake in middle W section of Lauderdale County. 12 mi E of Ripley.
Sunshine Lake	Lake in E Central area of Carroll County E of Smyrna.
Swafford Pond	Pond in central section of Bledsoe County. 1 mi NE of Pikeville.
Swan Lake	Lake in NW section of Lauderdale County, NW of Chisholm Lake.
Tatlock Lake	Lake in NE section of Tipton County. Approx. 2 mi SW of Covington.
Taylor Creek	Creek in NW central section of Franklin County. Runs N to S through Estill Springs.
Tellico Lake (Little Tennessee River)	Located in Monroe County NE of Madisonville.
Tellico Lake	Lake in Monroe County located S SE of Tellico Plains.
Tennessee River	The Tennessee River begins where the Holston and French Broad Rivers join in Knoxville. It flows along the Knox and Blount County lines into Loudon County where the Little Tennessee River flows into it, flows into Roane County, South into Rhea and Meigs Counties where it forms county lines and is backed up by the Watts Bar Dam. Flows southward into Hamilton County where it is backed up by the Chickamauga Dam forming Lake Chickamauga, flows into Marion County where it is backed up by the Nickajack Dam forming the Nickajack Lake. Flows through the Northern portion of the States of Alabama and Mississippi and re-enters Tennessee in Hardin County where it is backed up by the Pickwick Dam. Flows Northward forming county lines for Decatur and Perry Counties, Humphrey and Benton Counties and for Stewart and Henry Counties and then flows into Kentucky where it flows into the Ohio River. Total length of the Tennessee River is 652 miles.

Terra Atra Lake	Lake in E section of Fayette County, E SE of Somerville.
Thompson Lake	Lake in S SE section of Williamson County. 11 mi S SE of Franklin.
Timber Lake Lake	Lake in central section of Lincoln County. 1 1/2 mi SE of Fayetteville.
Tims Ford Lake	Lake in Mid W area of Franklin County on Elk River.
Todds Lake	Lake in SE section of Murfreesboro, in Rutherford County.
Toliveer Lake	Lake in middle SW section of Coffee County. 2 mi S SW of Manchester.
Tollett Lake	Lake in N Central section of Bledsoe County S of Ninemile.
Tompkins Lake	Lake in NW section of Shelby County. N NW of Cuba.
Trace Creek	Creek in W section of Humphreys County. Begins W NW of Denver.
Travis McNatt Lake	Lake in SW section of McNairy County. In Big Hill Pond State Park.
Tullahoma Lake	Lake in SW area of Coffee County. N of Tullahoma.
Turkey Creek	Creek in NW corner of Humphreys County. 10 1/2 mi NW of Waverly.
Turner Lake	Lake in S SW section of McNairy County. 12 mi S SW of Selmer.
Twin Lake	Lake in middle E section of Dickson County. 3 mi E NE of Dickson.
Twin Lakes	Lake in middle SW section of Carroll County, NE of Howley.
Tyree Lake	Lake in E section of Gibson County, N of Concord.
Vaughn Pond	Pond in Hardeman County N NE of Bolivar near Shandy.
VFW Lake	Lake in middle W NW section of Lawrence County. W of Center.
Walker Pond	Pond in S SW section of Tipton County. Approx. 1 mi S of Crosstown.
Waller Pond	Pond in SW area of Lauderdale County, in the

Waller Pond, (Cont.)	Anderson-Tully Wildlife Area.
Walnut Grove Lake	Lake in middle SE section of Shelby County. S of Cordovia.
Wartrace Lake	Lake in center of Robertson County.
Watauga Lake	Lake in middle N section of Carter County, S of Horseshoe.
Watauga River	In E central area of Carter County on Watauga Lake. 5 mi S SE of Elizabethton.
Water River	River in NE section of Rhea County, off Watts Bar Lake at Spring City.
Webb Lake	Lake in N central section of McMinn County. 3 mi NW of Athens.
Webbs Creek	Creek in middle E section of Sevier County. E of Laurel.
Wells Creek	Creek in SE section of Stewart County near Cumberland City Steam Plant.
Whale Pond	Pond in SW section of Lauderdale County, in the Anderson-Tully Wildlife Area.
Whiteoak Creek	Creek in SW corner of Houston County, off Tennessee River.
Whiteoak Lake	Lake in E NE section of Roane County. 11 mi E NE of Kingston in Oak Ridge.
Whites Lake	Lake in NW section of Dyer County. 10 mi W NW of Dyersburg
Whiteville Lake	Lake in W central section of Hardeman County. 8 mi W NW of Bolivar. 6 mi N NE of Newcastle.
Wilber Lake	Lake (Watauga River) in N central section of Carter County, NE of Dogtown.
Wildwood Lake	Lake in S Central area of Bradley County. Just SE of Cleveland.
Williams Lake	Lake in W NW section of Shelby County. W SW of Ramsey.
Willow Lake	Lake in middle NW section of Sumner County. S of Fountain Head.
Wolf Creek	Creek in E NE section of of Rhea County. 14 mi NE of Dayton.
Wolf Pond	Pond in E NE section of Hamilton County, E of Grasshopper.

Wolf River	River in N NW section of Pickett County (Dale Hollow Lake).
Wolf River	Begins in the State of Mississippi and flows N into Fayette County and then W through Fayette and Shelby Counties where it flows into the Mississippi River.
Wolftever Creek	Creek in E area of Hamilton County (Harrison Bay Area), flows into the Tennessee River.
Woods Reservoir	Lake in N section of Franklin County part of Elk River, backed up by the Elk River Dam.